P9-DWP-683

GUIDE TO CAREERS IN WORLD AFFAIRS

Third Edition

Foreign Policy Association (ed.)

Riverside Community College
Library
4800 Magnolia Avenue
Riverside, California 92506

IMPACT PUBLICATIONS
Manassas Park, VA

GUIDE TO CAREERS IN WORLD AFFAIRS

Third Edition

Copyright © 1985, 1987, 1993 Foreign Policy Association

Special Editor: The special editor of this edition is Pamela Gerard, associate editor of the Foreign Policy Association from 1990 to 1992. She revised and expanded the 1987 edition of the guide, organized the research, supervised the work of student interns and wrote the introduction as well as most of the entries. A 1990 graduate of Rutgers University, where she was a staff writer on the university newspaper and a staff assistant on the radio station, Ms. Gerard is currently a graduate student at the Fletcher School of Law and Diplomacy.

Foreign Policy Association: The Foreign Policy Association is a private nonprofit, nonpartisan organization dedicated to the education of American citizens on matters of foreign policy. Through its publications—the annual *Great Decisions* study and discussion guide, the quarterly *Headline Series*, and special reports on timely topics—and through meetings and discussion groups that it sponsors in communities across the nation, FPA seeks to stimulate more effective participation in and greater understanding of world affairs among American citizens.

Chairman of the Foreign Policy Association, Michael H. Coles
President, R. T. Curran
Editor-in-chief, Nancy L. Hoepli
Senior Editor, Ann R. Monjo
Special Projects Editor, K.M. Rohan

All rights reserved. Printed in the United States of America. No part of this book may be used or reproduced in any manner whatsoever without written permission of the publisher: Impact Publications, 9104-N Manassas Drive, Manassas Park, VA 22111.

Library of Congress Cataloguing-in-Publication Data

Guide to careers in world affairs / Foreign Policy Association (ed.) ;
   [special editor, Pamela Gerard].—3rd edition
      p. cm.
   Includes bibliographical references and index.
      ISBN 0-942710-17-7 (hard): $32.95.—ISBN 0-942710-89-4
(paper) : $14.95
      1. Americans—Employment—Foreign countries—Handbooks, manuals,
etc. 2. Vocational guidance—Handbooks, manuals, etc.
   I. Gerard, Pamela. II. Foreign Policy Association.
HF5549.5.E45G79   1993
331.7'02—dc20   93-25815
                                                         CIP

CONTENTS

ACKNOWLEDGMENTS

Without the help of interns, this book could not have been completed. The Foreign Policy Association is indebted to the following for their contributions: Christopher E. Abbruzzese, Mark Boote, William Brenner, Melani Cammett, Holly Denniston, Adam Michael Handler, Timothy M. Johnson, Camilla R.G. Rees, Elyse Sashin, Jennifer M. Walden and Catherine A. Wright.

FPA also wishes to thank Judith L. Biggs and the other members of the Governing Committee of the Off-the-Record Luncheon Series for their generous support of this publication.

NOTE TO USERS

While we have attempted to provide accurate and up-to-date information in this book, please be advised that names, addresses and phone numbers do change, that organizations do move, go out of business or change management and that deadlines for submitting applications may also change. We regret any inconvenience such changes may cause to your international job search.

If you have difficulty contacting a particular organization included in this book, please do one or all of the following:

- Consult the latest edition of the *National Directory of Addresses and Telephone Numbers* (Omnigraphics: Detroit, MI).

- Contact the Information or Reference section of your local library.

- Call Information.

Inclusion of organizations in this book in no way implies endorsements by either the Foreign Policy Association or Impact Publications. The information and recommendations appearing in this book are provided solely for your reference. As indicated in Chapter Twelve on job-hunting strategies, it is the reader's responsibility to take initiative in contacting and following-through with employers. The names, addresses and phone numbers appearing in this book provide one important component for conducting a successful international job search.

INTRODUCTION

Welcome to the third edition of the *Guide to Careers in World Affairs*. In her introduction to the 1987 edition, editor Laura Schisgall wrote, "there is scarcely a profession, trade or occupation in the U.S. that is not affected–directly or indirectly–by decisions made in Riyadh, Frankfurt, London, Mexico City, Moscow, Beijing, Rio de Janeiro, Tokyo, New Delhi or the world's other major cities." This statement is even more applicable today. In the five years since the last edition of the book was published we have witnessed a sea change in the economic, political and social state of the globe. International trade and shared environmental problems are drawing the peoples of the world into an ever more interdependent relationship. The destruction of the Berlin Wall and the breakup of the Soviet Union signaled an end to the cold war and made the prospect of international cooperation a reality again.

Together these international developments have created, if not a new world order, a global society that demands a new type of international affairs professional. Both the public and private sectors need talented individuals with the training, skills and knowledge of international affairs that will enable them to rise to new challenges and opportunities. According to a seasoned international business executive, "There is no comparison between the growth of the international job market during my lifetime and the growth it will experience in your lifetime. It is a great time to want an international career."

WHAT IS A CAREER IN WORLD AFFAIRS?

When most people think of international careers they envisage the U.S. Foreign Service or, perhaps, the United Nations. Although these are major sources of international employment, the market is much more diverse, encompassing almost every field of endeavor. Red Cross relief workers bringing needed food and medical services to the people of war- and drought-devastated Somalia, researchers studying the effects of nationalism in the republics of the former Soviet Union, trade specialists helping companies sell their products and services abroad, foreign correspondents relaying news and images from around the world, and educators facilitating cultural and professional exchanges are just a few of the many different types of international workers, each requiring specific qualifications. All of these occupations, and the credentials needed for them, are discussed in the guide.

The allure of living overseas draws many students to seek work in international affairs. Although some may spend most of their careers living or traveling abroad, others may never work outside their employer's home office. There are many internationally oriented occupations in the U.S., for example in finance and banking, that may not require, or offer the opportunity for, living abroad and may entail only infrequent travel. Others, like the U.S. Foreign Service, international development-assistance fieldwork, foreign consulting and foreign news coverage, necessitate living abroad for a certain amount of time.

Because overseas posts are few in number and sought by many, competition is tough. However, as the globalization of financial markets, the geographic diversification of industrial and corporate activities and the exportation of U.S. services continue, new opportunities arise. Of the 84 businesses, media and organizations surveyed in the guide, 85% have offices abroad. Thirty-one percent of the nonprofit organizations and 57% of the state and federal agencies had overseas branches—a significant increase since the last edition. Although many employers in recent years cut back the number of U.S. citizens they sent overseas for economic reasons and relied more heavily on the networks, cultural understanding and know-how of local foreign nationals, this trend seems to have stopped. Presently, 60% of the organizations with overseas staff listed in the guide hire both foreign nationals and U.S. citizens; 30% hire only U.S. citizens; 10% hire only foreign nationals.

If you are just starting a career, you will probably have to prove yourself in the domestic operations of the business or in the international division of U.S. headquarters before being considered for an overseas assignment. If you are looking for a shortcut to landing an overseas post, there aren't any, but there are skills that can help speed the process.

These include proficiency in a language, particularly an uncommon one or a dialect, and technical expertise. Some of the more adventurous move to the country in which they wish to work and begin the job hunt there, becoming what is affectionately known as an ex-patriot. A word of caution. If you have never spent an extended period of time abroad and you are looking for an overseas position, give careful thought to the challenges and hardships that living in a different culture and being separated from friends and family can present. One writer suggests, "if you don't have the sense of adventure and patience, curiosity, emotional stability, flexibility, good humor, tolerance, sensitivity, independence, self-discipline and tact needed for overseas work," you might be happier remaining where you are.

Building credentials for international work can be difficult, but it is not impossible. A deliberate, well-planned approach, combining internships, work experience and education, is best. International resolve (the strong desire to do something international) is sometimes as important as work experience. Foreign languages are frequently essential. Reading the guide carefully will give you an idea of what it takes to be successful, or at least land a job, in your chosen field.

USING THE GUIDE

Whether you have already decided that a career in international development, for example, is your destiny or you are simply interested in exploring the many different fields that offer international careers, we advise the same approach to using the guide. In addition to reading the chapter or chapters you think are relevant to your interests, read (or at least scan) those chapters that you think are not. You might find organizations, for example, doing important development work in the consulting, government and nonprofit chapters, or opportunities in finance and banking with the UN and the U.S. federal government. Quite possibly, you might discover a company, firm, organization or even a field you would not have otherwise considered.

The guide looks at the following fields that are good sources of international employment: business, consulting, finance and banking, journalism, law, translating and interpreting, nonprofit (research and education; development assistance, environment and relief; health and population; youth programs), government, the UN and other international organizations. The introductions to the chapters by outstanding leaders in their fields provide inside information about the nature of the work, qualifications and prospects for employment and offer job hunting advice. The profiles of representative companies and other organizations, compiled from questionnaires filled out by the people who do the hiring, give a description of the organization and information about the staff, qualifications for employment, availability of internships and application procedures. Because of frequent personnel changes, we do not provide contact names. Although companies are sometimes reluctant to give out names of personnel directors, we advise you to try to get them. Applications addressed to an individual, not a title, show initiative and are more likely to get attention. They also make following up on your application easier.

Chapter Ten lists internships in the fields covered by the guide and Chapter Eleven, graduate programs in international relations, public policy and related fields. Because we believe internships are the building blocks of any promising international career, these chapters have been substantially expanded. The graduate study chapter now includes detailed information about the master's degree programs such as areas of specialization, financial aid, internships, study abroad, and 1992 application and enrollment figures. Finally, for those who want to do further research, Chapter Thirteen provides an annotated bibliography.

Organizations listed in the guide are only a representative sampling of the rich variety of opportunities in the international arena. For every organization profiled here, there are many more which have comparable openings. Today, the mid-size and small companies are offering virtually the same employment opportunities that the large corporations and organizations provided in earlier years. According to *U.S. News & World Report,* downsizing by *Fortune* 500 companies has claimed over 750,000 jobs since the last edition of this book. The good news is that 1.9 million new jobs will be created this year, of which 80% will be at companies with fewer than 100 employees. They are looking for qualified people to help them achieve their goals. Don't be afraid to knock on different doors.

We hope that this third edition of the guide provides you with as inspiring a look at the many possibilities for a "career in world affairs" as its predecessor did for this writer. Researching it has convinced us that this is truly a fascinating and advantageous time to be launching an international career.

Pamela Gerard
New York City
January 1993

Chapter One

INTERNATIONAL BUSINESS

Introduction by Barry MacTaggart

Since international business is a wide field representing such industries as consumer products, automotives, cosmetics, oil, communication, aerospace, pharmaceuticals and others, career opportunities can be as diverse as the companies doing business. However, there are some similarities in the type of job opportunities and responsibilities just as there are similarities in the nature of international businesses themselves.

U.S. companies are increasingly aware that there now exists a global marketplace and that U.S. industry must strive for its share of the market. Industries and companies that fail to identify the potential of the international market may be limiting their opportunities for growth.

Barry MacTaggart, until his retirement, was chairman and president of Pfizer International. An Australian Chartered Accountant, Mr. MacTaggart joined Pfizer International as an auditor in 1959. In 1965 he assumed responsibility for administration at the Management Center in Tokyo. In 1969 he was appointed president of Pfizer Asia with headquarters in Hong Kong. He moved to New York headquarters in 1972. Mr. MacTaggart is a former member of the board of governors of the Foreign Policy Association.

Successful entry into a foreign market is not easy. It takes time, perseverance and long-term dedication. To establish a foreign subsidiary that will become a viable competitor and a good corporate citizen in the host country, the parent company must develop marketing plans, arrange distribution systems, secure local financing, make government and industry contacts, recruit employees, etc.

Once the firms have made the commitment to develop an offshore business, the recruitment of U.S. nationals for overseas assignment (expatriates, as they are known in business) begins. For many firms—but by no means all—the recruitment process goes through three phases: the expatriate, the local national and the integrated phase. In each stage there is a difference in the type and number of overseas job opportunities, and anyone aspiring to an international career should be aware of those differences.

THE EXPATRIATE PHASE

In the start-up phase, when a company has decided to expand into a foreign market and is beginning to establish an overseas regional headquarters or a subsidiary, it tends to recruit employees from its domestic staff. It knows little about the foreign market and has no local staff. Therefore it relies on a large number of U.S. expatriates, selecting those who have had a successful domestic career with the company, or those who have a good understanding of the local market.

During this phase, there is a lot of movement between domestic and international operations, particularly if a regional headquarters is being established, and many domestic employees at all levels can expect to be tapped for international assignments. Those assignments vary: some will be for very specific jobs of fixed duration, such as an engineer who is sent abroad to build a plant. Others will be more general and for a longer period of time, such as a general manager who is sent abroad for five to fifteen years. There is no better time for overseas career opportunities than when a company is launching a new subsidiary or headquarters.

The expatriate phase tends to carry the seeds of its own destruction. It is costly for headquarters to sustain a large staff of Americans abroad. It is also in the interest of the parent company to build up the overseas subsidiary with local talent so that it will be viewed as a local rather than a foreign enterprise. How long a company remains in the expatriate phase is determined in part by such factors as the political and economic structure of the host country and the cooperation of the host government.

LOCAL NATIONAL PHASE

As the foreign enterprise matures, more and more local nationals are placed in positions of authority, and the number of expatriates is scaled back significantly. There are fewer opportunities for two- to three-year overseas assignments, and the overseas vacancies that do occur are filled from the ranks of a small group of career expatriates, usually general managers who are transferred from country to country every few years.

In this stage, if all goes well, the foreign subsidiary has taken on a local coloration that enhances business prospects, and the parent company has begun to pare expenses by reducing the size of its expatriate staff. It may also have begun to dismantle or severely curtail the regional headquarters. This phase offers very limited opportunities to those who wish to launch an international career. The few overseas assignments that do occur are usually to fill a specialized need and last several years.

INTEGRATED PHASE

In the third stage, the parent company or its international division has acquired a truly international outlook, and it draws on a worldwide body of talent to meet its manpower needs. U.S. employees must now compete with employees in all the overseas subsidiaries rather than just the parent company for an international assignment. Increased competition reduces the opportunities; therefore, this is the bleakest phase for those seeking overseas careers.

The lesson for someone wishing to pursue an international career is, first, try to find out which phase a company is in. (Bear in mind, however, that not all international businesses follow the same three-stage pattern or use the same terminology to describe the phases.) If you are just leaving school and the company you are interviewing appears to be moving into an integrated phase, keep looking. Your chances of going overseas will be better with a firm either entering or already in the expatriate stage. Even in this phase, the total number of expatriates is only a fraction of the company's total work force. Moreover, a new graduate's chances of getting picked for overseas work are small. A typical U.S. expatriate is someone with an established, successful track record in his or her field who has been with the company for a number of years. Since expatriates must operate more independently than domestic employees, companies tend to choose people who have proven themselves. In general, the number of expatriates has diminished over the last decade and a half because most of the major U.S. multinational corporations have already progressed from the expatriate stage to the local national phase, and a few to the integrated stage.

The best route to an overseas career is via a very successful domestic career in a company with an expanding international business. This does not mean that knowledge of foreign languages, experience living abroad and an academic background covering aspects of international business are not helpful. They are. But being an outstanding performer in your domestic position, having enough tenure to have established yourself in the company and making sure that management knows of your desire for an international assignment are key ingredients that will lead to an overseas post.

This may not be an optimistic picture for those who want to pursue an international career, but it is a realistic and challenging one. The business world will need your help during the next decades, and I can assure you that the rewards, both tangible and intangible, are gratifying.

AMERICAN INTERNATIONAL GROUP
New York, NY

Founded in 1919, AIG is the leading U.S.-based international insurance company. Operating in approximately 130 countries and jurisdictions, member companies write property, casualty, marine, life and financial services insurance, and they are also engaged in a range of financial-services businesses. AIG's net income in 1990 was $1.4 billion and assets were $58.1 billion.

The company has six operating divisions: domestic general/ brokerage, domestic general/agency, life, specialty companies, reinsurance and foreign. Within the foreign division are subgroups working in most areas of the world. Some of the other divisions also have internationally oriented subgroups. One half of AIG's pretax income comes from non-U.S. sources, including Europe, Asia, Australia, Latin America, the Middle East and Africa. The international department coordinates all human-resources functions worldwide. Principal duties of the overseas staff are insurance and financial activities.

Professional Staff: AIG has a U.S. staff of 15,000, with an additional 19,000 staff members overseas. In the last 12 months, 475 professionals were hired, 35 of whom were hired for the international department.

Qualifications: The company prefers candidates with a BA, MBA or an MIA. Knowledge of Spanish and French is preferred, but German and Japanese are also desirable. Willingness to travel is a prerequisite for employment, as is living abroad, but neither previous work experience nor overseas experience is required for entry-level positions. For higher-level positions, experience in underwriting, claims, accounting and finance is useful. AIG recruits on college campuses and from graduate programs.

Training Program: College graduates with up to two years experience are eligible for the two-year training program. Through on-the-job training and selected courses, the program provides exposure to the insurance business both domestically and internationally. The number of applicants accepted each year varies.

Application Procedure: Persons interested in the training program may obtain more information by writing to Human Resources. Other applicants should contact Director of Staffing:

> American International Group
> 72 Wall Street
> New York, NY 10027
> (212) 770-7000, ext. 3561

THE BOEING COMPANY
Seattle, WA

Boeing is the largest producer of commercial aircraft in the world. The nation's 13th largest corporation also produces helicopters, defense electronics and space systems. Boeing is the largest exporter in the U.S., earning over $16 billion in foreign sales in 1991. The company is organized into three major business segments: commercial airplanes, defense and space, and computer services, and it has two international subsidiaries: Boeing International Corporation, which is responsible for sales and marketing abroad, and Boeing Operations International, which oversees foreign contracts. Staff sent abroad work mainly in marketing and sales.

The corporate international department is quite small. It monitors the operation of the foreign offices and overseas expatriate employees, but does not hire them. Hiring is done by the U.S.-based divisions. Individuals sent abroad have usually already worked with Boeing's foreign clients, and they are typically senior-level employees, although occasionally Boeing hires someone without in-house experience but with considerable experience in a particular overseas area.

Professional Staff: In all, Boeing employs over 160,000 people. About 80 U.S. professionals are based abroad. The company usually hires foreign nationals as support staff. About 20% of the overseas staff have been sent abroad within the past year. Staff normally go abroad for two-year rotations.

Qualifications: Generally, Boeing seeks applicants with degrees, preferably advanced, in the legal, technical and financial fields. Foreign languages are preferred but not necessary. Japanese, Chinese, Arabic, French, German, Russian and Spanish are useful. Employees must be willing to travel and live abroad. The company desires previous professional experience either in the aerospace industry or in related work. Overseas experience is helpful but not necessary.

Application Procedure: Interested persons seeking more information may write to:

> Director of Employment
> The Boeing Company
> PO Box 3707
> Seattle, WA 98124
> (206) 393-8479

CHUBB & SON, INC.
Warren, NJ

Through its agents and brokers, Chubb provides business and personal insurance worldwide. Chubb operates in over 100 countries through its 70 branches in the U.S., Canada, Europe, South America and the Pacific. The International Department provides property/casualty insurance to U.S.-and Canadian-based multinational corporations. It also provides coverages for exporters of goods and services. To provide insurance, loss control, claims and underwriting services for North American clients, Chubb International relies principally on its own offices in major insurance markets in Europe, the Caribbean, South America and the Pacific Rim.

Professional Staff: Chubb employs over 4,000 people in the U.S. and 250 overseas. Both U.S. and foreign nationals are hired for the underwriting, claims, loss control, operations, actuarial and information resources departments. In 1990, Chubb hired 400 people, including 44 for overseas positions.

Qualifications: Chubb seeks qualified college graduates, and recruits from college campuses in the U.S. and overseas. Knowledge of Spanish, French, Italian or German is helpful.

Training Program: Chubb offers a five-phase training program that accepts approximately 200 trainees yearly. Training begins in a local branch, followed by three weeks at the Chubb School of Insurance, then a three-to-six- week specialty school and on-the-job training at the assigned branch.

Internships: Paid internships are offered to college students with excellent communications skills and the ability to work with others as a team. They are offered in the summer and during the year. During the summer, or a series of summers, interns may rotate through a variety of departments to gain a complete understanding of the insurance business.

Application Procedure: Those interested in professional or internship positions should contact:

> Human Resources
> Chubb & Son Inc.
> 15 Mountain View Road
> PO Box 1615
> Warren, NJ 07061-1615
> (908) 580-2063

COOPERS & LYBRAND
New York, NY

For over 90 years, Coopers & Lybrand (C&L) has aided its clients in identifying business risks and opportunities. A diversified financial services company, C&L provides a variety of services from its 710 offices located in 112 countries overseas and 101 offices in the U.S. These activities range from general financial services, such as accounting and auditing, to consulting in strategic and resource management, and insurance and tax planning. The international directorate, located in the New York national office, is the firm's international division in the U.S. It is involved in new international business initiatives, liaisons with international member firms and the management of international transfers for business and training.

Professional Staff: C&L employs some 65,000 people overseas, of whom about 5,000 are partners and 60,000 are staff members and administrative personnel. In the U.S., C&L has over 1,000 partners and 10,994 professionals. The international directorate is comprised of 25 professionals, 5 of whom are partners.

Qualifications: Qualifications for employment vary according to position and location. Typically, recruitment is handled within each country by its local office. There is no formal international recruitment function in the U.S.; however, overseas positions are filled by U.S. as well as foreign nationals. Often, C&L partners and staff will fill temporary overseas positions through a rotation system. Persons with special expertise or foreign language proficiency are often recruited from the general human resources office for the international directorate.

Application Procedure: Those interested in applying should contact:

> Human Resources
> Coopers & Lybrand
> 1251 Avenue of the Americas
> New York, NY 10020
> (212) 536-2000, ext. 2849

ELI LILLY INTERNATIONAL CORPORATION
Indianapolis, IN

Eli Lilly International, a research-based corporation, is one of the world leaders in the pharmaceutical industry. The company started its international operations in 1918 in Shanghai and has since expanded its operations all over the world, with an especially strong concentration in member countries of the European Community. Lilly focuses on the development, manufacture and marketing of pharmaceuticals, medical instruments and diagnostic and agricultural products.

Professional Staff: Eli Lilly employs about 28,000 people, 10,000 of whom are assigned outside the U.S. The company's overseas staff is mostly made up of foreign nationals, although opportunities for Americans to work overseas are available. The international department hired 25 professionals last year.

Qualifications: Eli Lily International prefers applicants who have an academic background in health care, business, liberal arts, or engineering. Fluency in at least one foreign language is required, and applicants must be willing to travel and live abroad. Applicants should have two years of previous work experience.

Training Program: Lilly has a rigorous training program, which runs from 18 to 24 months. Each year, 25 trainees are accepted to complete three assignments in the U.S. and one overseas. Almost all trainees have a graduate degree.

Internships: The company has a paid summer internship program for graduate students interested in international business. Interns are given assignments in marketing and international finance and may be located in the U.S. or abroad.

Application Procedure: Interested interns or job applicants should write to:

> International Recruitment
> Eli Lilly International Corporation
> Lilly Corporate Center
> Indianapolis, IN 46285
> (800) 338-9656

In Europe:

> European Recruitment
> Eli Lilly International Corporation
> Lilly Corporate Center 1047
> Lilly House
> Hanover Square
> London W1R 0PA
> England
> 71-409-4841

EXXON CORPORATION
Irving, TX

The principal business of Exxon Corporation is energy. This involves the exploration for and production of crude oil and natural gas and petroleum products; the manufacturing and marketing of petrochemicals; and the exploration for and mining and sale of coal and other minerals.

Exxon's international business is assuming an increasingly larger share of its total business. Several of Exxon's divisions, rather than one international department, are responsible for much of the company's international activity. They include: Exxon Company International, Exxon Chemical Company, Exxon Exploration Company and Exxon Coal and Minerals Company.

Professional Staff: Exxon and its divisions employ 18,000 professionals in the U.S. and about 26,000 overseas in 79 countries, including most of Europe, Southeast Asia, South America and Canada. Most overseas positions are filled by foreign nationals. Exxon Company International, the company's largest U.S. division, in Florham Park, NJ, employs over 35,000 people. The Irving, TX, corporate headquarters has a staff of about 300 professionals, of whom a half dozen were hired in the last year.

Qualifications: Exxon looks for applicants with a college or graduate degree in engineering, geology, geophysics, computer sciences or business. While willingness to travel and live abroad are not required, both are desirable. Foreign language proficiency is considered helpful, especially French, German and Spanish. Previous work experience is not necessary. Exxon recruits in colleges and graduate schools.

Training Program: Exxon offers a multitude of formal training programs in specific functional programs. However, its primary method of training is "on-the-job."

Internships: Paid summer internships are offered in most of Exxon's divisions. Both college and graduate students may apply.

Application Procedure: Applications for employment and internships may be addressed to:

> Exxon Corporation
> Professional Employment Office
> PO Box 2180
> Houston, TX 77252-2180
> (713) 656-3636

THE GOODYEAR TIRE & RUBBER CO.
Akron, OH

Goodyear produces—in addition to tires and a host of other rubber products—plastics and chemicals for the industrial and consumer markets of the transportation industry. However, its principal business is the research, development, manufacture, distribution and sale of tires.

Goodyear has offices worldwide with a major presence in Europe, Latin America, Asia and Canada. Its international division located in the Akron, Ohio, headquarters, helps coordinate the activities of overseas offices.

Professional Staff: Goodyear has a staff of 650 in its Akron headquarters, 100 of whom were hired in the past year. Overseas offices employ about 51,000 people, 165 of whom are expatriates. Its foreign offices hire both U.S. citizens and foreign nationals.

Qualifications: Applicants with a BA and an MBA in business or a technical field and expertise in manufacturing, finance and sales are preferred. Knowledge of Spanish, Japanese, German, French, Russian, Chinese or Arabic is helpful. Previous work experience is not required for employment although willingness to travel and live abroad is necessary. Internships are not offered.

Training Program: Goodyear offers a one-year training program that accepts three to six college graduates yearly. The trainee becomes acquainted with the company's employees, products and plants through an assignment at a U.S. manufacturing plant.

Application Procedure: Applications for the training program and entry-level positions should be sent to the Manager of Corporate College Relations. For other positions write to the Personnel Department at the following address:

> The Goodyear Tire and Rubber Company
> 1144 East Market Street
> Akron, OH 44316
> (216) 796-7900

GRUMMAN INTERNATIONAL, INC.
Bethpage, NY

Grumman International is a subsidiary of the Grumman Corporation, a manufacturer of high-technology aerospace products (such as the F-14 fighter plane), electronics systems, data systems and space systems. Grumman does approximately 80% of its business with the government; the international subsidiary markets products abroad. According to the corporation's annual report, Singapore, Egypt, Japan, Israel and Taiwan are its primary customers. Overseas staff are based in Japan, Singapore, Taiwan, Thailand, Belgium and France.

Professional Staff: Grumman International has a staff of 45 at its Bethpage, New York, headquarters, two of whom have been hired within the past year; 16 people, both U.S. citizens and local nationals, are stationed overseas. There are approximately 8,000 professional positions in the Grumman Corporation.

Qualifications: A BS or an MS in aerospace engineering, course work in international business, or an MBA are useful for employment. Knowledge of a foreign language is preferred, with French, Italian, German and Japanese being the most useful. A minimum of 10 years experience in foreign military sales or aerospace marketing is required for employment in Grumman International, which does not recruit. Employees must be willing to travel but not necessarily to live abroad.

Application Procedure: Write to:

> Administrator
> Grumman International, Inc.
> 1111 Stewart Avenue
> Bethpage, NY 11714-3590-A32-GHQ
> (516) 575-6859

HONEYWELL, INC.
Minneapolis, MN

Established in 1885, Honeywell is a publicly owned, global enterprise that creates automation and control products, systems and services for homes, offices and factories, aviation and space. In the U.S. more than 3 million commercial buildings and 60 million homes have Honeywell controls. In Europe, Honeywell controls are found in 40 million homes and apartment buildings.

In 1991, international operations accounted for more than a third of the company's $6 billion annual revenues by generating sales of $2.1 billion, 34% of the company's total sales, and a profit of $248 million, 37% of Honeywell's total profit. International sales are expected to approach 50% of the company's total sales by the end of the decade. Honeywell has its international headquarters in Minneapolis and maintains a presence in over 90 countries. Honeywell's overseas employees work with 75 distributors and sales agents worldwide and are responsible for the research, development, marketing and distribution of products.

Professional Staff: Honeywell employs 60,000, of whom 17,000 are in international operations; fewer than 150 are U.S. citizens assigned abroad. Those assigned abroad have an average of 10 years experience with the company and are top-level managers or technical experts. The international department, Honeywell International, is staffed by about 20 senior professionals, 1 of whom was hired within the last year. Those on international assignments have generally begun their careers in the U.S.

Qualifications: Undergraduate degrees in engineering, computer science, accounting or business administration are generally sufficient for employment, although the company does hire people with PhDs in the sciences for some positions. Foreign-language and international affairs training are useful, but people are usually not hired directly for international work. Work experience in industry or a technical field is useful; previous experience abroad is not necessary but would help career development leading to an international assignment. The company does not recruit nor does it have a formal management-training program.

Internships: Some summer internships are available to college students. Interns are paid and their duties depend on their fields of interest. Most, but not all, of the internships are in technical areas.

Application Procedure: Applicants for both professional positions and internships should contact:

> Manager, Corporate Staffing (MN12-3166)
> Honeywell, Inc.
> Honeywell Plaza, PO Box 524
> Minneapolis, MN 55440-0524
> (612) 951-1000

JOHNSON & JOHNSON
New Brunswick, NJ

Johnson & Johnson, with 82,200 employees and $12.5 billion in sales, is the world's largest and most comprehensive manufacturer of health-care products. Johnson & Johnson has three worldwide business segments: the consumer segment, the company's largest; the pharmaceutical segment, the most profitable; and the professional segment, producing medical and surgical equipment and devices.

Like most global corporations, Johnson & Johnson has a decentralized structure. The company's international business is conducted by subsidiaries manufacturing in 49 countries outside the U.S. and selling in more than 150 countries around the world. The company generates approximately 57% of its revenues outside the U.S. Johnson & Johnson has 32 company/affiliate offices in the U.S.

Professional Staff: Approximately 12,000 professionals are employed in the U.S. and 17,000 overseas in over 50 countries. Overseas staff, who are mainly foreign nationals, perform marketing, sales and operations functions. In the last 12 months 250 professionals were hired for the New Brunswick headquarters. The international department has a staff of about 200, 50 of whom were hired in the last year.

Qualifications: A college degree in marketing, operations or finance or an MBA is most desirable. Willingness to travel and work abroad is required. Foreign-language proficiency is preferred, with Spanish, Chinese, Japanese, Russian and Portuguese deemed most useful. Previous work experience is not necessary. Johnson & Johnson recruits from college campuses.

Internships: Paid summer internships are available to college and graduate students in various Johnson & Johnson divisions, including accounting, public relations and others. Interns should have a strong academic record.

Application Procedure: For internship and professional positions write to:

> Vice President, Headquarters Human Resources
> Johnson & Johnson
> One Johnson & Johnson Plaza
> New Brunswick, NJ 08933
> (908) 524-0400

JOHNSON CONTROLS, INC.
Milwaukee, WI

Founded in 1885, Johnson Controls is a market leader in four industries: facility-control systems and services for nonresidential buildings; automotive seating; automotive batteries; and plastic containers. Some of its better-known products include Diehard and Eveready batteries, car seats for Renault, Ford and BMW, as well as plastic bottles for Folgers coffee and Gerber juices. Johnson Controls has manufacturing offices in six countries and 220 offices worldwide, including Eastern and Western Europe, the Pacific Rim and Mexico.

Professional Staff: Johnson Controls has a professional staff of 40,000, 11,000 of whom are stationed overseas. Both foreign nationals and U.S. citizens are employed abroad.

Qualifications: Applicants should have either an undergraduate degree in engineering, finance or business, or an MBA. Previous experience in auditing, finance, engineering or manufacturing is useful. Knowledge of German, French, Spanish or Japanese is preferred, and a willingness to live and travel abroad is required. Johnson Controls occasionally recruits from college campuses.

Internships: Semester-long paid internships are available in the company's accounting and internal auditing departments. Applicants can be either undergraduate or graduate students with good academic standing and course work in the appropriate field of study. Previous work experience is a plus.

Application Procedure: Persons interested in both professional positions and internships should contact:

> Manager, Corporate Staffing
> Johnson Controls, Inc.
> PO Box 591
> Milwaukee, WI 53201-0591
> (414) 228-2339

MINNESOTA MINING AND MANUFACTURING (3M)
St. Paul, MN

Number 32 on the *Fortune* 500 list, 3M produces an array of over 50,000 products, including Scotch brand tape, data cartridges, reflective materials, photographic paper, overhead projectors, surgical masks, sandpaper and videocassettes. Sales to foreign countries represent about 50% of 3M's total. 3M has plants in 53 countries; most of its 40,000 employees abroad are foreign nationals. All of the professional staff working in the international department or abroad are hired from within the corporation. Most have served with the company for 10 or more years.

Professional Staff: The company has 450 professionals in international departments spread throughout its domestic operations. There are some 100 U.S. citizens in professional positions abroad. Each year 3M hires about 300 recent college graduates for a variety of positions.

Qualifications: 3M hires people with undergraduate degrees and top undergraduate records in fields such as chemistry or engineering. Previous technical, marketing or sales experience is not necessary. The staffing department is also interested in people with a PhD in technical fields or an MBA in marketing. They recruit on both college and graduate-school campuses.

Training Program: The company runs informal and formal short training programs for its new employees. Manufacturing and sales have a two- to four-week training program, the length depending on the employee's previous experience.

Application Procedure: Applications may be addressed to:

> 3M
> 3M Staffing and College Relations
> Building 224-1W-02
> St. Paul, MN 55144-1000
> (612) 733-1755

NIKE, INC.
Beaverton, OR

Nike is a major sports and fitness company, producing footwear, apparel and accessories. With business, manufacturing and distribution facilities in 67 countries worldwide and international revenues in 1990 at $480 million, Nike calls itself "truly an international company, as opposed to one just doing business internationally."

Nike International, located in the Oregon headquarters, coordinates the worldwide marketing, sales and distribution of products.

Professional Staff: Of its 4,000 employees, 1,500 are based overseas. Nike hires both foreign nationals and U.S. citizens for overseas positions. In the last 12 months, 500 professionals were hired, 75 for the international department alone.

Qualifications: Nike prefers candidates who have a college degree in international business, liberal arts, computer science or textiles, or an MBA. Expertise in marketing sales, product development, finance, human resources or computer systems is desirable as well as at least one year of experience in sports and fitness consumer products. Overseas experience in Europe, Latin America or Asia is preferred and in some cases required. Proficiency in Chinese, French, German, Japanese, Spanish or Dutch—for the Nike European headquarters in the Netherlands—is preferred for most positions and required for some.

Training Program: Close to a dozen people a year participate in Nike's training program for managers and supervisors. Trainees have a college degree and previous work experience. The program length varies.

Internships: Paid fall semester and summer internships are available for college and graduate students. Interns assist professionals in research and organizational projects. Recruiting for internships is done during the "internship season," which runs from February through April.

Application Procedure: Applications are accepted for open positions only. To apply call the Job Hotline at (503) 644-4224. Interns can contact the employment office at:

> Nike, Inc.
> Employment Office
> One Bowerman Drive
> Beaverton, OR 97005
> (503) 671-6495

PEPSI-COLA INTERNATIONAL
Somers, NY

Pepsi-Cola International (PCI) is the international beverage division of PepsiCo, Inc., a worldwide consumer-products corporation with 1991 revenues of $19.3 billion. PCI makes concentrates for soft-drink production in more than 600 plants in over 165 countries and territories, not including the U.S. headquarters in Somers, NY. PCI sets the strategic agenda for its five overseas operating divisions. Overseas staff are responsible for the sale and marketing of Pepsi brands.

Professional Staff: The overseas staff of 3,500 professionals is stationed in 150 countries worldwide. This staff is mostly comprised of foreign nationals but includes some U.S. citizens. The Somers headquarters employs approximately 250 people.

Qualifications: PCI looks for applicants with a college degree or MBA and some expertise in consumer products. Three-to-ten years experience in marketing or finance and knowledge of Spanish, Arabic, Chinese, French, German, Japanese or Russian, in that order, is preferred. Willingness to travel and live abroad is necessary. Pepsi-Cola International recruits from colleges and graduate schools.

Training Program: The Designate Program is designed to build skills in U.S. bottling assignments prior to transfer abroad. A graduate degree and/or previous work experience qualifies applicants for this six-to-twelve- month training program. There are currently 20 trainee slots available each year.

Internships: Graduate students in business may apply for paid summer internships.

Application Procedure: Interested interns or job applicants should contact:

> Director of Personnel
> Pepsi-Cola International
> 1 Pepsi Way
> Somers, NY 10589
> (914) 767-6000, ext. 7445

PHILLIPS PETROLEUM COMPANY
Bartlesville, OK

Phillips Petroleum, the company that drilled the first successful oil wells in the North Sea, exported over $300 million worth of liquefied natural gas, petrochemicals and plastics to customers worldwide in 1990. However, only some 3% of its profits come from export sales. Phillips, rated 27th in the 1991 *Fortune* 500 listing, is divided into five operating groups and has no international department per se. Exploration and Production explores for and produces oil and gas in 16 countries. Gas and Gas Liquids processes and sells natural gas worldwide. Minerals locates and markets an array of petroleum-related minerals. Petroleum Products buys and markets oil and gas. Chemicals manufactures petroleum-based products and has facilities in 21 countries. Phillips also has subsidiaries in 23 countries in Europe, Asia and Latin America, although these foreign operations have been trimmed somewhat in the last five years.

Professional Staff: Most Americans working for Phillips spend three-to-five years with its U.S.-based operations before receiving international assignments. Out of a total international staff of 4,650, approximately 115 U.S. citizens are stationed abroad. The company hired 184 recent college graduates in the past year.

Qualifications: Although Phillips prefers people with technical degrees in research- and development-oriented sciences, it does sometimes hire applicants without graduate degrees and, in some cases, without technical degrees. Some, but not all, employees are put through training programs, but Phillips has such a diverse range of programs that it cannot specify which employees will be put through what programs. The company does not require previous work experience, foreign languages or a willingness to travel.

Application Procedure: Write to:

>   Director of Employment
>   Phillips Petroleum Company
>   180 Plaza Building
>   Bartlesville, OK 74004
>   (918) 661-4400, ext. 6467

PROCTER & GAMBLE INTERNATIONAL
Cincinnati, OH

Crest toothpaste is sold in almost 50 nations around the world, including countries in the former Soviet Union, Latin America and Asia, as well as Canada. Crest is one of many products the multinational has marketed abroad since 1967. Procter & Gamble (P&G) has over 70 U.S. brands and sells over 160 brands in nearly 140 countries. Today, its international organization contributes more than 40% of the company's total sales and profits. International is the fastest growing part of P&G, with over 50 overseas operations.

The company has three major regional headquarters: Caracas, Venezuela; Brussels, Belgium, and Osaka, Japan. The international headquarters in Cincinnati provides support for overseas operations in all business areas. Each function, e.g., legal, tax, personnel, etc., has staff dedicated to supporting international operations. These individuals provide strategic, planning and coordination services to operating management. Most employees in overseas offices are foreign nationals.

Professional Staff: Currently, worldwide staff consists of about 96,000 people, half of whom work in the U.S. Although exact figures are not available for the U.S. international division, last year about 3,000 people were recruited to join international operations around the world.

Qualifications: Prerequisites for employment vary by location, function and position. Candidates with an MBA or other advanced degrees—both foreign and U.S. students—are preferred. This is true for both full-time and summer positions. P&G is willing to consider starting assignments outside of the applicant's home country if the candidate has the necessary language skills. Because P&G prefers to fill higher-level jobs by promoting from within the company, most employees come directly from college or graduate school. Regardless of prior experience, all employees start at entry-level positions, but experience could contribute to more rapid advancement. Second-language fluency is a significant plus and is almost always required.

Training Program: There is no official program; most of the training received at P&G is on-the-job, supplemented by classroom instruction conducted by P&G managers.

Internships: Paid summer internships are offered to graduate students in business as well as other fields.

Application Procedure: For more information, write to:

> International Recruiting Manager
> Procter & Gamble International (SY-4)
> PO Box 599
> Cincinnati, OH 45201-0599
> (513) 983-1100

ROCKWELL INTERNATIONAL
Pittsburgh, PA

Rockwell International is a $12 billion conglomerate with businesses manufacturing products for the aerospace, automotive and graphics industries. For 17 consecutive years Rockwell's Space Systems was the National Aeronautics and Space Administration's number one contract award winner for projects like the Space shuttle program.

Rockwell has four U.S. corporate offices: in Dallas, TX; Washington, DC; Pittsburgh, PA, and its world headquarters in Seal Beach, CA. The company also has corporate offices in Tokyo, Japan; Riyadh, Saudi Arabia; Moscow, Russia; London, England, and Hong Kong. International sales accounted for 26% of Rockwell's gross earnings last year. Rockwell's international department provides business unit support for international marketing activities.

Professional Staff: The international divisions in Rockwell's U.S. offices are usually small. The Pittsburgh international division has 15 professionals; Washington has 9. No professionals were hired for the Washington or Pittsburgh international divisions in the past year. There are 15 U.S. citizens overseas in Japan, Hong Kong, the U.K., Russia (Moscow), Brazil, Canada, Australia, France, Germany, Spain and Italy. The remainder of staff in the overseas offices consists of foreign nationals.

Qualifications: A college degree in management or finance as well as an MBA or an MS are desirable. Knowledge of foreign languages is preferred, particularly German, Japanese or French, although skills in Spanish, Chinese, Russian and Arabic are also useful, depending on the position and its location. Two-to-five years previous work experience in a technical field is required for employment but the applicant need not be willing to travel.

Training Program: Rockwell offers a training program that requires both college and graduate degrees, as well as previous work experience. A varying number of trainees are accepted each year, and the program's length depends on the field of training.

Internships: Rockwell offers semester-long paid internships in the engineering and finance sectors of the company for college students. Interns are chosen on the basis of their technical field of study. Interns are also placed in international departments.

Application Procedure: Applicants interested in internships in the Washington office should contact:

Human Resources
Rockwell International
1745 Jefferson Davis Highway
Arlington, VA 22210
(703) 553-6600

Applicants interested in internships in other parts of the company should contact:

Director of College Relations
Rockwell International
2201 Seal Beach Blvd., PO Box 4250
Seal Beach, CA 90740-8250
(310) 797-3311

Those interested in permanent employment should write to the Director of Human Resources at:

Rockwell International
625 Liberty Avenue
Pittsburgh, PA 15222-3123
(412) 565-7401

SPRINT INTERNATIONAL
Reston, VA

Sprint International is a subsidiary of United Telecom/Sprint which, after five years of operation, is the nation's third-largest long distance company with more than 6 million customers worldwide and $5.1 billion in annual revenues in 1991.

Sprint International is an expanding telecommunications company with wholly owned and joint ventures in Britain, Japan, the Netherlands, Belgium, France, Italy, Norway and the former Soviet Union. Activities of Sprint International include providing telecommunications products, support and services to the international marketplace.

Professional Staff: Sprint International is a growing subsidiary, with 1,500 professional employees in the U.S. and 200 abroad. Both foreign nationals and U.S. citizens are hired for overseas positions. In the last 12 months, 100 people were hired.

Qualifications: Applicants with a BS, BA, MBA or MS in engineering, math, sciences, international business, international finance or languages are preferred. Knowledge of Japanese, Russian, Spanish, French, German, Chinese, Arabic or other languages is generally preferred, and sometimes required, depending on the position or country of activity. Two to three years previous work experience in a telecom environment or international business is generally required for employment, but willingness to travel or live abroad is not.

Internships: Semester-long unpaid internships are available to graduate or third-year undergraduate students throughout the year. Interns generally assist program managers and their support staff.

Application Procedure: Applicants interested in internships should contact the College Intern Coordinator. Applicants for permanent positions should contact the Staffing Department. The address is:

Sprint International
12490 Sunrise Valley Drive
Reston, VA 22096
(703) 689-5469

R.J. REYNOLDS TOBACCO INTERNATIONAL, INC.
Winston-Salem, NC

Tobacco International is the RJR Nabisco subsidiary that manufactures, markets and sells tobacco products internationally as well as engaging in export licensing and joint ventures. It is a highly decentralized operation, with each of its marketing companies or subsidiaries operating independently.

Professional Staff: The U.S. staff comprises 175 people. Overseas, a staff of 6,500 is stationed in Europe, South America, the Middle East and Asia. In the last year, approximately 50 people were hired. Both foreign nationals and U.S. citizens are stationed abroad.

Qualifications: An undergraduate degree in finance, marketing, sales, development or human resources or an MBA is preferred. Knowledge of Spanish and French is also desirable, as is a willingness to travel and live abroad. Previous experience is required for certain positions. Most of those employed overseas have worked for RJR Tobacco International for at least five years; all international employees are middle to senior level.

Training Program: Some departments offer informal training programs for college graduates or those with previous work experience.

Internships: Paid summer internships are offered to graduate students and those with previous work experience or a particular area of interest. Interns usually work in the finance, marketing or human resources departments.

Application Procedure: Those interested in professional employment, internships or training programs should contact:

Director of Human Resources
R.J. Reynolds Tobacco International, Inc.
401 North Main Street
Winston-Salem, NC 27102
(919) 741-5000

UNISYS CORPORATION
Blue Bell, PA

Unisys Corporation makes and markets computer-based information systems, networks and related software on a worldwide basis. It specializes in providing mission-critical solutions, based on open information networks, for organizations such as banks, insurance companies, airlines, telephone companies, government agencies and other commercial enterprises with high-volume distribution activities.

One of the largest information-technology companies in the world, Unisys employs more that 65,000 people and operates in some 100 countries. In 1991 Unisys' total revenue was over $10 billion. Its annual engineering, research and development expenditures exceed $1 billion. Nearly 80% of Unisys' revenue is derived from commercial information systems and services, with the remainder originating from defense-oriented systems and services. Slightly more that one half of Unisys' revenue is from overseas operations. Principal duties of overseas staff include sales, manufacturing, distribution, finance, accounting and general support activities.

Professional Staff: Approximately 50,000 people work in Unisys' U.S. offices, including its corporate headquarters in Blue Bell, PA, and its defense subsidiary in McLean, VA. Twenty thousand employees are based overseas in Central and South America, Europe, Africa and Asia. Unisys hires both U.S. citizens and foreign nationals for overseas positions.

Qualifications: Because Unisys is such a large and diversified corporation, qualifications for applicants vary greatly. Generally, applicants should have an undergraduate degree in engineering or business. For some positions an MBA or other advanced degree is required.

Application Procedure: To find out what qualifications are currently being sought, contact:

> Vice President, Human Resources
> Unisys Corporation
> PO Box 500
> Blue Bell, PA 19424
> (215) 986-3527

U.S. CHAMBER OF COMMERCE
Washington, DC

The U.S. Chamber of Commerce is the world's largest federation of companies, chambers of commerce, and trade and professional associations. With more than 180,000 members representing the broad spectrum of business interests, the U.S. Chamber of Commerce is the principal advocate of the American business community.

The chamber's international division responds to global economic and business issues affecting U.S. enterprise. The chamber shapes legislative and regulatory policies at home and abroad that promote open competition. A network of bilateral and multilateral councils around the world complements the chamber's efforts in the U.S. and helps produce agreements and trade policies that improve business conditions in other countries to benefit American enterprises. This network provides a channel through which the Chamber of Commerce can communicate to foreign governments and business leaders American business views on key economic and commercial issues.

Professional Staff: The international division comprises 35 individuals, 4 of whom were hired in the chamber. Professional staff members conduct research, formulate policy, lobby members of Congress and work with the media in promoting the free-enterprise system.

Qualifications: The international division seeks candidates with undergraduate and graduate degrees in international relations and international economics. Applicants with an MA in a geographic specialization are also sought. Knowledge of Arabic, French and Spanish is preferred, but foreign languages are not necessary for policymaking and research positions. Experience in foreign affairs (public or private sector) is required for employment. The chamber rarely hires entry-level employees. Openings are sometimes offered to former interns.

Internships: The chamber offers unpaid semester-long internships to college juniors and seniors. Interns work on research projects, monitor bilateral economic issues, prepare directories of organizations, write articles for a monthly newsletter, attend congressional hearings and follow legislation. To be considered for the internship program, the applicant must have good writing and research skills and be studying international relations, economics or a geographic specialization.

Application Procedure: Those interested in internships should contact the International Division, Internship Program. For other applications, write to the Personnel Department:

The U.S. Chamber of Commerce
1615 H Street, NW
Washington, DC 20062
(202) 463-5731

Chapter Two

INTERNATIONAL CONSULTING

Introduction by James W. Fay

Over 4,000 international consulting firms are registered with the World Bank. The U.S. Agency for International Development (AID) maintains records on 1,000 U.S. consulting firms. Similarly, regional development finance institutions like the Asian Development Bank in Manila, the Inter-American Development Bank in Washington, DC, and the African Development Bank in Abidjan have files listing hundreds of consulting firms. For individuals seeking employment with either U.S. or non-U.S. consulting firms, the opportunities would seem to be extensive.

There are two things to remember about international consulting firms. First, they are as varied as different types of bread. There are engineering,

---

James W. Fay is Senior Vice President of International Operations for Nathan Associates, Inc., an economic consulting firm based in Washington, DC. Dr. Fay, who has a PhD in economics, joined Robert R. Nathan Associates in 1972 after spending five years working abroad as an economic consultant, primarily in Southeast Asia. In the last 25 years he has worked or lived in over 25 developing countries in Africa, South America, the Middle East and Asia.

economic, planning, architectural and a host of other types of firms offering specialized services, for example, energy planning, urban development, agriculture, transport planning, remote sensing, etc. While some of the larger firms in the U.S. may cover the whole range of consulting services, most firms consist of just a few experts in a narrow discipline. In fact, expertise is what consulting is about; anyone with detailed knowledge of a particular field or topic is a potential consultant.

Second, consulting firms for the most part do client research. That is, they provide individuals and services in response to what clients such as the World Bank or the government of Bangladesh, already has determined to be the requirements. As a result, consulting firms by and large are limited in whom they select to work on any given international assignments. A consulting firm may propose a specific individual, but in the final analysis staff selection is approved or vetoed by the client.

OVERSEAS EXPERIENCE: CATCH 22

Individuals seeking entry-level positions with consulting firms are often told that they cannot work overseas until they have worked overseas. This variant of catch-22 has been faced by all of us who now work for international consulting firms, and somehow we managed to overcome it. Some of us went to work initially for the U.S. government or an international organization like the UN, while others spent two years in the Peace Corps. Many had to spend time—two to three years—in the home office of a consulting firm working on proposals or doing backstopping work until an appropriate overseas opportunity presented itself.

Most people in consulting have advanced degrees, but employers are reluctant to send them on an overseas assignment until they have learned to apply their theoretical knowledge of, say, economic development to the firm's projects. Most consultants serve an apprenticeship of at least two to three years before they are considered qualified to work overseas in a position of responsibility. [Note: For further discussion of how to get overseas experience, see Chapter Eight.]

QUALIFICATIONS

Many entry-level opportunities in international consulting are biased toward individuals with advanced degrees and foreign-language capabilities. A master's degree is almost always required by most firms now, even for entry-level employees, although experience can be substituted for a degree in some cases. Common fields of academic specialization include engineering, economics, planning, public administration, agriculture, sociology and anthropology. Since most consulting firms do not specialize regionally, language capability in French or Spanish is often felt to be more useful than, say, Thai or Urdu. In general, fluency in at least one foreign language is considered a requirement.

In screening and hiring, especially for entry-level positions, consulting firms, like any business, are looking for intelligent persons who possess good common sense, flexibility in the areas or countries they are willing to work in and an appreciation that they must serve time in the home office before being assigned overseas. Writing skills, quantitative skills and, increasingly, hands-on-computer experience are also basic requirements.

You should not consider international consulting firms if high starting salaries and 9-5 workdays are important factors. Starting salaries are typically low, and the work load, particularly in the field, can at times exceed 12 hours a day, 6 days a week. As you take on more responsibility, you will have to travel as well. Individuals generally choose careers with consulting firms because they believe their efforts can make a difference in the quality of life for people in developing countries, and they are interested in job variety and exposure to different cultures.

Unlike entry-level applicants, experienced professionals usually have an established track record in a fairly well-defined area of expertise. For such persons finding the right project may be more important than finding the right firm. Their salaries will be higher than those of entry-level persons and will normally be in line with what they earned in their previous job.

Entry-level consulting staff start as research assistants, collecting and interpreting data and working on teams with more-senior staff. Training programs for new personnel are rare. The next step up is research associate, who begins to do some traveling. Associates may take long-term overseas positions and, upon return, be promoted to senior staff and may own shares in the company. In general, the more senior the staff, the more client contacts they have and the more they are expected to bring in new business. More-senior staff oversee parts of projects and eventually entire projects.

FINDING A CONSULTING JOB

For either entry-level applicants or experienced professionals who are seeking opportunities with international consulting firms, the critical requirement is a good resume and a list of appropriate firms to contact. If you lack overseas experience, your resume must highlight academic courses and areas of interest. Your resume—or cover letter—should indicate that you have the ability to undertake a variety of assignments in order to gain the requisite experience for overseas work. For experienced professionals, succinct summaries of past experience and areas of expertise are most important. Although you must be prepared for rejections, individuals interested in an overseas career with a consulting firm should not get discouraged. It is the nature of the business that staffing needs arise frequently and unpredictably as new projects emerge The fact that there is no opening today does not mean that there may not be one tomorrow.

Professional women have overcome most of the barriers that previously existed to their employment overseas. Still, there are some countries, principally Arab countries, where opportunities for women are limited. Offsetting this limitation is an increased emphasis by development finance institutions on the need to address the role of women in developing countries, and hence more projects are being undertaken in areas that should favor the involvement of female professionals.

The demand for international consultants continues to grow in the Third World. However, opportunities in Asia and Latin America for outside consultants can be expected to decline as indigenous personnel become qualified and take over the work done previously by international consulting firms.

The life blood of any consulting firm is good people, both at entry-levels and at professional levels. Probably no other industry is so dependent for its reputation on the individual performance of its employees as is the consulting business.

Thus, in spite of the many obstacles that entry-level applicants face, the message should be: "If you are well educated, competent and dedicated to pursuing a career in consulting, persevere." Eventually you will be given the opportunity to join a consulting firm. After the initial barrier is overcome, however, you will need to demonstrate very quickly that you have the "right stuff." [Reprinted from the second edition.]

ACADEMY FOR EDUCATIONAL DEVELOPMENT (AED)
Washington, DC

Founded in 1961, AED is a multifaceted, independent, nonprofit organization dedicated to promoting human development through education, communication and information. AED's activities are organized into three program areas: exchange and student services, higher education and technical training, and social development. Activities within these program areas include providing consulting expertise in education, exchange programs, vocational training, child survival, maternal and child health, family planning and environment and natural resources. Clients include educational institutions, foundations, corporations and governmental and international agencies in more than 50 cities throughout the U.S. and in more than 60 countries in the developing world. AED maintains project offices in Africa, Latin America, East Asia, South Asia, the Middle East and the Near East as well as offices in New York City and Washington, DC.

Professional Staff: AED employs 270 people, 70 of whom are stationed overseas. In the past year, 35 people were hired, 17 for the international department.

Qualifications: AED prefers applicants with graduate backgrounds in health, business, public affairs, economics, sciences, education or development. Knowledge of Spanish, French, Arabic or Russian is preferred. Typical qualifications of AED employees are two-to-ten years previous experience living, working, or studying in a developing country or experience in international development, administration, financial management and budgeting, research, writing, training or quantitative and qualitative analysis. Willingness to live abroad is required for certain positions.

Internships: Semester-long paid and unpaid internships are available for college and graduate students. Applicants must be enrolled in programs in communications, education or international development. Interns are involved in research and writing, financial tracking and management, coordinating travel arrangements, itineraries, meetings and conferences as well as the preparation and production of proposals.

Application Procedure: Persons interested in either professional positions or internships should contact:

> Recruitment Manager
> Academy for Educational Development
> 1255 23rd Street, NW
> Suite 400
> Washington, DC 20037
> (202) 862-1900

AGRICULTURAL COOPERATIVE DEVELOPMENT INTERNATIONAL
Washington, DC

ACDI, a nonprofit consortium of U.S. agricultural cooperatives, farm-credit banks, farmers' associations and independent farm experts, provides advisers to farm cooperatives, agricultural banks, government agencies and donor organizations in the Third World to help them prepare project proposals and secure financing, often from the U.S. Agency for International Development. It has helped farming communities in Africa, Asia, Central America, South America and the South Pacific increase productivity, and it conducts regional workshops and participates in international seminars on Third World agricultural development.

Professional Staff: ACDI employs 27 people in the U.S. and 20 abroad. In the past year, approximately 20 were hired for overseas positions. Advisers to farmer cooperatives and credit institutions are stationed in Bolivia, Costa Rica, Egypt, Guatemala, Honduras, Jamaica, the Philippines, Tanzania, Tonga and Uganda.

Qualifications: An MA, MBA, MIA or PhD in agricultural economics, business or financial management is necessary for employment. Four or more years of hands-on experience managing farm cooperatives, training in finance and accounting, or consulting on agricultural work in developing countries is required. Knowledge of French, Spanish, Arabic or local African languages is preferred. Employees must be willing to travel and live abroad.

Application Procedure: Applications should be addressed to:

> Executive Assistant
> Agricultural Cooperative Development International
> 50 F Street, NW
> #900
> Washington, DC 20001
> (202) 638-4661

ARTHUR D. LITTLE, INC.
Cambridge, MA

A.D. Little provides technical and management consultancy on a global basis, including contract research and product/process development, as well as environmental and health consulting. The international department is involved in human-resource management, including recruiting, staffing, hiring, transferring benefits, compensation, tax planning and expatriate administration.

Professional Staff: A.D. Little maintains a staff of 2,500 in the U.S. and has 500 employees stationed abroad. Overseas staff members are stationed in Australia, Belgium, Brazil, Denmark, France, Germany, Hong Kong, Japan, Mexico, Saudi Arabia, Singapore, Spain, Taiwan, the U.K., Venezuela and elsewhere. Last year 100 professionals were hired.

Qualifications: Qualified applicants hold MBA, MS or PhD degrees in various fields. Knowledge of Chinese, Spanish, French, German or Japanese is helpful and is required for some positions. Qualified applicants have three-to-five years of overseas experience.

Internships: Paid positions are offered during the summer to first-year MBA students with three-to-five years of experience in industry.

Application Procedure: Address applications to:

> Human Resources Department
> A.D. Little, Inc.
> 25 Acorn Park
> Cambridge, MA 02140
> (617) 864-5770, ext. 2249

CHECCHI AND COMPANY
Washington, DC

Checchi is an economic consulting firm specializing in international development. Its projects focus on agricultural production, business management, education and training programs, the growth of small industry, capital generation and the expansion of tourism. Clients have included international organizations, federal agencies, state and local governments, foreign governments and nonprofit organizations. Checchi currently has overseas staff in 20 countries and has had staff in 110 countries over the past 40 years.

Professional Staff: Checchi's headquarters in Washington, DC, maintains a staff of 20 professionals. Overseas staff comprises approximately two dozen people. During the past year, the firm hired 3 people for the home office, 7 for long-term overseas projects and 35 free-lance overseas consultants. Both U.S. citizens and foreign nationals are represented on the staff, and free-lance consultants are often used.

Qualifications: Although academic requirements vary according to specific projects, a background in economics, business or international relations is most frequently sought. Previous international development work, especially in the Third World, is preferred. The stateside staff includes experts in rural development; agricultural economics; development banking; administration, education and training; economic and financial analysis; information systems; and tourism. Knowledge of foreign languages is required for most project work. Languages vary according to project; usually local dialects—especially Asian ones—are desired.

Application Procedure: Persons interested in professional positions should contact:

> Recruitment Coordinator
> Checchi and Company
> 1730 Rhode Island Avenue, NW
> Suite 910
> Washington, DC 20036
> (202) 452-9700

DATA RESOURCES, INCORPORATED/McGRAW-HILL
Lexington, MA

DRI/McGraw-Hill provides businesses with information concerning market planning, financial-market opportunities, regional investments, government-policy implications and global-market developments. DRI/McGraw-Hill has staff stationed in Germany, Toronto, Brussels, London, Milan and Paris.

Professional Staff: The U.S. staff numbers 470, with 50 professionals hired last year. Both U.S. and foreign nationals are hired overseas.

Qualifications: Qualified applicants have a background in economics or another quantitative discipline, business or marketing, with an MA, MBA, MS or PhD degree. Individuals with expertise in various fields including energy, government, chemicals, telecommunications, transportation and insurance are sought. Experience in a specific industry is required, and placement varies according to experience. Foreign language requirements vary according to position.

Internships: Positions are occasionally open to graduate students.

Application Procedure: Direct application correspondence to:

Human Resource Representative
DRI/McGraw-Hill
24 Hartwell Avenue
Lexington, MA 02173
(617) 863-5100

EXPERIENCE, INC.
Minneapolis, MN

Experience, Inc., has provided analysis and counseling in all aspects of agribusiness—including natural resources, production and marketing—to over 50 developed and developing countries since 1967. The international department works mainly with foreign governments managing projects, adapting technology and training indigenous people to improve agricultural techniques and production. Personnel in Bolivia, Uganda, Ecuador and Mali are also responsible for proposal design, preparation and business development.

Professional Staff: The U.S. office maintains a staff of 5, with 10 people stationed overseas. During the past year, five people were hired for the international department.

Qualifications: Experience, Inc., provides advanced technical and business expertise, and its staff is therefore highly educated and experienced. An MA, MS or PhD in agricultural economics, marketing, agronomy or natural resources is preferred. At least 10 years experience in agricultural development, production, processing or marketing, food technology or processing and farm management is necessary. Experience in Third World development is preferred but not required. Knowledge of Spanish and French is useful. Employees must be willing to travel and live abroad.

Internships: Graduate students may apply for paid internships at the Arlington, VA, office. Applicants should have an undergraduate degree in international or agriculture-related fields. Knowledge of a foreign language is useful.

Application Procedure: Individuals interested in professional positions and internships should contact:

Personnel Office
Experience, Inc.
1200 2nd Avenue South, #400
Minneapolis, MN 55403
(612) 338-7844

MEDICAL SERVICE CORPORATION INTERNATIONAL (MSCI)
Arlington, VA

MSCI is a diversified health-care management firm involved in a broad range of health activities, ranging from highly focused analytical studies to complex multimillion-dollar primary health-care delivery projects. Currently, MSCI is working on projects in El Salvador and Egypt, and has recently begun a new project in Bulgaria. MSCI's principal activities include recruiting long-term and short-term consultants to work on international health-care projects and maintaining a computerized data base of consultants. MSCI also manages the U.S. Agency for International Development's Vector Biology and Control Project (VBC), a worldwide program of vector-borne disease-control activities.

Professional Staff: MSCI currently maintains a staff of 47 in its U.S. office, 34 in El Salvador, and 4 in Egypt. Both U.S. citizens and foreign nationals are hired for overseas positions. In the past year 10 people were hired, 3 for positions overseas. The number of employees to work in Bulgaria has not yet been determined.

Qualifications: MSCI seeks applicants with advanced degrees (MA, MBA, MD, MIA, MPA, MS, PhD or MPH) in the fields of public health, public administration, international economics and finance, business administration or biomedical maintenance. Preferred fields of expertise are international health-related areas such as public health and tropical diseases, medicine, biomedical research and equipment maintenance. Knowledge of foreign languages, including Spanish, French, German, Russian, Bulgarian and Arabic, is preferred. For overseas positions, at least three-to-five years of previous overseas experience is required. Except for some of the corporate staff, travel and living abroad may be required.

Internships: A limited number of internships is offered by the Vector Biology and Control Project. Internships last three months and are offered on a semester basis and during the summer. Graduate students with a background in vector-borne diseases are preferred. Interns are provided a stipend.

Application Procedure: Individuals interested in professional and internship positions should contact:

> Personnel Manager
> Medical Service Corporation International
> 1716 Wilson Boulevard
> Arlington, VA 22209
> (703) 276-3000

MORAN, STAHL AND BOYER INTERNATIONAL (MS&B)
Boulder, CO

MS&B, a subsidiary of The Prudential, is a consulting firm specializing in international human-resources management. For over 25 years MS&B has provided consulting and tailored assessment, research and training services to senior executives, expatriate personnel and their families, international business travelers and foreign employees. Services include consulting and seminars on business globalization, assessment and selection of potential expatriates, cross-cultural training for expatriates, learner-centered foreign-language instruction, repatriation training and counseling, programs on foreign-business practices, training for multicultural work-force management and team-building, and workshops on intercultural sales, marketing and negotiations. Programs have been conducted in 87 different countries at MS&B's facilities in New York, Boulder, Houston, London and Tokyo, as well as at clients' locations worldwide.

Professional Staff: MS&B has a staff of 33 in its U.S. offices and 6 employees stationed in offices in London and Tokyo. Principal duties of overseas staff are international training and consulting. Both U.S. and foreign nationals are hired for overseas positions. Two people were hired in 1991, both in the international department.

Qualifications: MS&B prefers applicants with a PhD and expertise in either international business or intercultural communications. Knowledge of foreign languages is required, and Japanese, Russian, Chinese, German, French, Spanish, Arabic and Eastern European languages are preferred. Successful overseas living and work experience is also required. Employees must be willing to travel and live abroad.

Training Program: MS&B has an ad hoc training program, averaging two-to-three days, that acquaints trainees with the theory and practices of the organization. The number of trainees accepted varies from year to year.

Internships: Internship positions are offered on a yearly, semester or summer basis to qualified graduate students with background and experience in international or intercultural studies. Duties involve assisting with training, materials development and marketing. Positions are unpaid.

Application Procedure: Address applications for internships to Director, Program Design and Development. Address applications for professional positions to:

> Moran, Stahl & Boyer International
> 900 28th Street
> Boulder, CO 80303
> (303) 449 8440

NATHAN ASSOCIATES
Arlington, VA

Nathan Associates, Inc., established in 1946, is one of the oldest and most experienced economic and management consulting companies in the world. It conducts economic development studies for and provides advisory assistance to countries throughout Africa, Asia, the Middle East, Europe, Latin America and the Caribbean. International projects make up about two thirds of Nathan Associates' work, focusing on national and regional planning, agricultural-sector studies, energy, transportation, private-sector development, trade-development banking and urban planning. Nathan Associates concentrates on economic issues and contracts with other international firms to provide engineering and other technical assistance. Recent clients include the African and Asian development banks, the U.S. Agency for International Development, the Inter-American Development Bank, the UN Development Program and the World Bank. Staff are currently stationed in Bangladesh, Bolivia, Cameroon, Egypt, Ghana, Honduras, Indonesia, the Philippines and Zambia.

Professional Staff: The Arlington, VA, office has a staff of 70 professional economists; an additional 35 people work on overseas advisory teams. Approximately a half dozen people were hired in 1991 for the professional staff. In addition, Nathan Associates hires free-lance consultants for international projects of both short and long duration.

Qualifications: Nathan Associates mainly employs professionals with an MA, MBA or PhD in economics or finance. A strong candidate should have approximately five years previous business or overseas development experience. Fluency in a foreign language, particularly Spanish, French, Arabic, Indonesian, Thai, Chinese or Urdu, is preferred. Employees must be willing to travel and live abroad.

Application Procedure: Interested individuals should contact:

Recruiter, International Operations
Nathan Associates Inc.
2101 Wilson Boulevard, Suite 1200
Arlington, VA 22201
(703) 516-7700

TOWERS PERRIN
New York, NY

Towers Perrin, an international firm of management consultants and actuaries, advises organizations on the design, funding and administration of benefit, remuneration and other human-resources programs. In addition, it provides general, management and risk-management consulting services and offers counsel on insurance company actuarial issues. Towers Perrin serves more than 8,000 clients in the private and public sectors from 60 offices throughout the U.S., Latin America, the Netherlands, Canada, Europe, the Far East and Australia. The international department is comprised of specialized international consulting units that assist multinational employers in managing their benefit, remuneration and other human-resources programs worldwide.

Professional Staff: The combined domestic and overseas staff totals 5,000. During the past year, 100 were hired, 50 for the international department. Both U.S. citizens and foreign nationals are employed. Overseas offices are staffed primarily by nationals.

Qualifications: Towers Perrin seeks candidates with undergraduate or graduate degrees in business, law, engineering, mathematics, computer science and economics. Potential employees are expected to have two-to-three years professional experience in the fields of communications, energy, financial services, information processing, government, education, insurance or general business/industry. Preferred languages include French, German, Spanish, Japanese, Chinese and Portuguese. Overseas experience in Japan or Europe is helpful.

Internships: A limited number of paid summer internships are available for graduate students. Applicants should be interested in gaining actuarial qualifications or have experience in human-resources management. Interns conduct research, write reports and perform analysis.

Application Procedure: Towers Perrin recruits from international departments on college campuses as well as graduate programs. Persons interested in internships or professional positions should contact:

> Manager, International Recruiting
> Towers Perrin
> 245 Park Avenue
> New York, NY 10167
> (212) 309-3400

TRANSCENTURY
Arlington, VA

TransCentury is an internationally recognized consulting group that assists domestic and international development and investment in the context of multicultural cooperation. The group consists of TransCentury Corporation and the New TransCentury Foundation. TransCentury Corporation was founded in 1967 as a profit-making research and operations firm. Initially focused on U.S. youth and community development projects, the corporation has expertise in a wide range of areas, including international development, investment and procurement. The corporation also offers recruitment service to people seeking positions in the field of international development and contracts with the U.S. Agency for International Development in the area of Third World development. The international department's activities include procurement services, microenterprise and small-business development, career counseling for nonprofit professionals and international executive search. New TransCentury Foundation was founded in 1968 as a nonprofit organization to promote democratic and innovative social development and to inquire into the nature of the innovative process. Creative human-resources development remains a key focus of the foundation's technical assistance and research. During its 20-year history, TransCentury has worked in all 50 states and has assisted 80 countries worldwide. TransCentury currently has four overseas projects.

Professional Staff: TransCentury currently has an overseas staff of 30 and a U.S. staff of 7 employees. Overseas staff members are presently stationed in Egypt and Senegal. Their duties involve health procurement, enterprise development and participant training. Both U.S. and foreign nationals are hired.

Qualifications: Applicants with advanced degrees in various fields are sought. At least two years of overseas development experience, preferably in a Third World country, is required. Knowledge of a foreign language, preferably French or Spanish, is required.

Application Procedure: Interested individuals should contact:

TransCentury Recruitment Center
1901 N. Fort Myer Drive
Suite 1017
Arlington, VA 22209
(703) 351-5500

Chapter Three

INTERNATIONAL FINANCE AND BANKING

Introduction by Richard A. Debs
and Tarek Abdel-Meguid

Banking and finance offer a variety of opportunities for both entry-level and experienced professionals interested in internationally oriented careers. The range of possibilities has never been greater and, if anything, promises to grow. This is true for a number of reasons, the most important of which is the continuing trend toward the globalization of

---

Richard A. Debs is advisory director of Morgan Stanley & Co. Inc. and former president of Morgan Stanley International, Inc. He previously served as first vice president and chief administrative officer of the Federal Reserve Bank of New York. Mr. Debs graduated summa cum laude from Colgate University in 1952, and holds an MA and a PhD from Princeton University. He is also a graduate of the Harvard Law School as well as of the Advanced Management Program at the Harvard Business School. He was a Fulbright Scholar in Egypt. Mr. Debs is a member of the board of governors of the Foreign Policy Association.

Tarek Abdel-Meguid is managing director of the merger and acquisitions department of Morgan Stanley & Co. Inc. He received a BS from McGill University, Montreal, and an MBA from Columbia University.

financial markets and the geographic diversification of industrial and corporate activities. The volatility of financial markets, the continuing deregulation in the financial-services industry worldwide, and advances in communications technology all point to the rapid development of interdependent, integrated global markets where national boundaries will be less and less significant.

Those institutions that have been active in bringing about the globalization of the financial-services industry are the most obvious prospective employers of individuals with international-affairs backgrounds. The institutions include the large money-center commercial banks and a number of investment banking firms, most of which are headquartered in New York City. However, as discussed below, there is a great deal more to both entering and being successful in international banking or finance than simply an understanding of "things international."

Most commercial banks hire at the undergraduate level at liberal arts colleges, and some have a preference for majors such as economics or political science. They also recruit graduates with an MBA, a law degree or even an MIA in one of many subjects. Banks recruit at the most prestigious schools, and seek qualities such as common sense and good judgment as well as quantitative and analytic skills.

Most commercial banks and some investment banks have formal training programs. These vary from bank to bank and last from two months to two years. The programs, which are usually very structured in the commercial banks, combine classroom experience (including courses in accounting, corporate finance, credit analysis and international finance) with on-the-job training, in which the trainee is often expected to participate in daily activities from the outset. Training programs are sometimes highly competitive, and as much as 10 percent of the trainees may not complete the course. In other programs, the entire class is assured permanent employment. Trainees may be placed in one department or rotated among departments.

Virtually all organizations with international capabilities have anywhere from one to dozens of foreign offices. The principal foreign office is usually London, but many firms have other European, Canadian, Far Eastern, Middle Eastern and Australian operations of varying magnitude. Job openings overseas depend on the particular bank and the volume of business it does in a particular region.

The criteria for transferring U.S. personnel to overseas offices vary with the needs of each bank. Consideration is given to the performance of the individual. It must be remembered that headquarters handles many vital functions of a company's overseas work; thus those who hope to work overseas should expect to spend some time at the company's nerve center.

Securing a position in investment banking tends to be more competitive than in commercial banking. Most firms focus their recruitment at business schools, seeking MBAs with some business experience. In some firms, undergraduates may be recruited for a one- or two-year program, after which they are expected to go to business school for an MBA. They may or may not return to the same firm after completion of their degrees, and there is no commitment on either side to do so.

Most firms in the field are organized along two broad functional lines: investment banking, which includes corporate finance and merger and acquisition activities; and capital markets, which includes securities sales and trading activities. Successful candidates generally have distinguished themselves either academically or in other ways. An MBA degree from a school like Harvard or Wharton is a plus, although it does not guarantee you a job. A less-traditional background is sometimes an advantage Among the people Morgan Stanley has hired for the investment banking program are a former movie producer and an oil-rig operator. The point, of course, is never to write yourself off as a possible investment banker because you have not followed a traditional path.

Relocation abroad and promotion operate in much the same way as in the commercial banks: they vary with each firm's needs as well as with the ability of the individual. (It should also be noted that many commercial banks have significant investment banking activities, particularly overseas.)

A career in investment banking has recently offered the promise of high compensation over the years, but it is coupled with longer hours, unpredictable demands on time and generally greater stress. However, more and more commercial banks are developing investment banking groups that offer similar monetary rewards with similar demands.

Regardless of whether one's interest lies in commercial or investment banking, both require individuals who possess strong interpersonal skills, a high energy level and a reasonable degree of quantitative fluency.

ADVENT INTERNATIONAL
Boston, MA

Advent International is a private equity/venture capital investment firm that manages over $650 million in corporate and institutional investments. Investments are made in the U.S. and internationally, often in conjunction with member firms of the Advent Network, one of the largest venture-capital networks in the world.

The firm's overseas staff, stationed in the U.K., Italy, Germany, Canada and Hong Kong, is primarily involved with venture-capital investments and ongoing management of existing investment portfolios. Advent describes its international activities as growing.

Professional Staff: Advent International currently has 45 professionals in its Boston office and 20 professionals working abroad. Mainly foreign nationals fill overseas positions. In the last 12 months, five professionals were hired.

Qualifications: Candidates with an MBA combined with scientific graduate or undergraduate work are most desirable, although those with an MS or PhD with expertise or at least two years experience in venture capital, investment banking, finance, accounting, technology or marketing are also considered. Knowledge of Chinese, French, German, Japanese or Spanish is preferred, as is a willingness to travel.

Training Program: Advent accepts one or two "junior hires" annually into its two-year training program. The analyst position is offered to individuals with two-to-three years work experience after completing an undergraduate degree. Analysts support investment managers, vice-presidents and senior vice-presidents.

Application Procedure: Contact:

> Personnel Department
> Advent International Corporation
> 101 Federal Street
> Boston, MA 02110
> (617) 951-9400

ALLIANCE CAPITAL MANAGEMENT
New York, NY

Alliance Capital Management is a fully diversified global-investment adviser providing asset management for institutions—pension funds, endowments, foundations—and for individuals. Alliance has offered investment management for 20 years, amassing $62 billion in assets since 1991 and providing investment-management services to 21 of the top *Fortune* 100 companies.

Professional Staff: Alliance has a professional staff of 237 in the U.S. Thirty-one overseas employees are stationed in the U.K., Germany, Spain, Luxembourg, Japan, Australia, Canada and India. Overseas staff engages in investment management, marketing and sales. In the past year, 53 professionals were hired, 19 for the international department only.

Qualifications: Alliance seeks applicants with college or graduate degrees in finance, business and economics and those with some expertise in investment management and research marketing. Six-to-ten years experience in international investment, management or marketing is required, as is a willingness to travel and live abroad. Knowledge of Spanish, Japanese or German is preferred.

Application Procedure: Write to:

Vice President of Human Resources
Alliance Capital Management Corporation
1345 Avenue of the Americas
New York, NY 10105
(212) 969-1000

AMERICAN EXPRESS BANK
New York, NY

Through its 87 offices in 39 countries, American Express Bank (AEB) offers international financial services for individuals and businesses. These services include global treasury services, commercial services, correspondent banking and private banking. AEB recently expanded its global network with three new locations in Athens, Geneva and Pusan, South Korea.

Professional Staff: AEB employs over 2,000 people worldwide, with 1,459 employees working in overseas offices. Both U.S. and foreign nationals are hired, and their duties may involve sales and marketing, credit, finance and systems services.

Qualifications: AEB seeks applicants with advanced degrees in finance, economics or international studies. Work-experience requirements depend on the position. Generally, AEB seeks applicants with three to four years of experience in banking, international business or finance. Knowledge of foreign languages is desirable, depending on the geographic region of the assignment. Willingness to travel and live abroad is preferred.

Training Program: AEB offers a 10-month training program. From 12 to 15 trainees are accepted yearly, and are trained in finance, credit and financial-statement analysis.

Internships: Summer internships are offered to qualified college students. Positions are paid and are project-oriented or clerical in nature. These involve work in various areas in the accounting, operations, systems and treasury departments.

Application Procedure: Those interested in professional or internship positions should contact:

> American Express Bank Ltd.
> Human Resources Department
> American Express Tower
> World Financial Center
> New York, NY 10285
> (212) 298-5000

CRÉDIT SUISSE
New York, NY

Crédit Suisse, the third-largest Swiss bank, is a globally active full-service bank based in Zurich, with branches all over the world. Crédit Suisse provides both retail and wholesale banking, commercial banking, securities and investment business, specialty finance, consumer credit, leasing and international finance. International business is assuming increasing importance for Crédit Suisse, representing more than 30% of the bank's gross profit (up from 18% two years ago). Internationally, the bank seeks to provide specialized wholesale banking services. Overseas staff, in addition to performing their job-related duties, are looked upon to transfer know-how and skills; to gain exposure on an international level; to foster corporate identity and to ensure Crédit Suisse standards; and to otherwise internationalize Crédit Suisse.

Professional Staff: Crédit Suisse branch has a professional staff of 285 people, of whom 28 were hired in the last year.

Qualifications: Crédit Suisse looks for applicants with at least a college degree in finance, accounting, economics or other relevant subjects. MBAs are desirable. Employees in the international department must be willing to travel and live abroad. Foreign-language proficiency is required, with the language depending on the place of assignment. Crédit Suisse normally recruits only at the graduate level.

Training Program: For those with previous work experience, Crédit Suisse offers six-to-eight month training programs. There are 48 trainee positions open each year for the following programs: investment advisory, logistics; operations, corporate finance; and capital markets.

Internships: Paid internships are available in most of Crédit Suisse's branches. Qualifications for internships depend on purpose, skills and potential as a future employee.

Application Procedure: For information about opportunities in any of Crédit Suisse's overseas offices, contact the Human Resources Department of the respective branch. For employment and other inquiries for the New York office, contact:

> Human Resources Department
> Crédit Suisse
> 100 Wall Street
> New York, NY 10005
> (212) 612-8000

EXPORT-IMPORT BANK (Eximbank)
Washington, DC

Eximbank, operating since 1934 as a government-owned corporation, is designed to aid in financing and facilitating exports from the U.S. Opportunities in international commerce are extended to businesses through a program of loans, export-credit insurance and guarantees aimed at reducing risk for exporters. The economic feasibility of loan applications is evaluated by bank teams of economists, financial analysts, engineers and lawyers.

Professional Staff: Eximbank employs 350 people, 20 of whom were hired in the past year. Most are loan officers, accountants and economists. No employees work abroad.

Qualifications: Most employees have an MA, MBA, JD or PhD. Knowledge of a foreign language is a plus although foreign-language training is provided by the bank. Spanish and French are most useful. Previous work experience is not a prerequisite, but related experience is an asset. International travel is required of most professional staff members. After working one year for the bank, employees can receive tuition support to obtain advanced degrees.

Internships: See Chapter Ten, Internships.

Application Procedure: Although Eximbank recruits on a few college and graduate campuses, most positions require Office of Personnel Management (OPM) competitive eligibility and are filled from a federal listing of qualified candidates. For information and forms, write to:

> The Job Information Center
> U.S. Office of Personnel Management
> 1900 E Street, NW
> Washington, DC 20571

You might also write directly to Eximbank, especially if you are interested in a specific opening.

> Vice President—Human Resources
> Export-Import Bank of the United States
> 811 Vermont Avenue, NW
> Washington, DC 20571
> (202) 566-8834

GOLDMAN, SACHS & CO.
New York, NY

Goldman, Sachs & Co. conducts comprehensive and diversified investment banking and investment-services business in the U.S. and abroad. The firm is a member of the principal exchanges trading stocks and commodities, and it is one of the largest managing underwriters of corporate and government offerings in the world. It has been a major participant in fixed-income and equity markets, mergers, international arbitrage, block trading, swaps and convertible securities. Overseas staff are stationed in Australia, Canada, France, Germany, Grand Cayman, Hong Kong, Japan, Singapore, Spain, Switzerland, Taiwan and the U.K. Principal duties of the overseas staff vary by position level.

Professional Staff: There are 2,272 professional staff members in the U.S. and 912 overseas, of whom 265 are U.S. citizens. The firm hires both U.S. citizens and foreign nationals for overseas positions. The firm hired 262 professionals in the last 12 months. Ninety professionals were hired for the international offices only. The international department is growing.

Qualifications: The firm looks for many different degrees: JD, MA, MBA, MS and PhD. The desired field of expertise, and the kind and number of years of experience will vary with the position level.

Willingness to travel and live abroad and foreign-language proficiency are required.

Training Program: Goldman, Sachs & Co. has many different training programs, for example the Equities Associate program. Applicants with appropriate graduate degrees train in New York for six to nine months. Forty to sixty trainees are accepted yearly. Also the firm offers an Investment Banking Associate program. As in the Equities Associate program, the applicants must have a graduate degree. This year, the firm hired about 50 Investment Banking Associates. Of this number, 60% were hired for offices in the U.S. and 40% for the international offices. The training program lasts five weeks.

Internships: The firm offers paid summer internships to college and graduate students. The type of internships available varies; undergraduates usually perform clerical and analytical work, and MBA candidates perform corporate finance work.

Application Procedure: Write to:

> Manager of Employment
> Goldman, Sachs & Co.
> 85 Broad Street
> New York, NY 10004
> (212) 902-1000

THE INDUSTRIAL BANK OF JAPAN, LTD.
New York, NY

IBJ, founded in 1902, is Japan's largest long-term credit bank and one of the leading banks in the world. IBJ is rated the seventh-largest bank in Japan and ninth in the world. IBJ's years of experience in the U.S. began with the establishment of the New York representative office in 1956, which is now the New York branch. Headquartered in Tokyo, the bank operates 29 branches in Japan and 51 overseas offices as well as subsidiaries throughout the world.

IBJ and IBJ-affiliated locations in Europe, the Americas, Asia and the Pacific Rim provide a full range of financial and advisory services. Financial services include lending operations, funding and treasury operations, capital-markets activities and securities underwriting. IBJ is a major securities trader, ranking 12 in Eurobond underwriting. Advisory services include mergers and acquisitions, investment management and arrangement of tax-oriented lease financing.

Professional Staff: IBJ has a professional staff of 250 in the U.S. and 3,000 overseas. In the last 12 months, 21 professionals were hired for the New York branch. Mostly U.S. citizens staff the New York branch.

Qualifications: Previous experience is not required for employment. Experience and educational requirements vary with each position. Knowledge of foreign languages is unnecessary.

Application Procedure: All applications for employment should be addressed to the Personnel Department.

> The Industrial Bank of Japan, Ltd.
> 245 Park Avenue
> New York, NY 10167
> (212) 557-3500

J.P. MORGAN & CO., INCORPORATED
New York, NY

J.P. Morgan, the nation's fourth-largest banking and financial-services institution, is the holding company for subsidiaries engaged globally in a wide range of activities, including financing, advising, securities trading and underwriting, trust, agency and operational services and investment management. J.P Morgan's clients are mainly corporations, governments and financial institutions. The company also offers banking and asset-management services to individuals, privately held companies, professional firms and nonprofit organizations.

Professional Staff: J.P. Morgan & Co. employs 7,064 people worldwide. The overseas staff of 2,471 is comprised mainly of foreign nationals stationed throughout Europe. Activities of overseas staff include corporate finance, private banking, financial advisory, sales, trading and research. In the past 12 months, 65 graduates and undergraduates were hired for the New York office.

Qualifications: Applicants for work at J.P. Morgan come from a range of academic backgrounds but are expected to have strong quantitative skills. No previous work experience is required although a willingness to travel and live abroad is. essential. Knowledge of Japanese, German and French is preferred. J.P. Morgan actively recruits from colleges and graduate schools.

Training Program: The Morgan finance program introduces trainees to corporate finance and accounting, as well as global, capital and money markets. Both undergraduates and graduates are accepted into the program which lasts from 10 to 18 weeks.

Internships: Paid summer internships are offered to college students with a strong quantitative background. Interns assist in all aspects of bank operations.

Application Procedure: Those interested in internships or professional positions may contact:

> College Relations
> J.P. Morgan & Co., Incorporated
> 60 Wall Street
> New York, NY 10260-0060
> (212) 483-2323

MERRILL LYNCH & CO., INC.
New York, NY

Merrill Lynch & Co., Inc., is a holding company that through its subsidiaries and affiliates provides investment, financing, insurance and related services. The primary subsidiaries of the company are Merrill Lynch, Pierce, Fenner & Smith Incorporated (MLPF&S), one of the largest securities firms in the world; Merrill Lynch Asset Management, Inc., which manages mutual funds and provides investment advisory services; Merrill Lynch Government Securities, Inc., a primary dealer in obligations issued by the U.S. government or guaranteed or issued by federal agencies. Other subsidiaries provide financial services outside the U.S. similar to those of MLPF&S and are involved in international banking, lending and providing other investment and financing services. The international department in the New York office is divided into five main business groups: investment banking, debt markets, equity markets, private clients and asset management.

Professional Staff: The company has a professional staff of 30,000 in the U.S., of whom 213 (107 MBAs and 106 BAs) were hired in the last year, 48 for the international department only. Overseas, Merrill Lynch employs 9,000 professionals, mostly foreign nationals, stationed in 28 countries.

Qualifications: Merrill Lynch prefers candidates to have college degrees or MBAs with course work in finance. Expertise in accounting or international relations is favored. A willingness to travel is required for employment, but living abroad is not. Applicants with foreign-language skills, especially in Japanese, Spanish, French and German, are preferred. MBA candidates should have two to three years of meaningful work experience. BA candidates should have several years of summer work experience. The company recruits from international departments on college campuses.

Training Program: About 100 college graduates and 100 graduate students enter the company's five-to-six week training program each year. The program consists of orientation, socializing with fellow recruits and an academic review of accounting, finance and economics.

Internships: Graduate students are accepted for paid summer internships. Applicants should have an interest in Merrill Lynch and finance.

Application Procedure: Applications for professional positions and internships may be sent to:

> Director, Recruiting
> Merrill Lynch & Co., Inc.
> 250 Vesey Street
> New York, NY 10281-1331
> (212) 449-9836

U.S. TRUST CO. OF NEW YORK
New York, NY

U.S. Trust is a commercial bank and trust company. The bank primarily provides services in investment management, estate and trust administration, financial counseling, trusts and securities, and personal and corporate banking. The international department focuses on international investment administration. Since U.S. Trust does not compete in international banking, the international staff serves in the limited capacity of meeting domestic customers' overseas needs. Although there are no overseas offices, U.S. Trust does have subsidiary companies in the British West Indies, the Bahamas and Switzerland, all of which do their own hiring. It also engages in joint ventures with companies in London and Saudi Arabia.

Professional Staff: Of the 1,000 employees, 100 were hired during the past year. Eight to ten people work in the international department. Turnover in the international department is minimal. The subsidiary companies hire only foreign nationals.

Qualifications: Employees in U.S. Trust typically have an undergraduate degree in economics or finance. Experience in trust, estate or investment management is also helpful. Willingness to travel overseas is not a requirement for employment nor is living abroad.

Application Procedure: Those interested in professional positions may contact:

> Human Resources Department
> U.S. Trust Co. of New York
> 114 West 47th Street
> New York, NY 10036
> (212) 852-1000

THE WORLD BANK GROUP
Washington, DC

The World Bank Group is a multilateral organization comprising four institutions: the International Bank for Reconstruction and Development (IBRD), the International Development Association (IDA), the International Finance Corporation (IFC) and the Multilateral Investment Guarantee Agency (MIGA). Each institution is supported by member countries.

Founded in 1944 at the Bretton Woods Conference in New Hampshire, the IBRD is the oldest and largest of the four. Its purpose is to lend funds, provide advice and stimulate investment The bank emphasizes projects and programs that improve the well-being of the poorest people in developing countries. It has invested in agriculture and rural development, education, health and family planning, water supply and electrification. Its loans are financed primarily from its borrowings in world markets but also from retained earnings and repayments from other loans.

Sharing staff with the IBRD is the IDA, which is the bank's concessional financing arm. IDA was established in 1960 when it became apparent that there was a need for lending to poor countries on easier terms than the IBRD could provide. IDA issues credits that are long-term and interest-free. In addition, there is a 10-year grace period before the principal has to be repaid.

The IFC has its own staff, is funded separately and constitutes a legal entity, even though it shares with the bank a wide variety of administrative and other services. The IFC's purpose is to promote the growth of the private sector in its less-developed member countries. It does this by providing loans, making equity investments and stimulating private capital flows. The IFC neither requires nor accepts government guarantees.

MIGA, the newest member of the World Bank Group, helps developing countries attract productive foreign investment by both private investors and commercially operated public-sector companies. Its facilities include guarantees against noncommercial risks and a program of consultative and advisory services to promote improvements in member countries' environments for foreign investment.

IBRD/IDA maintains more than 50 overseas offices, mainly in developing countries; the IFC has about 20. Professional IBRD/IDA positions include country economists, research/policy economists, project/sector economists, financial analysts, technical specialists, attorneys and investment/financial officers. The main professional positions at the IFC include engineers, economists, attorneys and investment officers.

Professional Staff: Most of the staff are located at the bank's headquarters in Washington, DC. The IBRD/IDA has over 3,500 professional staff of whom about 200 are hired each year from approximately 70 member countries. The IFC has a smaller staff, about 400, with about 40 new employees annually. Appointments are normally to nonmanagerial jobs, as managerial openings are usually filled from within the bank. While most staff members are appointed on a career basis, the bank also offers fixed-term appointments, usually for a period of two to three years.

Qualifications: The World Bank Group typically recruits an international corps of professionals who have extensive experience in their fields, as well as graduate degrees from leading academic institutions throughout the world. Knowledge of foreign languages, especially French, Spanish, Arabic, Portuguese or Chinese, is considered an advantage. A willingness to travel is usually essential since staff members may spend as much as one quarter of their time on overseas business. Applicants must also demonstrate an interest in development and issues related to the work of the bank. The recruitment process is highly selective. Important factors are technical knowledge, analytical skill, communications ability, professional judgment and cultural sensitivity.

Training Program: About 30 individuals are hired annually through the Young Professionals Program (YPP). The program is aimed at people under the age of 32 who have very strong master's or doctorate backgrounds in economics or finance, plus some related work experience and foreign language capability. The program provides an opportunity for professional development through on-the-job learning. Program participants are usually given two six-month assignments in different departments and afterward are given a permanent position.

Internships: The bank has a summer employment program for continuing graduate students in economics, finance and technical fields such as public health, agriculture, engineering, education and environmental science. These are paid positions and generally run from June to September. Applicants should have quantitative abilities, computer skills and a good command of English. The assignments usually entail statistical analysis, data collection, research and report writing. A familiarity with development issues is an advantage, and a knowledge of foreign languages is useful. The bank receives about 2,000 applications a year for about 160 summer assignments. Those interested in the program are advised to submit an application in December or January.

Application Procedure: Individuals interested in employment should send a resume and cover letter. State the type of position you are applying for. Formal application forms will only be given to candidates who are of potential interest to the World Bank Group. Although openings are very limited, the bank annually receives about 20,000 inquiries.

To apply for the YPP, address letters to Administrator, YP Program; to apply for a summer position, write to Administrator, Summer Employment Program; to apply to the IFC, write to the IFC Personnel Department. To apply to the IBRD or MIGA, contact the Recruitment Division.

The World Bank Group address is:

1818 H Street, NW
Washington, DC 20433
(202) 477-1234

Chapter Four

INTERNATIONAL JOURNALISM

Introduction by Francis X. Clines

The entry point for a foreign correspondent's career is human curiosity and a belief in storytelling as the best way of marking each day of life and involving others in the common tale of existence. This is what keeps a reporter going in any beat, from a Manhattan police shack to the White House. When the beat is foreign coverage, the possibilities for indulging this curiosity are wider and more dynamic than anywhere else. Formal education enhances this process, but a correspondent's daily mix of travel, investigation, witness and writing ultimately is energized by that same engine of curiosity that got the reporter through storytelling in a dozen earlier jobs back in the U.S.

Francis X. Clines has worked for The New York Times *since 1958. Born in Brooklyn, NY, he has covered various aspects of government and politics in New York and at the White House, written a feature column on New York City, and served overseas, most recently as Moscow bureau chief during the collapse of the Soviet Union.*

Curiosity, not careerism, is what turns the task into an adventure and promises readers something special. For my money, Chaucer is a better inspiration for a foreign correspondent's range of interests than Bismarck—not for any hope of literary immortality but for his unfailing faith in ordinary human characters and events as the stuff of extraordinary stories.

To make curiosity a tool, of course, the craft of reporting must be mastered, and the best way to do this is in on-the-job experience. To leap from graduate school to foreign correspondence is virtually unheard of, although a few ambitious young souls regularly manage to travel to places normally uncovered by the news media and make serendipitous breakthroughs for their careers, story by story. Luck plays a part in everyone's life, but it can't be fashioned, only exploited.

Journalism school is of limited value in getting to the major foreign posts in print and broadcasting. At best, J-schools provide some worthwhile mock reporting experience and maybe a job interview at the small provincial newspapers that can be invaluable in trying to work your way to major papers and finally overseas. At my newspaper, reporters are mainly hired on the basis of outstanding experience at other newspapers. But there is also a trainee program by which a few promising young clerks can earn a trial in the field, report and write and, depending on the results, be promoted directly to the news staff.

Salaries have gotten more competitive in journalism, but the big money—aside from a relative few eye-catching jobs in print and broadcasting—cannot routinely compete with the lucrative levels of lawyering or business.

Whatever the larger fates, get experience as early as possible in the knack of being fast, accurate and original in fashioning events into singular stories. Most likely you must begin provincially, domestically, on your local paper, your high school or college papers—wherever events and opportunity allow. Write about anything that is needed by whatever editor might finally yield to your pleas for a chance. No topic is minor if you can make other people share your curiosity. Submit a piece unsolicited if you believe in it enough; the writing of something you care for is worth the effort, even if it goes unpublished.

Even working on a newspaper, a correspondent will sooner or later discover that his or her own personal curiosity and standards are the only reliable ones across time, whatever guidance is available from editors and the paper's style. This isolation is most especially the environment of the foreign correspondent working alone overseas. One of the best ways of practicing the craft is as a reporter for a wire service, where an on-the-job, guild approach to learning is most intense. Some of the best correspondents I know have moved on to individual newspaper or broadcasting correspondent jobs from the run-and-gun experience of working for such services as the Associated Press and Reuters, first at home, then overseas.

Through all this, read as well as write, letting your curiosity range well beyond mere reportage. Personally I prefer the reading to reach as far as possible away from journalism. Fiction provides both relief from journalism and an affirmation of the sheer power of imagination as something compelling that we all share. You can make use of vacation travel to spot oddities and propose stories as a free-lancer, paid or unpaid.

Foreign correspondents must be able to write stories about the arts, finance, government, politics, the environment and a dozen more specialties. In each of them, as with each story, the comforting little secret is that a correspondent's product is usually cobbled hurriedly, adrenally. That's the fun, the dash into the unknown, with ignorance as a starting point—learning to be wary of flashy expertise in the process, especially in oneself.

Reporters discover and readers know that the best stories are those witnessed directly, and a perch overseas holds great promise for wandering exotically and witnessing directly. A friend of mine covered the assassination of Egypt's head of state Anwar Sadat with the same honest eyewitness verve that he had honed a decade earlier in telling of the dramatic public gunning down of an underworld don in New York City. The stories were equally moving and, a case could be made, equally important. They artfully answered the irrepressible question we all share daily: Have you heard what happened?

The working conditions of foreign correspondents are unpredictable and range from dank and occasionally dangerous to splendid and pampered. A casual mastery of laptop computers and telephone splicing tricks is part of the routine these days for filing, but so is a working knowledge of the old-era telex typing machines. More importantly, fluency in a foreign language more and more is a minimal requirement, though major news organizations will invest in schooling for a correspondent preferred for a particular posting. Blessedly, print journalism seems to have turned 180 degrees on the once controversial question of sending out spousal competitors and colleagues. Management is coming to appreciate the logistical twofers of married journalists working together overseas, sometimes for the same paper, sometimes not, sometimes with one in print, the other in broadcasting.

The foreign correspondent's job used to be easier when it was rooted more simply in a sense of personal adventure and curiosity about the daily implications of established world politics. Now the job is far more miasmic and challenging because it is literally waiting to be redefined by a new generation of post-cold-war journalists suddenly freed from the old parameters. The vocation has never been so exciting because of the scrapping of most of the dominant definitions, presumptions and us-versus-them conceits of the old bipolar world politics.

In Moscow, my last overseas post, you could witness how swiftly the global agenda was being wrenched apart in the crash of the Soviet empire in 1991. A new sort of denseness quickly swept the globe. The dust cloud of so much upheaval and its implications caught journalists as much as world leaders by surprise. The immediate discovery, of course, was that life had instantly become more complex, if less apocalyptic, with long-suppressed entities of the empire rushing forth to blossom, some-times darkly, always unpredictably. There were fresh unknowns to be fathomed everywhere as a result. In this lay the freedom to define anew, a freedom as much a part of the role of correspondents as political leaders. The world itself is the fresh story, and a new generation of foreign correspondents is being invited to get to it and file it.

They could, for example, be among the first to discover, interview and explain the "good Communists" venturing into pluralistic politics amid the shambles of the Soviet empire, or, then again, to describe the reactionaries cleverly exploiting the postmortem. Even more inviting, they could be among the first to supply a fresh look well beyond Moscow and Washington at the many other nations overlooked in the superpower era, all of them ripe with news.

As we round out the century, the post-cold-war stories such as genocide in the rubble of Yugoslavia or famine relief in Somalia are rightly perceived as hedged with new rings of complexity: Can a surviving superpower turn solitary world policeman? Can it be a donor nation and get away with mere charity and moral preachments? Or must it plunge more fully into political collegiality through the United Nations, risking a new foreign policy era of protectorate to guarantee political promise in nations debilitated from cold-war colonialism? Such questions are often being raised first and most vividly by journalists groping on the scene. Here is the new state of the craft, a fresh blank tablet. The job has never looked more inviting for those young men and women willing to range into the world on the strength of their curiosity and to satisfy it daily in behalf of all the rest of us.

THE ASSOCIATED PRESS (AP)
New York, NY

AP gathers and disseminates state, national and international news and photographs to over 15,000 newspapers and radio and TV stations in 116 countries. AP, the oldest and largest news-gathering agency in the world, is a not-for-profit cooperative, owned and operated by its American newspaper and broadcast members. Members contribute local and regional stories that may be of interest to a larger audience; they may use any story AP puts on its wire service.

Professional Staff: AP employs approximately 1,600 journalists (reporters, photographers and editors) in 142 U.S. bureaus. It has over 700 people in 83 bureaus overseas. Most of those overseas are journalists, but some are technical and clerical workers, since AP develops, constructs and maintains its own communications equipment worldwide. About 100 overseas personnel are U.S. citizens; the rest are foreign nationals.

Qualifications: A minimum of 18 months of experience in daily news—either on a newspaper or in a broadcast outlet—is required. In order to be posted abroad, an AP journalist must have worked in a domestic bureau and on the general or foreign desk at AP's world headquarters in New York. Knowledge of a foreign language is required for overseas assignment but experience abroad is not necessary. Regional expertise is also useful.

Internships: AP offers a 13-week summer internship program for minority students. Fifteen paid internships are offered both to college and to graduate students wishing to pursue a career in journalism.

Application Procedure: Inquiries about application for employment and internships may be made to any of AP's bureaus or may be sent to:

> Director of Recruiting
> The Associated Press
> 50 Rockefeller Plaza
> New York, NY 10020
> (212) 621-1777

THE CHRISTIAN SCIENCE MONITOR
Boston, MA

The Christian Science Monitor is an international daily newspaper with 5 U.S. bureaus and 14 overseas bureaus, as well as special correspondents. *The Monitor* was founded in 1908 and is published by The Christian Science Publishing Society, the publishing arm of the First Church of Christ, Scientist. The paper is the center of the publishing society's full range of news operations, which include radio, television and a monthly magazine. *The Monitor* is allied to no political party or ideology, but attempts in its news coverage to foster a sense of the dignity of each individual, and to work on behalf of individual freedom. The daily paper is 20 pages long—18 pages of news and features and two pages of advertising. No other U.S. newspaper devotes as large a percentage of its space to international news as *The Monitor.* The international department produces and manages the paper's international news coverage. International writers, however, write for all pages of the newspaper as well.

Professional Staff: The professional staff is comprised of 100 employees in the U.S. and 13 journalists overseas. Overseas correspondents, stationed in China, Russia, Japan, Thailand, Kenya, Israel, Australia, France, Mexico, South Africa and Germany, are mainly U.S. citizens. Four professionals were hired in the last 12 months.

Qualifications: *The Monitor* looks for applicants from a broad range of backgrounds, with information-gathering and writing skills and a college degree. Recent college graduates are often hired, but some newspaper writing or editing experience is helpful. Knowledge of foreign languages is preferred, but *The Monitor* provides language training for specific assignments when needed.

Internships: Generally, *The Monitor* offers paid summer internships to college students. Applications for other times are also welcome. Interns perform the same tasks as entry-level employees: compiling reports and story lists, preparing copy for editing and other tasks related to the production of the paper. Interns should have an interest in *The Monitor* and, if possible, some journalistic experience, for example, on their school newspaper.

Applications for both internships and professional positions should be sent to:

> Business Manager
> *The Christian Science Monitor*
> One Norway Street
> Boston, MA 02115
> (617) 734-5600

CNN
Atlanta, GA

CNN is a 24-hour news channel covering world and national events. It is produced out of its Atlanta headquarters, and has reporters throughout the U.S. and the world.

Professional Staff: CNN's foreign news desk employs a professional staff of 25 in the U.S. and approximately 200 worldwide. CNN has bureaus in Amman, Bangkok, Beijing, Berlin, Brussels, Cairo, Jerusalem, London, Managua, Manila, Moscow, Nairobi, New Delhi, Paris, Rio de Janeiro, Rome, Santiago, Seoul and Tokyo. Staff members travel within their surrounding areas to cover events. There are nine U.S.-based domestic news bureaus that employ about 475. In the past year, the CNN international operation hired 15 for U.S. and 25 for overseas positions. Both U.S. citizens and foreign nationals are hired for overseas assignments.

Qualifications: For correspondents, CNN seeks applicants with a college degree and at least five to seven years of television work in a major market as a reporter. Knowledge of a second language is required for overseas work; Spanish, French, Arabic and Russian are the most useful. Overseas experience is desirable.

Entry-level Positions: CNN's Atlanta headquarters offers an entry-level position called a Video Journalist, or VJ. College graduates are eligible. Most employees begin their careers as VJs and, as positions become available, advance along a technical or editorial career path.

Internships: CNN offers unpaid, overseas summer internships to aspiring journalists. Interns should be graduate students (often in journalism school or international affairs) with journalism experience. Several overseas bureaus take interns. There is also an internship program in the U.S. Applicants should be college juniors or seniors and have a desire for a career in television journalism.

Application Procedure: Applications for professional positions overseas and on the international desk should be addressed to the Vice President, International Newsgathering. Video Journalist applications should be sent to the CNN Recruiter. If interested in interning in one of the international bureaus, resumes should be sent to the International Desk. The address is below. All inquiries for internships in the U.S. should be directed to the desired bureau.

Videotapes accepted only upon request.

> CNN
> 1 CNN Center
> Box 105366
> Atlanta, GA 30348-5366
> (404) 827-1500

DOW JONES & COMPANY, INC.
THE WALL STREET JOURNAL
New York, NY

Founded in 1882, Dow Jones is a leading publisher of business and financial news and information. *The Wall Street Journal* is Dow Jones's major publication and the country's largest newspaper, with a daily circulation of about 1.8 million and an estimated readership of about 5 million. The domestic edition is complemented by *The Wall Street Journal Europe,* published in Brussels, and *The Asian Wall Street Journal,* published in Hong Kong. In 1991, a classroom edition of the newspaper for high school students was introduced. Dow Jones also publishes *Barron's,* a weekly financial magazine aimed at people who make investment decisions; *Far Eastern Economic Review,* which is Asia's leading English-language news weekly, and *The Asian Wall Street Journal Weekly,* which is published in New York for readers with Asian interests.

Professional Staff: Dow Jones has over 9,500 employees stationed around the world engaged in newsgathering, sales, technical, production, administrative and distribution activities. Its professional staff numbers approximately 475, and its 10 overseas bureaus in Rio, Moscow, Paris, Tokyo, Vienna, Seoul, Jerusalem, London Hong Kong and Mexico City employ 21 correspondents. During the past year, 27 professionals were hired for the domestic departments and 1 was hired as a foreign correspondent.

Qualifications: *The Wall Street Journal* requires a college degree and prefers applicants to have an advanced degree in law, business, journalism or liberal arts, but such degrees are not always necessary or sufficient qualification for employment; applicants normally have previous experience as well. Knowledge of foreign languages, especially French, German, Japanese, Spanish or Chinese, is preferred.

Internships: Summer internships are offered to graduate students of journalism. Responsibilities include copyediting and proofreading. Positions are funded.

Application Procedure: Those interested in professional and internship positions should contact:

> Personnel Manager
> Dow Jones & Company, Inc.
> 200 Liberty Street
> New York, NY 10281
> (212) 416-2000

GAMMA LIAISON
New York, NY

Gamma Liaison is a worldwide photo-news agency. It acts as the agent for photojournalists who cover news events in the U.S. and abroad and send their negatives to the agency. The agency normally sells one-time usage of the photographs to magazines, newspapers and other media. Though some of its photographers work on a freelance basis, the majority work exclusively for Gamma Liaison.

Professional Staff: The U.S. staff comprises 30 people, 10 of whom are part of the international department. Seventy-five professional photographers, based in major cities overseas, cover events. In the past year, 10 professionals were hired. U.S. citizens and foreign nationals are employed overseas.

Qualifications: Gamma Liaison seeks photographers who have five years experience as photojournalists and have had their work published. Knowledge of foreign languages and experience abroad are required for overseas work.

Application Procedure: Applications should be addressed to:

> Gamma Liaison
> 11 East 26th Street
> New York, NY 10010
> (212) 447-2500

THE LOS ANGELES TIMES
Los Angeles, CA

The Los Angeles Times provides regional, national and international news for the greater Los Angeles community. It maintains 29 international bureaus in major cities throughout the world.

Professional Staff: The staff includes 1,000 editors, reporters, photographers and artists, 34 of whom are foreign correspondents. Approximately 68 people were hired for all positions in the past year.

Qualifications: Journalists hired as reporters or editors on the regular news staff must have professional experience with a daily newspaper. Although many of the reporters and editors are journalism school graduates, a degree in journalism is not necessary for employment. Foreign languages are preferred for overseas assignments; Spanish, Russian and Asian languages are needed most frequently.

Training Program: An intensive, two-year, career-entry program, the Minority Editorial Training Program (METPRO), is sponsored by *The Los Angeles Times* and the Times Mirror Company for minority candidates who want to work as reporters or photographers on metropolitan daily newspapers. METPRO selects 8 trainees from over 500 applicants for training and placement as copy editors at Times-Mirror newspapers. Applicants must be able to demonstrate writing and other skills necessary for a career in journalism. Prior training, in journalism, however, is not required. Trainees receive a weekly stipend, housing and medical benefits. The program does not necessarily lead to jobs with *The Los Angeles Times,* although it assists trainees in finding suitable jobs elsewhere. Deadline for application is January 1. Applications are available in August.

Internships: Academic-year internships and summer internships are available to college students or recent graduates. Previous newspaper experience, especially for summer interns, is highly desirable. Academic interns (fall and spring) may receive credit and must work a minimum of 16 hours a week. They are paid an hourly wage. Summer interns work full-time and are paid a weekly salary. Deadlines for applications, which should include a cover letter, resume, four references and at least eight samples of published work: Nov. 1 for the spring term, Dec. 1 for the summer, and July 1 for the fall.

Application Procedure: For METPRO, write to METPRO Director. For internships, write to the Editorial Internship Director. For professional editorial positions, write to Editorial Hiring at:

> The Los Angeles Times
> Times Mirror Square
> Los Angeles, CA 90053
> (213) 237-7397

NATIONAL BROADCASTING CORPORATION (NBC)
New York, NY

NBC is a national network providing entertainment, sports and news services. Its primary news presentation is "NBC Nightly News with Tom Brokaw" that provides reports and analysis of the day's national and international events. NBC's news coverage is bolstered by 6 domestic news bureaus and 18 foreign bureaus and offices. International news is coordinated in the New York headquarters by two news directors and a researcher. These staff members conduct research, write and gather information from the many foreign bureaus and offices and decide what international news will be featured in the nightly broadcast. NBC, like many networks, also relies on the international news and image gathering of independent international news agencies like Visnews and the BBC.

Professional Staff: NBC news has approximately 1,100 professional staff members stationed abroad. Overseas staff consists of correspondents, producers, technical and support staff and is comprised of foreign nationals and U.S. citizens. NBC employs approximately 30 correspondents in its domestic bureaus and approximately 10 correspondents in its foreign bureaus. International news is coordinated in New York by a staff of three and domestic news by a staff of 11. In the past year 7 correspondents were hired for the domestic staff; no correspondents were hired for overseas posts.

Qualifications: Before obtaining an overseas post, many correspondents work for several years in NBC's domestic bureaus; some are hired directly for overseas assignments. For overseas posts, correspondents must have an interest in international stories and how they affect U.S. interests; education that supports his/her interests in international affairs; and language skills.

Internships: NBC hires approximately 300 unpaid interns companywide. The number of interns working in the news division varies. Interns must be undergraduates who receive academic credit for the internship. Interns perform various tasks, including research and other work on stories or assist with general "production assistant" duties such as running tapes.

Application Procedure: For professional positions, contact the Director of Organization and Management, Resource Planning. For internships contact the internship office at:

NBC
30 Rockefeller Plaza
New York, NY 10112
(212) 664-4444

NATIONAL PUBLIC RADIO (NPR)
New York, NY

NPR is a noncommercial, satellite radio system. A nonprofit, private corporation, NPR provides programming, distribution and representational support services to 400 radio stations. It produces *All Things Considered, Morning Edition* and a variety of performance programs, including operatic, symphonic, jazz and dramatic presentations.

Professional Staff: There are 400 professionals based in the U.S. and 1 overseas correspondent in London. U.S.-based correspondents travel overseas to cover world news and features. During the past year, approximately 95 professionals were hired.

Qualifications: NPR seeks college graduates and, preferably, applicants possessing advanced degrees. A minimum of one to three years of previous radio experience is necessary for employment. Knowledge of foreign languages is preferred but not necessary.

Internships: Paid semester and summer internships are available for college juniors or seniors and graduate-school students. Interns work on programming, editing, research and writing projects.

Application Procedure: Applications for both professional and internship positions should be addressed to:

Director of Personnel
National Public Radio
2025 M Street, NW
Washington, DC 20036
(202) 822-2909

THE NEW YORK TIMES
New York, NY

The New York Times, published every day, covers national, international, cultural, business and regional affairs. The foreign news desk, in New York, supervises and monitors the foreign correspondents and edits stories from abroad.

Professional Staff: *The New York Times* maintains a professional news staff of 950. The full-time overseas staff consists of 36 correspondents based in Brazil, Britain, Canada, China, Egypt, El Salvador, France, Germany, Greece, India, Israel, Italy, Japan, Mexico, Nicaragua, the Philippines, Poland, West and Southern Africa, Thailand and Russia. *The New York Times* also maintains reporters for international news in Washington, DC, and at the UN in New York. Some correspondents are bureau chiefs, others are stationed in the bureaus; all travel widely to cover news developments in their regions. In addition to these correspondents, *The New York Times* also works with a number of "stringers," people who write articles freelance and sell regularly to a given media. Two to three positions open up annually overseas, but are frequently filled by a foreign correspondent from another overseas bureau.

Qualifications: A college education is considered but is not required. Expertise in specific areas, such as the Far East, or in technical or business fields is useful. *The New York Times* does not hire recent graduates from journalism school unless they have previous experience, nor does it require applicants to have a journalism degree. Five years experience on a major U.S. daily newspaper is normally required for employment as a reporter.

The New York Times does not hire correspondents through its foreign news desk. Foreign correspondents generally begin as reporters for the Metropolitan or Business sections. Editors of *The New York Times* believe that there is nothing more demanding than being an overseas correspondent. Many foreign correspondents choose their own stories, are essentially their own editors, and must frequently work alone without daily guidance from an editor. Reporters selected for overseas posts have generally shown excellence in the Metro or Business sections in New York for 18 months to 2 years.

The best qualifications an aspiring foreign correspondent can have are professional writing skills, overseas experience and fluency in a foreign language. Many of *The New York Times'* foreign correspondents have been previously employed by other newspapers, frequently overseas. Journalism school can be beneficial, but more important is a portfolio of impressive clippings and bylines. The foreign desk does, on occasion, hire individuals because of their knowledge of an exotic language or culture. While knowledge of any foreign language is helpful, fluency in exotic languages is likely to be more valuable.

Training Program: Each year about 10 college graduates with one year of experience in reporting with a daily newspaper are accepted as news clerks. News clerks write news stories and try for a job as a reporter-trainee after two years. Three may succeed.

Application Procedure: All applications should be addressed to:

>   Assistant Managing Editor
>   News Department
>   *The New York Times*
>   229 West 43rd Street
>   New York, NY 10036
>   (212) 556-1234

NEWSDAY
Long Island, NY

Newsday is a regional, national, and international newspaper serving the Long Island and metropolitan New York region.

Professional Staff: *Newsday* employs 750 professionals in the U.S. and 4 correspondents stationed in Germany, Egypt, Japan and the former Soviet Union. The paper hired 35 journalists in 1991, all for domestic posts.

Qualifications: *Newsday* seeks applicants with at least three-to-five years experience on a daily newspaper. Some of that experience should be on a daily that has a circulation greater than 200,000. Many writers have journalism degrees, although *Newsday* is more concerned with experience than formal degrees. There is no language requirement for hiring, but foreign language proficiency is preferred for foreign posting.

Training Program: *Newsday* also participates in the METPRO program (see description above under *The Los Angeles Times* listing).

Internships: *Newsday* maintains one of the most extensive summer internship programs in the country, hiring 32 interns each summer. Interns are paid and work on reporting, copyediting, research or photography projects. College students who apply must pass a test given by the newspaper and must have some college or professional journalism background.

Application Procedure: Applications for professional positions should be addressed to:

> Vice President
> Editorial Administration
> *Newsday*
> 235 Pinelawn Road
> Melville, NY 11747-4250

Those interested in applying for METPRO should contact the METPRO Director at the above address.

To apply for internship positions contact:

> Newsday/NY Newsday
> 2 Park Avenue
> New York, NY 10016-5695
> Attn: Internship Program

THE WASHINGTON POST
Washington, DC

The Washington Post provides regional, national and international news to the District of Columbia, Virginia and Maryland. Its overseas staff members are stationed in 19 countries.

Professional Staff: *The Washington Post* has a professional full-time staff (editors, photographers, artists, etc.) of 520, 260 of whom are reporters. The international department has 19 correspondents overseas and 15 editors at the Washington, DC, headquarters. During the past year 25 professionals were hired for varying jobs, including one for an overseas post.

Qualifications: A college degree, newspaper experience and general interest and expertise in a region or area are preferred qualifications. The typical path for a foreign correspondent is a couple of years reporting for another paper and five years work on the metropolitan or national staff of *The Washington Post*. Foreign languages are required for overseas assignment. Experienced reporters with the appropriate language for an available opening have some advantage.

Internships: Paid summer internships are available for college or graduate students. Some newspaper experience is required. College newspaper experience is acceptable. Responsibilities include reporting, editing and photography.

Application Procedure: Applications for both professional and internship positions should be addressed to:

Director of Recruiting, Newsroom
The Washington Post
1150 15th Street, NW
Washington, DC 20071
(202) 334-6000

Chapter Five

INTERNATIONAL LAW

Introduction by Paul B. Ford, Jr.

The prospect of a career in international law is likely to conjure up notions of travel to, and perhaps residence in, exotic parts of the world and interaction with different cultures. To be sure, there is more than a small element of truth in this picture, but it is important to remember that the practice of law is fundamentally a domestic profession requiring a U.S. law degree, passing a state bar examination, satisfaction of character and fitness requirements and adherence to a code of professional ethics. Many lawyers would also say that membership in the profession brings with it an obligation to perform public service. These requirements apply to all U.S. lawyers whether they practice in the domestic or international arenas. In the international context, lawyers have a particular duty to promote the "rule of law" as the basis for relations among nations, the

---

Paul Ford is a partner, policy committee member and chairman of the International Practice Committee of Simpson Thacher & Bartlett. A graduate of Boston College and Duke University School of Law, Mr. Ford specializes in international finance and banking. He is secretary of the Board of Governors of the Foreign Policy Association.

smooth functioning of the global economy and the protection of human rights.

Before describing in some detail opportunities to practice law in the international arena, two additional general observations may be in order. Men and women seeking a law degree come from a wide variety of educational backgrounds and, in many cases, working careers. Second, the legal profession has traditionally been a springboard to a wide variety of other careers. Lawyers regularly occupy senior positions in government, business and international organizations, as well as teaching positions in the U.S. and abroad. It is not unusual for an international lawyer to enjoy one or more of these experiences during his or her career, in addition to the practice of law.

Twenty years ago only a handful of U.S. law firms regularly practiced law in the international arena. Today virtually every law firm of size is involved. Many domestic clients have expanded overseas and law firms have followed, advising on U.S. law aspects of acquisitions, joint ventures, global securities offerings and international dispute resolution and interfacing with foreign lawyers on local law issues. This has led to a proliferation of law-firm branch offices and, in some cases, the practice of foreign law in combination with foreign lawyers in Western and Eastern Europe, the Far East and Latin America. U.S. law firms also increasingly represent foreign corporations and financial institutions in the U.S. as well as abroad through their branch offices. Indeed, foreign clients who use in-house lawyers may represent the most significant opportunity for growth in the U.S. legal profession. The result of this trend is that any lawyer joining a U.S. law firm of size will likely have some international experience during his or her career.

The opportunities offered by law firms in the international arena vary widely and so will the experience of the young attorney. Choosing the right firm can prove to be a challenging task. Fortunately, most firms today publish detailed information regarding the nature of their international practice, and the legal press produces a wealth of information to help law students select firms they wish to interview.

Over the past decade, U.S. corporations and financial institutions have greatly expanded their in-house legal staffs, in many cases hiring associates from large law firms. Some legal departments now compare in size with large law firms and post lawyers around the world to serve their client's international operations. Increasingly, foreign enterprises with U.S. operations are also hiring U.S. legal staff. In some instances, these staffs have grown quite large. Thus large institutions with international business undertakings present excellent opportunities for a legal career with an international dimension as well as an opportunity over time to participate in management of the enterprise. It is not unusual for the in-house general counsel to be a senior executive officer.

Like private practice, government service today provides a broad array of opportunities to gain international experience. All governmental agencies provide useful career information upon request (see Chapter Nine).

International organizations such as the United Nations and its many agencies provide some of the best opportunities for the practice of international law, that is, a practice which involves laws created among nations by treaty or other international convention (see Chapter Ten). Some prior international experience is generally a prerequisite to securing a position with one of these organizations.

There are some common factors that contribute to a successful legal career in the international arena. First and foremost is mastering the discipline and critical thinking that is essential for success in any area of legal practice. There is no shortcut to obtaining these skills. Most successful lawyers strive to improve them throughout their careers. Second, the day of the generalist lawyer is rapidly passing. This is increasingly true in the international arena. Today's successful international lawyer is more likely than not a specialist in one or two areas of the practice. This trend toward specialization presents particular challenges to lawyers stationed abroad who are called upon to answer questions in areas in which they do not regularly practice. Access to a strong home base with professionals willing and able to provide the requested expertise has become essential to effective representation of clients abroad. The ability to speak, read and write at least one foreign language will greatly increase the likelihood of being selected for international assignments. In addition to its practical aspects, the mastery of a foreign language demonstrates an interest and a commitment to dealing with foreign cultures. While not critical to success, it is also very helpful to have spent time abroad to develop the patience and understanding required to practice in a cross-border context.

Student Advisory by David J. Scheffer

The practice of international law can be painstakingly difficult yet richly rewarding, intellectually as well as financially, but not every student of international affairs is suited for it. It is the purpose of this essay to help students determine whether, and how, they should pursue a career in international law.

That pursuit is an unpredictable exercise at best. The student is well advised to concentrate on the fundamentals during college and law school and to explore options in international law when seeking employment. The key is to maintain flexibility, avoid irreversible commitments and keep an open mind.

The term international law as used in this essay embraces four distinct areas:

- public international law (the rules governing relations among nations and peoples);

- transnational law (the laws of nations governing international transactions such as international trade and investment);

- foreign and comparative law (the laws of a particular country, for example France or China, and the comparative study of how a particular area of law is dealt with in different countries);

- conflict of laws (the rules of a particular country, for example the U.S., determining which country's law should apply to a transaction when key elements cover more than one jurisdiction).

State Department lawyers deal regularly with public international law, such as the interpretation of bilateral and multilateral treaties (including the UN Charter), the preparation of UN Security Council resolutions, litigation before the International Court of Justice, and state responsibility

---

David J. Scheffer is a senior associate in international and national security law at the Carnegie Endowment for International Peace and an adjunct professor in international law at Georgetown University Law Center. He formerly worked on the professional staff of the House Committee on Foreign Affairs, and was associate attorney with Coudert Brothers, an international law firm, from 1979 to 1986. Mr. Scheffer is a graduate of Harvard College and has law degrees from Oxford University (Britain) and Georgetown University Law Center.

for injuries to nations and the taking of foreign property. The sources of public international law are international agreements and customary international law, that is, those rules that have evolved from the practice of nations. Lawyers in private practice may occasionally represent private parties or governments before *ad hoc* international arbitral tribunals, the Iran-U.S. Claims Tribunal or the International Court of Justice. Since public international law is part of U.S. law, they sometimes deal with public international questions in cases before U.S. courts.

International lawyers in private practice are normally concerned with transnational law, foreign law and conflict of laws. Typically they represent foreigners investing in the U.S. (where American law will be applied) or Americans investing in a foreign country (where that country's laws will apply). American lawyers who describe themselves as international lawyers actually practice a great deal of American law and typically work closely with local counsel overseas to facilitate their client's foreign business. Usually the international lawyer is concerned with the laws of the particular jurisdiction where his or her client is active and the conflicts that may exist between different systems of law.

Keep in mind that:

- International lawyers do not emerge from a single mold. There is no upbringing, course curriculum, particular college or law school or intellectual type that defines the makings of an international lawyer.

- An intrinsic interest in other cultures and peoples and in world affairs is essential. If one is not interested in problems and issues that have transnational impact, then international law may not be the right career.

- As with most careers, international law is what you make of it. It is not a tidy, well-defined career that one typically starts practicing the first day on the job. It is a career that usually takes years to nurture and gain expertise in. Some luck is involved in terms of being in the right place at the right time. A lawyer can work for years on domestic law matters without seeing a single international case or project. Then, suddenly, the expertise he or she has developed practicing domestic law becomes invaluable to a client involved in an international project. Within weeks or months, that lawyer is practicing international law full-time.

Qualifications for Law Schools

It is a safe bet that most practicing international lawyers had little inkling when they were applying to law school that their careers would veer toward international law. In fact, a large percentage of lawyers do not settle on a particular legal career until they have practiced law for several years. The first hurdle for the college student is simply getting into law school.

Although an individual may enter law school with a degree in any discipline, common degrees are English, political science, economics and history. Some law-school admissions officers take more interest in an individual who has earned a rigorous academic degree in such fields as physics, chemistry, Greek classics, philosophy, foreign languages, engineering or mathematics. One of my college roommates graduated *summa cum laude* in physics from Harvard and went on to Yale Law School. One of the nation's foremost constitutional law professors, Laurence Tribe of Harvard Law School, has a doctorate in mathematics.

More important than the discipline that one studies in college are the skills that one develops in the study of that discipline, including the ability to analyze and pinpoint the main issues of problems, to write clearly and succinctly, to speak articulately and to work diligently. An interesting mix in college would be a major in mathematics, a minor in English and extracurricular work as a reporter on the school newspaper. Throw in a little debating or a rhetoric class and you will be well prepared for law school.

Law-school admissions officers typically look, first, for a high grade-point average and, second, at performance on the Law School Admissions Test, which is critical. LSAT scores assist in weeding out the "less qualified." A college student is strongly advised to take a preparatory course for the LSAT in order to become familiar with the types of questions that will be asked, the strategy to employ in taking the exam and how to get into the right frame of mind for it. Admissions officers also consider the candidate's degree and extracurricular activities, which include anything from sports to debating society to student council. Most officers look for individuals who can express themselves, who can work with other people and who are not afraid to get involved. Law school and the practice of law are *participatory* exercises, and students are expected to *speak up*. Finally, work experience can be relevant but is not too important, unless the student has worked for a year or more before applying to law school.

Law School

The most practical advice I ever received about becoming an international lawyer came from one of Washington, DC's, top international lawyers: "To become an international lawyer, first become a darn good domestic lawyer." A solid background in American law is essential.

The first year in law school is critical. A student should take seriously such fundamental courses as contracts, torts, civil procedure, criminal law, legal drafting and property. First-year grades can be a determining factor in where you obtain summer work during law school, and they will be important in a law firm's consideration of your application for permanent employment. The legal principles learned in the first year continue to be applied by practicing lawyers for their entire careers. A second tier of fundamental courses particularly important for the aspiring international lawyer includes constitutional law, administrative law, corporation law, tax law (including corporate international taxation), securities regulation law, the law of secured transactions, antitrust law and accounting. The primary business of international law is commercial transactions, so a law student should focus on learning the fundamentals of corporate and commercial law.

Now we come to a third tier of courses. I would recommend that the aspiring international lawyer take four fundamental international law courses: public international law, international business transactions, international organizations and conflict of laws. Many law students take at least one additional course, one that gives them an opportunity to delve into the laws of foreign countries. It could be a course on civil law or Japanese law or European Community law. The international lawyer will spend much of his or her time communicating with and working with foreign attorneys and their legal systems, so some academic exposure is warranted.

A number of law schools in the U.S. provide a strong international law curriculum, among them Columbia, Harvard, Yale, Georgetown, New York University, Chicago, University of Virginia, Michigan, Stanford, the University of California at Berkeley and Duke. However, other private and state university law schools have highly qualified professors who can adequately prepare the law student.

An excellent way for students to immerse themselves in international law is to work on the staff of an international law journal. Participation in the Jessup Moot Court competition each year can also expose law students to a whole range of international legal issues. Further, obtaining a position as a summer associate with an international law firm is one of the best means of exploring your interest in the practice of international law.

Another way to broaden your academic experience in preparation for a career in international law is to enroll in a dual-degree program, which combines a degree in law with a master's degree in international relations, foreign languages or business administration.

Finally, law students interested in a career in international law might consider spending a year or two after graduation immersing themselves in a foreign culture, either through a fellowship or through further education or employment overseas. It is often possible for the graduating law student to accept a position with an American law firm and defer entering the firm until after one or two years abroad. The law student might consider working in the offices of a foreign law firm, especially in a civil law jurisdiction, where he or she may gain an understanding for the style and substance of practice by foreign lawyers. Although the young American attorney may perform paralegal work for the foreign law firm, it can be a professionally satisfying experience.

Law Firms

Most international law is practiced in private law firms handling international business transactions. Thousands of law firms at one time or another handle transnational matters, but there is a group of law firms that handles a large amount of international work and some firms that specialize in it. The largest number of international law firms is in New York City, followed by Washington, DC. But "international" law firms can be found in all major cities of the U.S. Identifying those firms is not always an easy task: law firms do not usually broadcast their client work to the world. Career placement advisers at law schools can advise law students which law firms to consider. Also, firm resumes available to law students should give the student some idea of the scope of the law firm's work.

The criteria law firms use to select their lawyers vary from firm to firm. A common denominator is a solid academic background, meaning high grades in the fundamental first- and second-tier courses mentioned above. Those firms that specialize in international law also typically look for foreign language capability, evidence of the applicant's interest in international affairs (such as travel, course work, extracurricular activities on campus) and flexibility. Those law firms with overseas offices often like to attract candidates who are willing not only to travel but also to spend a number of years working overseas in one of the firm's branch offices.

A word of caution: The law student is well advised not to express too much enthusiasm for international law or travel during the interview process. This is simply because a law firm is looking for a good lawyer, first, and an international lawyer, second. An interviewee should show his or her "legal thinking" skills, for example, by talking about a particular course or a law review article he or she wrote. Other impressive qualities would be a rich background of foreign languages, cultures, academic degrees and, on top of all that, a sound legal background.

The trek into a law firm often begins as a summer associate during a student's law-school years. Firms interview law students for summer (as well as permanent) positions. An excellent performance as a summer associate (which typically will involve legal research and drafting) can translate into an offer for permanent employment upon graduation. Once employed on a full-time basis, the novice attorney will spend five to nine years working as an associate on salary. Starting annual salaries at major New York law firms range from $82,000 to $86,000. Each year the associate's salary should increase until in the seventh year, for example, it may top $180,000. It is best, however, to check with your law school's career adviser to obtain up-to-date information. First-year salaries in other cities can be considerably lower, but keep in mind that the cost-of-living in New York is very high. You may find yourself worse off in real terms in New York than elsewhere, even though your New York salary looks more impressive.

Some associate attorneys will be selected as partners in their respective law firms. The ratio is typically small, meaning that out of a major law firm's starting class of perhaps 25 associate attorneys, two may make partner. Typical qualities and talents that make a partner are excellent legal skills, consistency in quality work, success at client development, the respect of colleagues and a pleasant personality. Partners' income at major law firms ranges from $150,000 to $600,000 to much higher, although actual figures vary widely from firm to firm.

Most major law firms are structured so as to take full advantage of their attorneys' specialized skills. This means, for example, that some attorneys will specialize in tax matters, others in corporate law and still others in litigation. International lawyers, however, typically do not specialize to the same degree because transnational business transactions usually involve numerous fields of law. A typical transnational business deal, for example, will include legal issues that bear upon the law of corporations, tax, banking, secured transactions and contracts, not to mention a working knowledge of the foreign law that may be part of the transaction.

Of the 250 largest law firms in the U.S., 84 have foreign offices, and the number is growing, according to the September 28, 1992, issue of *The National Law Journal.* American law firms have discovered over the last 30 years that not only American business overseas but also European, Asian and Latin American companies and banks look to American lawyers for their drafting skills, their extensive network of offices and correspondent attorneys around the world and their efficiency. Also, since so much transnational business is transacted with American entities (in particular U.S. banks), a lot of contracts and loan agreements are governed by New York law, which is recognized for its international commercial application.

Law firms with foreign offices typically send mid-level associates overseas for two- or three-year periods. Unless the foreign country is predominantly English-speaking, law firms will look for language skills in the attorneys they send overseas. It is not possible to represent effectively a client in Beijing without speaking Mandarin. Many of these mid-level associates never return to the U.S. to work. They recognize, as do their firms, that their expertise and client contacts are overseas. Many eventually become partners of their firms and, even as partner, they remain overseas.

If you have an opportunity to move overseas to a firm's foreign office, it can be a truly challenging and fulfilling experience. The law student should be careful to look at the nature of the law firm's overseas offices. Some are staffed almost entirely by American lawyers practicing American law, and attorneys working in the domestic office may find little opportunity to travel overseas. Other law firms run a quasi-franchise operation: they lend their name to a foreign office staffed primarily with foreign lawyers. Another category of law firms purports to have foreign offices, but in fact the firms have simply placed one or two attorneys in a foreign law firm's offices.

Returning to the U.S. after an overseas assignment also can be an adjustment professionally. You may have to catch up with changes in the American legal scene and develop a new client base within the firm. You may have to reintroduce yourself to partners who have forgotten you. But you can also bring to the U.S. office invaluable skills and foreign contacts, which, in the long run, should work to your advantage.

International lawyers serve many types of clients—from multinational corporations to international banks to wealthy individuals seeking tax havens to foreign governments. Some international law firms' client rosters include may of the companies on the *Fortune* 500 list, but the work being done for those companies is exclusively overseas work. General Motors may use one large firm in the U.S. for its primary domestic work but numerous international law firms to conduct its business overseas. Likewise, major American banks often split their international work among a number of international law firms, depending upon the geographical region in which business is being conducted.

Federal Government

The largest single employer of international lawyers in the U.S. is the federal government. Many of its lawyers work full-time on international legal problems. The departments of State and Defense handle the greatest volume of public international law work on a daily basis. Other agencies actively involved in transnational matters include the departments of Agriculture and Commerce and the Treasury Department, the Federal Reserve system, the Agency for International Development, the Office of the U.S. Trade Representative, the Overseas Private Investment Corporation, the Export-Import Bank of the U.S. and the U.S. Information Agency. The Department of Justice handles a lot of private international law matters, especially in the Foreign Litigation Section of the Civil Division. The Office of International Affairs in the Criminal Division of the Justice Department works on such public international law subjects as extradition, mutual international assistance in law enforcement, prisoner exchanges and foreign corrupt practices.

The State Department Legal Adviser's Office is perhaps the best known enclave of public international lawyers in the federal government. The work undertaken there can be most challenging, including the drafting and negotiation of treaties and representation of the U.S. before the International Court of Justice at The Hague and at other international tribunals and diplomatic conferences. State Department attorneys can find themselves on the cutting edge of policymaking, especially during a foreign crisis, when legal advice is quickly sought by the Secretary of State, the U.S. ambassador to the United Nations and the White House and quickly rendered by lawyers in the Legal Adviser's Office. They also are increasingly involved in advising policy-makers in the post-cold-war work of the UN. Attorneys should be prepared to represent their client, the U.S. government, and, in particular, the administration of the day without much opportunity to challenge basic policy once it has been set.

In the Department of Agriculture, attorneys are involved with a variety of foreign transactions, including export credit sales to other countries through the programs of the Commodity Credit Corporation, maritime claims and cases, international agreements on agricultural trade, representation before the Federal Maritime Commission and the International Trade Commission, review and drafting of international agreements in connection with agricultural matters, and coordination with the State and Treasury departments on a host of international financing issues.

The Department of Commerce employs many lawyers to interpret and administer the General Agreement on Tariffs and Trade, the Export Administration Act of 1979, federal anti-boycott rules, import-relief provisions of U.S. trade legislation, trade-promotion activities and representation at administrative proceedings to impose sanctions for export control and anti-boycott violations. At the Export-Import Bank, lawyers practice a good deal of international banking law. Lawyers in the office of the Assistant General Counsel for International Affairs at the

Department of Treasury handle an array of international financial matters, including U.S. relations with multilateral financial institutions, international trade policy, foreign direct investment in the U.S., foreign assets and the international debt crisis.

Two other federal agencies that use international lawyers are the U.S. International Trade Commission (ITC) and the Office of U.S. Trade Representative (USTR). The ITC investigates matters relating to U.S. foreign trade policy and makes recommendations to the President for enforcement. The ITC's attorneys advise the commission on the legal implications of its proposed actions. This is one agency in which an attorney will be involved in a substantial amount of litigation work. The USTR has some of the most interesting trade-related work for attorneys in the federal government because it is the President's top adviser on international trade policy.

Government offices typically do not offer the comforts of private practice nor the type of counseling that senior associates and partners of a law firm can offer a young private attorney. The young government attorney may be given a tremendous amount of responsibility at a young age, and that in itself may be very attractive, but the government lawyer typically will not command the same salary as a private attorney and may become quite specialized. Nonetheless, some of Washington's most successful international lawyers started their careers as government attorneys. Keep in mind, however, that moving from government to private practice may be subject to legal restrictions to avoid conflict of interest.

Corporate Counsel

Some of the most active international lawyers today are found in corporations. Law students contemplating an in-house position must have a solid grounding in corporation law, antitrust, tax, contracts, securities regulations, accounting and patents, trademarks and licensing. Corporations may not look for any specialized international courses or foreign language skills in a law student's background. Corporations are more prone to hire well-educated "domestic" lawyers and give them opportunities to learn on the job.

Much of the legal work previously done by law firms has now moved in-house at corporations. This extends even to international work. The hours can be grueling, especially because so much of what corporations are engaged in overseas is deal-making. That can mean all-night negotiations, 24-hour flights from New York to Bombay, "seat of the pants" negotiating and drafting, and the frustrations that may accompany dealing with foreign attorneys in exotic locations.

While most corporations look to senior associates in law firms for their in-house legal staff, some are now looking to law schools for new lawyers. Law students should carefully investigate the corporate counsel's office before making any decision to accept employment. Questions to ask are whether the in-house attorneys work well together, whether the general counsel has a final say on personnel matters, how and under what conditions attorneys are transferred among the domestic and international offices of the corporation, how much international legal work attorneys on the staff handle during the course of the year, and whether lawyers with a particular interest in multinational legal problems have the opportunity to specialize in working on those problems. The law student should be particularly inquisitive about opportunities for promotion which, in corporations, can be a very complex affair with less degree of predictability than in law firms. The law student should ask whether lawyers can move from legal work to management within the company, and what happens to lawyers who seek to stay permanently in the legal counsel's office. Often lawyers who prove themselves within the legal counsel's office rise to assistant general counsel or general counsel of the corporation. The general counsel often assumes other hats as well, such as senior or executive vice-president and sometimes will rise to the top of the corporation. But each company should be examined on its own merits.

The attitude of management toward the legal department also is important. If management shuns the advice of its in-house attorneys and rarely consults them, then the attorney may find work in the corporation frustrating and lacking in intellectual appeal. In-house counsel of a major corporation can acquire a vast amount of experience and knowledge, which can be very attractive to a law firm, particularly if that corporate counsel can bring some of the corporation's business to the law firm.

Finally, while many corporations interview on campus, a law student should approach corporations directly. Letters should be directed to the attention of the president or general counsel of the corporation.

International Organizations and Nonprofit Groups

The range of international legal positions in international organizations and nonprofit groups is far-reaching and sometimes difficult to discover. In most cases, law students are best advised to start out in private practice or the federal government. There is very little legal training in international organizations, and attorneys are usually expected to hit the ground running upon commencement of employment. Moreover, previous experience in private practice leaves the young attorney greater opportunity to return to the private sector.

The most active legal shops in international organizations are the UN Legal Counsel's Office and the legal departments of the World Bank Group and the International Monetary Fund (IMF). The UN Legal Counsel's Office is deeply involved in legal problems before the Security Council and the General Assembly, particularly the activities of the assembly's Sixth Committee (which handles legal affairs) and legal problems arising from the administration of UN operations. Attorneys working closely with the Sixth Committee and its subcommittees negotiate and draft documents on such matters as rules relating to the non-use of force, the peaceful settlement of disputes, the maintenance of international peace and security, improving the efficiency of UN procedures, codifying offenses against the peace and security of mankind, international trade, international treaty-making conferences, relations between the UN and its host country, the U.S., the safety and protection of diplomats and their missions, various treaties governing the law of outer space, the host of projects before the International Law Commission and numerous other legal issues.

At the World Bank Group and the IMF, attorneys' activities correspond to a large degree to those in the private sector. Most of the attorneys in the legal department of the World Bank are assigned to lending operations. Others participate in the settlement of investment disputes between member countries, World Bank borrowings in international capital markets and participation in specialized technical assistance programs for member countries and other international organizations. (For information about hiring practices in international organizations, see Chapter Ten.)

Legal positions can also be found in certain private nonprofit organizations, such as Amnesty International USA, CARE and Catholic Relief Services. Again, it may be advisable to start one's legal career in private practice before exploring these particular options. Salary scales are quite low and the young attorney may want to leave open the option of returning to private practice.

The Future of International Law

International law is hardly a static profession. New areas of practice in international law emerge every year, making it increasingly difficult for attorneys to describe themselves as all-purpose international lawyers. There are continuing developments in capital markets (trading in stocks, bonds and money-market instruments) throughout the world. Lawyers with a solid grounding in securities-regulation law will continue to be sought out for this field of international practice. The international debt problem and the profusion of financial instruments, such as swap agreements for interest rates and foreign currencies, are making knowl-

intellectual-property rights, including patents, trademarks and copyright, especially for high-technology products such as computers and biotechnology. International trade will continue for the foreseeable future to employ legions of attorneys in the U.S. Every time there is a change in any aspect of U.S. trade law or in international agreements on trade, it can have a tidal-wave effect on the operation of businesses (and consequently the work of lawyers) in the U.S. and overseas.

One thing is certain. Despite the skepticism that people typically express about whether or not there is "international law," the fact is that it exists and lawyers will continue to practice it every day of the year.

CLEARY, GOTTLIEB, STEEN & HAMILTON
New York, NY

Cleary, Gottlieb is a large international law firm, with more than one third of its attorneys practicing abroad. The firm engages in general private practice with special emphasis on corporate, financial, tax, antitrust, regulatory and litigation matters. It maintains offices in Washington, DC, London, Paris, Hong Kong, Brussels, Frankfurt and Tokyo. Some of its partners and attorneys are foreign nationals who serve abroad and have the same responsibilities and benefits as their U.S. counterparts. U.S. lawyers, especially those with prior foreign language training or international experience, may also serve abroad.

Clients include multinational corporations, financial institutions and governmental and international entities. The firm offers associates the opportunity to take a four-month paid leave of absence to do pro bono community action work.

Professional Staff: The firm currently employs 84 partners and 231 associates in the New York office and 34 partners and 69 associates overseas. The international staff is growing.

Qualifications: A law degree and superior academic performance, maturity of judgment, independence and the ability to work with clients are the prime qualifications for employment. For those interested in international work, knowledge of French, German, Japanese, Russian or Spanish is helpful.

Summer Programs: About 30 summer associates are hired annually to work in all areas of the firm's practice. The firm places strong emphasis on high academic performance and generally hires candidates in the top 10% of their law-school classes. The program lasts for eight weeks.

Application Procedure: Contact:

Legal Personnel Coordinator
Cleary, Gottlieb, Steen & Hamilton
One Liberty Plaza
New York, NY 10006
(212) 225-3150

COUDERT BROTHERS
New York, NY

Coudert Brothers provides U.S.-law services to clients in the U.S. and abroad as well as foreign-law services in the U.K., France, Australia and Belgium. It has offices in Washington, DC, Los Angeles, San Francisco and San José, CA, but most of its personnel are located either at New York headquarters or abroad. The foreign offices are in Paris, London, Brussels, Moscow, Hong Kong, Beijing, Singapore, Tokyo, Sao Paolo, Sydney, Shanghai, Bangkok and Jakarta.

Coudert is organized into functional departments—corporate, litigation, real estate, tax, estate planning, customs, bankruptcy, employee benefits and international banking. Most of the firm's corporate attorneys work in regional groups. There are French, European, Italian, Russian and East Asian groups. Most associates begin their work with the firm at the New York office, although from time to time lawyers are hired directly by the other offices.

Professional Staff: The firm has 130 partners and 217 associates. Of these, 32 partners and 92 associates serve abroad. Some, especially those in the Paris, Brussels, London and Sydney offices, are foreign nationals. The firm hires 20–25 new attorneys each year, most of whom have served as summer associates.

Qualifications: Coudert looks for academic achievement in law school and, to some extent, undergraduate school. With very few exceptions, the firm hires lawyers who have been educated in the U.S. rather than foreign attorneys admitted to practice in the U.S. It is interested in attorneys with initiative, maturity and innovativeness. It has continuing need for attorneys fluent in French, Indonesian, Japanese, Chinese, Korean, German, Spanish, Portuguese, Russian or Italian. Regional experience and knowledge of legal systems of other countries are helpful for attorneys interested in working in international law, but are not absolute prerequisites.

Summer Program: Coudert hires 20–25 law students for its summer associates program. (See qualifications section for requirements.)

Application Procedure: Applicants should submit a transcript and a resume that emphasizes any foreign-language skills, overseas work or study experience and foreign-law expertise. Writing samples and references are also relevant. Write to:

Hiring Committee
Coudert Brothers
200 Park Avenue
New York, NY 10166
(212) 880-4400

DEBEVOISE & PLIMPTON
New York, NY

Debevoise & Plimpton, founded in 1931, is a preeminent international law firm. The firm, which now has over 370 lawyers, provides services for corporate, international, litigation, real estate, tax and trust and estates law. The firm has local offices in Washington, DC, Los Angeles, Paris, London, and Budapest. Debevoise & Plimpton regularly assists major non-U.S. companies and individuals investing in U.S. businesses, American firms investing outside the U.S., and firms engaging in overseas mining or commercial joint ventures. Much of the representation of U.S. and European clients in transnational acquisitions, divestitures, investments, financing and other commercial transactions is handled by the Paris and London offices. The Washington, DC, office assists in the firm's international work, concentrating on international communications, trade and intellectual property issues.

Professional Staff: Debevoise & Plimpton has a staff of 354 in the U.S. and 24 overseas. Attorneys are stationed in England, France, Hungary, Czechoslovakia and the former Soviet Union. The international department is growing. Last year, 53 attorneys were hired.

Qualifications: Applicants must have a JD or the equivalent. Knowledge of a foreign language is preferred.

Summer Program: The summer program is designed to give those interested in permanent employment the opportunity to learn about the firm and its practice. Participants are actively involved on the same basis as regular associates and work with a number of lawyers on a variety of matters in one or more practice groups. Debevoise & Plimpton seeks students whose personal qualities, academic records and other achievements demonstrate exceptional ability, motivation and potential for growth.

Applications: Applicants for the summer program or permanent employment should contact:

> Manager of Associates and Recruitment
> Debevoise & Plimpton
> 875 Third Avenue
> New York, NY 10022
> (212) 909-6000

GIBSON, DUNN & CRUTCHER
Los Angeles, CA

Gibson, Dunn & Crutcher, California's largest law firm, has four departments: corporate and business, tax and probate, litigation, and labor. The firm has 18 offices worldwide—12 domestic and 6 foreign offices in London, Paris, Brussels, Riyadh, Tokyo and Hong Kong. Gibson, Dunn & Crutcher's foreign offices practice U.S. law for foreign clients and help U.S. clients who are doing business abroad. New associates rotate through the firm's four departments; after this rotation period, some may work in international law. All attorneys in the foreign offices are American citizens.

Professional Staff: The firm has 700 lawyers worldwide. There are usually at least 2 experienced U.S. lawyers (11 in London) in each of the six international offices. Each year, 90 attorneys are hired.

Qualifications: Top-ranking graduates from many of the nation's best law schools are sought. Foreign languages are not required, but attorneys interested in working abroad should know European languages.

Summer Program: There is a broad-based training program, and the opportunity to work on international cases depends on the office in which an associate is located. Approximately 90 associates are hired each year.

Application Procedure: Contact:

Recruitment Coordinator
Gibson, Dunn & Crutcher
333 S. Grand Avenue
Los Angeles, CA 90071
(213) 229-7631

MUDGE ROSE GUTHRIE ALEXANDER & FERDON
Washington, DC

Mudge Rose, founded in 1869, is a major international law firm headquartered in New York City, with offices in Washington, DC, Los Angeles, West Palm Beach, Paris, and a newly established one in Tokyo. The firm conducts an extensive and varied law practice and is equipped to provide a broad array of legal services to American and foreign clients in the U.S. and abroad, including corporate, business, and securities law; finance and taxation; banking; antitrust; litigation; intellectual property; real estate; and trusts and estates.

Mudge Rose has one of the largest international trade-law practices in the U.S. devoted principally to the representation of U.S. importers and overseas exporters. The international trade practice is concentrated in Washington, DC, where the firm represents the interests of clients in antidumping, countervailing duty, customs, unfair competition, export-control and other trade-law proceedings before the U.S. International Trade Commission, the Department of Commerce, the U.S. Trade Representative, the U.S. Customs Service and the federal courts. In addition, the firm's lawyers have broad administrative law experience before a number of federal agencies.

Professional Staff: Mudge Rose has 270 professionals working in its U.S. locations and 10 overseas, in France and Japan. Mainly U.S. nationals are hired for overseas positions. In the last 12 months, two lawyers were hired for the Washington, DC, office.

Qualifications: Mudge Rose seeks applicants with advanced degrees in law, international business and economics, especially those with a background in dumping and countervailing-duty law, export controls and multinational negotiations. Experience in international trade is preferred, but not required. Proficiency in Japanese, Chinese or Spanish is also helpful.

Application Procedure: Contact:

Recruitment Coordinator
Mudge Rose Guthrie Alexander & Ferdon
2121 K Street, NW
Suite 700
Washington, DC 20037
(202) 429-9355

PATTON, BOGGS & BLOW
Washington, DC

Much of the practice of Patton, Boggs & Blow, founded in 1962, involves public policy issues. Typically, the firm represents clients on several levels—from litigation before federal courts or regulatory agencies to advocacy before Congress and the executive branch. The firm's principal areas of practice are: litigation, taxation, government contracts, federal, administrative, environmental, corporate, trade, international and legislative law. The firm also has offices in Maryland, Colorado, Florida, North Carolina and Texas.

Professional Staff: Patton, Boggs & Blow has 93 partners, 15 lawyers of counsel and 94 associates. In the last year, 14 associates were hired.

Qualifications: In addition to a law degree, a knowledge of foreign languages is desirable. Arabic, French, German, Italian, Spanish and Farsi are most useful. Previous work experience is not required.

Summer Program: Patton, Boggs & Blow hires approximately 15 trainees for their summer program. Summer associates are hired after their second year in law school.

Application Procedure: Contact:

Recruiting Committee
Patton, Boggs & Blow
2550 M Street, NW
Suite 800
Washington, DC 20037
(202) 457-6000

PENNIE & EDMONDS
New York, NY

Pennie & Edmonds is one of the largest firms in the U.S. specializing in domestic and international law as they apply to the securing, protection and commercial exploitation of intellectual property rights (better known as patents, copyrights and trademarks). The firm represents clients ranging from individual inventors to large corporations. Its international department works on foreign matters for domestic clients and domestic matters for foreign clients. There is an office in Washington, DC, with one partner and three associates.

Professional Staff: Pennie & Edmonds has 98 attorneys, 33 of whom are partners. The legal staff also includes 17 law clerks and 4 foreign interns.

Qualifications: The firm has specialists in fields such as chemistry, physics, molecular biology, metallurgy and electronics. Most staff have JD degrees in addition to a BA, BS, MA or PhD degree. Applicants should have knowledge of foreign languages, especially Spanish, German, French, Japanese, Chinese, Arabic or Russian, in that order. Willingness to travel, but not live abroad, is necessary; work experience is not.

Summer Program: Ten summer associates are hired for the entire summer. Those with technical backgrounds work on patent prosecution. Others work on the less technically oriented copyright and trademark practice.

Application Procedure: Contact:

>Hiring Partner
>Pennie & Edmonds
>Counselors-at-Law
>1155 Avenue of the Americas
>New York, NY 10036
>(212) 790-9090

SULLIVAN & CROMWELL
New York, NY

Sullivan & Cromwell conducts a national and international general legal practice and provides legal advice and services in virtually all areas of U.S. law, cross-border transactions and French and European Community matters. Many of the firm's clients are foreign governments and enterprises.

Professional Staff: The firm has a professional staff of 340 in the U.S., 60 of whom were hired in the past year. Thirty-two associates/partners are stationed overseas in Australia, Britain, France, Hong Kong and Japan, two of whom were recently hired.

Qualifications: Sullivan & Cromwell prefers its lawyers to have foreign language skills. French, Chinese, German, Japanese, Russian and Spanish are most useful. A willingness to travel and live overseas is not obligatory.

Summer Program: Sullivan & Cromwell considers law students for its summer program after they have completed two years of law school. Program participants are paid and perform general legal work.

Application Procedure: To apply for permanent positions or for the summer program, write to:

Director of Legal Recruiting
Sullivan & Cromwell
125 Broad Street
New York, NY 10004
(212) 558-4000

Chapter Six

TRANSLATION, INTERPRETATION AND TERMINOLOGY

Introduction by Barbara Moser-Mercer

From politics to poetry, international and intercultural communication would be doomed to failure were it not for the skilled services of translators, interpreters and terminologists. Their expertise has facilitated many a breakthrough in difficult diplomatic meetings and has helped save lives when doctor and patient did not speak the same language. Most international development programs would never produce results if training and documentation were not available in the recipients' language, and our lives in general would certainly be lacking in the enrichment we derive from learning about other peoples' ideas through their literature. Translation and interpretation have become so much a part of our daily lives that we tend to forget about the professionals responsible for such "effortless" communication.

Barbara Moser-Mercer, Dean of Translation and Interpreting of the Monterey Institute of International Studies, received a diploma in translation, an MA in conference interpretation and a PhD in linguistics from the University of Innsbruck. A former Fulbright research scholar, she was vice president of the Ecole de Traduction et d'Interprétation of the University of Geneva before going to Monterey.

WHAT IS TRANSLATION?

The term "translation" is usually reserved for rendering a written text, such as a book, a manual, or a scientific article, into another language. Translators will usually specialize in certain fields: some will translate fiction and poetry, others legal documents and patents, and still others will translate mostly scientific and technical texts. Such specialization is often determined by a translator's previous education—some of the very best technical translators started out as engineers, but a number of outstanding software translators acquired such a good background in software engineering that they switched careers. Common to all translators is a love for language, intellectual curiosity and considerable patience in working out seemingly unresolvable problems of meaning and style.

WHAT IS INTERPRETATION?

"Interpretation" refers to the oral rendition of statements spoken in one language into another language. This can be carried out in a variety of settings: a hospital, a court of law, a business meeting, an international conference, on TV, or even over the telephone where, by means of a conference call, two parties communicate with the help of an interpreter. Interpreters are usually characterized as outgoing individuals, interested in communicating orally, ready to master a given topic in a very short period of time and able to put themselves in the shoes of the speaker at all times.

WHAT IS TERMINOLOGY?

Speed and a high degree of specialization have made it difficult for today's translators and interpreters to keep up with the technical vocabulary they need to use every day. The advent of computerized databases has provided a multitude of options to collect, organize and update the specialized terms used in international technical exchanges today. Terminologists represent an important link between translators and interpreters on the one hand and technical writers and the scientific community on the other. Their task consists in screening the technical literature in many fields for newly coined terms, phrases and expressions, and organizing the result of their research systematically on the computer, where it becomes available to translators and interpreters.

PROFESSIONAL TRAINING

From the brief job descriptions given above it is evident that today's language professionals can no longer rely on language education alone to meet the diverse needs of their work. Nowadays, specialized training built upon a solid foundation of general education is almost always required for landing one's first job. Translation, interpretation and terminology call for outstanding skills in the native language, since this is the language one usually works into, and an excellent command of the foreign language(s) one intends to use professionally. Such competence can normally be achieved only by supplementing foreign language studies with extensive stays abroad. While the U.S. market still offers opportunities for translators with one foreign language, at least two foreign languages are now generally required on the European market.

Professional programs are available in many countries. Listings can be obtained from the American Translators Association (ATA), from the International Association of Conference Interpreters (AIIC) for reputable interpreter-training programs around the world, and from the Interuniversity Conference of Institutes of Translation and Interpretation (CIUTI) for programs in translation and interpretation in many countries that meet the stringent criteria established by this association. (Addresses are given at the end of the chapter.)

A good professional program will make admission contingent upon a high degree of linguistic competence in all the languages a candidate intends to use professionally, proof of residence in the countries where these languages are spoken, and some type of admission exam designed to screen applicants with regard to the skills required for successful completion of the training program. Most admission tests emphasize analytical skills, language competence, sound general knowledge and knowledge of world affairs.

Instruction should be given by practicing professionals. Most translators and interpreters know that even a few months away from exercising their profession will make them feel "rusty" and in need of practice. A good training program will make a clear distinction between translation and interpretation and require additional testing for interpretation. Although both skills rely on some of the same intellectual prerequisites, interpretation requires an additional set of aptitudes for which students should be tested before embarking on training. In a well-balanced curriculum a student should find translation courses dealing with a variety of subjects, such as politics, economics and the natural sciences, unless the program specializes in only one type of translation (literary or technical, for example). A student should also be able to acquire a theoretical understanding of the field of translation, interpretation and terminology and be exposed to the modern tools of the trade: multilingual word processing, terminology database software, computer-assisted translation software and the operation of modems and fax machines. Most reputable programs will make the awarding of a degree contingent upon the passing of a set of exams. Most employers still rely on additional testing before offering work to graduates in the field. (Competitive exams are the rule at the UN, the various institutions of the European Community, the U.S. Department of State, etc.)

In some cases qualified university graduates may be accepted for in-house training by a large corporation or the Commission of the European Community. There is a preference for university graduates in law, economics, international relations or another field relevant to the corporation offering such training and, in the case of the European Community, strong foreign-language competence.

Internships are another way to build professional competence. Good professional training programs will offer a variety of translation- and terminology-related internships to qualified students. Internships are usually for students approaching the end of their professional training and are thus an excellent opportunity to break into the market. They last anywhere from 2 to 18 months and are offered by large corporations with significant translation and terminology needs, as well as translation agencies interested in providing further training to future professionals. While internships offered by the UN and its agencies are not remunerated, other internships provide adequate remuneration, visa and work-permit services, if required, and sometimes health-insurance coverage.

Many professional associations hold annual conferences and thus offer the membership a chance to brush up on certain skills and to learn about the most recent developments in a field of specialization. Many professional training programs offer continuing courses in translation, interpretation and terminology. These are usually offered workshop-style on weekends or during the summer. These courses are not designed to help interested people become translators or interpreters overnight, but to help professionals gain expertise. For those unable to participate in such programs, there are still ample opportunities to enhance professional expertise: professional journals in translation, interpretation and terminology, specialized journals in science and technology, or publications in any other field of interest to the professional linguist.

PROFESSIONAL PRACTICE TODAY

Most people interested in the field have already undertaken extensive studies in one or more foreign languages, with many intent on adding another foreign language over the years. In the U.S., demand is quite high for translation to French and German as well as from English into Japanese and from Japanese into English, and from English into Spanish and from Spanish into English. Russian and other Slavic languages have gained in importance since the end of the cold war. In conference interpretation, language needs do not vary as much: on the private market most of the demand is still for English, French, Spanish, German, Japanese; the UN and its various agencies work with English, French, Spanish, Russian, Chinese and Arabic (in addition German is used at the International Labor Organization and the World Health Organization); the official languages of the European Community and its institutions are English, German, Spanish, Portuguese, Italian, Greek and Dutch. The European Community is the world's largest employer of conference interpreters, with about 250 meetings to be staffed every day. A conference interpreter's combination of languages will often determine where he or she will reside professionally: thus, if a translator or interpreter's strength is in English and French, he or she may decide to live in Canada, for example.

Most professionals work as free-lancers. They work from their home or share an office with other professionals. Given the high cost of equipment today, the latter solution can be advantageous. Up-to-date computer equipment, state-of-the-art software, a modem and a fax machine are absolutely essential for getting started in translation. A good answering machine and a fax machine are important for breaking into the interpreting market. Free-lancers receive their work mostly from agencies specializing in translation, and it is not uncommon for Americans to sell their native-language expertise in an overseas market: they receive the original texts to be translated via fax and send their translated texts out via modem. Working with agencies is advantageous since one does not have to advertise one's services all the time, and the agency will normally provide a final edit of one's work, thus reducing the chance of serious translation errors going uncorrected. Agencies can also offer desktop publishing and printing services that are often beyond the resources of an individual translator. All of these services have to be paid for, however, and the rate a translator receives from an agency reflects that. Sending one well-written resume to a large number of agencies will almost certainly yield work. Usually, agencies will send out a sample translation to test whether an applicant has the skills he or she lists on the resume.

Many translators, usually the more established ones, will work directly with clients. These professionals have almost always developed expertise in the client's field of specialization, and can usually rely on a steady stream of work. They are free to set their own rates, which are higher than what they could charge an agency.

The most important markets in the U.S. are the U.S. government and its agencies, U.S. and foreign multinational corporations and their subsidiaries, U.S. importers and exporters, commercial and nonprofit research institutions, pharmaceutical, chemical and machinery manufacturers not covered by any of the above categories, engineering and construction firms with foreign connections, patent attorneys, the publishing industry, the news media, municipal governments in bilingual U.S. cities, graduate schools of U.S. universities, and foreign diplomatic, commercial, scientific and other representatives in the U.S.

Large corporations, international organizations and many governments have ongoing translation needs and have therefore established their own language services. The UN employs translators also as précis-writers. These specialists sit in UN meetings, take notes on everything that is being said and then produce summary records of such meetings. In-house translators are fully employed with full benefits. While such permanent positions are advantageous for a number of translators, others prefer the variety and the flexible working hours that come with free-lancing, even if that means giving up some of the security.

Terminologists work almost exclusively in-house, either in international organizations, governments of multilingual countries, large corporations or translation agencies. The need for trained terminologists has risen considerably over the past eight years as machine-assisted translation systems and terminology data banks have become more widely used. Terminologists will usually be called upon to help develop a company's terminology data bank, thus ensuring that multilingual terminology needs are consistently met. Regular screening of technical and company publications for technical terms is a must for terminologists; as such they are always at the cutting edge of an industry's development.

The market for interpreting services is highly varied. Court interpreters will make their services known to the courts in their area. Several states have enacted legislation requiring court interpreters to be certified. However, the demand is often so high, or the language combinations so variable, that certification requirements cannot be met. Examinations are offered at the state or federal level for a number of language combinations. The demand is highest in the Spanish/English combination; Vietnamese, Laotian and Cantonese are also very much in demand. Immigration patterns will usually dictate the needs in various language combinations.

Medical interpreting is becoming increasingly important, with some legislation in the offing that would require all hospitals to offer interpreting services to its patients. Many hospitals rely on volunteers, but as the need increases, trained professionals will most likely be in a better position to provide reliable service. The language combination currently most in demand is Spanish/English.

Telephone interpretation links two parties with an interpreter via a conference call. The agency providing the service will require its free-lance interpreters to be "on call" during specified days of the week. This work quite often involves interpreting for business partners, hospitals or police departments.

The State Department uses escort interpreters to accompany foreign visitors while they tour the U.S. These interpreters must prove that they are truly bicultural as they are often called upon to explain aspects of American culture to their clients. Escort interpreters travel extensively, with most tours lasting between two and five weeks.

Conference interpreters work either for international organizations or in the private market, i.e. for a variety of clients. Many of them belong to professional secretariats, groups of interpreters who advertise together and service international meetings. Officially bilingual countries, such as Canada, have a continuous need for highly qualified conference interpreters, whereas the demand in the U.S. is highly regionalized, with most international meetings being held on the East Coast. The European market has its main centers in Brussels, Paris, Geneva and Vienna; all of these cities are host either to institutions of the European Community or to international and intergovernmental organizations that are known to hold meetings regularly. International trade patterns influence the conference interpretation market as well; thus Japanese/English interpreters find a ready market in Japan and on the West Coast of the U.S., and Chinese/English conference interpreters are in high demand in Taiwan, whereas language combinations involving the Scandinavian and Baltic languages rarely come into play beyond the countries bordering on the Baltic sea. Although interpretation via satellite has been tried and found to be feasible, conference interpreters must still be willing to relocate to where their market is and ready to travel at the drop of a hat to a conference site often thousands of miles away from home.

A very special kind of mix between the security of full-time employment and the freedom of the free-lancer's life is the retainer contract, an agreement between a free-lance translator and a translation agency by which the agency guarantees the translator a certain amount of work each month, and the translator is obligated to give preferential treatment to any translation coming from the agency. This enables the free-lancer to secure a minimum amount of work each month and the agency has the advantage of always having a translator available in a certain language combination or for a specific subject field.

ALL-LANGUAGE SERVICES, INC. (ALS)
New York, NY

ALS provides translating services in over 60 languages to a variety of technical and professional entities, including engineering concerns, businesses and the medical field.

Professional Staff: ALS employs more than 150 translators, interpreters, revisers and editors. It has a very low turnover rate. ALS rarely hires free-lancers but will do so when necessary (for example, when there is a demand for an exotic or unusual language). All staff members are based in the U.S, but travel frequently. All employees are encouraged to travel abroad to keep up their languages.

Qualifications: The overriding qualifications for employment are linguistic ability and the expertise to translate technical and professional material. Almost all ALS employees have had experience in another profession. ALS gives a language test to potential employees.

Application Procedure: For more information or to apply for a position, contact:

> Personnel Director
> All-Language Services, Inc.
> 545 Fifth Avenue
> New York, NY 10017
> (212) 986-1688

BERLITZ TRANSLATION SERVICES (BTS)
Woodland Hills, CA

Berlitz, well-known for its language-training schools, also operates a language-translation service. BTS offers many languages, ranging from Arabic to Vietnamese, Spanish, Greek, Russian and Korean. It offers full-service graphics production in all languages, audiovisual production services for the industrial or consumer markets, and conference, court and business interpretation services. It maintains 19 main translation centers in 14 countries. The four production sites in the U.S. are in Miami, Los Angeles, New York City and Washington, DC.

Professional Staff: BTS maintains a computerized "resource bank" containing the names of more than 3,000 contract translators, editors, interpreters, narrators and language consultants. There are approximately

100 permanent staff members, most of whom are professional translators, language and project managers and graphics production staff.

Qualifications: BTS requires a college degree (or the equivalent), previous experience as a translator or interpreter as well as in a profession or technical field, and refined linguistic ability. Translators and interpreters must successfully complete a series of tests.

Internships/Temporary Positions: BTS offers paid internships for high school, college and graduate students. Interns without significant foreign language skills work as entry-level production assistants and in clerical positions. Those with foreign language skills do work that helps them train to be translators. BTS works with schools to design appropriate internships. Should no academic credit be required, a temporary assignment may be available. While most of its four U.S. offices will accept interns or offer temporary work, no set number are available annually.

Application Procedure: Submit your application in writing to the national production headquarters at:

> Berlitz Translation Services
> 6415 Independence Avenue
> Woodland Hills, CA 91367
> (818) 340-5147

RENNERT BILINGUAL TRANSLATIONS
New York, NY

Rennert offers translating and consecutive as well as simultaneous interpreting for large companies and individuals. It also has private foreign language classes. The firm translates a wide variety of documents, including speeches, contracts, articles and catalogues, and deals with many subjects, including engineering, advertising and foreign trade.

Professional Staff: Rennert maintains a roster of 50–60 free-lance interpreters. This number includes a core group of 20 that the agency uses regularly, usually once or twice a week. The agency calls on the other free-lancers once or twice a month. There are 7 full-time administrators.

Qualifications: Rennert requires an undergraduate degree and prefers applicants to have graduate degrees or experience in legal, financial, technical, scientific or medical fields. Romance languages are most in demand, followed by German, Japanese, Chinese, Arabic and Russian. Rennert requires that an applicant have work experience as an in-house translator or proofreader or in a multilingual context. Previous overseas experience is helpful but not necessary; some free-lancers must travel. Rennert rarely recruits from colleges or graduate schools. Unsolicited resumes are submitted frequently, and applicants are generally chosen on the basis of previous experience and recommendations.

Application Procedure: Applications should be addressed to:

> Rennert Bilingual Translations
> Assistant Director, Translations
> 2 West 45th Street
> 5th Floor
> New York, NY 10036
> (212) 819-1776

TRANSLATION ACES, INC.
New York, NY

Formerly known as Linder Translations, Translation Aces offers translation and interpreting services on subjects as diverse as automotive engineering, admiralty law, telecommunications and insurance. All languages are offered.

Professional Staff: Translation Aces' core of several hundred professional free-lancers is always expanding. Each translator specializes in a particular technical field and works only in his or her native language.

Qualifications: Translation Aces requires extensive professional experience in specialized fields such as chemistry, physics, finance, telecommunications or law. German, the Romance languages, Russian, Arabic, Japanese and other Asian languages are most frequently requested. Knowledge of English is also required.

Application Procedure: All applications and inquiries should be mailed to:

> Translation Aces, Inc.
> 29 Broadway
> New York, NY 10006
> (212) 269-4660

TRANSLATION COMPANY OF AMERICA (TCA)
New York, NY

TCA is a full-service foreign language company providing document translation and interpreters.

Professional Staff: TCA maintains a full-time staff as well as approximately 100 free-lancers.

Qualifications: In addition to knowledge of foreign languages and attention to accuracy, applicants should have a field of expertise. Among the preferred fields of expertise are law, medicine, advertising, education and transportation.

Languages in order of current demand: Spanish, German, French, Japanese, Russian, Chinese and Arabic. Previous experience is not required.

Internships: Unpaid summer internships are available to college students with an interest and abilities in various foreign languages. Interns do office work and, depending on ability, some editing and proofreading.

Application Procedure: For both internships and professional work, contact:

> Manager, Translators
> Translation Company of America
> 10 West 37th Street
> New York, NY 10018
> (212) 563-7054

PROFESSIONAL ASSOCIATIONS
AND EDUCATIONAL ORGANIZATIONS

> The American Association of Language Specialists (TAALS)
> 1000 Connecticut Avenue, NW
> Suite 9
> Washington, DC 20036
> (301) 657-2545

American Translators Association (ATA)
1735 Jefferson Davis Highway
Suite 903
Arlington, VA 22202-3413
(703) 892-1500
Fax: (703) 892-1501

Association Internationale des Interpretes
de Conférence (AIIC)
10, avenue de Sécheron
CH-1202 Geneva
Switzerland
+41 22 731 33 23
Fax: +41 22 732 41 51

Association Internationale des Traducteurs
de Conférence (AITC)
15, route des Morillons
CH-1218 Le Grand-Saconnex
Switzerland
+41 22 791 06 66

Conference Interuniversitaire des Instituts
de Traduction et d'Interprétation (CUITI)
c/o I.S.T.I.
Rue Joseph Hazard 34
B-1180 Bruxelles
Belgium
322/770 62 87
Fax: 322/346 21 34

International Information Center for
Terminology (INFOTERM)
Heinestrasse 38
Postfach 130
A-1021 Vienna
Austria

National Association of Judiciary Interpreters
and Translators (NAJIT)
Plaza II, Executive Center
125 Lincoln Ave, Suite 400
Santa Fe, NM 87501

School of Languages and Linguistics
Division of Interpretation and Translation
Georgetown University
Intercultural Center 225
Washington, DC 20057
(202) 687-5848

Chapter Seven

NONPROFIT ORGANIZATIONS

Introduction

"What unites nonprofit groups is a decision to be guided
by a particular idea, whatever it may be, and to keep
other considerations secondary."
The New Yorker, 1991

Nonprofit organizations (NPOs) are not in the business of making
money, for themselves or for the corporations, foundations, government
agencies or individuals who support them financially. NPOs are in the
business of addressing some of the most pressing social problems of our
time—refugees, hunger, chronic poverty, inadequate health care and
education, disasters, environmental degradation and even political
development. Because nonprofits often work at the grass-roots level with
the people they wish to serve, they are often in the best position to
achieve their goals and are an important source of information and ideas
that stimulate social change. Nonprofits are taking an increasingly
important place in worldwide development, effectively bridging the gap
between governments and people by providing services directly to those
in need.

Nonprofits are sometimes called nongovernmental organizations (NGOs). The term NGO usually refers to organizations involved in development. It was first used by the UN in recognition of the importance of independently organized groups of professionals, experts or interested private citizens in the overall development process.

The world of nonprofits has grown to include between 500,000 and 1 million organizations worldwide and employs approximately 10 million. Although nonprofit organizations active internationally comprise a relatively small percentage of all nonprofits, they offer excellent career opportunities. Some people find work in the "third sector" attractive because of the heightened job satisfaction and personal rewards gained from working for something in which they believe. For others, like development workers, international public-health professionals and researchers, etc., nonprofits simply provide many of the jobs in their chosen fields. Nonprofit work, however, is not for everyone. It offers neither the market-oriented excitement and perks that many business people thrive on nor the competitive salaries. Although entry-level salaries are low in many fields, middle-range salaries in nonprofits may stagnate at $25,000-$30,000 and senior-level salaries often do not exceed $50,000.

This chapter focuses on international nonprofits, many of which you may already be familiar with. It is not an exhaustive list, so we suggest you do some research of your own. You may want to concentrate your job search in New York, Washington, Chicago or Los Angeles, the areas in which nonprofit activity is currently concentrated. The nonprofit organizations have been divided into four substantive categories: research and education; development assistance, environment and relief; youth-oriented; and health and population. There is some overlap among organizations.

Research and Educational Organizations

Foreign policy research organizations, or think tanks as they are sometimes called, are interested in formulating and communicating ideas. They seek to influence or educate people and thus affect the direction of foreign policy. Some do this by lobbying and disseminating their publications. Others take a more passive approach. Some research organizations are nonpartisan and publish only objective educational materials, while others promote a political or ideological cause. Still others focus on a particular geographic region or country. The research organizations listed in this chapter run the gamut from nonpartisan to overtly partisan; their missions range from education to advocacy. Their audiences also vary—from policymakers and academics to average citizens.

Most research organizations have a similar structure: a board of directors or governors, which has at least nominal control over the organization; a president responsible for administration and development; senior managers or vice-presidents in charge of public affairs, outreach, development (that is, fund-raising) and lobbying. Some organizations have staff who arrange seminars, conferences, meetings or trips. Most also have research departments, which may consist of senior fellows or senior researchers/analysts, junior researchers, research associates and assistants and editors.

Senior research staffs are frequently made up of former government officials or academics who have devoted their careers to international relations and who are considered experts in their fields. They serve as spokespersons for their organizations, often generating publicity by their participation in TV talk shows and radio programs and appearances before congressional committees and influential groups, as well as by articles on the op-ed pages of newspapers and periodicals. International research organizations rarely have overseas staff, although their work may involve travel.

Research organizations are generally small. Turnover can be slow and promotions rare. Research organizations offer a small number of entry-level positions, as research assistants or associates, to recent recipients of BAs or MAs. They also hire support staff for their outreach or educational programs, including speakers' forums, conferences, workshops and symposia.

Development Assistance,
Environment and Relief Organizations

In many instances the poorest countries in the world, where development activities are most concentrated, also have ominous environmental problems. The combination of poverty, environmental exploitation and political instability often leave the peoples of these countries more vulnerable to the ravages of man-made and natural disasters. Thus, the work of development, environmental and relief agencies is often interconnected.

"Development is not a cluster of benefits 'given' to people in need, but rather a process by which a populace acquires greater mastery over its own destiny," according to a person in the field. Most development and relief agencies focus on the "processes" that can improve the quality of life most dramatically: health, education, food (agriculture), income and employment. But within these areas, the range of development assistance activities and relief organizations is phenomenal. There are organizations that offer small-business loans to people who would not otherwise be eligible to borrow; teach and train indigenous people in nutrition and health care, agricultural and livestock methods and community planning and teach the appropriate technologies. They also support and encourage political development in the countries in which they are working.

There are few differences between the work of development organizations and that of relief organizations. The large development NGOs are involved in both emergency relief and long-term projects, and those organizations that consider themselves primarily relief-oriented also provide training and other self-help services.

The methods of the development NGOs have, at times, been criticized. In the past, some development assistance organizations have omitted local people in their planning and implementation. They have used a staff from the developed world to analyze a problem, suggest a remedy and carry out a solution. In some cases this approach has worked, but in others it has harmed local ecosystems or economic patterns, alienated the local community, wasted money, or simply failed to correct the original problem.

Today, this approach has for the most part been replaced by programs planned with input and help from locals and local NGOs that are designed to promote self-reliance. Helping people to help themselves is the operative catchphrase of the development assistance field, even among organizations that specialize in providing disaster relief and emergency aid.

The structure of development and relief organizations is similar to that of research organizations, except instead of having a large research staff, they have field (or overseas) staff. Support staff and coordinators usually are based at headquarters, and area managers and fieldworkers, based abroad. Development assistance NPOs use only experienced specialists in their field operations. Specialization in this case means a PhD or MA, plus overseas experience in a technical field such as agriculture, nutrition, community planning or social work.

Because almost no fieldworkers are hired without significant experience abroad, technical assistance is a difficult field to enter. Finding the first job abroad is the hardest. One way to gain field experience is through the U.S. Peace Corps. (See Chapter Eight for a full description.) The Peace Corps trains Americans who have had no experience working abroad and sends them overseas for two-year assignments in developing countries. Personnel managers of the NPOs listed in this chapter consider the Peace Corps experience an excellent preparation for development assistance.

Although interning for the headquarters office is good experience for someone interested in development, very few interns are sent overseas. A few organizations, however, do offer internships abroad. See Chapter Ten and the development assistance section below for more information.

Contrary to the image most of us have of environmental advocates floating in tiny rafts between whaling ships and the whales they wish to protect or creating a human chain around ancient trees about to be cut down, most international environmental organizations are not involved in such "fieldwork" lobbying or advocacy, but concentrate instead on providing information on which others can act. For the most part, international environmental organizations engage in two activities: research and education and development assistance.

Environmental research organizations compile and analyze data and offer policy solutions to environmental problems. Through their publications, educational programs, conferences, policy proposals and contact with the international media, these institutions hope to foster awareness that they hope will eventually lead to action. Many consider themselves nonpartisan and do not advocate any particular point of view, but as one worker said "the facts often speak for themselves."

In the field of development, environmental NGOs have taken on an increasingly important role. In 1987 an environment department was set up within the World Bank. Now, proposed development projects must undergo extensive assessments on their impact on the environment. "Sustainable development," a concept that incorporates environmental planning into economic development, is another persistent catchphrase among NGOs. Overseas, environmental NGOs provide technical assistance and work with other NGOs and local governments to create sound environmental policy.

Generally, most environmental NGOs are small and are involved with a multitude of environmental issues. Thus—especially at the entry-level —they look for generalists with a social science background and a demonstrated interest in environmental issues. Previous field experience, volunteerism, internships and some course work or a specialization in environmental studies are the best ways to demonstrate commitment to environmental issues. Internships are also valuable because environmental organizations have a strong tendency to fill positions from within or from the volunteer ranks. Of course, experts in a variety of ecological and technical fields are critical to their sustainable development, research and education programs.

Health and Population Organizations

The main difference between health-related organizations and the ones included in the development, environment and relief section is the nature of the fieldwork. The organizations listed in this section exclusively provide medical care, training of medical staff and health-related counseling to people in developing countries. Their salaried employees are doctors, nurses, laboratory technicians and people with both experience and graduate degrees in nutrition, public health/public planning, maternal and child care, epidemiology or family planning. Health-related work experience is almost always required, except for some medical students who work abroad as part of their training.

The health-care field is unique in that it frequently accepts volunteers for its programs abroad. Volunteers generally have not had experience working abroad but do have accredited health-care-work experience and graduate degrees. For both volunteer and permanent positions, health-care credentials are more important than international experience or foreign language proficiency.

Youth-Oriented Organizations

The organizations in this section arrange exchange programs and educational and work-study experiences abroad. Their programs are aimed mainly at young people, high-school through college age. However, most of the organizations also sponsor shorter programs for young adults and older groups.

Some of the programs listed provide useful work experience for budding internationalists. Others at least provide international exposure, which is a prerequisite for anyone considering an international career.

The organizations below have been included not only because they provide opportunities to work or study abroad; they are also a source for internationally related employment. "Many of our current employees are former Peace Corps volunteers who wanted to help others have the same experience and work in an international field," commented an employer in one of the organizations. Someone interested in international education or intercultural relations would also find work at one of these organizations satisfying.

RESEARCH AND EDUCATION

ACCESS: A Security Information Service
Washington, DC

Access is a nonpartisan clearinghouse established to broaden and improve understanding of foreign policy, peace and security issues by providing access to authoritative information and resources representing a full spectrum of views. Access operates an inquiry and speaker referral service on international affairs issues and produces directories and special guides. Access also publishes issue summaries.

Professional Staff: Access has a staff of three, which is based in the U.S. In the past year, the staff size has remained the same.

Qualifications: An undergraduate or graduate degree in international affairs and three years work experience in the field of international affairs is required. Knowledge of foreign languages is preferred, but not essential.

Internships: College juniors and seniors as well as graduate students may apply for paid year-round internships. Interns assist researchers with ongoing projects and handle office duties.

Application Procedure: Individuals interested in professional positions should contact the office manager. Applications for internships should be addressed to the intern coordinator. The address is:

> ACCESS: A Security Information Service
> 1511 K Street, NW, Suite 643
> Washington, DC 20005
> (202) 783-6050

THE AFRICAN-AMERICAN INSTITUTE
New York, NY

The African-American Institute's mission is twofold. First, to further African development by strengthening its human resources and promoting trade and investment between Africa and the U.S. Second, AAI seeks to encourage African-American understanding by bringing African exchange students to the U.S. to study and through publishing the bimonthly *Africa Report*.

Professional Staff: The institute employs 95 people in the U.S. There are 26 employees overseas in numerous countries in sub-Saharan Africa and Portugal. Overseas staff recruit students for higher education programs in the U.S. During the past year, 10 people were hired, 3 for overseas positions.

Qualifications: An MA, MBA, MIA, MS or PhD in international affairs is preferred. A background in democratization, trade issues, education or journalism is useful. Previous work experience is preferred and may be necessary depending on the position available. A willingness to travel or live abroad is generally not required. Knowledge of French and Spanish is preferred. Arabic and Portuguese are also helpful.

Internships: Unpaid internships are available for undergraduates on a semester, summer or yearly basis. Candidates should have an interest in African affairs and the ability to assist in various administrative and research tasks.

Application Procedure: Inquiries relating to professional positions and internships should be directed to the Director of Personnel and Administration. The address is:

> The African-American Institute
> 833 United Nations Plaza
> New York, NY 10017
> (212) 949-5666

AMERICAN ENTERPRISE INSTITUTE
FOR PUBLIC POLICY RESEARCH (AEI)
Washington, DC

AEI is a private research organization "dedicated to preserving and improving the institutions of a free society—open and competitive private enterprise, limited and public-spirited government, strong and well-managed defense and foreign policies and vital cultural and political values." The Foreign Policy Studies division approaches international issues by seeking to understand how American interests, and those of political and economic freedom, can be advanced.

Professional Staff: AEI has a professional staff of 120, 10 of whom were hired in the past year.

Qualifications: Senior employees usually have advanced degrees, experience in high-level jobs and have published. Research associates and assistants should have an MA or PhD in international relations, with expertise in Soviet and East European studies, defense and arms control, or regional and development issues. Research associates must have some research experience; assistants need not. Proficiency in Chinese, German or Russian is preferred.

Internships: College and graduate students may apply for fall, spring or summer unpaid internships. Interns provide research support to scholars, research associates and managers. Applicants with high grades in a relevant major should send a writing sample, resume and transcript.

Application Procedure: Candidates for internships should contact the Internship Coordinator. Other inquiries should be directed to the Director of Administration.

> American Enterprise Institute for Public Policy Research
> 1150 17th Street, NW
> Washington, DC 20036
> (202) 862-5800

AMERICA-MIDEAST EDUCATIONAL AND TRAINING SERVICE, INC. (AMIDEAST)
Washington, DC

The objectives of Amideast are to develop human resources in the Middle East and North Africa and to promote understanding between the Arab world and the U.S. The objectives are carried out, in part, through education, information and development programs. Overseas offices in Bahrain, Egypt, Jordan, Kuwait, Lebanon, Morocco, Syria, Tunisia, Yemen, the West Bank and the Gaza Strip offer educational counseling and testing for Arab individuals and institutions interested in study and training in the U.S., as well as technical assistance Other activities include administration and training programs for sponsors of Arab and American students, trainees and visitors and public outreach projects.

Professional Staff: Amideast has a professional staff of 65, 52 of whom are based overseas. Both foreign nationals and U.S. citizens work overseas. In the past year 20 have been hired.

Qualifications: An MA or MS in international relations, Middle Eastern studies, international development, international education or student counseling is desired. Foreign language ability is preferred. Arabic and French are the most desirable languages. Applicants should have one to two years work experience. Experience working in the Middle East or North Africa is also helpful.

Internships: Two to three people are hired each year for the summer or during the school year. High school, college and graduate students enrolled in programs relating to Arab/Middle East studies, international education or international development may apply. Interns are involved in research, writing and administrative work. Interns with special skills are offered a modest stipend.

Application Procedure: Send applications to:

Director of Personnel
AMIDEAST
1100 17th Street, NW
Suite 300
Washington, DC 20036-4601
(202) 785-0022

AMNESTY INTERNATIONAL U.S.A. (AI-USA)
New York, NY

AI-USA is the U.S. arm of Amnesty International, an umbrella organization that sponsors groups in over 50 countries who campaign for the release of "prisoners of conscience," fair and prompt trials for political prisoners and an end to torture and executions. It monitors how well governments preserve individuals' fundamental civil, political, economic, social, religious and cultural rights.

AI's approaches include researching human-rights violations in a large number of countries, sending delegates on research, observation and advocacy missions, and documenting and publicizing individual prisoner of conscience cases. It appeals to government authorities by writing letters detailing abuses and by sending petitions. It also provides information to UN agencies and other international organizations, and it is widely considered to be a preeminent source of information on human-rights abuses throughout the world. A network of thousands of volunteer groups worldwide organize work on behalf of some 55,000 prisoners. There are 410 local groups and 2,000 student groups in the U.S.

AI publishes reports on rights violations, a bimonthly newsletter profiling prisoners of conscience and a yearbook summarizing allegations against each country.

Professional Staff: AI-USA's staff is comprised of 80 professionals. Seven were hired in the past year and all work in the U.S. The London headquarters employs some 250 people and does its own hiring.

Qualifications: An undergraduate degree in the social sciences, especially in international relations or political science, is preferred.

Knowledge of foreign languages is useful, particularly French and Spanish. Computer skills, especially word processing, are essential.

AI-USA is a grass-roots membership organization. Thus, candidates with grass-roots experience in a nonprofit organization, with a local group or with political-organizing experience are preferred. At least five years work experience is required. Foreign study or employment is a plus, but not essential. Employees must be willing to travel.

Internships: College students may spend a summer or more working in any of AI-USA's departments. Students should have some political science and international relations course work and a good GPA. Students who have worked with an AI-USA group on their campus often serve as interns. Positions are not paid.

Application Procedure: Candidates for either professional or internship positions should contact:

> Personnel Department
> Amnesty International U.S.A.
> 322 Eighth Avenue
> New York, NY 10001
> (212) 807-8400

ARMS CONTROL ASSOCIATION (ACA)
Washington, DC

The Arms Control Association is a nonpartisan, nonprofit organization dedicated to promoting public understanding of effective policies and programs in arms control and disarmament. The association works with the media, interested members of Congress and the general public to create broad public understanding of the need for positive steps toward the limitation of armaments to reduce world tensions. In addition, ACA publishes a monthly journal, *Arms Control Today*.

Professional Staff: ACA has a staff of 11 people, 3 of whom were hired in the last year.

Qualifications: Depending on the position in question, an MA or PhD in international relations, security policy or public policy, is required. Previous work experience is required including a familiarity with research and general office skills. Language abilities are not required, but knowledge of Russian, German or French is helpful.

Internships: ACA offers summer and semester-long internships to college students with good interpersonal and writing skills, some general office experience, and knowledge of related issues. Interns are primarily support staff, doing some research for ACA analysts, assisting with the production of their magazine, maintaining ACA's library, and performing some clerical work.

Application Procedure: For professional positions contact the address below. Those interested in internships should contact the Internship Coordinator at the same address.

> Arms Control Association
> 11 Dupont Circle
> Suite 250
> Washington, DC 20036
> (202) 797-4604

THE ASIA FOUNDATION
San Francisco, CA

The Asia Foundation is a grant-making organization that supports Asian initiatives to strengthen institutions concerned with representative government, the administration of justice, human rights, market economies, an independent media, regional cooperation and other nongovernmental organizations that encourage broad participation in public life. It sponsors exchange programs that bring Asian legislators, judges, civil servants and journalists to the U.S. to receive training or advanced degrees in their fields and in the American political system. It administers the Luce Scholars program, which sends Americans to Asia, and also holds meetings on Asian geopolitical issues. It also sponsors a large book distribution program called Books in Asia. The program provides about 1 million books a year to Asian libraries; most are donated by U.S. publishers.

Professional Staff: There are 42 people stationed in the U.S. and 32 overseas, in Bangladesh, Indonesia, Fiji, Japan, Korea, Malaysia, Nepal, Pakistan, the Philippines, Sri Lanka, Thailand and Taiwan. During the past year, 11 people were hired. Both U.S. citizens and foreign nationals are employed.

Qualifications: An MA or PhD in Asian studies, international relations, political science, economics or law is required. Knowledge of Chinese or South or East Asian languages and overseas experience are preferred. At least two years previous experience in U.S. governmental agencies, nongovernmental organizations, educational institutions or international organizations are required. Employees are required to travel and possibly live abroad.

Internships: The foundation offers paid internships to undergraduate or graduate students, usually in the summer. Depending on the projects available, interns assist in research and writing, preparing grant documents and proposals, and arranging details of international exchanges.

Application Procedure: Those interested in either internships or employment should contact:

> Director of Personnel
> Asia Foundation
> 465 California Street
> 14th Floor
> San Francisco, CA 94119
> (415) 982-4640

THE ASIA SOCIETY
New York, NY

The Asia Society was established in 1956 by John D. Rockefeller 3rd to promote cross-cultural understanding between Asia and the U.S. By sponsoring a variety of events on political, economic, social and cultural issues, the Asia Society hopes to improve Americans' understanding of the Asia-Pacific region. The public affairs department offers courses and lectures, issues publications, holds conferences and conducts public education programs on contemporary developments in Asia. The education and communications department develops learning materials. In addition, the society holds art exhibits in its galleries and introduces U.S. audiences to both traditional and contemporary Asian arts through its performing arts program.

The Asia Society has regional offices in Washington, DC, Houston and Los Angeles. and a newly opened office in Hong Kong.

Professional Staff: The Asia Society has a professional staff of 52, 2 of whom work in Hong Kong. This overseas office plus the regional offices organize events and assist in program development. Six people were hired for the New York office in the past year.

Qualifications: The Asia Society usually requires a graduate degree for employment, preferably in Asian studies or international relations. Knowledge of Chinese and Japanese is preferred. For some jobs, two or more years work experience is required, preferably with an international or nonprofit organization. Willingness to live or travel abroad is not required.

Internships: Unpaid internships can be arranged on an ad hoc basis for the summer, semester or year. Interns may be undergraduates or graduate students; all should have an interest in Asian studies. Interns perform some administrative duties and work on ongoing projects.

Application Procedure: Applications for internships or full-time paid positions should be addressed to:

> Director of Personnel and Administration
> The Asia Society
> 725 Park Avenue
> New York, NY 10021
> (212) 288-6400

THE BROOKINGS INSTITUTION
Washington, DC

The principal purpose of the Brookings Institution, founded in 1927, is to conduct research, publish and educate the public on public policy issues. Scholars in Brookings' three research programs—economic, governmental and foreign policy studies—conduct approximately 75 projects annually. The Foreign Policy Studies group addresses issues in areas of national security and defense analysis, international economics, and trade and regional studies on the former Soviet Union, East Asia and the Middle East.

Brookings analyzes and assesses policies and attempts to convey its findings to policymakers, scholars and the public. It also encompasses the Center for Public Policy Education, a program providing conferences and lectures for 3,000 corporate and government executives each year. Brookings publishes books, papers and the *Brookings Review*, a quarterly public policy journal. Research-assistant positions for college graduates and graduate students are offered in the economic studies program and the foreign-policy studies program. Brookings also awards resident fellowships for predoctoral study in economics, government and foreign policy. Candidates must be nominated by their university graduate department. No individual applications are accepted. Last year, 10 fellowships were awarded.

Professional Staff: Total staff numbers about 250. The foreign policy studies staff has about 20 professionals. There are normally five or six people in entry-level research staff positions. The rest are research associates or senior fellows. The economics division employs eight to ten research assistants, each for a year. Brookings hired 15 people in the last year, 3 for the foreign affairs division. No one is stationed abroad.

Qualifications: For the foreign-policy studies staff, research assistants should have an MA or MIA and foreign language skills. Russian, Arabic and Chinese are the most desirable, followed by Japanese. For people interested in working as research assistants in defense studies, background in this field is required. In the economics division, research assistants need only a BA in economics or math. Most research associates and senior fellows hold PhDs, have had previous research or teaching experience and have published works in their field.

Internships: Brookings does not have a formal internship program, although the governmental studies division hosts unpaid college interns on a semester basis. Prospective interns should have an academic background and an interest in public policy or domestic issues.

Application Procedure: Inquiries relating to professional positions should be directed to the Personnel Coordinator. Persons interested in internships should contact the Administrative Assistant—Government Studies. The address is:

> The Brookings Institution
> 1775 Massachusetts Avenue, NW
> Washington, DC 20036-2188
> (202) 797-6000

CENTER FOR DEFENSE INFORMATION
Washington, DC

CDI is a nonprofit, nonpartisan research organization, founded and directed by retired officers of the U.S. military. The center is dedicated to providing up-to-the-minute, accurate information on and appraisals of the U.S. military. It strives to provide information free of the special interests of any government or military, political or business organization. CDI regularly publishes the *Defense Monitor* and produces a weekly television program, American Defense Monitor. CDI also conducts military-related international conferences.

Professional Staff: CDI has a staff of 25 in its Washington, DC, office, 2 of whom were hired in the last year.

Qualifications: A BA, MA or PhD in international relations, national security studies or foreign area studies, with expertise in military issues and arms control, is preferred. A willingness to travel and live abroad and foreign language ability are not necessary. Demonstrated writing ability and a background in security issues is desirable. Military experience is also useful.

Internships: Semester and summer paid internships are offered to college and graduate students. Interns should have some background in international relations or national security studies. Interns assist in preparation of the *Defense Monitor* and other written materials and in the *American Defense Monitor* TV program. Interns also assist in the day-to-day administrative work. Interns often join the regular research staff.

Application Procedure: To apply for internships and professional positions contact:

> Director
> Center for Defense Information
> 1500 Massachusetts Avenue, NW
> Washington, DC 20005
> (202) 862-0700

THE CHICAGO COUNCIL ON FOREIGN RELATIONS
Chicago, IL

The council promotes public education, conducts research and issues publications on foreign policy topics. Its conference series provides a private forum for leaders to discuss important issues of foreign policy. The Corporate Service Program examines various economic issues of interest to the business community. In the field of general education, the council sponsors varied activities, including numerous public lectures and seminars for high-school teachers. The council issues reports every four years on American public opinion and foreign policy and publishes occasional papers and books.

Professional Staff: The Council has a staff of 20, all of whom are based in the U.S. In the past year, the staff size has remained the same.

Qualifications: Applicants with an MIA or MA in international relations are generally sought for program officer positions. Knowledge of foreign languages and work experience are preferred but not essential.

Internships: Internships are occasionally available to students. Interns perform clerical work and do some research.

Application Procedure: Applications for internships and other positions should be addressed to:

> Vice President and Program Director
> The Chicago Council on Foreign Relations
> 116 South Michigan Avenue
> Chicago, IL 60603
> (312) 726-3860

CHINA INSTITUTE IN AMERICA
New York, NY

The China Institute in America works to advance Americans' understanding of China and serves as a meeting place for the Chinese community in the U.S. The institute organizes conferences, symposia and workshops, and a lecture series, sponsors an exchange program for physicians, distributes films, publishes studies and holds art exhibitions. The institute also provides advice and support services for Chinese scholars and students in the New York area. It offers courses on a wide variety of China-related topics.

Professional Staff: The institute has a professional staff of 15. In the past year three people were hired.

Qualifications: A degree, usually advanced, in Chinese studies, Asian studies or international relations is required. Expertise in Chinese culture, contemporary China, administration, fund-raising or public relations is desired. Knowledge of a Chinese dialect is preferred. Previous work experience is not required. Travel or study in China is preferred. Computer literacy is a plus.

Internships: Unpaid internships are available during the summer, a semester or an academic year to college students with an interest in

China. Small stipends are provided. Interns help to implement institute programs. They may work in the gallery, school or with the student/scholar services. Clerical work should be expected.

Application Procedure: Letters of inquiry, along with resume, should be sent to:

> Office of the President
> China Institute in America
> 125 East 65th Street
> New York, NY 10021-7088
> (212) 744-8181

CITIZENS DEMOCRACY CORPS (CDC)
Washington, DC

CDC is a private, nonprofit organization established at President George Bush's request in 1990 to encourage the flow of private American assistance to the countries of Central and Eastern Europe and the former Soviet Union. Activities include assisting American companies to design and undertake *pro bono* programs in the region; maintaining a volunteer registry, a database of U.S. citizens who wish to serve as skilled volunteers in the region (CDC then refers volunteers to organizations in the U.S. and overseas). The CDC databank contains profiles of U.S. nonprofits with active or planned programs in Central and Eastern Europe and the Soviet Republics.

CDC published the *Compendium of U.S. Nonprofit Organizations Providing Voluntary Assistance to Central and Eastern Europe and the Soviet Union* as well as individual directories with the same information for other East European countries.

Professional Staff: CDC has 14 professionals in its Washington, DC, office and 10–15 overseas in Hungary, Czechoslovakia, Poland, Bulgaria and Romania, three of whom are U.S. citizens. The rest are local nationals. During the past year, six people were hired, three for overseas positions.

Qualifications: CDC looks for applicants with at least a college degree. Russian and other languages indigenous to Eastern Europe and the former U.S.S.R., including Czech, Slovak, Hungarian and Polish, are preferred. Previous work experience is usually required.

Internships: Semester and summer internships for college and graduate students are offered. Interns undertake special research projects about the activities of various organizations in Central and Eastern Europe and the former Soviet Union. Applicants should have an interest in Central and East European and former Soviet Union activities, and promotion of relations between the U.S. and the republics of the former Soviet Union.

Application Procedure: For information on, or to apply for, professional positions, internships or the volunteer registry, contact:

> Administrative Officer
> Citizens Democracy Corps
> 2021 K Street, NW
> Suite 215
> Washington, DC 20006
> (202) 872-0933

THE COUNCIL ON FOREIGN RELATIONS
New York, NY

The Council on Foreign Relations, established in 1921, is one of the foremost think tanks dedicated to improving the understanding of American foreign policy and international affairs through the free exchange of ideas. The council conducts meetings for members at its headquarters in New York City, in Washington, DC, and in other cities in the U.S. and occasionally abroad. The council's Studies Program examines major foreign policy questions through individual research projects, group discussions and conferences in which both council members and nonmember experts participate. The council also publishes books and papers, frequently the result of its deliberations. Since 1922, it has published *Foreign Affairs,* the leading journal in the field.

Professional Staff: The council has a professional staff of 40. Most of the positions are staff assistants or program assistants. In the last year, 15 professionals were hired.

Qualifications: For staff assistant positions, a college degree or related experience is required. For program assistant positions, usually a master's degree or several years of work experience is required. Senior staff, such as senior research fellows, directors, etc., usually have graduate degrees or PhDs in international relations, political science, history, economics, and English or journalism. A willingness to live or travel abroad and foreign language ability are not necessary.

Internships: College and graduate students can apply for summer and semester unpaid internships. Undergraduates do a combination of administrative office work, project work and research. Graduate students who intern at *Foreign Affairs* edit. Students selected are those studying international relations or related topics who are willing and able to help out with office administrative tasks and research.

Application Procedure: For professional positions write to the Director of Personnel; for internships write to the Assistant Director of Personnel at:

> Council on Foreign Relations
> 58 East 68th Street
> New York, NY 10021
> (212) 734-0400

EAST-WEST CENTER (EWC)
Honolulu, HI

The East-West Center is a major research institution founded by the U.S. Congress in 1960 to promote better relations and understanding between the U.S. and the nations of Asia and the Pacific through cooperative study, training and research. Organized around eight problem-oriented programs—culture learning; business; resource systems; population; environment and policy; communications; energy; and education—the center brings together academic, governmental, business, civic and media leaders to explore issues and to identify possible solutions. EWC annually gives 250–300 awards in the form of stipends to advanced students, scholars and professionals to finance research programs. In 1990, the center was selected to host the Pacific summit between President George Bush and the leaders of 11 Pacific island nations.

Professional Staff: EWC has a staff of 80 researchers and 300 support personnel, all of whom are based at the Honolulu headquarters. In the past year no researchers were hired; there is always a high turnover in support staff.

Qualifications: An MA or PhD, preferably in the social sciences, is essential for researchers. A BA is useful for those applying for support positions. Knowledge of Asian languages is preferred; work experience within the Asia/Pacific field is required. A willingness to travel is necessary, but living abroad is not.

Internships: Internships are available to graduate students. Interns participate in data processing and research assistance. Positions are paid and can last several months to a year.

Application Procedure: Applicants for internships, professional and support positions should contact the

> Personnel Officer
> East-West Center
> 1777 East-West Road
> Honolulu, HI 96848
> (808) 944-7111

FOREIGN POLICY ASSOCIATION (FPA)
New York, NY

FPA, currently celebrating its 75th anniversary, is a national, nonpartisan organization dedicated to the education of American citizens on foreign policy. Through its publications—the annual *Great Decisions* study and discussion guide, the quarterly *Headline Series* and special reports on timely topics—meetings, lectures and special events, FPA seeks to stimulate wider interest, more-effective participation in and greater understanding of world affairs among American citizens. FPA's major events are open to the public. *Great Decisions,* FPA's largest educational program, involves citizens in study and discussion of foreign policy issues in communities across the nation. More than 250,000 individuals take part in the *Great Decisions* program each year and thousands more increase their understanding of the issues from radio, television and newspaper articles, audio- and videocassettes on the eight annual *Great Decisions* topics.

Professional Staff: The professional staff numbers 21, 9 of whom were hired in the past year.

Qualifications: Professional staff openings, including some entry-level positions, require an undergraduate or graduate degree in political science, history, government, international relations, education or business administration. Knowledge of foreign languages and experience abroad are not necessary.

Internships: Undergraduate and graduate students may apply for unpaid internships offered during the summer and academic year. Interns may be placed in the editorial, events, education and/or community programs departments, depending on need.

Application Procedure: Inquiries relating to professional positions or internships should be directed to:

>Director of Business Administration
>Foreign Policy Association
>729 Seventh Avenue
>New York, NY 10019
>(212) 764-4050

FREEDOM HOUSE
New York, NY

Freedom House was established in 1941 to galvanize U.S. public support for the struggle against fascism. For over 50 years Freedom House has been committed to monitoring political rights and civil liberties worldwide. Programs include on-site election monitoring, supporting democratic institutions, making policy recommendations and giving congressional testimony. Freedom House also sponsors conferences and seminars for nongovernmental institutions worldwide, issues special briefings on current events and organizes roundtable discussions featuring international newsmakers.

Professional Staff: Freedom House has a professional staff of 25 in the U.S. No employees are stationed abroad. During the past year, 2 people were hired.

Qualifications: Applicants with a college degree and a graduate degree in international affairs, history, languages, communications and law or with excellent computer skills are most sought after. Minimal work experience is required for employment. Proficiency in Chinese, Russian or Spanish is preferred.

Internships: See Chapter Ten for details.

Application Procedure: Write to the Executive Director:

>Freedom House, Inc.
>120 Wall Street, Floor 26
>New York, NY 10005
>(212) 514-8040

THE HERITAGE FOUNDATION
Washington, DC

The Heritage Foundation is a research organization with a public policy agenda based on the principles of a free-market economy, limited government and strong national defense. The organization functions as the nerve center of conservative policymaking in Washington through a variety of publications and activities directed at Washington legislators and policymakers and the national news media. Researchers working in the domestic and foreign policy divisions, the United Nations Assessment Project, the Congressional Assessment Project and the Asian Studies Center prepare papers on current policy issues. The foundation puts out a variety of publications, including the quarterly *Policy Review,* the *Critical Issues* monograph series and more than 200 *Backgrounder* policy papers and lectures each year. It also sponsors lectures, debates and seminars. The Heritage Resource Bank is comprised of 1,600 scholars and 400 research organizations that assist the organization in reaching out to Washington policymakers.

Professional Staff: The Heritage Foundation employs about 150 individuals. There are approximately 40 people in domestic and international research positions. Approximately 25 are policy analysts, 8 are research assistants and the rest are senior scholars and management staff. In addition, Heritage has resident- and visiting-scholar programs.

Qualifications: Most senior scholars have advanced degrees and significant academic and government experience. Policy analysts generally have MA or PhD degrees. Analysts do not normally need prior work experience to be considered for employment. Research assistants are entry-level personnel who often have only a BA. Some are hired directly out of college. Knowledge of foreign languages is desirable but not always necessary.

Internships: Undergraduate and graduate students may participate in semester or summer internships in one of the research departments. Work involves assisting policy analysts by doing basic fact-gathering, library research and clerical duties. Prospective interns should demonstrate a commitment to the conservative philosophy of the Heritage Foundation as well as an interest in world affairs. Summer positions are paid, semester positions are not.

Application Procedure: Individuals qualified for professional positions should contact the Director of Personnel and/or Vice President for Foreign Policy and Defense Studies. Those interested in scholar status or internships should contact the Director of Academic Programs; internship applicants should send a resume and cover letter. The address is:

> The Heritage Foundation
> 214 Massachusetts Avenue, NE
> Washington, DC 20002
> (202) 546-4400

HUDSON INSTITUTE
Indianapolis, IN

The Hudson Institute is a policy research organization. Under the leadership of the late Herman Kahn, its founder, Hudson pioneered the use of "scenarios" to help policymakers analyze issues and reach long-range decisions. Currently, Hudson Institute research is focused on the areas of defense strategy, foreign policy, technology, competitiveness, education and training, and political and social institutions. The institute conducts both contract research and noncontract studies.

Professional Staff: Hudson employs a professional staff of 33 in the U.S. Two staff members run affiliated offices in Canada and Belgium. During the past year, three people were hired.

Qualifications: Professional staff members have advanced degrees in a variety of social science disciplines, including economics, political science, international relations and law, and expertise in Russian studies, national security affairs, arms control, trade policy, and other areas depending on the institute's current needs. For work with international issues, a knowledge of foreign languages is preferred, with Spanish, French, German, Japanese and Russian being the most useful. A willingness to travel is required for employment. Previous work experience is not necessary for entry-level positions. Senior staff must have policy-related experience in government or other research organizations.

Internships: Semester and summer internships are offered to undergraduates. For the most part, interns perform administrative work, with the exception of occasional research internships on specific projects. Internships are nonremunerative.

Application Procedure: Internship applications should be directed to the Intern Coordinator; for professional positions direct applications to the Director of Personnel at:

Hudson Institute
5395 Emerson Way
PO Box 26-919
Indianapolis, IN 46226
(317) 545-1000

HUMAN RIGHTS WATCH
New York, NY

Human Rights Watch conducts systematic investigations of human-rights abuses in over 60 countries around the world. It addresses the human-rights practices of governments and defends freedom of thought and expression, due process of law and equal protection of the law. It also documents and protests murders, disappearances, torture, arbitrary imprisonment, exile, censorship and other abuses of internationally recognized human rights. In internal wars, it documents violations by both governments and rebel groups.

Human Rights Watch has a staff of over 30 country specialists who are sent on more than 100 investigative missions annually. Staff members who are stationed overseas, or sent overseas on assignment, meet with government officials, opposition leaders, journalists, scholars, lawyers, relief groups, doctors and others with information on human-rights practices. Frequently they interview victims, members of their families and witnesses to abuses. They also attend court proceedings and examine court records.

Professional Staff: Human Rights Watch has a professional staff of 40 in the U.S. and 4 overseas, stationed in El Salvador, Hong Kong, and the U.K. In the last 12 months one person was hired.

Qualifications: Human Rights Watch usually hires individuals with a JD, MA, MS or PhD. While preferred fields of study vary according to the position, country specialists and persons with expertise in international law are frequently hired. Previous work experience is necessary, although the kind required varies depending on the positions available. A willingness to travel or to live abroad is not a requirement for employment. Knowledge of a foreign language is preferred.

Internships: See Chapter Ten for details.

Application Procedure: Persons seeking professional employment should apply to:

Office Manager
Human Rights Watch
485 Fifth Avenue
New York, NY 10017
(212) 972-8400

INSTITUTE FOR EAST-WEST STUDIES

The Institute for East-West Studies, founded in 1981, prides itself on being at the forefront of policymaking issues involving Eastern Europe. The institute specializes in economic and security issues of current concern, reviewing and researching the issues. The institute holds conferences and speakers' forums.

Professional Staff: The professional staff numbers 54. There are 35 people stationed in the U.S. and 19 overseas in the former Czechoslovakia, Poland and Hungary. All the offices engage in research, conference planning, editing and writing. In Budapest, Hungary, specific issues such as banking and finance are examined. Six people were hired in the past year, two for overseas positions.

Qualifications: A graduate degree in economics, national security studies or international relations is preferred. Knowledge of German or Russian is preferred, although Polish, Hungarian and Czech are also helpful. Experience requirements depend on the position to be filled. In most cases research and administrative experience is preferred.

Internships: Paid internships are offered during the summer and academic year to graduate students in international affairs programs specializing in Eastern Europe. Interns assist with various research projects, conferences and public affairs events, and editing and fact-checking.

Application Procedure: For professional and internship positions, the address is:

Personnel Director
Institute for East-West Studies
360 Lexington Avenue
New York, NY 10017
(212) 557-2570

INSTITUTE FOR FOOD AND DEVELOPMENT POLICY / FOOD FIRST
San Francisco, CA

Food First is a research and "education-for-action" organization using hunger as a measure of how societies are meeting the needs of their people. The institute's goal is to reveal the manifold ways that the links between economic development, democratic participation, economic justice and ecological equilibrium can be strengthened.

Professional Staff: There are seven people on the staff, one of whom is stationed abroad. In the past year one person was hired.

Qualifications: The institute looks for applicants with a BA, MA, MS or PhD in economics, sociology, anthropology, political science or international studies, and expertise in development and international economics. Experience in a developing country is also useful but not required. Knowledge of Spanish and Portuguese is preferred as is a willingness to travel. The institute recruits from international departments on college campuses.

Internships: Nonsalaried internships of varying lengths are offered to college and graduate students. Interns work on educational outreach and research and media projects. Interns should display commitment to the specific project, self-motivation and initiative.

Application Procedure: For permanent positions, write to the Executive Director. For internships, contact the Intern Coordinator.

> Institute for Food and Development Policy/Food First
> 145 Ninth Street
> San Francisco, CA 94103
> (415) 864-8555

INSTITUTE FOR INTERNATIONAL ECONOMICS
Washington, DC

Devoted to the study and discussion of international economic policy, the institute seeks practical new approaches to problems confronting the international economic community. It sponsors speakers and conferences and publishes its studies.

Professional Staff: The institute employs about 35 professionals in the U.S., none overseas. Professional research positions include senior fellows, research associates, visiting fellows and research assistants. During the past year, staff size has remained the same.

Qualifications: Research assistants typically have a BA or MA in economics, international relations or public policy and have little or no professional experience. Because they assist institute fellows in all aspects of their work, they must be familiar with the relevant issues. Desirable skills include report writing, computer programming and statistical analysis. Knowledge of Spanish, Japanese, German or French is preferred. The institute also encourages individuals who lack conventional background but have special academic or work experience to apply. There is little turnover in senior-level positions that call for advanced degrees or significant work experience.

Application Procedure: Write to:

> Deputy Director
> Institute for International Economics
> 6th Floor
> 11 Dupont Circle, NW
> Washington, DC 20036
> (202) 328-0583

INSTITUTE FOR POLICY STUDIES (IPS)
Washington, DC

IPS is a center for research and education with concerns focusing on military intervention, foreign policy, international economics, human rights, international development and domestic and women's issues. IPS conducts studies, holds conferences, publishes books, papers and a journal and sponsors the Washington School, which offers noncredit courses on public policy and political thought. IPS's sister organization, the Transnational Institute, based in Amsterdam, the Netherlands, employs European scholars and activists. IPS also offers a doctoral program in conjunction with Temple University's Union Graduate School in Washington, DC.

Professional Staff: IPS employs 35 people in its Washington, DC, headquarters. Half of these are research or administrative assistants; the rest are senior staff. In addition, 10 associate fellows are stationed in

Amsterdam. Two people were hired for Washington-based positions in the past year.

Qualifications: Positions as research and administrative assistants are entry-level. They typically require a BA. About half the assistants have MAs or MIAs. Specializations sought vary with projects. Foreign languages are not necessary for most positions, although in some cases a working knowledge of Spanish is necessary.

Internships: Internships throughout the year are open to college students who have an interest in U.S. domestic or foreign policy. Responsibilities include research, writing and administrative assistance.

Application Procedure: Applicants interested in staff positions should contact the Deputy Director. Inquiries pertaining to internships should be directed to the Intern Coordinator. The address is:

> Institute for Policy Studies
> 1601 Connecticut Avenue, NW
> Washington, DC 20009
> (202) 234-9382

INSTITUTE ON AFRICAN AFFAIRS
Washington, DC

The Institute on African Affairs is a nonpartisan organization dedicated to research, policy analysis and education on issues that affect the African continent. The institute publishes the *Analysis of African Affairs* (AAA) six times a year and the quarterly *Journal of African Policy Studies.*

Professional Staff: The institute has a staff of four based in the U.S. During the past year, staff size remained the same.

Qualifications: An undergraduate degree, MA, MIA or PhD in any relevant social science field is preferred. Previous work experience of two years in research and analysis on African affairs is required. Overseas experience in Africa is also helpful. Knowledge of French, Arabic or Portuguese is required. Willingness to travel or live abroad is required.

Internships: Unpaid internships can be arranged on an ad hoc basis for the summer, semester or year. Interns may be undergraduate or graduate students; all should have an interest in African studies. Interns work as research assistants.

Application Procedure: Applications for internships or full-time paid positions should be addressed to:

> Managing Director
> Institute on African Affairs
> 733 15th Street, NW, Suite 700
> Washington, DC 20005
> (202) 393-0150

INTERNATIONAL CENTER FOR DEVELOPMENT POLICY
Washington, DC

The International Center for Development Policy is a nonpartisan foreign policy think tank that examines major foreign policy issues facing the U.S. The center hosts conferences that bring together international fellows and high-level officials of the U.S. government. Conferences have explored policy options for regional disputes, human rights and environmental concerns. The center runs the U.S.-Vietnam trade council, a fact-finding project that monitors the economic and political situation in Vietnam. It also publishes the *New Forest News*, a quarterly publication that covers agricultural issues important to developing countries.

Professional Staff: The center has a professional staff of 15 at the Washington, DC, headquarters. Three people were hired in the past year.

Qualifications: For entry-level positions, a college degree and internship experience is necessary. For professional positions, a graduate degree in international affairs is preferred. Knowledge of Russian, Spanish or Chinese is helpful. A willingness to travel is not required.

Internships: Unpaid internships are available for undergraduate or graduate students on a semester or summer basis. Interns assist support staff and work on various research projects.

Application Procedure: For internship opportunities, contact the Internship Coordinator. For professional employment, write to Personnel:

> International Center for Development Policy
> 731 8th Street, SE
> Washington, DC 20003
> (202) 547-3800

INTERNATIONAL FOUNDATION
FOR ELECTORAL SYSTEMS (IFES)
Washington, DC

Founded in 1987, IFES is a foundation dedicated to analyzing, supporting and strengthening the election process in emerging democracies. IFES calls on international experts familiar with a wide variety of electoral systems to provide tailored assistance to countries seeking to establish an electoral system or to improve an existing process. The IFES Resource Center serves as a clearinghouse for information about all aspects of electoral systems and commodities essential to administering democratic elections. The IFES also offers training and other assistance to countries seeking information on citizen participation in the voting process and other aspects of the democratic process.

Professional Staff: The foundation has a professional staff of 16. There are no permanent overseas staff; temporary assignments include technical assistance, project and financial management and reporting. In the past year, three persons have been hired.

Qualifications: An MA, MIA or PhD in international relations or political science is preferred. One to two years previous experience and expertise in the election process, international development or international relations is required. Knowledge of French, Russian, Spanish or Portuguese is preferred. Willingness to travel or live abroad is not required.

Internships: Undergraduate or graduate students may apply year-round for paid or unpaid positions. Interns scan news sources for election-related news, assemble briefing books and reports, respond to information requests and process large mailings. Interns should have an interest in elections and international relations and possess foreign language and computer skills.

Application Procedure: Inquiries relating to professional positions or internships should be directed to the Director of Programs. The address is:

> International Foundation for Electoral Systems
> 1620 I Street, NW
> Suite 611
> Washington, DC 20006

JAPAN INFORMATION CENTER
New York, NY

The Japan Information Center is the information and cultural affairs department of the Consulate General of Japan. In addition to responding to inquiries concerning Japanese society, culture, politics and the economy, the Japanese Information Center provides U.S. media personnel with information on Japanese government policy and Japan-U.S. relations. The Japanese Information Center also organizes Japan-U.S. cultural events and recruits candidates for the Japan Exchange Teaching Program.

Professional Staff: The Japanese Information Center is a gradually growing organization that has a professional staff of 13 employees, 4 of whom are U.S. citizens. In the last 12 months one professional was hired for the international department.

Qualifications: The Japanese Information Center usually requires an MA in fields such as international politics, economics and journalism. Previous work experience is not required for employment. Knowledge of Japanese is preferred.

Application Procedure: The Japanese Information Center recruits from the international affairs departments of colleges and graduate schools. Individuals interested in employment should send a resume and cover letter to:

Deputy Director
Japan Information Center
299 Park Avenue, 18th Floor
New York, NY 10171
(212) 371-8222

THE NATIONAL COUNCIL ON U.S.-ARAB RELATIONS
Washington, DC

The council provides information to the public on issues of importance to U.S.-Arab relations. The goal is to stimulate a greater national awareness of U.S. interests in the region, thereby promoting and improving U.S.-Arab relations. The council administers nine programs, which include study visits for professors, high school students and congressional leaders; awarding small grants; sponsoring Model Arab Leagues; journalism internships; and a series of public affairs activities. The council is also involved in U.S.-Gulf Cooperation Council relations.

Professional Staff: There are 11 professionals on the council's staff. Three people were hired in the past year.

Qualifications: An MA or PhD in international relations, Middle East studies or political science is necessary for employment with the professional staff. Previous experience of one to two years in coordinating and administering international programs, working with foreign nationals and university faculty is also required. For entry-level positions, previous work experience is not required. Knowledge of Arabic or French is preferred. A willingness to travel is useful; living abroad is not required.

Internships: Internships for undergraduate and graduate students are available, assisting, coordinating and administering programs. Interns also write brief newsletter items on programs, update program manuals and do research and gather information on current events/issues. Positions are paid and are given on a semester, summer or yearly basis. To qualify for internships, participation in one of the council's international programs or recommendation by a previous participant in the council's international programs is required.

Application Procedure: Applications for internships should be addressed to the Internship Coordinator. For other positions, contact the Executive Director:

> The National Council on U.S.-Arab Relations
> 1735 Eye Street, NW
> Suite 515
> Washington, DC 20006
> (202) 293-0801

OVERSEAS DEVELOPMENT COUNCIL (ODC)
Washington, DC

ODC seeks to increase Americans' understanding of the economic and social problems of developing countries and to promote consideration of development issues. To meet these goals ODC does research, promotes public education and produces publications on issues such as energy, trade, agricultural development, foreign aid and international debt. It also organizes discussions and seminars for government officials and development specialists and gives press briefings.

Professional Staff: ODC has a professional staff of 26 in the U.S., none overseas. Three people are junior research staff. In the past year, five people were hired.

Qualifications: A graduate degree in economics (with emphasis on development, international finance or trade) or international relations is sought. Junior-level researchers usually have an MA in specific development— related fields, have often worked as ODC interns and do not have significant work experience. Senior researchers have either an MA or PhD and have had a good deal of research experience in less-developed countries.

Internships: Unpaid internships are available to graduate students or undergraduates with an interest in development issues and a strong academic background. Positions can be arranged throughout the year.

Application Procedure: For internships, write to the Intern Coordinator. For professional staff positions, write to the Business Manager:

> Overseas Development Council
> 1875 Connecticut Avenue, NW
> Suite 1012
> Washington, DC 20009
> (202) 234-8701

REFUGEE POLICY GROUP (RPG)
Washington, DC

RPG works to improve international and domestic refugee programs and designs new policies to counter the refugee crises occurring throughout the world. RPG serves as an institute for policy research and analysis and as a center for the exchange of ideas and information. RPG involves government officials, specialists and academics, advocates and activists, educators, the news media and the general public in an effort to voice refugee concerns. RPG issues reports and publishes a newsletter, *RPG Review.*

Professional Staff: RPG has a professional staff of 13 in the U.S. and 1 in Switzerland who works with an affiliate organization of the same name. In the past year, two support-staff members were hired.

Qualifications: An MA or PhD in international affairs, with experience in human rights, refugees, immigration, health, business or law, is useful.

Knowledge of French or Spanish is preferred. A willingness to travel is required for employment.

Internships: Undergraduate and graduate students may apply for internships available on a semester or summer basis. Work involves research and other administrative duties. Positions are not paid.

Application Procedure: Internship applications should be directed to the Director of Research Policy and Programs. Inquiries relating to professional positions should be directed to:

> Refugee Policy Group
> 1424 16th Street, NW
> Suite 401
> Washington, DC 20036
> (202) 387-3015

UNITED NATIONS ASSOCIATION OF THE UNITED STATES OF AMERICA (UNA-USA)
New York, NY

UNA-USA is a national organization that conducts programs to heighten U.S. public awareness and knowledge of global issues and their relationship to the UN. It seeks to encourage multilateral approaches in dealing with these issues, build public support for constructive U.S. policies on matters of global concern and enhance the effectiveness of the UN and other international institutions. It coordinates a national UN Day program, analyzes current international economic problems through its Economic Policy Council, and works with business executives through its Chairman's Council and Council of Fellows. It conducts parallel programs with the former Soviet Union, Japan and China and prepares background materials for the Model UN project. Publications include fact sheets on the UN, the annual *A Global Agenda: Issues Before the General Assembly, Washington Weekly Report* and *The Inter Dependent* newspaper, published six times a year.

Professional Staff: The professional staff numbers 15. Two people were hired in the past year. There are about five entry-level positions, which entail research and administrative work.

Qualifications: Besides a working knowledge of the UN, a college degree, preferably in international relations, is required for entry-level positions. A minimum of one year previous work experience in an international organization or other relevant institution is also necessary. Knowledge of foreign languages is not required. For directorial positions, an MA and substantial work experience are required.

Internships: Unpaid internships involving research on international issues can be arranged throughout the year for undergraduates in their senior year and graduate students. Interns should have good research skills and good writing ability.

Application Procedure: Resumes for internships and professional positions should be sent to:

> National Program Director
> United Nations Association of
>   the United States of America
> 485 Fifth Avenue
> New York, NY 10017
> (212) 697-3232

U.S. COMMITTEE FOR REFUGEES
Washington, DC

The goal of the U.S. Committee for Refugees is to assist refugees and displaced people. It is also concerned with ensuring that refugees are not forcibly returned to a place where their safety is threatened. By going to refugee crisis spots, testifying before Congress and publishing reports that appear in the national press, the committee hopes to bring refugee needs to the attention of policymakers and the public, in the hope that increased awareness will bring about increased assistance in dealing with refugee problems. The committee has worked in many areas around the world, most recently examining the refugee problems in Mozambique, Yugoslavia and Sri Lanka.

Professional Staff: Ten professionals, two hired within the past year, are based in U.S.C.R.'s Washington, DC, headquarters.

Qualifications: An undergraduate degree in history, sociology or international affairs is useful. Previous work experience is not required, however a background in journalism, international law, social work or teaching is preferred. Knowledge of French or Spanish is helpful. A willingness to travel is required.

Internships: Undergraduate students may apply for intern positions available on a semester or summer basis. Interns need to have an interest in and knowledge of international affairs and good communication skills.

Application Procedure: Address employment and internship applications to:

> U.S. Committee for Refugees
> 1025 Vermont Avenue, NW
> Suite 920
> Washington, DC 20005
> (202) 347-3507

U.S. COMMITTEE FOR UNICEF
New York, NY

The committee conducts fund-raisers for and promotes public awareness of worldwide hunger, underdevelopment and United Nations Children's Fund (Unicef) programs. It produces a variety of publications and educational materials concerning current Unicef projects and campaigns. The U.S. and other national committees throughout the world constitute one of the funding sources for Unicef; the other sources are direct government contributions and greeting-card sales.

Professional Staff: The headquarters in New York employs approximately 95 professionals. Most staff perform fund-raising, public affairs and administrative jobs. There are no full-time researchers.

Qualifications: All staff should have a basic understanding of the UN and its functions. Although a college degree is not always required, experience in an international organization, management, marketing, data processing or business administration is desirable. The committee does not require overseas experience, knowledge of foreign languages or willingness to travel.

Internships: Unpaid internships are open to high-school, college and graduate students. Interns are involved in marketing and research projects and assist in working with volunteer, community and campus groups.

Application Procedure: Individuals interested in professional positions should contact the Human Resources Department. Students interested in internships should write to the Internship Coordinator. The address is:

U.S. Committee for UNICEF
333 East 38th Street
New York, NY 10016
(212) 922-2582

WORLD POLICY INSTITUTE
New York, NY

The World Policy Institute is a public policy research and educational organization affiliated with the New School for Social Research in New York. Established in 1961, the institute publishes the quarterly *World Policy Journal* and other studies on world affairs, and conducts an ongoing program of forward-looking policy research. It also offers seminars, briefings and lectures for the public policy, political activist and university communities.

Professional Staff: The institute has a staff of eight. In the last year one professional was hired.

Qualifications: An undergraduate or graduate degree in international studies or economics with expertise in Latin American, Russian, African, Asian, European or Middle Eastern affairs is preferred, as are foreign language skills. For most positions, some experience in writing, editing, administration or fund-raising is required.

Application Procedure: Write to:

Managing Editor
World Policy Institute
65 Fifth Avenue
New York, NY 10003
(212) 229-5808

DEVELOPMENT ASSISTANCE, ENVIRONMENT AND RELIEF ORGANIZATIONS

ACCION INTERNATIONAL/AITEC
Cambridge, MA

Accion International/Aitec (Accion International Tecnica) is dedicated to generating new employment and income opportunities through credit and "microbusiness" programs in poor urban and rural communities in Latin America and the Caribbean. Microbusinesses are labor-intensive, small-scale, family-owned and operated with a limited amount of capital. Accion personnel stationed in Bolivia, Brazil, Colombia, Costa Rica, Dominican Republic, Ecuador, Guatemala, Mexico and Paraguay serve as technical advisers in programs focusing on the development of appropriate enterprises specifically geared to developing-country resources, markets and needs. Accion also sponsors workshops and development education programs in communities throughout the Americas. It publishes books, reports and manuals on enterprise projects.

Professional Staff: U.S. staff includes 18 people; overseas posts employ 9. In the last 12 months, four professionals were hired.

Qualifications: A BA or MA in business, international development, Latin American studies, foreign languages, economics or public administration is a general requirement for Accion employees. The ability to speak Spanish or Portuguese is required as is four years of previous work on small business or credit programs in Latin America or the Caribbean.

Internships: Semester-long unpaid internships are available in U.S. offices for undergraduate and graduate students. Qualifications include some knowledge of international development and basic Spanish. Interns should also have an interest in Latin America and specialized skills in writing and fund-raising.

Application Procedure: Persons interested in professional or intern positions should write to:

Executive Assistant
ACCION International/AITEC
130 Prospect Street
Cambridge, MA 02139
(617) 492-4930

AFRICARE
Washington, DC

The goal of Africare is to improve the quality of life in rural Africa through the development of water resources, increased food production and the delivery of health services. In over 23 African nations Africare works with host-country officials in coordinating and administering new and ongoing projects that benefit the general population.

Professional Staff: Africare has a professional staff of over 100 people, approximately 50 of whom work overseas. Twenty people have been hired in the past year, twelve for overseas positions.

Qualifications: An undergraduate degree in international studies or agriculture; an MA or MBA in those fields or expertise in health, child survival, irrigation, crop production, dams and forestation are all useful. Knowledge of French or Portuguese is required. Two to five years experience in related African fieldwork is essential for employment. Employees must be willing to live abroad and travel.

Internships: Paid summer or semester internships are available for undergraduates. Interns are involved in programming and administration.

Application Procedure: For the internship program and professional employment, contact Management Services.

Africare
440 R Street, NW
Washington, DC 20001
(202) 462-3614

AMERICAN JEWISH JOINT
DISTRIBUTION COMMITTEE (JDC)
New York, NY

Established in 1914 to provide aid to Jews in Palestine, the JDC has since served as the overseas arm of the American Jewish community, sponsoring relief, rescue, reconstruction and Jewish education programs. In Ethiopia, this past year, JDC helped to sustain the remaining Jewish population as it flooded into Addis Ababa seeking to be reunited with family members in Israel. In Eastern Europe, JDC provides life-sustaining assistance to elderly and infirm Holocaust survivors. In Latin America and Western Europe, the emphasis is on increasing self-sufficiency. In Israel, JDC is helping the country absorb its newest immigrants while continuing to enrich the lives of the disadvantaged and improve the quality of services for the aged, the handicapped and the disabled. Through the JDC-International Development Program and the "Open Mailbox" campaigns, JDC also enables the American Jewish community to provide nonsectarian disaster and development assistance worldwide. Overseas staff are responsible for managing local programs and for providing guidance and consultation in areas of program development and community organization. Overseas activities are expanding due to increased activities in the former Soviet Union and Eastern Europe.

Professional Staff: JDC has a professional staff in the U.S. of 27, 6 of whom were recently hired. Nineteen employees are stationed in Israel, Latin America, North Africa, Western Europe and the former Soviet Union. In the past 12 months, four people were hired for overseas positions.

Qualifications: JDC looks for people with graduate degrees in social work, public administration or studies relating to social service, planning and program management. Persons active in the Jewish community and experienced in providing services are especially good candidates. At least two to five years previous work in administration, program planning, finance and accounting is helpful. Knowledge of Hebrew, Yiddish, French, German, Russian or Spanish is essential. A willingness to travel and work abroad is obligatory.

Internships: A limited number of six-month internships are offered to graduate students through the Jewish Service Corps. All positions are overseas and offer a stipend to cover living expenses. Candidates should have a strong Judaic background and be dynamic, good with youths, self-starters, able to work independently and have extensive travel experience.

Application Procedure: Persons interested in internships should write to the Jewish Service Corps. Those interested in professional positions should contact the Personnel Administrator at:

> The American Jewish Joint Distribution Committee, Inc.
> 711 Third Avenue
> 10th Floor
> New York, NY 10017
> (212) 687-6200

AMERICAN NEAR EAST REFUGEE AID (ANERA)
Washington, DC

Established in 1968 after the Arab-Israeli Six-Day War, Anera provides financial assistance for social and economic development projects for Palestinians and other Arabs in the Middle East. Economic support takes three forms: funding for community and economic development projects; in-kind, cash and technical assistance for various health programs; and support for education through the provision of scholarships. Anera also seeks to promote peace in the Middle East by increasing Americans' understanding of the region.

Professional Staff: Anera has a professional staff of 28, 20 of whom, mostly foreign nationals, are based in the West Bank and Gaza offices. In the past year, Anera has hired two professionals for the Washington, DC, headquarters and two for overseas offices.

Qualifications: An undergraduate, MA or PhD degree in economics, engineering or agronomy is most useful for employment. Knowledge of Arabic is preferred. Applicants should have two to five years experience in overseas field work. For some positions, a willingness to travel and live abroad is required.

Application Procedure: Address applications to:

> President
> American Near East Refugee Aid
> 1522 K Street, NW
> Suite 202
> Washington, DC 20005
> (202) 347-2558

APPROPRIATE TECHNOLOGY INTERNATIONAL (ATI)
Washington, DC

ATI is a nonprofit development assistance organization with projects in Africa, Asia, Latin America and the Caribbean. Created in 1976 in response to an initiative of the U.S. Congress, ATI receives its principal funding for operations from the U.S. Agency for International Development. ATI works with and on behalf of small farmers and entrepreneurs in developing countries to boost their productivity and incomes, foster new enterprises and expand existing ones, and generate broad-based economic growth. ATI implements field projects in tandem with local partners, providing technical assistance and leveraging financial resources for targeted development programs with strategic and widespread impact.

Professional Staff: ATI operations are managed by a staff of 40 based in Washington, DC. Most functions, including finance and administration, technology and enterprise development, evaluation and field operations are directed through this office. ATI also has field offices in Dakar, Senegal; Kathmandu, Nepal; La Paz, Bolivia; and Manila, the Philippines. Fourteen people were hired in the past year, seven for international work.

Qualifications: An undergraduate degree in engineering, economics or business; an MA, MBA or MS in similar fields or a concentration in small business and rural industries development are all useful. Knowledge of Spanish or French is required. Three to five years previous work experience abroad or in rural industrial development is essential for employment. Employees must be willing to travel.

Internships: A limited number of paid and unpaid summer or semester internships for college or graduate students is available. Interns are primarily involved in research.

Application Procedure: For internship information or professional employment, write to:

Director, Finance and Administration
Appropriate Technology International
1331 H Street, NW
Suite 1200
Washington, DC 20005
(202) 879-2900

CARE, INC. (COOPERATIVE FOR AMERICAN RELIEF EVERYWHERE)
New York, NY

Dedicated to improving the lives of the poor throughout the world, CARE sponsors projects aimed at aiding developing countries achieve social and economic well-being and self-sufficiency. CARE is one of the largest and most diverse organizations providing technical assistance, with an annual budget of over $400 million. Its projects include emergency relief for disaster victims and a host of programs to improve nutrition, health, employment and educational conditions. CARE also advocates public policies that support its ends. Operations are based in 38 countries throughout Africa, Central and South America, South Asia and Southeast Asia. The U.S. headquarters and field offices are responsible for fund-raising and public relations while overseas staff monitor and administer CARE's many programs.

Professional Staff: The staff of CARE is divided into three sectors: New York headquarters employs 125 people; U.S. field offices employ 70; and overseas missions employ 280. In the past 12 months, 200 people were hired.

Qualifications: An undergraduate degree with specialization in international development or an MA, MS or MPH are required for employment. A minimum of two years fieldwork in a developing country, as well as the ability to speak French or Spanish, are essential qualifications. Employees must be willing to travel or live abroad.

Application Procedure: Inquiries relating to domestic positions and internships should be addressed to Human Resources. Overseas jobs are handled through International Recruitment. Both departments are at the following address:

Human Resources
CARE, Inc.
66 First Avenue
New York, NY 10016
(212) 686-3110

CHURCH WORLD SERVICE
New York, NY

Church World Service is the relief, development and refugee-assistance arm of the National Council of the Churches of Christ in the U.S. CWS works through some 100 local church agencies in over 50 countries in Africa, Asia, the Caribbean, Latin America, the Middle East and the Pacific. Through colleague agencies, CWS responds to persons suffering from the immediate effects of disasters and the long-term consequences of poverty, poor health and illiteracy. Through development programs, education and health care, local projects offer alternatives to help people help themselves. CWS is also active in community education in the U.S., and works to provide a global education for its constituents. CWS cosponsors an office in Washington, DC, which addresses development policy. CWS is also active in refugee resettlement and protection issues.

Professional Staff: The U.S. staff of 214 works in four main offices, the largest of which is located in New York City, with smaller offices in Washington, DC, Baltimore, Maryland, and Elkhart, Indiana, and some 24 regional offices around the country that do community education and fund-raising. During the past 12 months, 25 people were hired for domestic positions. Some two dozen technical specialists and consultative liaisons serve abroad. CWS also has 32 people teaching English in China. In the past year, 31 people were hired to work abroad, including 18 English teachers for China.

Qualifications: A graduate degree in the social sciences, appropriate educational fields or theology and experience in development technology are preferred qualifications. Additionally, knowledge of French, Spanish or Asian languages is expected. Three to five years experience in Third World development is required, especially for overseas applicants. Prospective employees must be able to live and travel overseas.

Application Procedure: Persons interested in overseas professional positions may contact:

> Director, Overseas Personnel
> Church World Service
> 475 Riverside Drive
> Room 668
> New York, NY 10115
> (212) 870-2368

ENVIRONMENTAL DEFENSE FUND
New York, NY

The EDF, a leading environmental organization with over 200,000 members, links science, economics and law to create innovative and economically viable solutions to today's environmental problems. With the help of public contributions, the EDF addresses environmental concerns by funding the creation of regulatory programs and promoting the development of legislation. The EDF sponsors the Pollution Prevention Alliance, which links state-level groups to environmental data. EDF's international program works on a variety of issues, covering endangered species, rain-forest destruction, international emission standards and Antarctica.

Professional Staff: There are approximately 130 staff in the national office and the five regional offices in the U.S. In the past year, a dozen people were hired.

Qualifications: A BA, MS, JD or PhD in area studies or relevant social sciences is generally preferred. Depending on the position, previous work experience is not always required. Knowledge of foreign languages and willingness to travel are not necessary.

Internships: Undergraduate and graduate students may apply for paid internships offered during the summer and academic year. Interns assist in clerical work and legal and scientific research.

Application Procedure: Inquiries relating to either professional or internship positions should be directed to:

Environmental Defense Fund
257 Park Avenue South
New York, NY 10010
(212) 505-2100

FREEDOM FROM HUNGER FOUNDATION
Davis, CA

The Freedom from Hunger Foundation provides resources and self-help information to families and communities to help them combat chronic hunger. It has two programs: (1) one that enables groups to provide their members cash credit and nonformal adult education, and (2) another that trains community and lay health workers to educate and motivate their peers to improve their families' health and nutrition and provides advice for problem solving. Currently the Freedom from Hunger Foundation has programs in Honduras, Bolivia, Thailand, Nepal, Ghana, Mali, Togo and the U.S.

Professional Staff: Overseas staff consists of 92 people, mostly foreign nationals. Its California headquarters employs 21 people, 5 of whom have recently been hired.

Qualifications: Formal educational qualifications are flexible and knowledge of foreign languages is useful, depending on the position. Prior experience in the field, preferably in the developing world, and some travel may be required.

Internships: A few graduate students are accepted as interns and work on a variety of projects.

Application Procedure: Those interested in internships or employment should write to the personnel officer:

> Freedom from Hunger Foundation
> 1644 DaVinci Court
> PO Box 2000
> Davis, CA 95616
> (916) 758-6200

HEIFER PROJECT INTERNATIONAL (HPI)
Little Rock, AR

The goal of HPI is to address causes of poverty and hunger by establishing successful livestock and poultry operations in underdeveloped areas of Africa, Asia, the Caribbean, the Near East and parts of the U.S. HPI provides quality farm animals appropriate for local conditions and conducts training workshops in animal care. Recipients of animals must share an offspring of that animal with others in that community. Recent programs in 34 countries have involved veterinary training, dairy projects, poultry cooperatives, marketing training and aquaculture models. HPI is also involved in research on breeding livestock.

Professional Staff: The six U.S. offices employ a total of 80 people. The offices in Cameroon, China, Ecuador, Guatemala, Honduras, India, Indonesia, Peru, the Philippines, Tanzania and Thailand are staffed by 13 professionals and many volunteers. Twenty-seven people were hired in the past year, eight for the overseas offices.

Qualifications: A graduate degree in animal husbandry or veterinary medicine is essential for employment. Knowledge of French, Spanish or Arabic is preferred. Previous work experience in developing countries is also preferred but not essential.

Internships: Unpaid semester internships are available for undergraduate students interested in agricultural development. Interns work on research, development and education.

Application Procedure: Address applications for staff positions and internships to:

> Director of Personnel
> Heifer Project International
> PO Box 808
> Little Rock, AR 72202
> (501) 376-6836

INTERACTION/AMERICAN COUNCIL FOR VOLUNTARY INTERNATIONAL ACTION
Washington, DC

InterAction is a coalition of U.S. private and voluntary organizations. Its diverse group of member-agencies work on a broad range of international humanitarian issues: long-term development; disaster relief; refugee protection, assistance and resettlement; public policy; and building a constituency for development assistance through education of the American public.

Professional Staff: InterAction has a professional staff of 12 people in its Washington, DC, headquarters. They do not engage in actual overseas fieldwork; domestically they act as a network for relief and development agencies. Two people have been hired in the past year.

Qualifications: An undergraduate degree is desirable. The background required depends on the position one is seeking, but generally previous work experience in humanitarian assistance, development, refugee issues, environment or public policy is useful. Knowledge of any foreign language is useful. Willingness to travel and live abroad is not required.

Internships: Unpaid semester or summer internships are offered to undergraduate or graduate students. Interns conduct research and perform administrative duties.

Application Procedure: For the internship program, contact the Office Manager. For professional positions, InterAction publishes a newsletter with job openings advertised by a variety of private voluntary organizations. For inquires about positions with InterAction, write to:

> InterAction/American Council for Voluntary International Action
> 1717 Massachusetts Avenue, NW
> Suite 801
> Washington, DC 20036
> (202) 667-8227

INTERNATIONAL EXECUTIVE SERVICE CORPS (IESC)
Stamford, CT

IESC is a global network of people working to upgrade management skills, improve basic technologies and increase the productivity of businesses in the developing world. IESC is a nonprofit organization that recruits retired, highly skilled U.S. executives and technical advisers to share their knowledge with business people in developing countries. The men and women selected by IESC work as unpaid volunteers and serve on short-term assignments. Travel and living expenses are paid. The major emphasis of IESC is on the development of private enterprise in the host nation. In the 25 years that IESC has been in existence, it has completed more that 13,000 projects in 95 nations.

Professional Staff: IESC has a professional staff of 100 who run the day-to-day operations of the agency. Most of these people are retirees who have embarked on a second career. All those sent abroad are volunteers. During the past year, 15 people were hired.

Qualifications: Individuals must be retired, experts in their business and willing to share their knowledge on a volunteer basis.

Application Procedure: For more information on IESC, please contact:

> International Executive Service Corps
> PO Box 10005
> Stamford, CT 06904
> (203) 967-6000

INTERNATIONAL VOLUNTARY SERVICES (IVS)
Washington, DC

International Voluntary Services (IVS) is a private, nonprofit development agency that encourages the principle of self-help and initiative. IVS provides voluntary technical assistance to local organizations in the developing world. Volunteers with skills in agriculture, animal husbandry, business or public health are employed most often. Field staff are based in Bangladesh, Bolivia, Ecuador and Zimbabwe. They work with local host organizations to develop project objectives and implement schedules for volunteer assistance. Projects include crop and livestock improvement; small-business and cooperative income generation; public health education and village health-worker training; and appropriate technology for agriculture, irrigation and potable water.

Professional Staff: In addition to its field staff of eight, there is a staff of eight at the Washington, DC, headquarters. There are over 40 volunteers overseas who are assigned to local organizations to provide technical assistance and training in their specialty. During the past year, 10 people were hired, 5 for the headquarters in Washington.

Qualifications: Potential volunteers should have a BA or MA in agriculture, business or nursing, as well as two years experience working in a developing country in their specialty. Fluent Spanish is required for positions in Spanish-speaking countries. Volunteers and their families receive a modest allowance, which covers all in-country expenses. In addition, they receive health insurance and international air-travel coverage.

Internships: Internships, usually nonpaying, are available. Undergraduate or graduate students may apply by sending a cover letter and resume. Interns are usually placed in the communications or program offices and assist communications staff in writing newsletters or provide administrative support to program staff. Some interns may work on recruitment.

Application Procedure: Persons interested in volunteer, field staff or intern positions may write to:

International Voluntary Services
1424 16th Street, NW
Suite 204
Washington, DC 20036
(202) 387-5533

MAP INTERNATIONAL
Brunswick, GA

MAP International is a Christian global health organization committed to providing services that promote total health for needy people in the developing world. Since its founding in 1954, MAP has provided over $500 million in donated medicines and medical supplies through Christian hospitals and clinics in over 90 countries. MAP focuses on both humanitarian assistance in times of crisis and development assistance through health training and leadership development conducted through its offices in Ecuador, Bolivia and Kenya, as well as at the U.S. headquarters in Brunswick, GA.

Overseas staff conduct workshops and courses on health-related topics, teaching adults interested in community development and management skills for hospital staff.

Professional Staff: The headquarters in Georgia employs 64 people in a variety of fund-raising, administrative, distribution and support-staff positions. Overseas staff in Kenya, Ecuador and Bolivia number 31, of whom 27 are nationals. In the past year, nine people were hired for the U.S. staff and six for overseas projects.

Qualifications: For a professional position at headquarters, MAP seeks applicants with graduate study in public health, international relations, business, nonformal education, community development or related fields. Foreign language skills, especially Spanish or French, are helpful but not required. For consideration for employment in a regional office overseas, at least four years work in a developing country in medicine, health or adult education is required. Domestic and international travel is required for all professional staff; however, living abroad is only required for those people stationed overseas.

Externships: Externs (interns assigned abroad) should be medical students, interns or residents in their fourth year of medical school. Students must be in good academic standing and demonstrate a strong interest in health services in developing countries. Externs assist with the medical needs of the hospital or clinic to which they are assigned. The program covers 75% of the most economical regularly scheduled round-trip airfare. Externships last from 8-10 weeks and are unpaid.

Application Procedure: For externships, write to the RDIF Coordinator. For professional positions, write to the Personnel Director at:

MAP International
2200 Glynco Parkway
PO Box 50
Brunswick, GA 31525
(912) 265-6010

NATIONAL COOPERATIVE BUSINESS ASSOCIATION (NCBA)
Washington, DC

NCBA is a national trade and membership association representing U.S. cooperatives. NCBA members include farm supply, agricultural marketing, insurance, banking, housing, health care, consumer goods, fishing, utilities and financial institutions. Besides serving its members, NCBA also promotes and helps establish cooperatives in developing countries. Cooperative, agricultural and credit advisers are stationed in Equatorial Guinea, India, Indonesia, Niger and Rwanda to assist communities in using indigenous resources to organize cooperative businesses.

Professional Staff: NCBA headquarters in Washington, DC, employs 35 people. There are 17 agricultural and credit consultants. In the past year, 11 people were hired for the international department.

Qualifications: Applicants should have a degree in areas related to livestock, food processing, economics, finance or international business administration. Knowledge of French, Spanish or Portuguese is desired. Three to five years previous community development experience in developing countries is necessary for overseas positions. Direct technical assistance work requires living abroad, while other work entails traveling overseas.

Internships: Paid internships are available on a semester, summer or yearly basis. Interns should have a background in cooperative industries, including housing, insurance, agriculture, trade and international development. Interns work on research projects.

Application Procedure: The NCBA headquarters handles all employment and internship inquiries. Write to:

Personnel Director
National Cooperative Business Association
1401 New York Avenue, NW, Suite 1100
Washington, DC 20005
(202) 638-6222

THE NATURE CONSERVANCY
Arlington, VA

The Nature Conservancy is an international membership organization devoted to the protection of the natural environment and its biological diversity. Conservation goals are pursued through a three-part approach that includes identification of endangered ecosystems, performance of various land-conservation techniques and the operation of land preserves to serve as laboratories for environmental research and education. The International Program works with foreign governments and conservation groups to establish wildlife and habitat preserves. Current regions receiving assistance are Latin America, the Caribbean, the South Pacific and Canada.

Professional Staff: The Arlington, VA, headquarters maintains a staff of approximately 300 people, 50 of whom were hired in the past year. The International Program includes 50 people, 5 of whom are stationed in Latin America. The rest work in Washington, DC, as country-program directors, scientists, fund-raisers, researchers and administrators.

Qualifications: The country-program directors are people with an in-depth knowledge of the foreign countries in which the conservancy has programs. The Latin American division covers 18 countries within Latin America and the Caribbean. This division works along with 30 partner agencies. The administrators have law or business backgrounds and most of the rest of the staff have MA or MS degrees. Fluency in Spanish is often required for international positions. At least three to five years previous work experience in either business or a conservation organization is required for domestic positions. Employees must be willing to travel.

Internships: Undergraduate and graduate students may apply for paid semester or summer internships. The number of internships available depends on the current needs of the conservancy. Interns assist in research. The conservancy welcomes numerous volunteers.

Application Procedure: Applications should be directed to:

> Director of Administration
> The Nature Conservancy
> 1815 North Lynn Street
> Arlington, VA 22209
> (703) 841-4860

NEAR EAST FOUNDATION (NEF)
New York, NY

The Near East Foundation supports community-level self-help initiatives in the Middle East and Africa. By offering opportunities to learn new skills and technologies, NEF helps build the local capacities and institutions needed to sustain development efforts beyond the life of a particular project. NEF provides qualified specialists to assist with the transfer of technical skills and training; funds projects which have strong local support; and actively seeks opportunities to extend its work through cooperation with other donor agencies. It concentrates on assistance in three main areas—agricultural productivity, primary health care and community development. Recent projects include establishment of the Center for Development Services, a training and support center in the areas of health and nutrition; income generation and small-business promotion; agricultural extension and development communications in Egypt; and beekeeping and honey production in Swaziland.

Professional Staff: NEF has a professional staff of three in the U.S. and fifteen stationed in Botswana, Egypt, Jordan, Lesotho, Mali, Morocco, Sudan and Swaziland. Overseas employees offer technical assistance, project management, monitoring and evaluation. Both foreign nationals and U.S. citizens fill overseas posts. In the past year no one was hired.

Qualifications: Generally, a degree in agricultural sciences, health sciences, nursing or sociology is required, but qualifications vary according to current projects. Knowledge of French, Arabic and local African languages is preferred. In most cases applicants should have at least two years previous overseas development experience. Employees must be willing to live and travel abroad.

Application Procedure: To apply, write to:

> President
> Near East Foundation (NEF)
> 342 Madison Avenue
> Suite 1030
> New York, NY 10173
> (212) 867-0064

OXFAM AMERICA
Boston, MA

Oxfam is an international agency that funds self-help development and disaster-relief projects in Africa, Asia, Latin America and the Caribbean. Oxfam believes in small-scale self-help projects, such as providing seeds and tools to farmers or supplying basic equipment to village-level health clinics, that improve long-term food security and rural development and foster self-management and community participation. Oxfam also produces and distributes educational materials for people in the U.S. on issues of hunger and development, conducts educational campaigns and speaks out on public policies that affect its grass-roots development work abroad. Unlike other humanitarian-aid agencies, Oxfam receives no government contributions. One hundred percent of its income comes from private sources.

Professional Staff: Approximately 40 people, among them fund-raisers, writers and community educators, work at the headquarters. Nine employees are based overseas in Africa, Asia and Latin America, supporting Oxfam programs and working to transfer resources overseas. In the past year, two people have been hired, one for the international department.

Qualifications: An MA or PhD in area studies, agricultural sciences or relevant social sciences is most useful. Project officers must have familiarity with the planning and implementation of development policy, three or more years of work-related experience in an area, plus the ability to communicate in the language of that area. U.S.-based desk officers who serve as liaison with overseas field officers and the public should have similar credentials, although they need not have as much work experience or an advanced degree. Willingness to travel is essential for employment, but living abroad is not.

Internships: Oxfam employs interns for semester, summer or yearly periods for a minimum of 10 hours a week. Interns should be undergraduate or graduate students with knowledge of or interest in development and good research, writing, grass-roots organizing or administrative skills. Knowledge of a foreign language may be required for certain internships in the Overseas Program Department. All internships are in the Boston headquarters and are unpaid. Oxfam also uses the help of nonstudent volunteers.

Application Procedure: For internships, contact the Internship Coordinator. For employment, contact the Human Resources Department. Both are at:

> Oxfam America
> 26 West Street
> Boston, MA 02116
> (617) 482-1211

THE PEARL S. BUCK FOUNDATION
Perkasie, PA

The Pearl S. Buck Foundation is dedicated to the education and general welfare of needy children in general, and especially Amerasian children abandoned overseas by American servicemen. Much of the foundation's work is carried out through its overseas offices in Okinawa, the Philippines, South Korea, Taiwan and Thailand (work is also carried out in Vietnam, but there is no office there). These offices provide education, nutrition services, preventive health care, medical assistance and vocational training in an effort to enable Amerasian and other children to become "healthy and productive citizens in their native countries." Programs are funded through individuals who donate $24 a month to sponsor a child. In addition to these activities, the foundation provides assistance to American fathers searching for their children in Asia. It is also involved in refugee work: it creates matches between Amerasians who hope to immigrate to the U.S. and families who wish to sponsor them.

Professional Staff: The foundation has a professional staff of 35 in the U.S. Approximately 10 Americans are employed in overseas offices, which are staffed by about 150 foreign nationals. Four people were hired in the past year.

Qualifications: The foundation prefers applicants to have an MA in international relations or an MA with administration or accounting backgrounds. Knowledge of languages is necessary, and Chinese, Japanese, Thai, Tagalog and Korean are listed as most important. Applicants should also have previous work experience; employment in developing countries is desirable. A willingness to live abroad is required of all employees.

Application Procedure: Applications should be sent to:

The Executive Director
The Pearl S. Buck Foundation
PO Box 181
Perkasie, PA 18944
(215) 249-0100

PLAN INTERNATIONAL (PLAN)
East Greenwich, RI

Formerly Foster Parents Plan International, PLAN distributes material aid
and services to more than 500,000 children and families in 26 countries
in Central America, South Asia and Southeast Asia, with financial
support from foster parents in eight industrialized countries. Projects,
which are decided on by locals and field staff, include mother/child
health care and nutrition instruction, literacy and vocational training,
community-infrastructure improvement, agricultural assistance and
small-business development. In addition to the international headquarters
in Rhode Island, there are national offices in Australia, Belgium, Canada,
Germany, Japan, the Netherlands, the U.K. and the U.S., which recruit
and provide services to sponsors and conduct informational and develop-
ment-education programs on the needs of the poor in developing
countries.

Professional Staff: Field offices abroad employ a staff of 130, 23 of
whom were hired as assistant field directors in the past year, and 11 of
whom are local nationals. The international headquarters employs 46
professionals. In the past year, five people were hired.

Qualifications: Undergraduate specializations in international studies,
economics or business are required for employment. Proficiency in
Spanish or French is most useful, as well as a knowledge of other
languages relevant to PLAN locations. At least two years experience
working in an integrated development program in a developing country
and managerial or administrative experience is required. Employees must
be willing to travel and live overseas.

Application Procedure: Address applications to the international
headquarters:

Recruitment Manager
Plan International
Box 804
East Greenwich, RI 02818
(401) 826-2500

SAVE THE CHILDREN
Westport, CT

Save the Children is dedicated to enriching the lives of children in underprivileged communities. Believing that children cannot be helped in isolation, Save the Children works to unite children, their families and communities in development projects, builds schools and houses, promotes reinvestment in communities and establishes small industries. The heart of the organization is the program department, which operates field offices in 35 countries throughout Africa, Asia, Latin America, the Middle East and the South Pacific, and in U.S. areas with American Indian populations. U.S.-based regional "desks" are staffed by a director, with supporting professional and clerical staff, who maintains contact with Save the Children's field directors. U.S.-based staff also design, monitor and evaluate overseas programs. Recent projects include well-digging projects in Cameroon, agricultural projects in the Dominican Republic and rainwater-catchment systems in the South Pacific nation of Kiribati.

Professional Staff: Of the 65 overseas field directors and assistants, about half are Americans; the remainder are local nationals, as are the volunteers who assist the projects. Overseas staff are stationed in over 35 countries. The total U.S. staff, including those at the Connecticut headquarters, is 344. In the past 12 months, the program department hired 9 people and domestic offices hired 39.

Qualifications: A BA or preferably an MA in areas pertinent to development is useful for employees. Ability to speak French, Arabic or Spanish is preferred. At least two years of community-development work abroad (such as experience gained in a program like the Peace Corps) is required, as is the willingness to live and travel overseas. Save the Children does recruit from the international departments on college campuses for entry-level positions.

Internships: The Mickey Leland Minority Internship for the summer is offered only to minority students in their junior or senior year of college. The internship offers a stipend and housing and transportation costs.

Interns work in the following areas: public information, finance, marketing/fund-raising and community development.

Application Procedure: Address internship and employment applications to:

Human Resources
Save the Children
54 Wilton Road
Westport, CT 06880
(203) 221-4000

TECHNOSERVE
Norwalk, CT

Technoserve provides business know-how to developing countries' agribusiness cooperatives. Technoserve's community-based enterprise-development process chooses businesses that have the greatest employment and income-generating potential. It evaluates requests for assistance and works with local managers. Recent projects have focused on agricultural productivity, crop processing, marketing and savings and credit management. Ongoing projects, mostly overseen by local nationals, are in Costa Rica, El Salvador, Ghana, Kenya, Nigeria, Panama, Peru, Rwanda and Tanzania.

Professional Staff: There are 35 people on the U.S. staff, 5 of whom were hired during the past 12 months. The 155 employees stationed abroad include both U.S. citizens and local nationals. Overseas employees oversee and manage the activities of the programs in Africa and Latin America. Recent overseas hiring figures were unavailable.

Qualifications: An undergraduate degree in a field related to business administration, management, agribusiness, agricultural economics or finance, and an MBA, MA, MIA, MPA or MS, are useful for employment. Knowledge of Spanish, French or Polish, as well as three to five years overseas experience in agribusiness or agricultural cooperatives, preferably in Africa, Asia or Latin America, is required of all Technoserve employees. A willingness to travel and live abroad is also required.

Internships: Graduate students working on their MBA may arrange for summer or semester internships. Applicants should have prior work experience in development. Knowledge of French or Spanish may be required. Both paid and volunteer internships are available. Work involves research on a specific project or topic.

Application Procedure: Persons interested in professional or intern positions should contact:

> Director, Human Resources
> Technoserve, Inc.
> 49 Day Street
> Norwalk, CT 06854
> (203) 852-0377

THE TRICKLE UP PROGRAM
New York, NY

The mission of Trickle Up is to help end poverty by helping poor people start and manage a business of their choice. Trickle Up offers encouragement, basic business training and seed capital of $100. Governments, international development agencies and nongovernmental organizations are encouraged to incorporate the Trickle Up process into their development strategies. The program has no staff overseas but works through hundreds of volunteers called coordinators. They implement the Trickle Up program in 92 countries: 33 in Africa, 22 in Asia, 34 in the Americas and the Caribbean, and 3 in Europe. The principal duties of volunteer coordinators are to identify potential grant recipients, introduce the groups to the Trickle Up process, help them step-by-step through the process of planning and operating a business and disburse grants to the groups. They also monitor the progress of the groups and report to Trickle Up.

Professional Staff: Trickle Up has a professional staff of 10 in the U.S., none overseas. In the past year, two persons were hired. Trickle Up has five positions in the program area: four Program Officers respectively for Africa, Asia, the Americas and the Caribbean, and Eastern Europe, and a Chief Program Officer who is also responsible for the Philippines. Two Program Officers were hired in the last 12 months.

Qualifications: An MA, MIA or MPA in the social sciences is preferred. For Program Officers a background in economics or development is an asset, as well as geographic specialization in the appropriate region. Two professional nonprogram positions involve information systems (computer-programming expertise) and fund-raising. Experience in nonprofit organizations is preferred. Work experience is required in the specific area of expertise called for in the position, for example in fund-raising.

For Program Officers, overseas field experience as a Peace Corps volunteer or service with an international development agency is preferred. For the professional staff, knowledge of a foreign language is useful. Program Officers should be fluent in the language of their assigned areas.

Internships: Graduate students may apply for internships on a semester or summer basis. Interns are paid a stipend. They help the Program Officers with regular work, research and writing country reports or country fact sheets that summarize Trickle Up activity. Interns should have background in a specific geographic region, as well as good language, computer, writing and research skills.

Application Procedure: Applications should be directed to:

> The Executive Director
> The Trickle Up Program
> 54 Riverside Drive
> New York, NY 10024-6509
> (212) 362-7958

VOLUNTEERS IN TECHNICAL ASSISTANCE, INC.
Arlington, VA

Founded in 1960, VITA is a private nonprofit organization dedicated to Third World development. Through a program of consulting, information and management services by volunteer specialists, VITA has helped small businesses, farmers, community workers and government agencies throughout Africa, Asia, the Caribbean and Latin America. VITA offers resource materials, mail and on-site consulting, training programs, new business services and technical information workshops. VITA focuses on low-level appropriate technology such as developing wind energy. Recent projects have included the improvement of food-processing systems in the Central African Republic, an enterprise-development program in Chad and construction of a water-supply system in Honduras. VITA publishes the quarterly *VITA News*, as well as newsletters and technical assistance books.

Professional Staff: The headquarters in Virginia has a staff of 30, 3 of whom were hired in the past year. Thirteen people are contracted by VITA to serve in overseas projects in Belize, the Central African Republic, Chad, Djibouti, Kenya, Mali, Pakistan and Zambia. VITA volunteers number 3,000 in the U.S. and 1,500 abroad.

Qualifications: For volunteers, a BA in a technical field such as engineering or knowledge of energy systems, agriculture, sanitation or housing construction is useful. Volunteers are recruited from college campuses and the corporate and business sector. They are contracted for one-to-two-year periods. Preferred languages include French and Spanish. Previous work experience is not essential.

For professional staff, an MA, MBA or PhD is preferred in agriculture, business, communications or engineering. VITA prefers at least one or more years experience in these related fields. At least five years overseas experience is required, preferably in the French-speaking regions of Africa. Ability to speak French or Spanish is required. Arabic and Portuguese are also desirable. A willingness to live and travel abroad is necessary for employment.

Application Procedure: Inquiries relating to professional positions should be addressed to the personnel manager. For volunteer positions, contact the manager of information.

> Personnel Manager
> Volunteers in Technical Assistance (VITA)
> 1600 Wilson Boulevard
> Suite 500
> Arlington, VA 22209
> (703) 276-1800

WINROCK INTERNATIONAL INSTITUTE FOR INTERNATIONAL DEVELOPMENT
Morrilton, AR

Winrock International was established in 1975 to help alleviate hunger and poverty through agricultural development. Winrock works in partnership with donors and other development assistance organizations to promote practices that produce more and better food, fiber and fuels. Winrock works with many institutions, universities, donor agencies and associated groups in the U.S. and worldwide to strengthen agricultural research and extension systems, improve food and agriculture policies, train agricultural scientists and leaders and increase the productivity of agricultural and renewable resources of developing countries. Winrock's overseas staff, stationed in 16 countries in Asia, Africa, the Middle East, Latin America and the Caribbean, implements approximately 100 major projects, programs and consultant assignments in some 50 countries around the world.

Professional Staff: The U.S. staff numbers 150, of whom 28 were hired in the past year. There are 66 field-workers, 10 of whom were recently hired. Both foreign nationals and U.S. citizens are hired for overseas assignments.

Qualifications: The professional staff includes specialists in socioeconomics, biological and physical sciences and program implementation. All have PhD, MBA, MA or BS degrees. Two years of previous overseas development work is usually required for employment. In some positions a willingness to travel and live overseas is required, and foreign language proficiency is preferred. French and Spanish are most useful.

Application Procedure: Write to:

> Director, Finance and Administration
> Winrock International
> Route 3
> PO Box 376
> Petit Jean Mountain
> Morrilton, AR 72110-9539
> (501) 727-5435

WORLD RESOURCES INSTITUTE
Washington, DC

Through policy research and technical assistance, the World Resources Institute (WRI) helps governments, the private sector, environmental and development organizations and others address what they deem one of our time's most pressing questions: How can societies meet human needs and nurture economic growth without destroying the natural resources and environmental integrity that make prosperity possible?

WRI aims to generate accurate information about global resources and environmental conditions, analyze issues and develop responses to both problems and opportunities. It publishes books, reports and papers, holds briefings, seminars and conferences and provides the media with perspective and background material. In developing countries, WRI provides technical support, policy analysis and other services for governments and nongovernmental organizations that are trying to manage natural resources and sustainable development.

Professional Staff: WRI has a professional staff of 95. In the last 12 months, 12 people were hired.

Qualifications: Qualifications vary according to the position. WRI employs specialists in many regional areas and environmental issues. Generally, a graduate degree and some work experience is required. Foreign language ability is preferred, with Spanish, French and Portuguese considered most useful.

Internships: Semester and summer paid internships are offered to college juniors and seniors and graduate students in the fields of economics or the sciences. Interns generally provide research assistance.

Application Procedure: Contact:

> Assistant to the Senior Vice President
> World Resources Institute
> 1709 New York Avenue, NW
> Washington, DC 20006
> (202) 638-6300

WORLD VISION INTERNATIONAL
Monrovia, CA

World Vision, a Christian organization founded in 1950, provides relief and development assistance to more than 80 Third World and 9 European countries, plus areas of Canada, Israel and the U.S. About 6,000 projects, including assistance to children and families, nutritional programs, emergency relief and rehabilitation, large-scale development and community development are in operation. World Vision also distributes emergency food, clothing and medical supplies, most recently in Mozambique, southern Sudan, Romania and Bangladesh. World Vision also brings the plight of developing countries before the U.S. public through television programs, a sponsorship program (which involves one million children worldwide) and several publications.

Professional Staff: The international headquarters in California employs 172 people, 84 of them hired within the last year, and 160 field staff, of whom 65 are American. Fifteen support offices, located in Australia, Britain, Canada, Finland, Germany, Hong Kong, Ireland, Japan, the Netherlands, New Zealand, Singapore, South Africa, Switzerland and the U.S., employ 1,528 people.

Qualifications: A graduate degree in business, medicine or public health or technical skills in related areas is most useful for employment. Knowledge of French or Spanish is preferred. Five or more years experience in Third World development, relief, research or missionary work is usually required. A willingness to travel is necessary for employment.

Application Procedure: Send application to the international office:

> Employment Manager
> World Vision International
> 919 West Huntington Drive
> Monrovia, CA 91016
> (818) 303-8811

WORLDWATCH INSTITUTE
Washington, DC

Founded in 1974, Worldwatch is a public-interest research institute concentrating on the global environment and environment-related issues. With its global research topics, the institute hopes to educate and raise public awareness of environmental threats in order to generate pressure for an effective public policy. The institute has several publications: the *Worldwatch Papers*, a series of six to eight monographs per year; *Worldwatch*, a bimonthly magazine; the *Environmental Alert* series that covers various topics; *Vital Signs*; and *State of the World* report, published annually. This single report combines information on the environment, population, development and agriculture into a single integrated analysis. Worldwatch research findings released to the international press corps are examined and used in lectures, television and radio programs, and testimony before many legislative bodies, such as the U.S. Congress.

Professional Staff: Worldwatch has a professional staff of 32 people, 5 of whom were hired in the past year.

Qualifications: Qualifications for Worldwatch vary according to position; generally a BS, BA, MA or MS in environmental studies is preferred. Background in population, development or agriculture is also useful. A willingness to live or travel abroad is not required.

Application Procedure: For employment opportunities contact:

Worldwatch Institute
1776 Massachusetts Avenue, NW
Washington, DC 20036-1904
(202) 452-1999

HEALTH AND POPULATION ORGANIZATIONS

AFRICAN MEDICAL AND RESEARCH FOUNDATION (AMREF)
New York, NY

Amref provides health care to remote rural African areas where such services are unavailable, promotes local health-care capabilities and works with African government ministries of health to alleviate long-term health problems. Amref's two arms are its Flying Doctors, airborne medical teams that deliver surgical and general health care and training to remote regions of Kenya, Tanzania and Uganda, and the Ground Mobile teams. These units work from tents treating nomadic groups, immunizing their children and providing care to mothers. In addition, Amref sponsors other health-personnel training programs in Uganda and Sudan, carries out research on African diseases in Kenya, puts on a health-related radio program and produces health-education materials and periodicals. Amref is based in Nairobi, Kenya, with affiliate offices in Europe and New York.

Professional Staff: Although only 3 people are on the staff in the U.S., approximately 500 are based in Kenya. Ninety-five are African, but there are also some Americans and Europeans. Ten people were hired in the last 12 months.

Qualifications: A graduate degree in medicine, public health, health planning and management, maternal and child care or nutrition is essential for employment. Knowledge of Swahili is preferred, and five years of health-related experience in Africa or developing nations elsewhere is required. Willingness to live and work abroad is essential.

Application Procedure: Applications may be sent to the New York office:

African Medical and Research Foundation
420 Lexington Avenue
Room 244
New York, NY 10170
(212) 986-1835

AMERICAN REFUGEE COMMITTEE (ARC)
Minneapolis, MN

The American Refugee Committee works for the survival, health and well-being of refugees and seeks to enable them to rebuild productive lives of dignity and purpose. ARC sends health professionals overseas for six months or more and conducts programs in the U.S. as well. Its volunteers, who act as medical trainers and health-care providers, work in refugee camps on the Thai-Cambodian (Kampuchean) border and in Malawi and with immigrants and refugees in Minnesota and Illinois.

Professional Staff: There are 10 permanent professional staff members in the Minneapolis headquarters; 9 in the Chicago office; 23 in the Thai office, 11 of whom are U.S. citizens; 19 in the Malawi office, of whom 3 are U.S. citizens; and 19 in the Cambodian office, of whom 7 are U.S. citizens. In the past year 12 professionals were hired for overseas positions. There are about 30 volunteers presently serving abroad.

Qualifications: ARC mainly hires doctors or residents, registered nurses or nurse practitioners, laboratory technicians, midwives, public-health specialists and administrators with several years experience. International work experience, especially development-based public-health work, is preferred. Proficiency in French, Khmer, Thai, Vietnamese or Portuguese is helpful but not required.

Application Procedure: Write to:

Director, International Programs
American Refugee Committee
2344 Nicollet Avenue
Suite 350
Minneapolis, MN 55404
(612) 872-7060

DIRECT RELIEF INTERNATIONAL (DRI)
Santa Barbara, CA

Founded in 1948 to provide medical assistance to postwar Europe, DRI now provides urgently needed medical supplies to health-care facilities and programs throughout the world to break the cycle of poverty, malnutrition and disease. DRI also assists refugees and other victims of disaster and civil strife. During the past year DRI donated $11 million in pharmaceuticals, medical supplies, nutritional supplements and medical equipment. These benefitted an estimated 4 million persons in over 40 countries. Ongoing programs are operated in conjunction with indigenous health-care systems in El Salvador, India, the Philippines and Thailand.

Professional Staff: International headquarters in California has a staff of 25, about half of whom work part-time. Medical volunteers do field assessment and evaluation. Six people were hired in the past year.

Qualifications: A master's or doctoral degree in public health, medicine or anthropology is preferred for staff employment. Although some positions require previous work experience in international public health, the majority of volunteer positions do not. Knowledge of French or Spanish is useful but not required. Over 100 domestic-based volunteers assist.

Internships: Undergraduates and graduate students may apply for semester or year-long internships. Prospective interns must show a concern for health in the international arena. Work includes research and program assistance. Positions are unpaid.

Application Procedure: Those interested in positions at the international headquarters should write to the Director of Personnel. The address is:

> Direct Relief International
> PO Box 30820
> Santa Barbara, CA 93130-0820
> (805) 964-4767

FAMILY HEALTH INTERNATIONAL (FHI)
Research Triangle Park, NC

Family Health International, based in Research Triangle Park, NC, is a 20-year-old organization engaged in research and technical assistance for contraceptive development, reproductive health, maternal and child health and AIDS prevention in developing countries. FHI is staffed by professionals skilled in public health, communications, social sciences, economics, biostatistics, epidemiology and infective-disease control. Since 1987, FHI has conducted AIDS intervention programs in over 40 nations. In August 1991 FHI received a $168 million five-year grant from the United States Agency for International Development to expand its work in AIDS prevention. The AIDS Control and Prevention Project (Aidscap) of FHI is located in northern Virginia, with regional offices in Africa, Asia, Latin America and the Caribbean.

Professional Staff: Two hundred and twenty-eight staff members are based in FHI's North Carolina headquarters, of whom twenty-five were hired in the last 12 months. Sixty-two staff members are based at FHI's Aidscap office in Arlington, VA.

Qualifications: Research experience is required for most FHI positions. An MD, MPA, MS, MA or PhD in public health, demography, epidemiology or statistics is required. Knowledge of French, Spanish or Portuguese is preferred and research experience in a developing country is useful. Most research staff travel as part of their work at FHI.

Application Procedure: Contact:

Human Resources
Family Health International
PO Box 13950
Research Triangle Park, NC 27709
(919) 544-7040

Human Resources
Family Health International
2101 Wilson Boulevard
Suite 701
Arlington, VA 22201
(703) 516-9781

INTERNATIONAL EYE FOUNDATION
Bethesda, MD

The International Eye Foundation helps developing countries set up effective eye health-care systems that stress blindness prevention. Its international staff trains local personnel in surgical and preventive care, provides mobile clinical services and establishes eye health-care systems. After training of staff is complete, programs are turned over to local personnel or governments. Personnel are stationed in Barbados, Honduras and Malawi.

Professional Staff: Eight people are in the Maryland office; ten are abroad. Six people have been hired in the past year.

Qualifications: An MD, especially in ophthalmology, an MA or PhD in epidemiology or public health or an MIA are all useful for employment. Foreign languages are helpful, depending on the country to which one is posted. Overseas field experience in developing-world health issues is useful but not essential. Some positions entail traveling and living abroad.

Application Procedure: Applications may be sent to:

> Executive Director
> International Eye Foundation
> 7801 Norfolk Avenue
> Suite 200
> Bethesda, MD 20814
> (301) 986-1830

INTERNATIONAL RESCUE COMMITTEE (IRC)
New York, NY

Founded in 1933, IRC's first assistance program helped anti-Nazis escape Hitler's Germany. IRC has since provided relief and resettlement programs for refugees who have fled from Afghanistan, Cuba, Cambodia (Kampuchea), the former Czechoslovakia, Ethiopia, Haiti, Iran, Laos, the former Soviet Union and Vietnam. IRC maintains health-care programs in refugee camps in El Salvador, Pakistan, the Sudan and Thailand. These projects provide primary health care to the most-needy refugee groups, with an emphasis on the training of refugee health workers. Personnel are stationed in Pakistan, Thailand, Turkey, Iraq, Sudan, Malawi, Sierra Leone, El Salvador, Costa Rica and Nicaragua.

Professional Staff: IRC has a staff of 65 professionals in the U.S. and 180 overseas. In the last 12 months, 80–100 professionals were hired.

Qualifications: A graduate degree in medicine, nursing, public health, immunology, infectious diseases or nutrition is required for employment. Expertise in refugee affairs and emergency relief are preferred, as is foreign language ability. One to three years overseas work experience in a developing country is required.

Internships: A limited number of internships are available to medical students attending affiliated medical schools.

Application Procedure: Eligible persons should write to:

Overseas Programs
International Rescue Committee
386 Park Avenue South
New York, NY 10016
(212) 679-0010

NATIONAL COUNCIL ON INTERNATIONAL HEALTH
Washington, DC

NCIH, a nonprofit membership organization, is a leader in policy analysis and health advocacy on a wide range of international health issues including women's health, child survival and AIDS. NCIH also acts as a link between private and public agencies, health professionals and policymakers involved in international health activities by hosting an annual international health conference. The NCIH monthly newsletter, *Healthlink,* highlights specific international health issues and provides updates on U.S. and international health policy. NCIH also publishes the *Directory of U.S.-Based Agencies Involved in International Health Assistance,* a resource for international health organizations. In addition, NCIH offers *Career Network*, a monthly job-announcements listing for international health positions. The annual NCIH conference has a career resource center for participants.

Professional Staff: NCIH has a professional staff of 11 in the U.S. In the last 12 months, six professionals were hired. No one is stationed abroad.

Qualifications: Applicants with a graduate degree in public health, public affairs, foreign policy, health care, medicine and business are all desirable, as are those with expertise in international public health. Foreign language skill in Spanish, French, German or Arabic is preferred. Although some employees may travel, a willingness to travel and live abroad is not necessary. Some international experience is required.

Internships: Unpaid internships for semester and summer periods are offered to college students. Interns conduct research, write, design, work in the archives and on marketing projects. Good research and writing skills and knowledge of public health issues is helpful but not required.

Application Procedure: Those interested in internships should contact the Communications Department; for professional positions, contact the Deputy Director at:

National Council for International Health
1701 K Street, NW
Suite 600
Washington, DC 20006
(202) 833-5900

PEOPLE TO PEOPLE HEALTH FOUNDATION (Project HOPE)
Millwood, VA

Project HOPE's goal is to train health-care professionals in the developing world. Its programs are aimed at setting up indigenous, self-sufficient health-education programs and health-care structures. HOPE is also involved in emergency programs for feeding children, teaching about nutrition and sanitation, and preventive medicine. Each year, it sends over 150 short-term volunteers abroad as teachers to supplement its long-term, salaried employees. Project HOPE currently has programs in Chile, China, Costa Rica, Eastern Europe, Egypt, the former Soviet Union, Guatemala, Honduras, Malawi, Nicaragua, Panama, Poland and Swaziland.

Professional Staff: Project HOPE maintains a staff of 60 at its Virginia headquarters and has 80 people stationed abroad. These long-term employees are mainly program and education directors. Project HOPE hires few permanent staff yearly but has taken on 200 volunteers in the past year. Most of these (approximately 180) have been sent abroad for a few months. Volunteers are not salaried, but their airfare is paid.

Qualifications: As in most health-related organizations, a graduate degree is required, and a specialized professional degree, such as an MD, MS, or PhD, is preferred. In addition, nurses, public-health educators and other allied personnel are hired as volunteers. Knowledge of foreign languages is preferred; Chinese, Russian and Spanish are the most useful. Two years previous work experience teaching health care is a desired qualification for employment, but overseas experience is not necessary.

Application Procedure: Applications may be addressed to:

International Recruitment Section
Project HOPE
PO Box 250
Millwood, VA 22646
(703) 837-2100

PLANNED PARENTHOOD FEDERATION OF AMERICA
New York, NY

Planned Parenthood, the largest and oldest voluntary family-planning organization in the U.S., maintains over 20,000 staff and volunteers nationwide to provide medical care, counseling and family planning to some 3 million Americans. Its international department, Family Planning International Assistance (FPIA), believes that "all individuals throughout the world have a basic right to control their own fertility." FPIA's staff assists foreign nationals in designing and initiating projects, monitors project performance and provides technical assistance. FPIA currently funds and monitors 52 family-planning projects in 20 countries.

Professional Staff: FPIA has a professional staff of 11 people at its New York headquarters, 4 people in its Latin American Regional Office in Miami, Florida, and 9 people in Thailand, Kenya and Nigeria. Three people were hired in the past year.

Qualifications: All applicants for the professional staff are required to have a college degree, preferably with a specialization in public health and public or business administration. An MA, MBA, MIA, MSW or MPH degree is desirable. French and Spanish are preferred languages, and fluency is often required for employment. Previous work experience is necessary for employment. Living and working abroad for two or more years in a developing country and involvement in family-planning and community health programs are typical qualifications for FPIA work. Although willingness to travel is required for employment, not all positions entail living abroad.

Application Procedure: Applications may be addressed to:

Chief Operating Officer
Planned Parenthood Federation of America
810 Seventh Avenue
New York, NY 10019
(212) 541-7800

POPULATION REFERENCE BUREAU, INC. (PRB)
Washington, DC 20009

PRB is a private, nonprofit educational organization that gathers, interprets and disseminates information on population. PRB seeks to increase understanding of population trends and their public-policy implications. Audiences in the U.S. and abroad include public officials, educators, students, the press, business leaders and the general public.

The international program at PRB provides technical support to organizations in developing countries to enable them to communicate critical population information to policymakers in their countries. Services include the design, production and dissemination of reports, booklets, wall charts, posters and other materials; conference support; assistance to journalists in covering population; organizing workshops, seminars, briefings and short courses on population topics; and consulting on needs assessment, project design and evaluation.

Professional Staff: PRB has a professional staff of 25 in the U.S. In the past year, two professionals were hired.

Qualifications: Most of PRB's professional staff hold advanced degrees in demography, but advanced degrees or expertise in economics, sociology, public health, communications, policy analysis, information sciences or journalism are also desirable. Knowledge of French is preferred and Arabic, Chinese and Japanese are used infrequently but considered an asset. Although some positions do involve travel, willingness to travel and work abroad is not obligatory. Work experience is not necessary for entry-level positions, but they are few. Mid- and upper-level positions require at least two to five years work experience with demography and policy analysis. Writing and computer skills are also extremely useful.

Internships: PRB offers paid internships to college and graduate students with a demonstrated interest in population and strong writing and computer skills. Course work in demography is a plus. Interns conduct research and data analysis, write, edit, produce computer graphics and give general project support. Semester, summer and year-long internships are available.

Application Procedure: To apply for an internship, write to the Internship Program, and for professional positions, contact the Vice President for Administration at:

Population Reference Bureau, Inc.
1875 Connecticut Avenue, NW
Suite 520
Washington, DC 20009
(202) 483-1100

YOUTH-ORIENTED ORGANIZATIONS

AFS INTERCULTURAL PROGRAMS/
AMERICAN FIELD SERVICE
New York, NY

AFS promotes worldwide intercultural exchanges for secondary-school students and young-adult professionals through homestays and educational experiences abroad. It is active in 70 countries throughout Western Europe, Latin America, Asia the Middle East and Africa. In the past year, AFS has organized over 10,000 exchanges, most involving high-school students. Student programs run for a summer, semester or a year. Programs for young adults vary in length and focus on professional exchange. Recent participants have included educators, lawyers and journalists.

AFS's staff is bolstered by the work of over 100,000 volunteers worldwide who help with fund-raising, recruitment, selection, orientation or counseling of students, or who act as host families. Volunteers are instrumental in implementing new programs and have the opportunity to participate in volunteer exchanges abroad.

Professional Staff: AFS has a staff of 200 people at the international headquarters in New York City and more than 200 in its overseas offices. Most overseas positions are filled by foreign nationals. In the past year, 33 people were hired, 5 for the international department, which supervises the operations of overseas offices.

Qualifications: A BA in liberal arts, previous international study and experience are good backgrounds for employment. For some positions, experience and an advanced degree in management, recruiting, finance, promotion, marketing and counseling are required. Knowledge of foreign languages is not required, nor is previous overseas experience; these are, however, useful. Some employees must be willing to travel.

To qualify for an exchange program, a student must be a sophomore, junior or senior in high school at the time of application and have a minimum B average. Some programs require two years or more of high-school French, German or Spanish. Qualifications for young adults vary. Families may apply to AFS for summer or year-long housing opportunities.

Internships: Unpaid internships are available to high-school, college and graduate students and are designed to accommodate students' schedules. Interns usually work on research projects.

Application Procedure: For internships, contact the Intern Coordinator. For employment, write to the Personnel Department. To become an exchange student/participant or to host an exchange student, call 1-800-AFS-INFO or write to the following address:

AFS International/American Field Service
313 East 43rd Street
New York, NY 10017
(212) 949-4242

COUNCIL ON INTERNATIONAL EDUCATIONAL EXCHANGE
New York, NY

The Council on International Educational Exchange (CIEE) is an international private, nonprofit membership organization, headquartered in the U.S., with international offices, affiliations and representation. Major contributions to the field of educational exchange throughout its more than 40 years of service to the academic community have established the council as one of the foremost organizations concerned with international education and travel.

The council's activities include the development and administration of international educational exchange throughout the world on behalf of both its national and international constituencies. In addition, CIEE provides a wide range of travel services for students and young people through two wholly owned subsidiary companies, Council Travel Services and Council Charter. Overseas offices help coordinate a multitude of council program activities and provide a wide range of services to educational institutions and organizations, as well as students, educators and professionals.

Professional Staff: CIEE has a professional staff of 130 in the U.S. and 30 overseas. Overseas staff are stationed in Britain, France, Spain, Germany, Japan, Italy and the former Soviet Union. Both foreign nationals and U.S. citizens are stationed abroad. Last year 12 people were hired.

Qualifications: A college degree in international affairs, political science or education or expertise in international education is preferred. Previous work experience that provided a work and/or study abroad experience, knowledge of office procedures, teaching or computer experience is required. Foreign languages are preferred, with French, Spanish, Japanese, Russian or Chinese considered the most useful.

Application Procedure: Contact:

> Personnel Department
> Council on International Educational Exchange
> 205 East 42nd Street
> New York, NY 10017
> (212) 661-1414

INTERNATIONAL ASSOCIATION FOR THE EXCHANGE OF STUDENTS FOR TECHNICAL EXPERIENCE (IAESTE)
Columbia, MD

Iaeste is an independent, nongovernmental organization that provides college or graduate students with on-the-job, practical training experience abroad. Iaeste is a confederation of over 50 member countries. The U.S. joined the international organization in 1950. In the U.S., the program is administered by the Association for International Practical Training (AIPT).

The Iaeste program provides opportunities for students of engineering sciences, agriculture, forestry, architecture, mathematics and other technical fields to work abroad with colleagues in the same profession. Placement may be in a research lab, design office, production department or field location, depending on the nature of the students' background and interests. Most placements are for 8 to 12 weeks during the summer, although some may be available for longer periods and at different times of the year. Employers usually pay a maintenance allowance to cover the trainee's living expenses. Students are responsible for their own travel and incidental expenses. In 1990, the Iaeste program worldwide provided practical training opportunities for over 6,300 students.

Professional Staff: The program has a professional staff of 20 in the U.S. In the last 12 months, three people were hired.

Qualifications: Iaeste exchange students must be enrolled in good standing at a college or institute of technology. They must have completed the sophomore year and major in one of the previously mentioned fields. Postdoctoral trainees are normally not accepted.

The Iaeste training program is reciprocal, therefore the chances of being accepted in the program are greatly enhanced if students can find an American employer willing to offer an international student a position. Most countries accept English-speaking students. However, some countries require some expertise in the local language.

Application Procedure: To apply, students must obtain an application from AIPT, complete it, secure academic endorsement and submit this package by December 10 (for the following year), together with a nonrefundable application processing fee of $75. To obtain application forms or more information, write to:

> IAESTE Trainee Program
> c/o Association for International Practical Training
> 10400 Little Patuxent Parkway
> Suite 250
> Columbia, MD 21044-3510
> (301) 997-2200

VOLUNTEERS FOR PEACE, INC. (VFP)
Belmont, VT

VFP coordinates international work camps in the U.S. for Americans and foreigners and helps place American volunteers in work camps in over 30 countries abroad. Work camps are two to three week programs, usually during the summer, in which international volunteers live and work together to carry out a community service project. Positions are unpaid, but room and board are free. Volunteers arrange their own transportation. They often apply to serve at more than one work camp in the same or nearby countries. Work camps are sponsored by an organization in the host country. Formal and informal discussion on issues of common concern are an integral part of every work camp. The work involved is often a construction, agricultural or environmental project or can be a community- or peace-oriented service. Conditions in the work camps vary. Housing may be in a local school or church or in tents. Meals are often prepared by campers on a rotating basis. Decision-making is by group consensus.

Professional Staff: VFP has a permanent staff of four. Turnover is very low. Most work is done by some 100 volunteers in the field.

Qualifications: Work camp volunteers should have an interest in promoting international goodwill and peace and must be able to pay their own transportation to and from the camps. The average age of volunteers is 21, but applications are accepted from anyone age 18 and up. There are limited opportunities for persons ages 13–18. No special skills or foreign-language proficiency is required, nor is a high-school, college or graduate degree.

Application Procedure: There is a $150 registration fee for foreign and U.S. work camps. Scholarships are available. People interested in work camps may request VFP's International Workcamp Directory, which includes the registration materials. This costs $10, postpaid. Write to:

> Volunteers for Peace, Inc.
> 43 Tiffany Road
> Belmont, VT 05730
> (802) 259-2759

WORLD LEARNING, INC.
Brattleboro, VT

World Learning was founded in 1932 as the U.S. Experiment in International Living. It is the oldest private, nonprofit, international education-services organization in the world. World Learning is the pioneer of the homestay concept, in which an individual learns about another culture by living with a family. World Learning hopes to give participants the knowledge, skills and attitudes needed to contribute to international understanding and development. This broad range of activities in international service includes the accredited undergraduate and graduate School for International Training; the Citizen Exchange Language Programs; the private, voluntary Projects in International Development and Training.

With more than 260 programs in 67 countries, World Learning provides services to some 54,000 participants and indirectly benefits more than 500,000 other people. Most positions available in the U.S. are dispersed among their headquarters in Brattleboro, VT, and other offices in Washington, DC; Belmont, CA; Jacksonville, FL; and Boston, MA.

World Learning's School for International Training was established in 1964 as an expansion of the original language training and teaching materials for the U.S. Peace Corps. Today, the school offers bachelor's-degree programs in international studies, master's-degree programs in intercultural management, and language study and college semesterabroad programs in more than 40 countries.

Professional Staff: World Learning has a professional staff of 636 in the U.S. and 622 overseas; however the number abroad varies. Most of the technical assistance work is done by foreign nationals, although some local nationals are hired for overseas projects. Professionals working in Third World countries usually hold one year renewable contracts.

Qualifications: Graduate degrees in international relations, educational administration, economic and social development or management are useful. A PhD is required for faculty positions at SIT. Two to three years experience in areas such as project management, teaching or intercultural work is generally required for most positions. Experience living or working abroad, preferably in developing countries, is very helpful. Knowledge of foreign languages is preferred, as is a willingness to travel or live abroad.

For leadership positions in the exchange programs, some degree of foreign language proficiency is almost always required. There are also academic requirements. Students participating in exchanges should also have some language training.

Application Procedure: People interested in professional staff positions should send a resume to the Human Resources Department. Those interested in leadership should write to the summer-abroad or college semester-abroad programs. Those interested in exchanges should contact the organization for a preliminary application. After this is reviewed, applicants must fill out and return a lengthier form. The address is:

World Learning, Inc.
PO Box 676
Kipling Road
Brattleboro, VT 05302-0676
(802) 257-7751

YOUNG MEN'S CHRISTIAN ASSOCIATION OF THE U.S.A. (The YMCA or the Y)
Chicago, IL

The Young Men's Christian Association (YMCA) is a worldwide Christian organization dedicated to developing leadership skills in youth, promoting international understanding and Third World development and strengthening family ties and community development. The Y serves about 25 million members in over 90 countries abroad and some 14 million in 2,400 local branches in the U.S. It sponsors many international programs, such as partnerships with Ys abroad, development aid for developing countries, exchanges for summer campers and counselors, international exchanges for business and community leaders and global-education programs.

The Y sponsors a volunteer program for American college graduates to teach English in Japan or Taiwan called the Overseas Service Corps of the YMCA (OSCY). Recruits spend a year in Taiwan or two years in Japan teaching noncredit English classes. Living stipends are provided, travel expenses are covered in part and housing is generally arranged.

The YMCA is a decentralized movement with a national headquarters—called the YMCA of the U.S.A.—in Chicago. Local Ys make their own policy and program decisions. The International Division of the YMCA of the U.S.A. works with seven regional offices—each devoted to a different part of the world—to coordinate and facilitate programs with Ys in the U.S. and abroad. Another office in New York, called International Program Services, organizes camp-counselor, trainee and other youth exchanges and a foreign-student arrival service.

Professional Staff: About 7,000 professionals nationwide work for the Y. Of these about 100 work on international programming at least half-time, some full-time. The YMCA of the U.S.A. has about 10 professional positions in its international division, none entry-level. The International Program Services office in New York has a professional staff of nine. About 50 persons are teaching in OSCY positions. Overseas, Ys are staffed by foreign nationals.

Qualifications: Qualifications vary according to position. OSCY teachers must be fluent in English, have an interest in teaching English as a second language and Asian studies and must have personal qualities such as tact and flexibility. Some background teaching English as a foreign language and volunteer experience with the YMCA or a similar organization are preferred. Knowledge of Japanese or Chinese is helpful but not required. Applicants must have a BA. Sponsorship by an American Y is not required.

For U.S.-based positions, the YMCA hires a wide variety of people with diverse backgrounds. For international programming positions, degrees carry less weight than experience in community development, recreation, camping, teaching and physical education. Languages such as Chinese, French, German, Japanese and Spanish are useful but not required. Previous international experience is highly desirable.

Internships: The New York office takes about five interns each summer. Positions are not paid, although some are work-study. Most interns are undergraduate students who help with administrative—not clerical—work. Interns should have international interests. Foreign language capabilities are also helpful.

Application Procedure: For internships, contact the Internship Coordinator at:

> YMCA International Program Services
> 356 West 34th Street
> New York, NY 10001
> (212) 630-9600

For OSCY, you must apply by March 15 for Taiwan, by March 15 or November 15 for Japan. Write to: Overseas Service Corps (OSCY), International Division. For more information, write to:

> YMCA of the U.S.A.
> 101 North Wacker Drive
> Chicago, IL 60606
> (312) 977-0031

For a list of Ys that sponsor international programs or to learn more about their international activities in general, write to the International Division at the address above.

YOUTH FOR UNDERSTANDING (YFU)
Washington, DC

YFU is an educational organization that organizes international exchange programs for high-school students. Students live with host families and are normally enrolled in local secondary schools. Programs last a semester, summer or year and usually start during the early summer. In 1991 approximately 3,700 students lived with host families in the U.S., and more than 1,800 American students became members of families in Europe, Latin America, Asia and the Pacific. In addition 800 students took part in programs offering exchanges between countries other than the U.S.

At present, YFU sponsors programs in Australia, Brazil, Canada, Chile, Colombia, Uruguay, Venezuela and throughout Western Europe. Its International Center in Washington, DC, and 10 regional offices are aided by many volunteers who screen candidates, provide orientation, promote the program and raise funds.

Professional Staff: YFU employs a full-time staff of 152 professionals in Washington and in its 10 regional offices. In the past year 10 people were hired. Overseas work is carried out by foreign affiliates, staffed by locals.

Application Procedure: Professionals seeking employment at YFU should send a resume to the Personnel Director. Applications for internships should be addressed to the Volunteer Office. Students interested in exchange programs may write or call YFU to receive application materials. To be considered, students must submit a completed application and a nonrefundable $50 application fee. The application procedure may originate with the Washington, DC, headquarters or with one of the U.S. regional offices. For information, write to:

Youth for Understanding
3501 Newark Street, NW
Washington, DC 20016
(202) 966-6800

Chapter Eight

FEDERAL AND STATE GOVERNMENT

FEDERAL GOVERNMENT

In the best of times and the worst of times, there is only one employer who offers over 300,000 openings a year: the U.S. government. The federal government employs more than 3 million people in jobs ranging from forest ranger to Foreign Service Officer. Federal employees work in every state and in almost every country. Their job is not only to serve their country, but to help run it.

About 80,500 U.S. federal civilian employees work abroad, including 7,000 for the Department of State. They fill almost as many different occupations abroad as they fill at home.

In addition to jobs overseas, the government offers many opportunities for internationally oriented work in the U.S. This chapter describes some of these federal positions.

Many federal agencies that deal primarily with national issues or implement domestic programs also have international departments or divisions. For example, the Department of the Interior's Fish and Wildlife Service began projects in 1989 in India and Pakistan researching herpetology, birds of prey and grasslands. The Department of Housing and Urban Development exchanges information with other governments, such as Canada, China and Mexico. This chapter concentrates on some of the larger offices and agencies with international employment opportunities, but there are many others. Some careful research could uncover additional unique job opportunities.

There are many ways to apply for work with the federal government. This chapter explains the procedures, but applicants should also contact the government's central personnel office, the Office of Personnel Management (OPM), or the agency to which they are applying for further information.

COMPETITIVE AND EXEMPTED SERVICE

The majority of federal jobs are offered through the *competitive service*, a frequently lengthy applicant-screening process run by OPM. In an effort to woo talented people, the government has changed some of its personnel practices, including application procedures. For example, some agencies now have "direct hire authority" for jobs that are hard to fill or exist in only in that particular agency. The best way to find these jobs is by watching federal job-vacancy advertisements. Another way to bypass the OPM process is through the Outstanding Scholar Program: students with a grade-point average of 3.5 or higher (out of 4.0) or who rank in the top 10% of their class may send applications directly to individual agencies. Appointees are guaranteed at least a GS-6 salary.

Although, more and more, individual agencies' personnel offices are responsible for announcing vacancies, rating applicants and training employees, the OPM is still a good place for most people to begin a federal job search by filing out an application, Standard Form 171 (SF-171). An OPM rating enables you to apply for positions in many different agencies, and 57% of all federal jobs are still offered through the competitive service, down from 81% in 1987.

OPM accepts applications for federal employment based on the number of jobs government agencies estimate they will need to fill in various locations over a period of time. Before applying to OPM, it is important to find out whether applications are being accepted in your field. If applications are being accepted, OPM will rate and rank your application and keep it on file. A government agency with a position to fill requests OPM to forward the names and backgrounds of the three top-rated applicants. The agency reviews the files and then hires the applicant[s] of its choice.

Some agencies are *exempted* from the competitive service and to apply for a job, you must follow that agency's application procedures. About 46% of the positions at the Department of State (including Foreign

Service Officers), 40% at the Department of Justice, 35% at the International Development Cooperation Agency, 22% at the U.S. Information Agency, and all the positions at the Library of Congress, the Federal Reserve Board, the Nuclear Regulatory Commission and intelligence agencies, congressional offices and committees are exempted, as are all teaching jobs at the Department of Defense Dependent Schools.

Some positions are *noncompetitive*, for example, attorneys, chaplains, summer interns, high-level policymakers or appointees, certain handicapped people and people claiming a 10-point Veterans Preference (disability, Purple Heart, widow, widower, spouse or mother of a veteran). These applicants do not need an OPM rating.

FEDERAL JOB HUNTING

Industrious federal jobseekers will not wait for OPM to call them. They will monitor job openings and also send applications to individual agencies, preferably with a resume and letter addressed to the head of the department or person responsible for hiring. Taking an activist approach to job-hunting is important: never assume that simply because you registered with OPM you will get a job. Registering is only the beginning.

OPM offices around the country provide information about which forms to fill out and which, if any, of the 30 tests to take. They also administer the tests. A Federal Job Information Center (FJIC) or one of the 54 regional or area OPM offices is probably located near you: check the white pages in the telephone directory under U.S. government.

When applying for a federal job, contacts—including friends, family, alumni, lobbyists and, for congressional positions, constituents, congressional staffers and party contributors—are extremely helpful. Keep in touch with acquaintances who work in the agency where you would like to work and publicize your job search to friends. Never forget to follow up on your inquiries, stay in touch with potential employers, cultivate contacts, network and consult vacancy announcements. It can take time to be hired for a federal job, so plan accordingly.

HOW TO FIND JOB INFORMATION

The *Federal Career Directory* published by the government informs prospective applicants about federal employment and answers the most commonly asked questions. It lists every federal agency and department and indexes job opportunities by major field, but it does not list vacancies. It can be ordered for $31.00 (Stock Number 006-000-01339-2) through the Government Printing Office:

Superintendent of Documents
U.S. Government Printing Office
Washington, DC 20401
(202) 783-3238

Most agencies have personnel offices or a "Dial-a-Job" recording that can inform you about existing vacancies for that agency. Each area OPM office publishes a "Federal Job Opportunities List" of openings in that locality and Washington, DC. This mimeographed list is updated every two weeks and is available free from OPM. Because most regional offices have automated telephone systems, applicants usually have to go in person to pick up a copy.

OPM's main switchboard telephone number is (202) 632-9594; its General Information Office number is (202) 653-8468, and the number of OPM's Federal Job Information Center is (202) 606-2700.

Federal Career Opportunities is a private publication that monitors and lists over 3,500 federal job openings, most at grades 9 through 12. (See Chapter Thirteen for further details.)

AFTER YOU ARE HIRED

If you are hired, you will be offered a temporary, term, or career-candidate appointment. Temporary appointments are for one year or less and offer few benefits. Term appointments are offered for work on a specific project that runs for more than one year and less than four years; such appointments carry benefits. Career-candidate appointments give full benefits and, after a three-year probationary period, lead to career status, which provides the most job security.

There are a number of federal pay systems designed to make government service comparable to the private sector. The *General Schedule (GS)* covers most professional, technical and other white-collar employees. OPM administers the entire GS scale, which runs from GS-1, the lowest grade, to GS-15. Each of the 15 grades has 10 pay steps. For GS-1 through GS-12, increases are normally given at one-, two- or three-year intervals. Raises at GS-13 to GS-15 are awarded purely on merit. The pay scale is indexed to the cost of living in order to maintain the government's competitiveness with the private sector. Raises may now vary by locality within the U.S., based on cost of living, and some overseas employees receive allowances to compensate for exchange rates.

Mid-level employees are hired at GS-9 to GS-12. Qualifications are generally four years of college or three years of professional work plus at least two years of specialized professional experience and/or an MA. For GS-11 and GS-12, three years of professional experience and three years of specialized experience are necessary. A graduate degree may be substituted for only two years of specialized experience.

Senior-level positions, GS-13 through GS-15, are normally filled by promotion and at least six years of "difficult" experience plus graduate education are required.

CENTRAL INTELLIGENCE AGENCY (CIA)
Langley, VA

The CIA has primary responsibility for the clandestine collection of foreign intelligence, for conducting counterintelligence abroad and for the research and development of technical collection systems. The CIA produces political, military, economic, biographic, sociological, and scientific and technical intelligence to meet the needs of national policymakers. It is one of the largest U.S. government agencies, offering internationally related employment opportunities for persons of almost every background and academic discipline.

The CIA has five directorates. The Intelligence Directorate uses information from a variety of sources to develop an analysis to be used by policymakers, including the President, Congress and the Cabinet. Issues addressed are as diverse as international terrorism, arms-control monitoring, narcotics trafficking, world energy, or technological breakthroughs. The Operations Directorate collects intelligence through personal contacts, which may range from clandestine meetings with foreign nationals to sessions with U.S. citizens who want to volunteer information about foreign events. The Science and Technology Director-ate develops and operates strategic technical collection systems. The Administration Directorate is the business arm of the organization. The Deputy Directorate for Planning and Coordination (DDP&C) coordinates the development of policies in all management areas, manages the agency's strategic-planning process, and fields any nonroutine official inquiries about the agency's activities.

Opportunities to serve abroad exist throughout the agency. Some personnel, including overseas intelligence and communications, spend a considerable portion of their careers overseas.

Qualifications: The CIA employs both experienced professionals and recent college graduates. All must be U.S. citizens. The Intelligence Directorate employs specialists, usually with advanced degrees, in the fields of economic and political analysis; scientific and military assess-ment; and geographic and biographic studies. Employment in the Operations Directorate as an overseas intelligence officer requires a minimum of a BA in a field such as economics, international relations, international finance or political science. Other desired qualities include foreign language capabilities or aptitude, a strong interest in foreign affairs and good communication skills. Individuals over 35 cannot be considered. The Science and Technology Directorate seeks engineers (electrical, aeronautical, optoelectronic), physical scientists, systems analysts, photo scientists and other individuals with a strong scientific or technical background. The Administration Directorate needs communications officers (radio operators, field engineers), security officers, computer specialists, logisticians, accountants and personnel officers. Many of these individuals serve on a rotational basis in the other four directorates.

Training Program: The CIA has a comprehensive training program. Depending on your assignment, you will be provided with classroom or on-the-job training ranging from one week to two years. The two-year Career Training (CT) program is like management training programs of other large corporations. The program is very competitive and selective.

Internships: The Agency participates in the Cooperative Education Program (CO-OP) for undergraduates majoring in accounting, computer science, economics, engineering, international studies, languages, photo science and printing/photography. CO-OPs must be able to work a minimum of three terms and maintain a 2.75 GPA. (See Chapter Ten: Internships.)

The Minority Undergraduate Studies Program provides promising students, particularly minorities and people with disabilities, the opportunity to gain practical summer work experience to complement their academic studies. Highly motivated students are encouraged to apply for this program early in their sophomore year.

The Graduate Studies Program is available for those students entering their first or second year of graduate study. Students must be studying fields related to agency requirements. Historically, most graduate fellows have interned in the summer; however, fall and spring internships are an option. Applications should be submitted nine months before the desired work period.

Application Procedure: The agency employs individuals from almost every academic discipline. Resumes are reviewed for all available openings and often referred to regional recruitment centers for action. The CIA will respond within 30 days to those judged to be of further interest. Qualifying applicants must undergo an extensive background investigation, medical evaluation and polygraph examination before a firm offer of employment can be made. The procedure may take six to nine months. For more information about career opportunities, write to:

Central Intelligence Agency
PO Box 1255 GCWA
Pittsburgh, PA 15230

CONGRESSIONAL RESEARCH SERVICE (CRS)
The Library of Congress
Washington, DC

Established in 1800 to provide Congress with library resources, the Library of Congress has since become America's national public library, stocking a copy of nearly every book and periodical published in the U.S. and abroad. CRS, a department of the library, provides nonpartisan research and reference assistance exclusively to Congress. CRS's Foreign Affairs and National Defense Division responds to congressional queries concerning U.S. foreign policy and national defense issues. Other CRS divisions also employ international specialists in the areas of economics, environment, international law, area studies and science policy.

Professional Staff: There are approximately 60 professionals within the Foreign Affairs and National Defense Division. One professional was hired permanently in the past year. Total CRS staff numbers 850.

Qualifications: A BA with some expertise in foreign affairs, defense policy or area studies is preferred. Previous work experience in related fields is required except at the entry level, but a graduate degree (MA, MIA, PhD) or superior academic achievements may be substituted for some or all of the required specialized experience. The number of years experience required depends on the position for which the candidate applies. Neither knowledge of a foreign language nor willingness to travel or live abroad is necessary. Employees must be able to work under deadlines and write objectively. U.S. citizenship is required.

Internships: Paid Foreign Defense Policy Research Associate positions are available for graduate students and college graduates for three-month terms. Interns respond to "quick-response" basic research requests on foreign and defense policy. Qualifications include a BA with emphasis on foreign or defense policy or the social sciences and at least three months previous research or graduate training in related fields. Interns must be nominated by their school or a policy research organization. Invitations are sent four times a year to nominating institutions composed of a core group of schools and research organizations, the list of which rotates on a regional basis to include a variety of organizations.

The Graduate Recruit Program is designed to recruit the nation's best graduate students—particularly minority students—for firsthand experience in a public policy organization and offers the possibility of being converted to a permanent position after completion of the initial temporary appointment. Initial appointments of 120 days begin the summer after completion of the recruit's current academic year. Appointments are made at a grade level commensurate with the selectee's educational qualifications. Conversion to a permanent position is based on a number of factors, including a participant's work performance, the need for staff members in certain subject areas, the availability of funds and vacancies.

The Student Volunteer Program places students throughout CRS, depending on the needs of specific divisions. To work in the Foreign Affairs and National Defense Division, prospective interns should have work experience and be studying some aspect of international relations. These nonpaying internships are offered throughout the year to students enrolled in an accredited educational program. Approximately five students are hired for summer positions and fewer for positions during the year.

Application Procedure: Information about the Foreign and Defense Policy Research Associate program can be obtained from:

> Foreign Affairs and National Defense Division
> Central Research Section, Room LM 315
> Congressional Research Service
> The Library of Congress
> Washington, DC 20540
> (202) 707-5064

Information about the Graduate Recruit Program can be obtained from:

> Graduate Recruit Program
> CRS Administration Office, LM-208
> Library of Congress
> Washington, DC 20540
> (202) 707-8803

Persons interested in the Student Volunteer Program should send Standard Form 171 (SF-171) with a cover letter stating date of availability. It is recommended that a course listing also be enclosed. The address is:

Administrative Officer
CRS Administration Office
The Library of Congress
Room LM 208
Washington, DC 20540
(202) 707-8803

CRS is exempt from the OPM system. Applications for specific vacancy announcements must be addressed to:

The Library of Congress
Human Resources Operations Office
Room LM 107
101 Independence Avenue, SE
Washington, DC 20540

CRS has a computerized recruiting system that generates mailings of vacancy announcements to potential applicants. Inquiries about this system or about other employment-related issues should be addressed to:

ALERT
CRS Administration Office
The Library of Congress
Washington, DC 20540
(202) 707-8803

DEPARTMENT OF AGRICULTURE (USDA)
Washington, DC

The Foreign Agricultural Service (FAS) is the USDA division which represents U.S. agricultural interests overseas, reports on international agricultural production and trade, promotes exports of U.S. farm products and works to improve world trade conditions. FAS is responsible for the policy direction, organization and management of a worldwide network of agricultural counselors, attachés and trade officers.

While FAS is charged with the task of coordinating USDA's role in international food aid programs, three fourths of its annual budget is allocated to building markets overseas for U.S. farm products. This includes funding for all FAS trade and attaché offices overseas, as well as its work with U.S. commodity associations on cooperative promotion projects. Remaining monies fund other trade functions, including the gathering and dissemination of market information and trade policy efforts.

Professional Staff: The Foreign Agricultural Service operates with a staff of 300 analysts, negotiators and marketing specialists in Washington, DC, and 125 representatives overseas. Stationed at 80 posts, these overseas personnel are responsible for covering more than 100 countries. FAS hired 26 professionals in the last year.

Qualifications: FAS seeks college graduates and applicants holding MA, MS and PhD degrees with expertise in agricultural economics, international economics, economics or international marketing. Foreign language skills are preferred but not required.

Training Program: The Foreign Agricultural Service accepts 25 to 30 trainees annually for a two- to three-year program.

Internships: Interns serve as economic assistants. Applications should be addressed to the Recruitment Specialist at the address below.

Application Process: Send all inquiries and applications to:

> Recruitment Officer
> USDA/Foreign Agricultural Service
> 14th and Independence Avenue, SW
> Room 5627-S
> Washington, DC 20250-1000
> (202) 720-1587

DEPARTMENT OF COMMERCE
Washington, DC

The Department of Commerce serves to strengthen domestic economic development, promote international trade and foster U.S. competitiveness in world markets. The department's foreign activities are managed by the International Trade Administration (ITA). ITA is divided into four subagencies: international economic policy, international trade development, import administration, and the U.S. and Foreign Commercial Service (U.S. & FCS, discussed separately below).

INTERNATIONAL TRADE ADMINISTRATION

> The **International Economic Policy** sector, seeking to increase U.S. trade and investment, identifies foreign barriers to commerce and takes part in negotiations to remove them. To this end, IEP gathers information on trade, investment and economic issues, and monitors worldwide

market conditions. IEP also gives seminars to U.S. businesses on the trade regulations of foreign countries.

> The **International Trade Development** sector provides major American industries with a point of contact in the Commerce Department to assist them in international trade. It handles the promotion of trade and focuses on the concerns and problems of individual industries. ITA publishes several booklets, guidebooks and the magazine *Business America*, all of which address international trade issues.

> The **Import Administration** provides an authority to which American manufacturers can turn to determine if they are the victims of unfair trade practices, and which can prescribe a remedy for them. The administration helps insure the competitiveness of American free-market businesses with foreign firms enjoying the benefits of government subsidies or protected home markets.

Professional Staff: All ITA staff serve domestically, except for Foreign Commercial Service Officers (see below). There are approximately 1,250 professionals. During the past year, 200 were hired.

Qualifications: ITA needs staff with academic backgrounds in international business, international economics and finance and international affairs. Students with specialized graduate degrees are recruited through the Cooperative Education Program (CO-OP) and through the Presidential Management Interns program. Knowledge of German, Japanese, Russian and other languages spoken in countries with which the U.S. has a high volume of trade is preferred, and a willingness to travel is required.

Internships: Internships are available through the Cooperative Education Program only. (See Chapter Ten: Internships.)

Application Procedure: To be considered for ITA domestic positions one must submit a SF-171 and be referred by the OPM. Applications should also be sent directly to:

> U.S. Department of Commerce
> ITA Personnel
> 14th and Constitution Avenue, NW,
> Room 4808
> Washington, DC 20230
> (202) 377-3808

> **Foreign Commercial Service** (FCS), the overseas arm of the U.S. and Foreign Commercial Service, is charged with representing and aggressively supporting U.S. commercial interests abroad. Created in 1980, the FCS works with governments, embassies and business representatives to increase the number of U.S. firms involved in international trade. Teams of FCS officers stationed in 127 cities in 68 major U.S. export countries worldwide conduct market research to identify potential trade opportunities for U.S. firms. FCS also resolves trade conflicts, conducts trade promotion activities overseas and assists U.S. firms in obtaining bids from major foreign contractors.

The U.S. Commercial Service (USCS), the domestic arm of US & FCS, works closely with U.S. businesses on international trade strategies. In addition, it assists small and medium companies in every phase of the exporting process.

Professional Staff: FCS employs 170 FSOs abroad and maintains a staff of 50 in Washington. USCS trade specialists operate 68 district offices throughout the U.S. Each office has a staff of five to seven. FCS hired 30 FSOs in the past year, and hires 10 to 15 trade specialists annually.

Qualifications: All FCS applicants must be willing to live overseas for the most of their careers. Half of the positions in 68 countries are filled by people formerly in private business, such as large multinational corporations and export firms. These people need not take the Foreign Service examination. FCS also accepts mid-level candidates through the Lateral Entry Program. Candidates must have prior Department of Commerce experience in a non-FCS position as a GS-12 or higher, have served abroad in a non-FCS capacity or be FSOs employed by the departments of State or Agriculture, USIA or AID. FSOs with an MA in business, international affairs or international business are preferred.

FCS also accepts newly appointed FSOs, known as Career Candidates. These are people who have passed the Foreign Service exam (including the Commerce "functional" section) and are thus qualified to become FSOs. Career Candidates must attain minimum professional proficiency in a foreign language.

Finally, the FCS annually appoints between five and ten people to noncareer positions overseas. These temporary jobs are reserved for candidates with specialized backgrounds in non-European languages, area studies or technical fields. Tours of duty normally last from two and five years. Applicants need not take the FSO exam and are eligible to apply for permanent FSO positions through the Lateral Entry Program. Of the 30 FSOs hired in the past year, 15 were noncareer appointments.

Training Program: US&FCS employees participate in an extensive training program to strengthen their language skills. Training lasts between six months and two years, depending on the language. During this time, employees become familiar with Department of Commerce issues and learn about the major issues affecting their work.

Application Procedure: Lateral entry personnel and non-career candidates participate in the FCS's own selection, commissioning and tenure process. Career candidates are selected from the FSO personnel registers maintained by the Department of State. (See Department of State entry for more information and addresses.) Persons desiring more information regarding FCS positions should contact:

> Attn: Recruitment
> U.S. and Foreign Commercial Service
> Office of Foreign Service Personnel
> Department of Commerce
> 14th and Constitution Avenue, NW
> Room 3813
> Washington, DC 20230
> (202) 482-3133

NATIONAL TELECOMMUNICATIONS AND INFORMATION ADMINISTRATION (NTIA)

In 1978 the Department of Commerce acquired the functions of the White House Office of Telecommunications Policy and subsequently created NTIA. In response to rapidly evolving technology and global competition, NTIA has recently placed greater emphasis on its Office of International Affairs (OIA). OIA works to maintain the efficient functioning of international trade in telecommunications and information services and products.

In conjunction with the Department of State and the Federal Communications Commission, OIA assesses foreign communication policies, reviews regulatory and legislative affairs, presents U.S. positions before international forums and oversees participation by the Communication Satellite Corporation, or COMSAT, in international organizations.

Professional Staff: Of the 311 staff members at NTIA, 110 are professionals. Twenty professionals were hired in the past year. Some 120 people are stationed at the NTIA laboratory in Boulder, CO. OIA has a staff of 20, all of whom are stationed in the U.S.

Qualifications: NTIA hires for entry- to senior-level positions. A college degree without significant experience is usually sufficient for an entry-level job, although approximately 40% of the employees have a master's degree and previous work experience in areas such as overseas telecommunications marketing and negotiations. A communications degree per se is not essential. NTIA hires professionals, primarily engineers, attorneys and economists, from the private, academic and government sectors.

Application Procedure: Interested persons should contact:

> Chief, Management Division
> U.S. Department of Commerce/NTIA/H-4890
> Washington, DC 20230
> (202) 377-1800

DEPARTMENT OF DEFENSE
Washington, DC

The Department of Defense is responsible for providing the military forces—the Army, Navy, Air Force and Marine Corps—to protect U.S. security. Nearly half of all government employees work for the Department of Defense: it employs more people overseas than any other government agency. The following is a sample of the many DoD offices involved in the international arena.

> Office of the Assistant Secretary for International Security Affairs (ISA). This office develops and coordinates DoD policies and research in international political, military and economic affairs. It studies general problems of international security, arms control and disarmament, administers foreign military aid and oversees arms sales. The ISA also provides policy guidance for U.S. military missions and for U.S. representatives to international conferences and organizations. ISA negotiates and monitors agreements with foreign bodies concerning equipment, facilities, operating rights and the status of forces. ISA does its own research into alternative defense strategies and policies for dealing with international security problems.

> Office of the Assistant Secretary for International Security Policy (ISP) is responsible for policy development on issues concerning nuclear forces, the North Atlantic Treaty Organization, East-West security negotiations, space, and multilateral negotiations on arms reductions. ISP is also charged with implementing nonproliferation mandates and other treaties and agreements, as well as general oversight of DoD activities regarding European security arrangements.

> Office of the Assistant Secretary for Special Operations and Low-Intensity Conflict. This office is responsible for advising the Undersecretary of Defense (Policy) in planning and preparation for special operations and low-intensity activities. Policy planning covers such areas as reconnaissance, unconventional warfare, foreign internal defense, civil affairs, psychological operations, counterterrorism and antiterrorism, search and rescue, and other activities.

Professional Staff: While many employees are military personnel, DoD also has approximately 375,000 civilians in Washington, DC, across the U.S. and around the world on its payroll.

Qualifications: The DoD and each one of its military services have their own personnel offices which recruit separately. The requirements for each vary, but generally a strong background in international affairs, history and economics is a good beginning. You will find certain offices have specific needs: for example, the Office of Secretary of Defense, Director for Personnel and Security, not only uses foreign affairs specialists but also program and budget analysts and security specialists. Several offices within the DoD provide the necessary training.

Internships: Most DoD offices have summer or semester internships available for high school, undergraduate and graduate students. Interns usually work as researchers or assist desk officers. Contact each office separately for availability and requirements.

Application Procedure: An application for employment in the Defense Department is made by presenting a completed SF-171 form to appropriate personnel. It is a good idea to call ahead to the particular office to which you are applying for current job openings. This will enable you to request the appropriate application forms and tailor your SF-171 to that job description. Because of the decentralized recruiting process and the organizational complexity of the DoD, applying to this federal department requires extra patience and perseverance.

> Office of the Secretary of Defense
> Directorate for Personnel and Security
> Room 3B347, Pentagon
> Washington, DC 20301
> (202) 697-9205

Department of the Army
Personnel and Employment Services, USA
Room 3D727, Pentagon
Washington, DC 20310
(202) 694-8494

Department of the Air Force
HQ USAF (1947 ASG/MPKS)
Room 5E871, Pentagon
Washington, DC 20330-6420
(202) 695-9028

Department of the Navy
Secretariat/HQ CPO
Civilian Personnel Office
Room 4D434, Pentagon
Washington, DC 20350-1000
(202) 697-6181

DEPARTMENT OF JUSTICE
Washington, DC

The Department of Justice is the nation's highest law enforcement agency
and the government's source of legal advice. The Attorney General, who
heads the department, has ultimate authority over the Federal Bureau of
Investigation (FBI), the International Criminal Policy Organization—U.S.
National Central Bureau, the nation's prisons, parole boards, Assistant
Attorneys General, U.S. Attorneys, U.S. Marshals, the Foreign Claims
Settlement Commission and the Immigration and Naturalization Service
(INS). The department also represents the U.S. government before the
U.S. Supreme Court.

Justice has one division monitoring criminal behavior and five
divisions that monitor compliance with civil laws. The five are antitrust,
civil, civil rights, land and natural resources, and tax. To a certain extent,
criminal matters may be handled in these divisions as well. The antitrust,
civil and criminal divisions handle most of the department's international
work.

The Foreign Commerce Section of the antitrust division preserves and
fosters competition in U.S. foreign trade; develops policy on issues of
trade and international antitrust enforcement; serves as division liaison
with competitive agencies of foreign governments and international
organizations; and coordinates the division's review of applications for
export trading-company certificates.

The civil division, divided into three branches, represents the government in all types of civil proceedings in foreign courts. The Commercial Litigation Branch defends the country's international trade policy; the Federal Programs Branch handles suits challenging the propriety, lawfulness or constitutionality of various governmental programs or actions; and the Torts Branch handles international aviation and admiralty law, including accidents and lawsuits, on behalf of the government.

The civil division's Office of Immigration Litigation conducts civil trial and appellate litigation under the immigration and naturalization laws, and represents the U.S. in civil suits brought against the INS.

There are two sections in the criminal division involved with international matters. The Office of Special Investigations detects, identifies and takes appropriate legal action leading to the denaturalization or deportation of Nazi war criminals. The Office of International Affairs supports the department's legal divisions, the U.S. Attorneys and state and local prosecutors in enforcing international criminal justice pursuant to treaties concerning extradition, mutual legal assistance and prisoner exchange. The office also engages in treaty negotiations in concert with the State Department.

Professional Staff: Six of the antitrust division's roughly 300 attorneys are employed in its Foreign Commerce Section, handling internationally related cases. Civil has 533 attorneys, 25 of whom are in the International Trade Office. Of the criminal division's 397 attorneys, 45 coordinate activities dealing with foreign governments in the Office of International Affairs. In the past year, antitrust has hired 40 lawyers, civil approximately 100, and criminal has added 109 attorneys.

Qualifications and Application Procedure:

> **U.S. Attorney's Offices.** Application for employment in any of the 93 U.S. Attorneys' Offices should be mailed directly to the office that you wish to have consider your application. For specific application information and mailing addresses, refer to the Legal Activities brochure available from the Office of Attorney Personnel Management at the address below.

> **Attorney General's Honor Program for New Attorneys.** The Attorney General's Honor Program, which is highly competitive, serves as the department's recruitment program for all its organizations except the U.S. Attorneys' Offices and the FBI. Each year, 100–125 attorneys are chosen from a field of outstanding third-year law students, graduate law students (who apply in the fall of their

last year of graduate law study) and judicial law clerks. Selection is based on academic achievement, law review and other publication work, extracurricular activities, such as moot-court competition, legal aid, legal clinic and student bar association, and summer and part-time employment. An Honor Program attorney who has recently graduated from law school enters at the GS-11 level. A judicial law clerk or Honor Program attorney with a graduate law degree enters at the GS-12 level. All JD graduates must pass a bar examination within 14 months of entry on duty and thereafter maintain an active bar membership. Honor Program applications must be received by the Department of Justice by the last Friday in September preceding the year of desired employment. All application materials should be sent to the Office of Attorney Personnel Management at the address below.

> **Experienced Attorney Program.** To apply for an attorney position with Justice under the Experienced Attorney Program, an applicant must be an active member of the Bar Association and have at last one year experience after graduation from a law school approved by the ABA. Resumes are accepted year round. Specific eligibility requirements under this program are outlined in Justice's Legal Activities brochure.

> **Summer Law Intern Program.** The Summer Law Intern Program is highly competitive. Each year the Justice Department hires about 125 students who have completed their second year at an ABA-approved law school. These appointees are assigned a GS-7 level. A number of first-year students are also hired at a GS-5 level. Summer law intern positions may also be offered to a law-school graduate the summer between graduation and the commencement of a judicial clerkship; graduates are usually assigned a GS-11 level, although the grade level is at the discretion of the employing organization. At the end of the summer, Summer Law Interns receive a performance appraisal. A favorable report greatly enhances an intern's chances for entrance into the Attorney General's Honor Program upon graduation from law school. Applications are due at the Department of Justice during September of the year preceding the desired year of employment. Specific deadlines are listed on the application form. All applications should be sent to the Office of Attorney Personnel Management at the address below.

For a Legal Activities brochure and application for the Attorney General's Honor Program for New Attorneys, Experienced Attorney Program, or Summer Law Intern Program, write to:

U.S. Department of Justice
Office of Attorney Personnel Management
Room 6150 Main
10th Street and Constitution Avenue, NW
Washington, DC 20530
(202) 514-3396

Under the Experienced Attorney Program, resumes may also be submitted directly to the division of desired employment. Addresses are available in the Legal Activities brochure.

FEDERAL BUREAU OF INVESTIGATION

The FBI handles its recruitment independently.

IMMIGRATION AND NATURALIZATION SERVICE

INS is responsible for administering and enforcing the immigration, naturalization, refugee and asylum laws concerning non-U.S. citizens. INS also provides information and counsel to those seeking U.S. citizenship, protects U.S. national borders against unlawful entry by aliens, and works in conjunction with other agencies to stem the flow of illegal drugs across international borders. In addition to maintaining regional offices in Vermont, Minnesota, Texas and California, INS has staff in various foreign locations, including Italy, Ireland, Britain, Greece, Germany, India, Russia, South Korea, Thailand and Mexico. Although INS employs some 350 attorneys, most positions are those of border patrol agent, immigration inspector, immigration examiner, criminal investigator, deportation officer or detention enforcement officer.

Professional Staff: INS staff includes over 18,000 individuals, including approximately 90 who are stationed overseas. Hiring power is dispersed among the four regional offices and the Washington, DC, district office. In the past year, 1,700 INS officers were hired, 3 of whom are stationed overseas.

Qualifications for Non-Attorney Positions: Although a college degree or previous work experience is not required, knowledge of immigration and nationality rules, laws, regulations and procedures is desired. Ability to speak Spanish, German or Italian is helpful.

Application Procedure: Interested persons should contact:

Headquarters Personnel Office
Room 6024
Immigration and Naturalization Service
425 I Street, NW
Washington, DC 20536
(202) 514-2530

DEPARTMENT OF STATE
Washington, DC

The State Department provides the background information and recommendations on which U.S. foreign policy is based, implements Administration policies and maintains diplomatic relations with over 155 nations The department is responsible for operating embassies and consulates overseas. It runs the Foreign Service selective examination process, which tests and chooses U.S. citizens to become Foreign Service Officers (FSOs). FSOs serve overseas for the departments of State, Commerce, Agriculture and the United States Information Agency (USIA).

Embassies, which range in size from fewer than 10 employees to a few hundred, are run by an ambassador, a deputy chief of mission and a "country team." The team usually includes four State Department section chiefs, as well as a staff from the USIA, the departments of Defense, Agriculture, Labor and Commerce, the Agency for International Development and the CIA. The four State Department sections, staffed by FSOs, are Administrative Affairs, Consular Affairs, Economic Affairs and Political Affairs. The Administrative Affairs section looks after budget and fiscal planning; general services such as shipping and maintenance; personnel management; security; communications and information systems. Consular Affairs issues visas, assists Americans overseas and helps those who wish to immigrate to the U.S. This section offers FSOs the opportunity for direct contact with foreign citizens and requires strong foreign language skills and sensitivity to foreign cultures. The Economic Affairs section monitors and reports on economic and scientific trends and events that may affect U.S. interests. FSOs in this section must maintain contact with foreign business representatives, bankers, economists and politicians as well as represent U.S. economic interests in negotiations. The Political Affairs section communicates U.S. policies on issues, seeks support for these issues and interests, and interprets the effect of political events. FSOs in this section are required to establish close contact with leaders of foreign countries. Area or labor specialists (either FSOs or from the Department of Labor) and technology experts are especially active in the Political Affairs section.

The Washington-based structure is divided into six geographic bureaus—African Affairs, Inter-American Affairs, East Asian and Pacific Affairs, European and Canadian Affairs, Near Eastern Affairs and South Asian Affairs—and 16 functional bureaus, which work to formulate policy, resolve conflicts and relay information to U.S. officials.

The functional bureaus focus on human rights and humanitarian affairs; intelligence and research; international communications and information policy; international narcotics; international organizations; legal matters; legislative and intergovernmental affairs; international communications and information policy; the oceans, environment and science; personnel; consular affairs; economics and business; administration; diplomatic security; politico-military affairs; public affairs; and refugee programs.

> Foreign Service

Professional Staff: The State Department has a staff of over 17,000 Americans, and also employs about 10,000 local nationals abroad. Two thirds of its American employees serve abroad in some capacity, although only about 4,500 are FSOs. Of the remaining staff, 4,400 are specialists (see qualifications, below). At any time, approximately 1,750 FSOs are based at Washington, DC, headquarters, helping to run the bureaus, and 2,750 officers are overseas. An average of 200 new FSOs are appointed each year by the State Department and 50 by USIA.

Qualifications: Overseas positions are filled by both commissioned FSOs, who have taken and passed the Foreign Service selective examination process, and foreign service specialists. These specialists are noncommissioned and work as secretaries; communications, budget, fiscal, security, engineering and personnel officers; physicians and nurses; construction engineers; facilities maintenance specialists; and couriers and information management officers. Specialists need not take the written Foreign Service exam, but they must go through a separate competitive selection process, and are paid on the FS schedule.

To qualify for FSO (commissioned) positions in the departments of State or Commerce or USIA, one must compete in a rigorous selection process. Of the 15,000 candidates who take the Foreign Service examination annually, some 200 become FSO appointees. Some enter the Foreign Service directly from college or graduate school; others have a background in education, business, law, science, journalism, military or government.

Over 65% of recently appointed FSOs have graduate degrees and 45% speak a foreign language. An advanced degree usually enhances the chance of obtaining a higher entrance classification. The median age of the entry-level FSO career candidate is 30.

The following fields of study are useful for the Foreign Service: history, political science, economics, international relations, geography and English. However, demand is increasing for scientists, systems analysts, language and area experts, business managers and industrial development specialists.

The Foreign Service places a strong emphasis on the ability to speak and write persuasively. Although knowledge of a foreign language is not required for employment, the departments of State and Commerce and USIA are particularly interested in persons with knowledge of languages such as Arabic, Chinese, Japanese and Russian. All accepted FSOs must acquire acceptable language competency before being stationed abroad. They usually attend language classes at the Foreign Service Institute in Washington, DC, for one to six months before leaving for their posts, where their language skills are periodically reviewed. Language competency is usually a factor in promotion and is a requirement for achieving tenure.

Career candidates are appointed at FS levels 6, 5, or 4 on a scale where FS-9 is the lowest (roughly equivalent to GS-5). Appointment at the FS-5 level usually requires an MA and the FS-4 level requires an MA and 18 months experience in a field closely related to one's foreign service work. A limited number of mid-level entry appointments may be made at the FS-2 or -3 levels, with FS-1 appointments being rare. Foreign Service specialists are appointed at FS-9 to FS-2, depending on their function, background and experience.

The Foreign Service Selective Examination: All FSO entry-level applicants, regardless of qualifications, must take and pass the Foreign Service written and oral examinations as the first steps toward being considered for an appointment.

Written examination. The Foreign Service written examination is given once annually, in either November or December, at numerous locations throughout the U.S. and overseas. Applicants must be U.S. citizens at least 20 years old on the date of the examination, and must be available for worldwide assignment. Applications for the exam must be filed by early October. The written examination, which takes a half day, is in three parts: the knowledge test measures the candidate's depth and breadth of knowledge and understanding of a range of subjects important to perform the tasks required of an FSO; the English expression test measures basic written English ability; and the third section is the biographic information questionnaire. Successful candidates must achieve passing scores in all three categories. There is no limit on the number of times the written exam may be taken. Tests may be retaken in consecutive years.

Oral assessment. An all-day oral examination may be taken only by those candidates who have passed the written examination. A panel of examiners rates individuals on their performance in the following timed exercises: an oral "démarche exercise" to measure knowledge of current political, cultural and economic issues; a written exercise designed to test ability to analyze and organize information into summary form; group exercise consisting of a simulated negotiation; and a written managerial/problem-solving exercise.

All candidates are notified in writing of their test results and the panel's decision. Candidates recommended by the panel must pass a security background investigation and submit the following information within six months: background investigation forms, medical clearances, university transcripts and a 1,000-word autobiography. A final review panel considers performance on the written examination and oral assessment as well as the autobiography, education, employment history and background investigation.

Potential applicants should be warned that this entire process can take up to a year. Acceptable candidates are placed on rank-order registers for possible appointments to USIA as information/cultural FSOs, to the Department of Commerce as commercial FSOs, to the Department of State as administrative, consular, economic or political FSOs. After 18 months on the rank-order register, the names of candidates not selected for appointment are removed.

Training Program: Before being posted overseas, new FSOs undergo three to seven months' instruction in language, area studies and other functional fields at the Foreign Service Institute in Washington, DC. State Department career candidates might initially have to spend two years performing consular work in a variety of geographical and functional areas prior to specialization. Officers remain career candidates for not more than five years of service, during which time they are constantly being evaluated, before receiving tenure as FSOs. Not all career candidates receive tenure, either due to the evaluation of their performance or because they choose to leave the Foreign Service.

Application Procedure: Applications for the Foreign Service examination process are available at university placement offices, regional offices of the OPM or by writing to:

Recruitment Division
Department of State
Box 9317
Rosslyn Station
Arlington, VA 22219
(703) 875-7490

The *Foreign Service Careers* booklet, which describes the work of the Foreign Service and the selection process and contains sample exam questions, may be obtained by writing to the above address. A State Department-sanctioned study guide may also be ordered.

> Civil Service

Surprisingly, the Washington-based, non-foreign-service arm of the Department of State is considered a small government agency. Professional civil service positions based at the Department of State number 2,000. Some positions are administrative—personnel, management, budget, finance and systems. Other positions include language interpreters (see Chapter Six), engineers, attorneys (see information of Office of the Legal Adviser, below), accountants and foreign affairs specialists (positions reserved for experts in international relations). Most civil service employees are permanently stationed in Washington.

Professional Staff: There are some 2,000 civil service professional working in the domestic bureaus of the State Department. Roughly 200 civil service professionals are hired annually.

Qualifications: Candidates for junior-level positions (starting at GS-5 level) should have either three years of general work experience or at least a BA. They are normally eligible for junior positions in personnel, management, budget, finance, engineering and accounting. For each year of work experience, and for graduate study, applicants may enter at a higher GS level. Administrative professionals normally work their way up through the Civil Service Merit Promotion Program. Under this program, current federal employees are given preference for vacancies. Supervisory positions at the GS-13 level and above are normally filled through competitive procedures in conjunction with the Office of Personnel Management.

Foreign affairs specialists usually enter the State Department at GS-9 to GS-15. Grades 9-11 are for foreign affairs specialists with MIAs or MAs and some professional work experience. At grades 12-15 most foreign affairs specialists hold a PhD and have teaching experience and expertise in specialized international affairs areas. Those interested in qualifying for these jobs are urged to register with OPM, and then submit a resume or SF-171 along with their civil service rating to the Office of Civil Service Personnel at the State Department. (See application procedure, below, and discussion of OPM.)

Internships: (See Chapter Ten.)

Application Procedure: Applicants interested in working in a Department of State domestic position should contact:

> U.S. Department of State
> Civil Service Personnel
> PO Box 18657
> Washington, DC 20036-8657
> (202) 647-7284

For a recording of civil service positions currently available with the Department of State, call the Department of State Employment Information Office at (202) 647-7284.

OFFICE OF THE LEGAL ADVISER

The Office of the Legal Adviser provides legal advice on all matters pertaining to the work of the Department of State, both in the U.S. and abroad. The office helps formulate and implement foreign policy and promotes the development of international law and international institutions upholding the law. Its specific responsibilities include drafting, negotiating and interpreting international agreements and representing the U.S. in meetings of international organizations, conferences and tribunals, such as the International Court of Justice.

The office's regional and functional bureaus correspond to those in the State Department. Attorneys are assigned to one bureau, but are encouraged to rotate every two to three years. While members of the office are under the direct supervision of the Legal Adviser, they usually submit their views directly to their "clients" (that is, other State Department offices).

Professional Staff: The office currently has 100 attorneys. Four attorneys are stationed overseas (in Berlin, Bonn, Geneva and The Hague) to provide legal advice on matters requiring quick response. The office usually hires between 8 and 10 attorneys each year.

Qualifications: All applicants must have law degrees and be members of (or applicants to) a state bar association. Each fall, the office hires third-year law students and recent law-school graduates who have served as judicial clerks. Some international legal training and a knowledge of one or more foreign languages are desirable. Junior attorneys must pass the bar examination within three years. Competition is fierce for these entry-level jobs.

The Office of the Legal Adviser hires all new attorneys for a three-year period; before the end of that period, a determination is made, based on performance, as to whether the attorney will receive a permanent appointment. Attorneys usually enter the Department of State at the GS-11 level.

The office hires attorneys laterally with one to five years of legal experience. For some positions, relevant international experience and a knowledge of one or more languages are desirable. Lateral attorneys are hired at grades 12 through 15, depending on experience.

Because of budgetary restrictions, on-campus recruiting and interviewing of second- and third-year law students are carried out only at a small number of top law schools each year.

Internships: The office employs five or six second-year law students each summer. The interns are assigned to various bureaus and generally perform the same work as the junior attorneys. Interns are paid at grade 9.

The office also accepts up to five third-year law students each fall or spring in the extern program. No remuneration is provided and externs must receive academic credit for their work. Externs generally assume responsibilities similar to those of the summer interns.

Application Procedure: Applications for all types of employment must consist of a comprehensive resume, including academic background, scholastic standing, honors, professional experience, active duty military experience, publications, references and law school transcripts. Applications should be sent to:

> Personnel Officer
> Office of the Legal Adviser/L/EX
> Room 5519
> Department of State
> Washington, DC 20520-6417
> (202) 647-8323

ENVIRONMENTAL PROTECTION AGENCY (EPA)
Washington, DC

The EPA develops, implements and enforces environmental and health protection regulations. It also conducts and coordinates research and monitoring in support of efforts to abate and control pollution. Broad goals covering the spectrum of EPA's international activities and programs include the protection of the global atmosphere; the protection of marine and polar environments; the conservation of species, habitats and ecosystems; sustainable development; the protection of human and ecosystem health; and the development of technical assistance for underdeveloped and developing countries.

The Office of International Activities (OIA) manages, coordinates and facilitates EPA involvement in international policy and technical activities. Nearly every program office and region is actively engaged in the international arena, and OIA serves as the focal point. OIA's mission abroad is to consult with UN and other international organizations' specialized agencies, foreign governments and U.S. embassies on a wide range of environmental and health issues. EPA does not hire staff specifically for overseas work but sends staff abroad on technical assistance assignments.

Professional Staff: About 60 professional staff are assigned to OIA. Due to budgetary constraints, OIA has limited hiring opportunities but has hired 12 professionals in the past year. Total EPA staff is more than 18,000.

Qualifications: Required background includes a BA, BS or MA in international affairs, environmental science, public policy or related fields, plus country-specific or multilateral expertise as well as expertise in international environmental issues such as deforestation, global climate change, trade and ocean pollution. Advanced graduate degrees in these fields are also helpful. Foreign language ability is useful, but is not required. Usually some previous experience is necessary. Overseas experience, although not essential, is a plus. Employees must be willing to travel abroad on one- to two-week assignments.

Internships: OIA is presently unable to hire any interns, but it benefits from the assistance of interns funded by other EPA offices.

Application Procedure: For information about when OIA may resume hiring, contact:

Program Operations Division
Office of International Activities
A-106
Environmental Protection Agency
Washington, DC 20460
(202) 382-2474

FEDERAL MARITIME COMMISSION
Washington, DC

The Federal Maritime Commission is responsible for regulating the waterborne foreign and domestic commerce of the U.S., assuring nondiscrimination in U.S. international trade and guarding against monopolies and collusion in U.S. waterborne commerce. In conjunction with the State Department, the commission works to eliminate discriminatory practices by foreign governments against U.S.-flag-bearing commerce. It investigates and analyzes shipping practices, reports on trade conditions, accepts or rejects tariff filings, and coordinates overseas shipping through its contacts with foreign embassies.

Professional Staff: Of the 140 professional staff, 2 were hired in the past year.

Qualifications: The commission primarily hires applicants with a law degree or an undergraduate or graduate degree in economics or maritime studies. Neither previous work experience nor knowledge of a foreign language is necessary for employment.

Application Procedure: Persons interested in a position with the Federal Maritime Commission should send applications to:

Personnel Office
Federal Maritime Commission
800 North Capitol Street, NW, 9th Floor
Washington, DC 20573
(202) 523-5773

FEDERAL RESERVE SYSTEM
Washington, DC

In functioning as the central bank of the U.S., the Federal Reserve System is responsible for formulating monetary policy, maintaining the commercial banking industry in sound condition and responding to both domestic and international financial needs. The system is supervised by the Board of Governors, which grants authority to member banks to establish branches in foreign countries and to invest in foreign banks. It also has the authority to regulate and supervise corporations and banks engaged in international banking. These international functions are managed by the board's Division of Banking Supervision and Regulation.

The monitoring and analysis of economic and financial developments abroad is conducted by the board's Division of International Finance. Current interests of this department include international banking regulations, the international monetary system and the relationship of foreign exchange to U.S. monetary policy.

Professional Staff: Of the 815 economists, financial and business analysts, attorneys, computer analysts and other specialists, the Federal Reserve System has hired 11 economists, 24 financial analysts and banking specialists, 26 research assistants and 13 computer specialists in the past year. Fifteen people were recently added to the international department.

Qualifications: Positions require at least an undergraduate degree in economics or finance. Persons with an MBA, JD or PhD have a better chance of being hired. No previous work experience is required for entry-level positions. Economists are hired at all levels depending on training and experience. Some research-assistant positions in economics or a related field are available for persons with a BA or MA.

The board is also interested in accredited attorneys, and law experience in a financial or consumer field is valuable. Law-school graduates who have worked on law review or have legal-writing credentials are highly desired.

The board also has a data-processing division, which employs computer programmers and analysts with a background in economics and statistical methodology. Board-sponsored training helps strengthen skills in these areas.

Internships: Summer or semester internship positions are available for PhD candidates in economics. Interns assist economists with research activities.

Application Procedure: Persons interested in an internship should forward their resume, a writing sample (preferably an economics term paper), transcript and three letters of recommendation from economics professors to the Recruitment, Planning and Placement Manager at the address below. Inquiries pertaining to professional positions should be directed to the Division of Personnel:

Board of Governors of the Federal Reserve System
Mail Stop 156
20th Street and Constitution Avenue, NW
Washington, DC 20551
(202) 452-3880 or (800) 448-4894

Those applying for professional positions must complete an application form (not an OPM form), available from the above address, or submit a resume.

INTER-AMERICAN FOUNDATION (IAF)
Arlington, VA

IAF is a government corporation funded by Congress and the Inter-American Development Bank and mandated to give financial support to social, economic and cultural development projects in more than 25 countries of Latin America and the Caribbean. IAF's development program has been supported by grants exceeding $100 million.

IAF's grants typically provide credit, training and technical assistance to poor farming organizations. Special IAF initiatives assist minorities, rural landless, women, youth and Native Americans and assess government policies affecting these groups. Because of IAF's broad mandate, small size and independence, it has the flexibility to accept grant proposals submitted by indigenous organizations otherwise excluded from federal aid programs. The average grant is $120,000.

Professional Staff: IAF employs 77 people, 3 of whom were hired in the past year. Only U.S. citizens are hired. There are no overseas offices.

Qualifications: An undergraduate degree in Latin American studies, economics, sociology, anthropology, international relations, a foreign language or business is useful, and most employees have an MA or PhD in one of these fields. Knowledge of Spanish, Portuguese, French or Creole is required. Previous field experience in Latin American development is necessary for employment. Employees must be willing to travel.

Internships: Graduate students with proficiency in Spanish, French or Portuguese are eligible for unpaid semester or summer-long internships. A typical assignment would be research and analysis of special short-term projects.

Application Procedure: Internship applications should be addressed to the Fellowship Officer. Job applicants should write to the Director of Personnel:

> Inter-American Foundation
> 901 North Stuart Street
> 10th Floor
> Arlington, VA 22201
> (703) 841-3800

INTERNATIONAL DEVELOPMENT COOPERATION AGENCY (IDCA)
Washington, DC

IDCA is the umbrella agency responsible for policy planning, policy-making and policy coordination for much of U.S. development work. It consists of three autonomous agencies, the U.S. Agency for International Development (AID), the Overseas Private Investment Corporation (OPIC) and the Trade and Development Program. IDCA has a very small staff and does not hire entry-level candidates. Its staff of 40 consists mainly of PhDs.

U.S. AGENCY FOR INTERNATIONAL DEVELOPMENT (AID)

AID was created by Congress in 1961 to administer the foreign economic assistance programs of the U.S. government. It operates from headquarters in Washington, DC, through field missions and representatives in approximately 70 developing countries in Africa, Asia, Europe, Latin America, the Caribbean and the Near East. AID development assistance includes agriculture, food and nutrition, family planning and health, education and human resources, energy, environment, natural resources and private enterprise. Through the Economic Support Fund, AID helps promote economic and political stability in regions where the U.S. has special security interests. AID also provides relief assistance to victims of natural disasters.

Professional Staff: The Washington, DC, headquarters employs 2,629 professionals (GS-9 and above), of whom 1,260 are stationed in Washington, DC, the rest overseas. Staff stationed abroad are responsible for planning and managing AID-supported projects and advising foreign government leaders and their staffs on development issues. Some AID field staff work with U.S. embassy personnel. AID hired 49 for their Foreign Service staff in the past year.

Qualifications: U.S. citizenship is required for employment, as is good health and availability to work anywhere. AID positions include agriculturalists; agricultural economists; commodity-management officers specializing in developmental economics, trade or commerce; educators and health, population and nutrition experts; housing/urban development specialists; and program and project-development officers who assist in managing AID programs and have financial management, developmental economics or international relations training. Most AID officials have graduate degrees, often PhDs.

Knowledge of French, Spanish, Arabic, Hindi or other languages used in developing countries is preferred upon entry and is required for tenure. Two years work experience in developmental or cross-cultural issues or a relevant technical field is required. Although previous professional overseas experience is not essential, it is an asset. Willingness to travel or live abroad is required for employment, as officers spend most of their careers abroad.

AID personnel overseas include both FSOs and civil servants, but the FSOs are not recruited, tested or ranked through the Department of State's Foreign Service selective examination process. Instead they go through an interview process with AID officials.

Training Programs: The International Development Intern (IDI) Program is the agency's entry-level program. It trains men and women to become Foreign Service Officers and assume positions of planning, implementing and managing AID's economic assistance activities overseas. AID normally recruits officers for positions in financial management, administrative management, agriculture/rural development/natural resources, contract/commodity management, education/human resources development, health/population/nutrition, housing/urban development, program economics and private enterprise, program and project development.

All positions require a BA or BS as well as two years of relevant professional experience; some require a graduate degree. Language proficiency is not required but is an asset. Applicants must be U.S. citizens dedicated to a career in international development to be spent, for the most part, overseas.

Selection for the IDI program is highly competitive. Candidates are screened initially to make certain they meet academic and work experience qualifications as well as the qualifications for an occupational specialty. Those passing the initial screening are asked to address four questions pertaining to general development issues in a second screening. Their responses together with the SF-171 forms are reviewed and rank-ordered by a technical review committee made up of Foreign Service Officers.

Following the second screening, the most qualified applicants for each occupational specialty are invited to come (at their own expense) to Washington, DC, for an interview. They will be asked to participate in a case-study exercise and a structured interview with another technical review committee made up of FSOs, including employees in the relevant job specialty. Interviews cover technical qualifications as well as managerial, interpersonal and communications skills and other factors.

Following the interview, applicants will, once again, be rank-ordered and the candidates with the highest scores will be scheduled for an IDI orientation class. All candidates must obtain security and health clearances and be subject to reference checks prior to entering on duty in the Foreign Service.

Training begins in Washington, DC, with formal group instruction. That is followed by a comprehensive, individually tailored on-the-job training program for up to one year in Washington. The purpose is to familiarize the intern with the requirements of the position, the operation of the geographic bureaus and the work of the field mission to which they will be assigned. This program is followed by several months of language training, if needed.

On-the-job training in Washington is followed by a year of training overseas designed to give interns the opportunity to become knowledgeable about the overall functions and specific operations of the field missions, to do substantive work and to assume increasing responsibilities relevant to their target positions.

Internships: Internships are available.

Application Procedure: AID personnel overseas are both FSOs and civil servants, but the FSOs, as indicated above, are not recruited, tested or ranked by the Department of State but instead go through an interview process with AID officials.

Because of budgetary constraints, hiring is limited. Resumes and applications will be reviewed as positions become available. AID occasionally hires mid-level personnel, although the number will be minimal in the foreseeable future. For professional positions and the IDI program, send your SF-171 to:

Agency for International Development
FA/HRDM/R
SA-02, Room 50
515 22nd Street, NW
Washington, DC 20523-0114
(202) 663-2400
IDI program: (202) 663-2639

OVERSEAS PRIVATE INVESTMENT CORPORATION (OPIC)

Although owned by the U.S. government and operated under the GS system, OPIC is organized as a private corporation with policy control vested in a board of directors composed of representatives from the private sector and from government agencies.

OPIC promotes U.S. private investment in more than 100 developing nations and emerging democracies. It provides political-risk insurance to protect investors against expropriation, currency-conversion conflicts and civil strife. OPIC also offers investment loans, guarantees and counseling to assist business projects that contribute to the economic or social development of the host country.

Professional Staff: The professional staff of 91 is headquartered in Washington, DC. There are no overseas offices, although travel within the U.S. and abroad is required of most professional staff. In the past year, 12 people were hired.

Qualifications: Most of OPIC's responsibilities fall within the fields of insurance, finance, investment development and law. Ideally, applicants should have a graduate degree in business, law, international relations or economics, and should have experience in one or more of these fields. Proficiency in a foreign language is preferred although not a prerequisite for employment. Many OPIC professionals have had several years of previous work experience in the private sector or government.

Internships: Internships are available for graduate and undergraduate students. Depending on the student's field of study, an intern may be placed with the legal, finance, investment development or insurance departments. Internships are available on either a semester or summer basis. While most internships are unpaid, paid internships generally are available in the summer.

Application Procedure: To apply for an internship, contact the Intern Program Coordinator at the address below. Employment applications and inquiries should be directed to the Director, Human Resources Management, at:

> Office of Human Resources Management
> Overseas Private Investment Corporation
> 1615 M Street, NW
> Washington, DC 20527
> (202) 336-8683 (Internships)
> (202) 336-8682 (Jobline)

NUCLEAR REGULATORY COMMISSION (NRC)
Washington, DC

The NRC is mandated by the Atomic Energy Act of 1954 to develop, implement and enforce standards governing domestic civilian nuclear activities. It also manages the licensing and regulation of nuclear energy facilities and materials with the objective of protecting public health, safety and the environment. The Office of International Programs has two primary functions. It designs programs for the licensing of nuclear exports and imports and the implementation of international safeguards. It also cooperates with regulatory organizations of other countries and participates in the exchange of information concerning nuclear regulations and safety.

Professional Staff: Of the 2,100 professional staff members of the NRC, 220 were hired in the past year. The international office has a staff of approximately 20 professionals. Turnover is very low.

Qualifications: Approximately 45% of NRC employees are scientists and engineers. Other employees include professional administrators and lawyers. Over 70% of the staff have at least a BA, while many hold advanced degrees in technical fields such as engineering, physics and, most important, nuclear engineering. Previous work experience should be in utilities, engineering or nuclear fields.

Internships: Undergraduate and graduate students may participate in the Cooperative Education Program (CO-OP). Students are placed in program offices and assist in the full range of activities, such as reviewing operating and construction licenses and assisting in inspections. Graduates with engineering or science degrees may participate in a technical intern program. The program comprises rotational and training assignments designed to provide maximum exposure to the work of the agency and a broad perspective concerning the role of the NRC and its various offices in the regulatory process. Positions are paid. For more information about the CO-OP program, see Chapter Ten.

Application Procedure: Persons interested in professional positions or internships may contact:

> U.S. Nuclear Regulatory Commission
> Office of Personnel, W-468
> Washington, DC 20555
> (301) 492-8234

OFFICE OF SCIENCE AND TECHNOLOGY POLICY (OSTP)
Washington, DC

Created during the Ford Administration, OSTP is charged with providing scientific, engineering and technological analysis and judgment for the President with respect to major policies, programs and plans of the federal government. OSTP advises the executive on issues of national concern, including the economy, health, foreign relations, national security, energy, resources and the environment.

Professional Staff: The office's staff of 40 is divided into four broad divisions: Policy and International Science and Technology; Life Sciences; Physical and Engineering Sciences; and Industrial Technology. Each division is headed by an associate director and has a maximum staff of six. An assistant director, two analysts and two secretarial staff fill out the division, with the remaining employees in administrative roles. In the last year, three people were hired, one for the Policy and International Science and Technology Division.

Qualifications: Most OSTP professionals have PhDs in scientific, public policy and technical disciplines, although some have JDs. The office seeks generalists rather than specialists because of the number and variety of issues dealt with by OSTP, and the frequency with which the issues change.

Application Procedure: Write to the Administrative Officer at:

> Office of Science and Technology Policy
> New Executive Office Building
> Washington, DC 20506
> (202) 395-7347

PEACE CORPS
Washington, DC

The Peace Corps was established by Congress in 1961 to promote world peace and friendship between the peoples of the U.S. and the developing world. Its objectives are to help people of developing countries meet their needs for trained personnel and to help promote mutual understanding. The Peace Corps has expanded greatly in recent years, with the fragmentation of the Eastern bloc and the emergence of many new countries.

The Peace Corps consists mainly of volunteers who serve two-year tours abroad. Volunteers have backgrounds in a variety of fields and are often hired without any significant previous experience or graduate study. Because of this, the Peace Corps is an excellent training ground for people interested in salaried work abroad with nonprofit organizations, with the Foreign Service or with an international organization.

Volunteers serve in the following positions: maternal and child health; family nutrition; fresh-water fisheries; agriculture; teacher training; math, science and language education; vocational training; conservation and energy; small-business consulting; public administration; natural-resource development; forestry; and construction and architecture. Volunteers are currently working throughout Africa, the Caribbean, Central America, Asia and the Pacific and Eastern Europe.

In addition to its Washington, DC, headquarters, the Peace Corps has three recruitment centers, 16 area offices and offices in most countries where volunteers serve.

Professional Staff: Total overseas and domestic staff numbers 1,280. In addition, there are some 6,000 volunteers in over 90 countries. Volunteers receive health benefits, travel expenses, a monthly living allowance and a monthly remuneration of $200, paid following the tour of duty.

Qualifications: Applicants must be U.S. citizens at least 18 years old. The Peace Corps is currently in need of people with experience or degrees in agriculture, teaching English as a foreign language, health and nutrition, secondary math and science education, forestry, environment, and business/small-enterprise development.

The median age of current volunteers is 31. More than half are women. Over 10% of the volunteers are over age 50. Married couples are required to work together on assignments, though couples with dependents are rarely accepted. Many handicapped people have served as Peace Corps volunteers.

Training Program: Language proficiency and cultural awareness are essential for all volunteers. Three months intensive language training is conducted in host countries. Cultural studies familiarize volunteers with the history, customs and social and political systems of host countries.

Internships: The Peace Corps accepts undergraduates as interns in the U.S., primarily for office work. If an intern has a particular interest in one country, he or she may intern at that country desk within the office. These nonpaid internships are usually one semester in duration. Interns should be interested in international development and have strong oral and written communications skills. Students should send a SF-171, a resume, writing sample and transcript at least six weeks prior to the time they would like to begin.

Application Procedure: Internship and staff inquiries and applications should be addressed to:

> The Office of Personnel
> United States Peace Corps
> 4th Floor
> 1990 K Street, NW
> Washington, DC 20526
> (202) 606-3170

Volunteer applications should be sent to:

> Recruitment
> United States Peace Corps
> 1990 K Street, NW
> Washington, DC 20526
> (202) 606-3387

U.S. CONGRESS
Washington, DC

As the U.S. legislative process became more complex, with new players and regulations, the U.S. Congress personnel roster grew rapidly—from 6,500 in 1960 to 18,300 in 1980. With the passage of the Gramm-Rudman-Hollings balanced budget act in December 1985, however, the rapid growth slowed. Congressional staffs were capped at their 1985 levels, and were even encouraged to cut back, leading to a total congressional staff size of 17,000 in 1992. Nevertheless, elections and staff turnover occur every two years. People willing to "get in at the ground floor" and help out with an election campaign may find themselves with a job on "the Hill," as it is fondly called.

The most important qualification of a Hill staffer is experience on the Hill, so one entry-level job with a member of Congress might lead to a career. Taking an unpaid internship with an established member is standard practice for any college graduate trying to get a foot in the door, establish contacts and gain experience. For those with a specific in foreign affairs, the following information on internationally related congressional jobs may be helpful.

> House Committee on Foreign Affairs
Senate Committee on Foreign Relations

The Committee on Foreign Affairs of the House of Representatives is a standing committee composed of 46 representatives and 56 professional staff members. The Senate counterpart, the Foreign Relations Committee, consists of 19 senators and 37 professional staff members. The committees have primary legislative and oversight responsibility in matters relating to international affairs. Both committees have a number of subcommittees which propose, critique or modify legislation before it is submitted to the full House or Senate.

> Subcommittees

The House subcommittees focus on specific regions and issues—Africa; Asia and the Pacific; Europe and the Middle East; Arms Control, International Security and Science; Human Rights and International Organizations; International Economic Policy and Trade; the Western Hemisphere; and International Operations. Each subcommittee is composed of 10 to 14 representatives. Each House subcommittee has a staff of five or six professionals. The subcommittee chairperson and ranking minority member are responsible for hiring. Competition among area specialists for these positions is very strong.

The Senate subcommittees are: African Affairs; East Asian and Pacific Affairs: European Affairs; International Economic Policy, Trade, Oceans and Environment; Near Eastern and South Asian Affairs; Terrorism, Narcotics and International Operations; and Western Hemisphere. Each subcommittee has 5 to 10 members. Senate subcommittees did not have individual staff until March 1991; they now have one to three staff members each.

Professional Staff: There is usually turnover in congressional staff only after a congressional election, especially one which changes House or Senate majorities or precipitates a change in committee leadership assignments.

Qualifications: Most committee staff have a graduate degree in international relations, international economics or law. Work experience is not required but highly preferred.

Internships: The committees do not participate in any internship program because all committee employees require security clearances. However, interns working for the congressional offices of committee members may participate in committee legislative activity.

Most congressional offices take interns, for both summer and year-long positions. Some offer internships in foreign affairs, but these are few in number and are thus very competitive. A prospective Hill intern should always contact his or her senator or representative first. Referrals or letters of recommendation from constituents, Hill staff members, contributors or local politicians supporting the application for an internship are generally useful.

While almost no House members offer stipends to interns, Senate offices may pay a small allowance to interns with previous experience, outstanding academic credentials or good political connections. It is common on the Hill for interns to wait tables or take other night jobs.

> Other Committees

International affairs is among the concerns of several other congressional committees—Commerce, Education, Banking, Finance and Urban Affairs, Armed Services and Intelligence, to name a few. There are also several subcommittees which focus on a particular international issue. The chairperson and ranking minority leader of each committee or subcommittee have primary control over hiring, but other committee members and senior staff also have some input. Applicants considering such positions should familiarize themselves with the composition of the various committees and contact the offices of those legislators whose concerns are in accordance with their own interests. The membership and staff of congressional committees are listed in the current Congressional Staff Directory as well as in the *U.S. Government Manual.*

Although these committees may not hire people specifically for international work, they often seek applicants with backgrounds in international economics or banking. Committees receive as many as four to five applications per month; they only do substantial hiring every two years.

SENATORS' AND REPRESENTATIVES' OFFICES

The primary function of a member's staff is to track legislation before Congress and committees, research bills, answer correspondence from constituents, write speeches and newsletters and meet with people when the member is not available. While some offices maintain a permanent, but small, foreign relations staff, others have no foreign-affairs specialists. This usually depends on a particular member's committee assignments and interests. In general, a member's staff must work on a range of domestic and international issues.

Every member has a legislative assistant (LA) and an administrative assistant (AA). The LA handles all legislative matters for the member and initiates, tracks and answers questions about legislation. The AA oversees the staff and keeps the member informed about legislative and campaign functions. The support staff includes office managers, schedulers, secretaries, press assistants, equipment operators and caseworkers. Note: the division of labor in a congressional office is often blurry, and staff responsibilities are often due more to talents than to titles.

Qualifications: Most offices look for background in international relations, economics or law. Some members' offices hire college graduates for entry-level research positions. These positions may serve as recruiting ground for higher positions. Someone right out of college who is willing to work as a receptionist or unpaid intern in a member's office and learn the ins and outs could advance to legislative correspondent (keeping track of the member's correspondence) or even legislative assistant; loyalty is usually rewarded on the Hill.

Applicants for Hill jobs should keep in mind that knowledge of the legislative process and issues plus excellent writing and speaking abilities are as important as academic degrees. Previous campaign experience or local government work is also very useful.

Application Procedure: Each congressional office has complete hiring authority and can select individuals to fill positions from a variety of sources, including contacts. Both the House and Senate have a placement office which serves an employment referral service for congressional members, committees and administrative officers. Congressional offices submit job orders, indicating education, experience and professional requirements, to the placement offices. The offices screen applications and resumes and send them to the requesting office for review. The placement offices will process applications received by mail. However, applicants are advised to apply in person so that their backgrounds, career goals and objectives can be assessed in an informal interview. Because of the highly competitive environment, career counselors routinely urge applicants to conduct their own networking campaigns to enhance their chances for obtaining employment. A first step to Hill networking is to visit the delegation offices of one's state, since most members prefer to hire individuals from their home state.

Each Thursday the Senate Placement Office publishes the Senate employment bulletin, which is a blind listing of some of the positions listed with them. Senate offices seeking unscreened resumes often use this method of advertising. Copies of the bulletin may be obtained in the Senate Placement Office but will not be mailed to applicants. For more information contact:

House Placement Office
Office of the Clerk
U.S. House of Representatives
219 Ford House Office Building
Washington, DC 20515
(202) 226-6731

Senate Placement Office
SH-142B Hart Senate Office Building
2nd & Constitution Avenue, NE
Washington, DC 20510
(202) 224-9167

Committee addresses are:

Committee on Foreign Affairs
U.S. House of Representatives
2170 Rayburn House Office Building
Washington, DC 20515
(202) 225-5021

and

Senate Foreign Relations Committee
U.S. Senate
SD-423 Dirksen Senate Office Building
Washington, DC 20510
(202) 224-4651

The phone numbers and office addresses of senators and representatives are listed in the *Congressional Staff Directory.* The number of the congressional switchboard is (202) 224-3121.

Another job-hunting angle to cover is the party job placement offices. Although you cannot be assured of and should not rely on finding a job through these services, they are a possibility.

Democratic Study Group (DSG): The DSG publishes a job listing, similar to a want-ad section in a newspaper, as a service to help Democratic members and House committees fill openings on their staff. DSG is not an employment agency or a placement office. It simply announces job openings, collects resumes from job applicants for those openings and forwards the resumes to the office with the opening. It will not hold resumes on file. DSG will not read the job list, which is published every Tuesday, over the phone, nor will it mail it to job seekers. Copies may be obtained at the House Placement Office:

House Placement Office
Democratic Study Group Job Service
219 Ford House Office Building
Washington, DC 20515
(202) 255-5858

Republican House Study Committee (RHSC): The RHSC maintains a resume clearinghouse to assist Republican House members or House minority staff in filling vacancies. Resumes are kept on file for three months. Internships are also available through the committee. To have a resume placed in the RHSC roster, it must be submitted in person along with a questionnaire (available from RHSC) specifying the applicant's field of interest. When RHSC is notified of a vacancy, it forwards the appropriate resume(s).

Republican House Study Committee
433 Cannon House Office Building
Washington, DC 20515
(202) 225-0587

Senate Republican Policy Committee (SRPC): The SRPC is a legislative and research service organization serving all Republican Senators and their staffs. The committee circulates summaries of all major bills and amendments considered on the Senate floor, prepares an analysis of every roll call vote, and distributes other materials reflecting Republican points of view on legislative and national issues.

The SRPC is also one of several informal clearinghouses for information about employment in Republican Senate offices. The committee maintains a current resume bank, and also publishes a job applicant's guide with information on contacts in Republican offices and in leadership and legislative committees. To be included in the bank, applicants need to fill out a questionnaire and submit a current copy of their resume. Resumes are kept on file for three months. SRPC forwards resumes to offices with vacancies.

Senate Majority Policy Committee
347 Russell Senate Office Building
Washington, DC 20510
(202) 224-2946

U.S. ARMS CONTROL AND DISARMAMENT AGENCY
Washington, DC

The agency is charged with providing the President, the Secretary of State and other officials of the executive branch and the Congress with recommendations concerning U.S. arms control and disarmament policy and assessing the effect of these recommendations on foreign policy, national security policy and the U.S. economy.

The agency also provides scientific, economic, political, military, legal, social, psychological and technological information on which realistic arms control must be based. ACDA conducts studies and provides advice on arms-control and disarmament policy formulation; prepares for and manages—under the direction of the Secretary of State—U.S. participation in international negotiations on arms control and disarmament, as well as the implementation of existing treaties; disseminates and coordinates public information about arms control and disarmament; and directs U.S. participation in the formulation and implementation of such verification systems as may come about through negotiations.

Professional Staff: The Arms Control and Disarmament Agency operates with a staff of 228, of whom approximately 10 were hired in the past year.

Qualifications: ACDA uses specialists in foreign policy, international relations, history, arms control, former Soviet studies and weapons technology. Willingness to travel is required, as ACDA supplies U.S. delegations in Geneva and elsewhere with technical support. Knowledge of a foreign language, however, is not required.

Training Program: ACDA provides training for its employees to broaden their knowledge and skills.

Internships: Due to budget constraints, ACDA has been unable to offer internships for the past several years.

Application Process: To apply for or inquire about the status of the internship program, contact:

> Personnel Office
> U.S. Arms Control and Disarmament Agency
> 320 21st Street, NW
> Washington, DC 20451
> (202) 647-2034

U.S. INFORMATION AGENCY (USIA)
Washington, DC

The USIA was established in 1953 as an independent agency within the executive branch to increase understanding between the people of the United States and the people of other countries, and to foster foreign awareness of U.S. society, culture and values. A primary function is to advise U.S. officials on the climate of public opinion abroad regarding the U.S., to ascertain foreign attitudes regarding global policy issues and to prepare daily summaries of worldwide reaction to issues of concern to the U.S.

The USIA recruits FSOs through the Department of State. All overseas positions are staffed by FSOs. USIA FSOs, stationed at U.S. embassies and consulates, engage in political advocacy for American foreign policy. Career opportunities are for public-affairs officers, information officers, cultural-affairs officers, technical specialists, librarians and English teachers for the English Teaching Fellow Program.

The public-affairs officer is responsible for advising embassy staff on issues pertaining to the press, education, cultural affairs and local public opinion. The information officer's role as embassy spokesperson entails conducting seminars and briefings and developing publications for local media. The cultural-affairs officer maintains contact with the academic and artistic communities of the host country and administers educational exchange activities.

At any time, about one third of USIA's FSOs are working in the Washington, DC, headquarters. There are four other domestic-based divisions—broadcasting, programs, management, and educational and cultural affairs—which produce exhibits, magazines, radio shows, television programs, telecommunications activities and research reports. These divisions also administer USIA's education and cultural exchange programs and provide the technical and engineering support for USIA's programs. USIA maintains an extensive press service that transmits daily information to USIA posts abroad and to foreign media, publishes 14 magazines in 20 languages and helps foreign correspondents cover stories in the U.S..

The USIA operates an international broadcasting service, the Voice of America (VOA), consisting of news, editorials and cultural programs. VOA broadcasts via radio in 43 languages to most countries in the world. It plans to add 18 other languages to its broadcasts.

USIA runs an English Teacher Specialist Corps. Candidates must have an MA in applied linguistics or teaching English as a foreign language (TEFL) and five years TEFL experience. Candidates must be willing to teach at any post abroad. For more information, write to:

U.S. Information Agency
English Teaching Fellow Division (E/EC)
Room 304
301 4th Street, SW
Washington, DC 20547
(202) 485-2869

Finally, USIA operates a global television network, WORLDNET, which enables U.S. policymakers to speak with foreign dignitaries and journalists via "video dialogues" and teleconferences. This TV-film service has recently expanded quite dramatically. There are frequent openings for communications specialists with approximately six years experience. Entry-level openings also occur from time to time in broadcasting, television and film production. Technical personnel are hired on a steady basis.

Professional Staff: USIA employs 4,265 professionals in the U.S. and 5,000 in embassies and consulates worldwide. Of those working overseas, 1,000 are U.S. citizens; the rest are local nationals. The USIA FSOs assess foreign attitudes through the local media and disseminate information with Voice of America broadcasts, television programs and videotape distribution services. USIA has hired approximately 100 U.S. citizens in the past 12 months.

Qualifications: Candidates for FSO positions must have at least an undergraduate degree. The only qualification beyond that is a passing grade on the FS written exam. Fields of study or expertise are unspecified: USIA trains its employees in preparation for each assignment. The 60-day training program also includes language instruction. Proficiency in a foreign language is preferred, and is necessary for tenured positions.

Application Procedure: The normal entry route for career candidates is through the Foreign Service written examination. Information regarding the exam is obtainable through the State Department:

Foreign Service Examination
U.S. Department of State
Recruitment Division
PO Box 9317
Arlington, VA 22219
(703) 875-7490

For a recorded listing of domestic employment opportunities in USIA, call (202) 485-2539 and (202) 472-6909 for VOA positions. To apply for these positions, send a SF-171, the standard government application form, to:

>   U.S. Information Agency
>   Personnel—Room 518
>   301 4th Street, SW
>   Washington, DC 20547
>   (202) 619-4656

U.S. INSTITUTE OF PEACE
Washington, DC

Created in 1984, the U.S. Institute of Peace is an independent, nonprofit government corporation charged with strengthening the nation's capacity to promote international peace and the peaceful resolution of conflict. The institute accomplishes this task with a three-tiered approach: by expanding basic and applied knowledge about the origins, nature and processes of peace and war; by disseminating this knowledge to officials, policymakers, diplomats, and others engaged in efforts to promote international peace; and by supporting education and training programs and providing information for secondary and university-level teachers and students, as well as the general public.

The institute promotes research, policy analysis, training and education on international peace and conflict resolution. Its programs include grantmaking, fellowships, conferences, research projects, library services, civic education activities and publications. While maintaining the ability to assist Congress and the executive branch with research, analysis and information, the Institute of Peace has been insulated from the political realm of policymaking and political pressures. In fact, stated in its charter is the stipulation that of its 15-member Senate-approved governing board, no more than 8 may be from one political party.

Professional Staff: The U.S. Institute of Peace staff includes 47 permanent positions. There are no overseas posts. The institute has hired five professionals in the past year.

Qualifications: Excluding support staff, all Institute of Peace employees hold at least a bachelor's degree, and many hold advanced degrees. While the institute is largely regarded as an international relations or foreign policy organization, its staff has its work and educational grounding in very diverse fields.

Internships: The U.S. Institute of Peace offers summer internships to undergraduate and graduate students with an interest in international affairs and a desire to work on a variety of projects. Interns are paid.

Application Procedure: Applications for both internships and employment should be addressed to:

> Personnel Office
> U.S. Institute of Peace
> 1550 M Street, NW, Suite 700
> Washington, DC 20005-1708
> (202) 457-1700

U.S. INTERNATIONAL TRADE COMMISSION
Washington, DC

The U.S. International Trade Commission is a quasi-judicial, independent agency established by Congress with broad investigative powers on matters of trade. It furnishes studies, reports and recommendations involving international trade to the President, Congress and government agencies. The commission makes determinations of injury or threat of injury by imports to U.S. industry, and serves as the government's think tank on trade.

Professional Staff: There are approximately 300 professionals working for the U.S. International Trade Commission. Forty were hired in the past year.

Qualifications: A BA with some specialized experience in international trade is an alternative to a graduate degree. However, graduate degrees in international trade, economics, business or international law, business administration, international relations or finance are desired. Depending on the level of the position, some experience may be required. Neither knowledge of a foreign language nor willingness to travel or live abroad is necessary.

Application Procedure: Applications may be sent directly to:

> Office of Personnel
> U.S. International Trade Commission
> 500 E Street, SW, Room 314
> Washington, DC 20436
> (202) 205-2561

U.S. TRADE REPRESENTATIVE

The Office of the U.S. Trade Representative is responsible for developing and coordinating U.S. international trade, commodity and direct investment policy, and leading or directing negotiations with other countries on such matters. The U.S. Trade Representative is a Cabinet member who acts as the principal trade adviser, negotiator and spokesperson for the President on trade and related matters. Through an interagency structure, the USTR coordinates trade policy, resolves agency disagreements and frames issues for presidential decision. "USTR" refers both to the agency and to the agency head, the U.S. Trade Representative, who holds the rank of ambassador. USTR has two offices, one in Washington, DC, and the other in Geneva, Switzerland.

The major areas of responsibility of the Office of the U.S. Trade Representative include all matters within the General Agreement on Tariffs and Trade (GATT); trade, commodity and direct investment matters dealt with by international institutions such as the Organization for Economic Cooperation and Development and the United Nations Conference on Trade Development (UNCTAD); export expansion policy; East-West trade; international commodity agreements and policy; and import policy.

Professional Staff: USTR's overseas staff in Geneva consists of 10 professionals. One ambassador, a deputy, two secretaries, one attorney and five international economists operate the Geneva office. In Washington, DC, 145 professionals, with a support staff of 10, run the Office of the U.S. Trade Representative. In the past year, 21 people were hired.

Qualifications: The Office of the U.S. Trade Representative seeks individuals with degrees and experience in economics and law. All international economists hold at least a BS, but many are PhDs. The turnover in the Geneva office is very small, and new staff is selected from within the Washington office.

Internships: USTR offers unpaid internships to undergraduate and graduate students. Internships are available for the summer, one semester or the entire year. Interns help prepare briefing books and may sit in on meetings, but must also perform some clerical duties. Interested students should contact the Personnel Division at the address below.

Application Procedure: Address all employment inquiries to:

Human Resources Manager
Office of the United States Trade Representative
600 17th Street, NW
Washington, DC 20506
(202) 395-7360

STATE GOVERNMENTS

INTRODUCTION

In April 1989, Illinois became the first state to open a trade office in
the Soviet Union. The state's Chicago-based International Business
Division screens businesses in the state to identify those with the greatest
potential for the new Russian marketplace, and it then provides them with
specialized assistance from their Moscow team. In March 1993, Kentucky
sponsored a national "post-Rio Earth Summit" on implementing the goals
of the international conference.

The involvement of state governments in foreign affairs, economic
development and international exchange is expanding dramatically,
presenting new career opportunities for those interested in internationally
oriented jobs. Today, states' international activities are primarily
economic in nature, e.g. promoting exports, attracting foreign investment,
promoting tourism. International exchange programs are also common,
ranging from sister city/sister state initiatives to technical assistance for
fledgling democracies.

A few states, however, have taken on a much broader role—one that
was traditionally filled by the federal government. These states have
created offices staffed by international negotiators, recruiters and goodwill
ambassadors. They offer one-stop service for all the state's international
activities. These states' concerns run the gamut from the environment to
health and drugs because these are national and international problems
with strong local repercussions—and local problems with major national
and international implications.

Although only three states currently have such offices, others will
probably soon follow their example. Because they are the "first-of-their-
kind" and thus experimental, no two have the same structure.

**Kentucky's Legislative Office of Federal and International
Relations** is the bipartisan arm of Kentucky's Legislative Research
Commission. The office's main goal is to "provide up-to-date information
to Kentucky's legislature and to regulate international issues that impact
the state," according to the office's assistant director for international
relations and creator, William A. Miller. A unique aspect of the division

is its networking activities with groups such as the area's schools of international relations, the State Department, regional organizations like the OAS and the OECD, private-sector groups and UN agencies. The ties sometimes result in joint projects. Other international activities of the office include: hosting international visitors and providing them with orientation programs on the Kentucky legislative process and general information regarding Kentucky; serving as a clearinghouse to complement the information service of the legislative committees; offering translation and interpretation services; providing technical assistance to legislators, including the drafting of resolutions on international issues; preparing cultural background papers on foreign countries; and developing briefing sessions on emerging international issues.

The office has a full-time staff of two but it is able to draw upon the human resources of the Legislative Research Commission with a professional staff of 90, most of whom are researchers. Most of the Legislative Research Commission's professional staff have master's degrees in a variety of fields, including public health, public administration, social work, agriculture, etc. Not many have international affairs degrees, but a growing number of applicants do. Turnover is very low.

The **Florida International Affairs Commission (FIAC)** has a broad mandate as the primary entity responsible for the oversight and coordination of policies and activities relating to the international affairs of the state. The commission has the authority to make policy for the state relating to international trade, investment, commerce, education and cultural affairs. FIAC analyzes and evaluates state programs in education, tourism, trade and investment and makes recommendations to improve them. It also advises the legislature regarding proposed legislation and appropriations in the area of international affairs. The principal focus of the commission is to develop a comprehensive strategic plan for the state to follow in international affairs. Its main programs include: award of grant monies for international business promotion; conducting consular relations between the state and all foreign governments doing business in Florida; negotiating sister-state and sister-city agreements; acting as the state's international trade data resource and research center; creating and running international language institutes, in cooperation with Florida universities and colleges.

FIAC is part of the Executive Office of the Governor, who chairs the commission. Cabinet members and other state officers serve on the commission together with 26 members from the private and public sectors. FIAC has a professional staff of three with three administrative support staffers. All professional staff have some international or public-service work experience.

Hawaii's Office of International Relations used the State Department as a model to structure its office. Staff members, like desk officers, are assigned regions of the world. Although the office's activities are primarily policy-oriented (formulation and implementation), other missions include international literacy, coordination with other state agencies on international issues and providing current analysis on international issues.

The office was elevated to cabinet level in 1992, and the director is a cabinet member. The office has a professional staff of 12, all of whom have had international experience. Common backgrounds include international business and consulting, U.S. Foreign Service and the Peace Corps. Most are conversant in a foreign language.

Although there are not many entry-level positions in these offices, many do offer internships, often to students at local universities and colleges.

INTERNATIONAL TRADE

Since state governments began independently promoting themselves abroad in the early 1960s and 1970s, some international programs have grown sufficiently to support 10 or more overseas offices. International trade divisions in state development agencies and their overseas offices are the liaison between the state government, the state's companies and the foreign business sector. In 1990, state spending on international programs totaled over $90 million and employed approximately 1,000 people. Between 1985 and 1988, state international trade staffs increased by 50% and averaged 13 people employed in international trade development.

Generally, the purpose of the state international programs is to attract foreign investment and promote trade development, exports and international tourism. State representatives in the U.S. and abroad accomplish this by assisting at trade shows, arranging appointments, supplying trade leads, providing market information, accompanying trade missions, and offering foreign-language assistance.

Although most state international offices—both in the U.S. and abroad—have small staffs, staffing levels are rising and most personnel offices describe the international departments as growing. Most of the opportunities to work in these international divisions or programs are in the U.S. However, there are over 125 state offices worldwide employing approximately 400 U.S. citizens and foreign nationals. Backgrounds in international business, marketing, business administration, economics and international relations are most common. Following is a sample of state trade-promotion programs and their staffs:

ALABAMA DEVELOPMENT OFFICE
Montgomery, AL

The international division of Alabama's development office works with international industrial clients and international markets to promote the state for industrial investment and tourist travel, find markets for state products, and encourage shipping through the Alabama state docks. Alabama has three overseas offices, in Japan, Korea and Germany.

Professional Staff: Of the ten people who work in the international division of the Alabama Development Office, six were hired in the past year. Eight people are employed overseas, only two of whom are U.S. citizens.

Qualifications: A college degree in business, international business or economics is preferred. Willingness to travel is required as well as fluency in a foreign language, especially German, Japanese or Korean. A business background with experience in industrial development and/or international trade is also required. The office does have a six-month training program for college graduates with work experience.

Internships: Paid internships are available for college students and recent graduates. Applicants must have some computer and typing skills and should have taken some business or economics classes. Interns are asked to gather data, prepare proposals and do other computer work. Contact the internship coordinator.

Application Procedure: Persons interested in working as a professional at the Alabama Development Office should contact:

> International Development Director
> Alabama Development Office
> 401 Adams Avenue
> Suite 600
> Montgomery, AL 36160
> (205) 242-0400

CALIFORNIA STATE WORLD TRADE COMMISSION
OFFICE OF EXPORT DEVELOPMENT
Long Beach, CA

California's Office of Export Development works with California exporters and development organizations and European, Latin American and Asian importers and investors to facilitate trade relationships. It assists California exporters in finding new markets, encourages joint business ventures, attracts foreign investors to opportunities in California, and advocates free-trade practices. California has offices in Japan, Germany, Britain, Mexico and Hong Kong.

Professional Staff: California's international department currently employs five people in the United States.

Qualifications: Applicants with an undergraduate degree in business or international affairs are desired. Two to four years of experience in international or domestic marketing, especially in a high-technology area, are helpful. Applicants could be asked to travel.

Application Procedure: Persons interested in professional positions should contact the office manager at:

> Office of Export Development
> California State World Trade Commission
> One World Trade Center, Suite 990
> Long Beach, CA 90831-0990
> (310) 590-5965

COLORADO OFFICE OF ECONOMIC DEVELOPMENT
International Trade Office
Denver, CO

The Colorado International Trade Office seeks to encourage, promote and assist in the expansion of Colorado exports. It also attracts and assists international companies interested in setting up facilities in the state. Colorado has offices in Japan, Taiwan, Korea and several countries in Western Europe where staff help identify investment opportunities and encourage investment missions to visit Colorado.

Professional Staff: Colorado's International Trade Office has a professional staff of eight people, all of whom work in the U.S. Two professionals were hired in the International Trade Office in the last 12 months.

Qualifications: Applicants should have an undergraduate degree in international relations. Fluency in a foreign language, especially Spanish, is preferred but not required. Experience in international trade is also helpful. Willingness to travel is a requirement for employment with the office.

Internships: The International Trade Office offers paid internships for college and graduate students. The internships can be arranged for the summer or during the academic semester. Interns are involved in assisting trade specialists in projects and doing research on the international market. Some clerical work is part of the job.

Application Procedure: Persons interested in internships should contact the internship coordinator, and those interested in professional positions should contact:

> Director
> Colorado International Trade Office
> 1625 Broadway, Suite 680
> Denver, Colorado 80202
> (303) 892-3850

ILLINOIS DEPARTMENT OF COMMERCE AND COMMUNITY AFFAIRS
International Business Division
Chicago, IL

Illinois claims the leading role among the U.S. states in international marketing activities. The International Business Division's primary purpose is to provide small- to medium-sized Illinois businesses with export assistance. The division attracts foreign investment and helps to build trade relationships. It has offices in Belgium, Hong Kong, Brazil, Japan, China, Mexico, Canada, Poland and Hungary.

Professional Staff: Although the division is temporarily shrinking, it employs 24 professionals in the U.S. and 24 overseas. No one was hired in the last 12 months.

Qualifications: Applicants should have at least a college degree but preferably a graduate degree in international business or marketing. Willingness to travel and live abroad is required as is fluency in some foreign language. Previous employment is not necessary, but experience in marketing, sales, international business or management is helpful.

Application Procedure: Applicants interested in professional positions with the division should contact:

Assistant Manager
International Business Division
Illinois Department of Commerce and Community Affairs
100 West Randolph, Suite 30400
Chicago, IL 60601
(312) 814-7164

INDIANA DEPARTMENT OF COMMERCE
International Trade Division
Indianapolis, IN

The Indiana Department of Commerce promotes awareness in the international community of business opportunities in Indiana and helps state companies seek trade opportunities abroad. The International Trade Division has six offices overseas which promote investment, foreign trade and tourism in Indiana. These offices are located in Canada, China, Japan, South Korea, Taiwan and the Netherlands.

Professional Staff: The Indianapolis office employs ten people, of whom two were hired the last 12 months. The overseas offices employ a combined total of nine professionals.

Qualifications: Applicants should have a college degree and knowledge of trade or geographic regions. A willingness to travel and live abroad is necessary, and language proficiency is preferred. Chinese, German, Japanese and Spanish are most desirable. Some international work experience is required.

Internships: Graduate students are eligible for semester, summer and year-long unpaid internships. Internships involve assisting trade specialists. Interns are required to work a minimum of three days a week.

To apply for an internships or a professional position, write to:

Director, International Trade Division
Indiana Department of Commerce
One North Capitol
Indianapolis, IN 46204-2288
(317) 232-8845

IOWA DEPARTMENT OF ECONOMIC DEVELOPMENT
International Division
Des Moines, IA

The function of the International Division of the Iowa Department of Economic Development is to strengthen Iowa's presence in the international marketplace. The International Division has four offices that work together to promote Iowa's products and services overseas, attract foreign investment into the state and educate Iowa's businesses on topics related to exporting and doing business in other countries. The department has offices in Germany, Japan and Hong Kong.

Professional Staff: Iowa's Department of Economic Development employs nine people, four of whom are located overseas. Two professionals were hired for the international department in the last 12 months.

Qualifications: Applicants should have an undergraduate degree in international relations or business. Fluency in a foreign language is only required for overseas positions. Previous professional experience in exporting is required. Applicants must be willing to travel.

Internships: Semester and year-long paid and unpaid internship positions are available throughout the year. They are available to undergraduate students working toward a degree in international affairs.

Application Procedure: Persons interested in internships or professional positions should contact:

> Division Administrator
> Iowa Department of Development
> International Division
> 200 East Grand Avenue
> Des Moines, IA 50309
> (515) 242-4743

MISSOURI DEPARTMENT OF ECONOMIC DEVELOPMENT
International Business Office
Jefferson City, MO

The purpose of Missouri's Department of Economic Development is to recruit foreign investment to the state of Missouri and export Missouri products, primarily to Taiwan. It also helps to facilitate trade relationships. The department has staff stationed in Germany, Japan, Taiwan and Korea.

Professional Staff: The Missouri Department of Economic Development has a relatively large professional staff, with eight located within the U.S. and seven working overseas. One professional was hired in the last 12 months.

Qualifications: Applicants should have a college degree in business focusing on international aspects and should be prepared to travel or possibly live abroad if hired. Fluency in French or German is preferred. Previous work experience in business is preferred but not necessary. The department offers a training program for those with a college education and previous experience.

Internships: The department offers semester-long unpaid internships to undergraduates interested in international business. Interns are usually assigned to do trade and investment research.

Application Procedure: Persons interested in internships or professional positions should contact:

> Business Development Coordinator
> Business Development Programs
> Department of Economic Development
> PO Box 118
> Jefferson City, MO 65102
> (314) 751-4855

STATE OF NEW JERSEY
Division of International Trade
Newark, New Jersey

The Division of International Trade assists New Jersey businesses by providing technical support on the mechanics of international trade as well as guidance on specific countries and industries. This assistance is provided through different education and trade programs. The division has an office in Japan which handles promotion, investment, travel and tourism for New Jersey.

Professional Staff: The division has ten professionals working in the U.S. and one working in Japan. It has not hired any professionals in the last 12 months.

Qualifications: The division looks for applicants with a college degree in international relations, international economics, foreign languages or political science. Willingness to travel abroad is a requirement. Foreign languages, especially Spanish and French, are preferred. No previous experience is necessary.

Internships: The division offers unpaid internships during the summer and academic semester for college students in their junior or senior year. A demonstrated interest in economics, international trade or political science is important. Applications should be addressed to the Foreign Trade Representative.

Application Procedure: Persons interested in a position should contact:

> Director
> State of New Jersey
> Division of International Trade
> 153 Halsey Street, 5th Floor, PO Box 47024
> Newark, NJ 07101
> (201) 648-3518

NEW YORK STATE DEPARTMENT OF ECONOMIC DEVELOPMENT
International Division
New York, NY

New York was the first state to create an international business unit to promote trade and investment. The purpose of the international division is to provide targeted assistance through various programs designed to improve the ability of New York State businesses to compete effectively in international markets. The division also works to attract investment by foreign companies. It has offices in Britain, Germany, Japan, Hong Kong and Canada.

Professional Staff: The international division continues to grow, with 25 professionals employed in the U.S. and 15 in its foreign offices. The international division hired one professional in the last 12 months.

Qualifications: Applicants should have at least an undergraduate degree in international studies, business or economics, but a graduate degree in international marketing, sales or finance is best. Willingness to travel is required for applicants, but living abroad is not. It is helpful but not essential to be fluent in French, German or Spanish. At least three years

previous experience in international sales, marketing or program
management is required. Overseas experience in Europe or Asia is also
helpful.

Internships: The division offers internships during the summer and
academic year. Most positions are for graduate students and are unpaid.
Interns are asked to do research, prepare surveys and assist with program
outreach.

Application Procedure: Persons interested in internships or professional
positions should contact:

> New York State Department of Economic Development
> International Division
> 1515 Broadway—51st Floor
> New York, NY 10036
> (212) 827-6200

OHIO DEPARTMENT OF DEVELOPMENT
International Trade Division
Columbus, Ohio

The International Trade Division of Ohio's Department of Development
helps to promote Ohio exports to overseas markets. The division focuses
on providing assistance to small- to medium-sized Ohio firms in the form
of export consultation, technical assistance and facilitating trade relations.
Ohio's international division has offices in Hong Kong, Japan, Canada,
Belgium and Nigeria.

Professional Staff: Although the international department is shrinking,
five professionals were hired in the last 12 months. There are 14 people
working for the division in the U.S. and another 8 working overseas.

Qualifications: Applicants should have an undergraduate degree in
international business or business administration but a graduate degree in
business administration is preferred. People with expertise in exporting
also stand a better chance of getting hired. One should have some
experience in international trade and must be willing to travel overseas.
Japanese is the preferred language in the international division. Experience in traveling and living abroad is also helpful.

Internships: Paid internships are available for college students majoring
in international studies. Interns assist staff personnel at a number of

events as well as in general office duties. The international division asks that interns stay for at least six months. Applicants should contact the Internship Coordinator at the address below.

Application Procedure: Persons interested in professional positions should contact:

> Ohio Department of Development
> Human Resources Division
> 77 South High Street
> 27th Floor
> Columbus, Ohio 43266-0101
> (614) 466-2072

OKLAHOMA DEPARTMENT OF COMMERCE
Division of International Trade and Development
Oklahoma City, OK

Oklahoma's Division of International Trade and Development helps small- and medium-sized Oklahoma manufacturers and service firms to export for the first time; expands international markets by providing export marketing information, assistance and consulting services; and promotes Oklahoma products and services in foreign markets. Oklahoma operates six overseas offices in Shanghai, New Delhi, Tokyo, Seoul, Frankfurt and Singapore. Only one U.S. citizen is employed overseas.

Professional Staff: Oklahoma's international division currently employs 10 people. No one was hired in the last year.

Qualifications: Applicants with an undergraduate degree in marketing, business administration or international relations or an MBA are favored. Language proficiency is preferred for some positions and required for others and is often a prerequisite for promotion. Previous work experience in international sales and marketing and in trade and export is desirable but not necessary. Applicants must be willing to travel.

Internships: Paid summer and semester internships are available to college students. Preference is given to applicants working toward a degree in international business or international relations and those with foreign language skills.

Application Procedure: Persons interested in internships or professional positions should contact the Personnel Office at:

Oklahoma Department of Commerce
6601 Broadway Extension
PO Box 26980
Oklahoma City, OK 73126-0980
(405) 841-9305

Chapter Nine

THE UN AND OTHER INTERNATIONAL ORGANIZATIONS

INTRODUCTION

The United Nations (UN) was founded in 1945 as World War II came to an end. The UN Charter outlines the world body's goals: maintaining international peace and security, promoting friendly relations among nations, resolving international economic, social, cultural, and humanitarian problems through international cooperation, and promoting human rights and fundamental freedoms. These are ambitious aims. However, the UN's successful involvement in the Persian Gulf war has led many diplomats to expect the organization to take on a larger, more useful role in the future.

The East-West conflict, which frequently paralyzed the Security Council, has ended, and there is a greater willingness among nations to cooperate in resolving their differences. Since 1988, the UN has succeeded in restoring peace in a number of military conflicts. In addition to mediating a termination of the Iran-Iraq war and facilitating the withdrawal of Soviet troops from Afghanistan, the UN helped to bring independence to Namibia, monitored elections in Nicaragua, and negotiated cease-fires in Central America, the Western Sahara, Angola,

El Salvador and Cambodia. The UN has also tackled global problems, including environmental concerns, never envisioned by the Charter.

UN work is not for everybody. International civil servants must be prepared to spend years away from their home countries, to work with people from diverse backgrounds, and to cultivate an impartial attitude in dealing with their own and other countries. For the internationally minded this can be challenging, thought-provoking and rewarding. Despite the conflicting ideologies of member states, the UN and its specialized agencies have always been involved in implementing successful projects worldwide. Their record in promoting human rights and the status of women, improving health care, providing technical assistance, doing disaster relief and compiling statistical data is impressive. With about 67,000 employees, the UN and its affiliated organizations are a huge source of potential international employment. However, because of geographic recruitment, and the preference of many specialized agencies to hire professionals from developing nations, it can be difficult for even highly qualified Americans to find work. **In addition, the current reorganization of the Secretariat has resulted in a temporary hiring freeze for most positions.**

THE UN ORGANIZATION

The UN has six main bodies. The *General Assembly* is its central organ. Each of the 180 member states of the UN has one vote in the assembly, where some issues are decided by simple majorities, others by consensus. All UN bodies report to the Assembly, which votes on their recommendations, approves budgets and elects the Secretary-General. Unlike congressional decisions, the General Assembly's decisions are nonbinding.

The Secretary-General is the chief executive officer of the UN. He heads the *Secretariat,* which does the UN's administrative work and has some 14,000 employees.

The *Security Council* has the power to take action against the threats to world peace. Its decisions are binding. It has 15 members, 5 of whom are permanent (China, France, Russian Federation, the UK and the U.S.) and have veto power.

The *Economic and Social Council* (ECOSOC) coordinates the UN's social and economic activities.

The *Trusteeship Council* oversees the only remaining non-independent trust territory, the Republic of Palau.

The *International Court of Justice,* located at The Hague in the Netherlands, decides international legal disputes between states that accept its jurisdiction. Its 15 judges are elected for 9-year terms.

In addition to these 6 bodies, there are 12 *specialized agencies* that are intergovernmental and autonomous:

- Food and Agriculture Organization of the United Nations (FAO)
- International Civil Aviation Organization (ICAO)
- International Fund for Agricultural Development (IFAD)
- International Labor Organization (ILO)
- International Maritime Organization (IMO)
- International Telecommunications Union (ITU)
- United Nations Educational, Scientific and Cultural Organization (UNESCO)
- United Nations Industrial Development Organization (UNIDO)
- Universal Postal Union (UPU)
- World Health Organization (WHO)
- World Intellectual Property Organization (WIPO)
- World Meteorological Organization (WMO)

Each specialized agency has its own charter, budget and staff, and each is funded by its member nations according to its own schedule of assessments. The specialized agencies are linked to the UN by individual agreements. Most of the specialized agencies report to ECOSOC or its commissions. The International Atomic Energy Agency (IAEA) is related to the UN but does not have specialized agency status.

There are also 14 *voluntary agencies*. These organizations, most of which have semiautonomous status, were created by and report to the General Assembly. They are funded, at least in part, by voluntary contributions from member countries or other fund-raising efforts. (The UN Children's Fund [UNICEF], for example, raises almost a quarter of its budget by selling cards and calendars.)

QUOTA SYSTEM, LANGUAGE REQUIREMENTS

The UN and several specialized agencies use a geographic distribution system of "desirable ranges" to make sure that all member countries are represented by at least some of their nationals. These formulas are based on factors such as the member state's financial contribution to the organization and the size of its population. Regardless of how little a nation is assessed or how small its size, the UN believes that all member states should be represented in the Secretariat staff by at least 2 to 14 nationals. This is not always possible; certain countries are underrepresented or not represented at all.

The U.S., as the biggest contributor to the UN, has the largest number of posts. Its "desirable range" in the Secretariat is 327–442. Currently the

U.S. has filled this quota, but it is seriously underrepresented in most of the specialized agencies, in particular the ILO, FAO, ICAO, and UNIDO.

The UN is making an effort to hire more women for its professional staff. In 1978, the General Assembly set 1982 as a target date when women would hold 25% of the UN professional posts. By 1992 they held 30%, and the goal has been raised to 35% by 1995. Most women, however, remain clustered in low-level administrative posts. The UN continues to try to place more Third World nationals in senior and policy-formulating posts, but due to the limited number of openings, budget constraints and internal promotions, it still has a long way to go.

Some positions are exempt from the geographical quotas. These include temporary appointees (for less than 1 year) and some appointees to overseas missions, technical assistance personnel and staff in posts with special language requirements. The latter are generally translators and interpreters. All UN Secretariat personnel are required to speak French or English. Staff are also encouraged to know one of the other official working UN languages: Arabic, Chinese, Russian and Spanish.

UN STAFF

Staff of the UN family of organizations are spread over more than 600 offices and stations throughout the world, although the New York office has the largest number. Their duties range from medical research to monitoring space activities.

Professionals who are hired for their specific expertise constitute 36% of the UN's staff. About one-third of the professional staff are technical-assistance experts who have "recognized standing" and extensive experience abroad. The UN employs few generalists. It mainly hires people with advanced degrees and three or more years experience, particularly in economics, development agriculture, statistics, finance, engineering, health services, demography, public administration and political affairs. Unlike businesses or banks, UN agencies rarely offer training programs.

The UN hires people with backgrounds in journalism, radio, film or publishing for public information positions. It also hires General Service clerical staff, Field Service staff, who handle communications and maintenance tasks for peacekeeping missions, and Military Observers from member governments who serve as peacekeeping staff.

UN salaries have not changed for a number of years and now lag behind those of the U.S. Civil Service. The discrepancy is greatest for UN employees at the D-1 level and above. Salaries range from approximately $22,000 (net of taxes) for an entry level P-1 position to $69,000 (net of taxes) for the top director D-2 position. Staff in the professional and higher positions receive expatriate benefits to compensate for the extra cost of living and working outside their home country. The UN also provides cost-of-living allowances to preserve equivalent purchasing power for staff in all UN duty stations. The rates are adjusted monthly, and for some high cost cities such as Geneva, Rome and Vienna they are significant.

APPLICATION PROCEDURE

For job hunting purposes, the substantive differences between autonomous, specialized, voluntary or subsidiary organizations are not important. What is important is to know where to apply for what job.

The UN has a temporary freeze on hiring and posting vacancies. When the freeze ends, for professional posts in the Secretariat, one may apply to:

Professional Staffing Service
Room S 2535
United Nations
New York, NY 10017
(212) 963-1090

Professional-vacancy announcements for Secretariat positions are usually sent to universities, professional and women's associations, member states' missions, international organizations and UN offices worldwide. All professional recruitment—either for positions in New York or abroad—is done internationally, and all candidates compete for positions. In New York, **when the freeze comes to an end,** vacancies will once again be posted at:

General Recruitment Office
Room 200
One UN Plaza
New York, NY 10017
(212) 963-8882

For nonprofessional positions with UN offices abroad, you must apply directly to the office in question. Likewise, for positions with specialized and voluntary organizations, which have their own separate and often different application procedures, you must apply directly. (For information concerning jobs with these organizations, see the entries below.)

Anyone applying for a UN position must fill out the P-11 form, which is available at this office. Most applicants for entry-level positions are required to take a standardized placement and qualification test. The office is open to the public between 10 A.M. and noon on weekdays.

General recruitment also accepts applications for clerical and secretarial positions, guides, messengers, etc. Applicants must have some work experience, and tour guides are required to speak English and have knowledge of a second UN language. People who are hired for these nonprofessional positions may try for promotion to professional status by taking a "General Service to Professional" test. This test may only be taken after five years of service by persons holding a permanent employment contract. The test, the G-2P, is usually given only once a year.

The U.S. Department of State, including its permanent mission to the UN in New York and its missions to other international organizations (in Vienna, Geneva, Rome and Montreal), as well as some other federal agencies, can advise Americans regarding employment opportunities and can refer candidates to the UN. Americans do not have to be sponsored to be eligible for a UN position. The IAEA, ITU and UNESCO are exceptions: they insist that applicants apply through and be supported by their country. (Note: the U.S. withdrew from UNESCO in 1984.) Final selection is up to the UN agency head. The most efficient way to apply for a UN position is directly to the UN. It is helpful to have an "in," either with a UN mission or friends inside the UN. For high-level jobs, government backing is important.

The Office of UN Employment Information and Assistance at the Department of State maintains a computerized roster of people who might qualify for professional UN positions. A staff member screens applications, scans vacancy announcements and, when appropriate, will write letters in support of American candidates for specific positions. The department also maintains a computerized list of people interested in receiving vacancy-announcement bulletins, which it sends out regularly. It welcomes detailed resumes from qualified Americans for its roster, and will gladly add names to the mailing list as well. It returns resumes to people whom it considers unqualified.

Write to:

Office of UN Employment Information and Assistance
Bureau of International Organization Affairs
IO/EA - Room 3536, NW
Department of State
Washington, DC 20520-6319
(202) 647-3396

If you are in the New York area, you may find it more convenient to contact the U.S. mission directly. The New York office supplies basic information about the UN and UN employment. The address is:

> Advisor
> Resources Management Section
> U.S. Mission to the United Nations
> 799 UN Plaza
> New York, NY 10017
> (212) 415-4328

When putting your name on a roster, it is advisable that you identify the position you are interested and for which you are qualified, contact the specific office to monitor personnel changes and let the U.S. Mission know your goals so it can advise you.

Another route to the UN is through U.S. government employment. U.S. government employees who qualify for and are offered a UN-related job may transfer to an international organization for a period of up to five years. This is subject to voluntary release from their federal agency.

FOOD AND AGRICULTURE ORGANIZATION
OF THE UN (FAO)
Rome, Italy

FAO is an autonomous, specialized UN agency that strives to eradicate world hunger. Its main concerns include raising levels of nutrition and standards of living, promoting rural development, improving the production and distribution of food and agricultural products, and developing fisheries and forestry. The FAO advises governments, promotes cooperation among member countries, collects and disseminates information and provides technical assistance. In addition, it cosponsors with the UN the World Food Program, which stimulates agricultural development and offers food assistance to developing countries. About two thirds of FAO professionals do field work, teaching people from developing countries a range of food-producing technologies.

Professional Staff: FAO has a professional staff of 3,157 drawn from its 160 member nations. Approximately 25 people work in the New York or Washington, DC, regional offices. The rest work at Rome headquarters, in other regional offices in Ghana, Thailand and Chile or in the field. Approximately 511 professionals were hired in the past year. U.S. citizens make up 12.5% of the professional staff.

Qualifications: FAO usually requires a graduate degree in agricultural sciences, rural planning, nutrition or other development-related fields. Knowledge of foreign languages is expected: Arabic, Chinese, French and Spanish are considered most important. FAO also requires previous work experience, usually about five years. Experience in agricultural development in a Third World country or with a national government is considered most desirable. FAO employees must be willing to live and travel abroad.

Internships: Instead of a formal internship program, the FAO hires qualified graduates, many of whom have advanced academic degrees and some limited professional experience, for the Associate Professional Officers program. The Associate Professionals are FAO staff members on one-year contracts, which may be extended to a maximum of three years. The associates gain experience in agricultural development and allow the FAO to increase its field staff by 20%. They become full members of the FAO project team, and are called to assist on projects in all areas of FAO's work.

Application Procedure: To apply for a professional position or an Associate Professional position, you must fill out a personal history form. Write to:

> Executive Officer
> Food and Agriculture Organization
> Liaison Office for North America
> 1001 22nd Street, NW
> Washington, DC 20437
> (202) 653-2398

or: FAO
> Via delle Terme di Caracalla
> 00100 Rome
> Italy

INTERNATIONAL CIVIL AVIATION ORGANIZATION (ICAO)
Montreal, Quebec, Canada

ICAO is a specialized agency of the UN that sets international standards, recommended practices and procedures on behalf of its 164 contracting states. Standards are aimed at ensuring safety and uniformity on matters affecting aircraft operations, telecommunications, air traffic, search and rescue, navigational aids and airport facilities.

CAO is also involved in regional planning, economic forecasting, fare and rate monitoring and a variety of air transport studies. It offers technical assistance to developing countries to train personnel and strengthen technical infrastructure and operations. ICAO headquarters are in Montreal, Canada; regional offices are in Bangkok, Thailand; Cairo, Egypt; Dakar, Senegal; Lima, Peru; Mexico City, Mexico; Nairobi, Kenya; and Paris, France.

Professional Staff: As of mid-1991, ICAO had an overseas professional staff of 87.

Qualifications: The majority of the staff come from civil aviation administrations of member nations. Specific educational requirements are not as important as experience and training in the technical, economic or legal aspects of civil aviation.

INTERNATIONAL LABOR ORGANIZATION (ILO)
Geneva, Switzerland

The ILO, a specialized UN agency, was founded in 1919 to improve living and working conditions, enhance employment opportunities, promote social and economic stability and advance the cause of social justice. These objectives are carried out through research, publishing, technical cooperation projects and the ILO's most important activity, setting international labor standards. Standards are set at annual ILO conference attended by worker, employer and government representatives of 154 member countries. Issues such as wages, social security and industrial safety are discussed and conventions are adopted. These become legally binding on the member states that ratify them. The ILO monitors compliance with these conventions.

Professional Staff: The ILO has a professional staff of 7 in the U.S. and 900 stationed overseas in field/branch offices in 40 countries. In the last year, 31 professionals were hired, including 4 for the Geneva headquarters.

Qualifications: The ILO usually requires a JD, MBA, MA, MIA, MPA, MS or PhD for employment, preferably in economics, law or the social sciences. A working knowledge of French or Spanish is frequently necessary. Persons seeking entry-level positions at the Geneva headquarters should have two to three years work experience in a related field. Individuals interested in field staff positions should have eight to ten years overall work experience, and have spent two to three years in a developing country.

Internships: Unpaid internships are available to graduate students on an ad hoc basis at the Geneva headquarters. Internships frequently involve research. Students should have good writing skills and preferably French language skills.

Application Procedure: Persons interested in applying should write to:

> Personnel Development Branch
> International Labor Organization
> 4, route des Morillons
> CH-1211 Geneva 22
> Switzerland

INTERNATIONAL MONETARY FUND (IMF)
Washington, DC

The IMF promotes international monetary cooperation and a more-open system of world trade. Consisting of 154 member countries, the IMF supports stable world economic growth by providing financial assistance to member countries suffering temporary balance-of-payments difficulties. It also plays a large role in managing international debt problems by issuing loans to help countries meet their interest payments and by directing austerity measures.

About two thirds of the IMF's international-projects staff are economists with proven skills in economic analysis. Most staff are based in Washington, DC, headquarters. Small offices are maintained in Paris and Geneva. Staff sometimes reside in member countries for varying periods in order to monitor economic developments and advise on economic matters. The IMF has 18 departments; five are area-related and the others are functional, such as Exchange and Trade Relations, Fiscal Affairs and Central Banking.

Professional Staff: The IMF has a professional staff of 2,000; 39 of the total are employed overseas. Approximately 26% are American citizens. In the past year, the IMF hired 90 people.

Qualifications: Applicants with a graduate degree in economics, preferably a PhD, stand the best chance of being hired. Knowledge of foreign languages is preferred, with Arabic, French and Spanish being most important. An appointment to the regular staff or to a fixed-term position usually requires experience in a government or in a financial or academic institution.

Training Program: Approximately 30 to 35 people are recruited—often from graduate programs—each year through the "Economist Program." The program is designed to acquaint candidates who have promising credentials with the policies, functions and operating methods of the fund. It runs for two years and involves assignments in both an area department and a functional department. At the conclusion of the program, some trainees are offered permanent employment. Candidates for the Economist Program should be under 33 years of age and have graduate training in economics. Applicants are selected on the basis of academic record, personal qualities and, in some instances, previous work experience.

Internships: Paid summer internships are available for graduate students in economics. Interns are involved in research activities and have the opportunity to acquire firsthand experience of fund operations Applications should be submitted no later than the end of January.

Application Procedure: Persons interested in applying for internships, the Economist Program, employment on the regular staff (permanent after a one-year probation period) or for a fixed term (two to three years duration) should be prepared to submit a sample of written work and graduate school transcript. They should write to:

> Recruitment Division, Room 6-525
> International Monetary Fund
> 700 19th Street, NW
> Washington, DC 20431
> (202) 623-7000

INTERNATIONAL ORGANIZATION FOR MIGRATION (IOM)
Geneva, Switzerland

The IOM works with governments, other international organizations and voluntary agencies to supply services to ensure the orderly migration of persons throughout the world. To fulfill global demands, the IOM provides resettlement assistance, medical services and language and cultural orientation to refugees, national migrants and displaced persons in search of a new home country.

The IOM is also dedicated to promoting the economic, social and cultural advancement of developing countries. In order to foster self-reliance and regional cooperation, the IOM assists in the exchange of government experts and the intra-regional transfer of professionals and technicians. Developing countries with a specific need for temporary expatriate expertise or the long-term services of professionals and skilled technicians are also assisted in selecting such persons. The IOM provides advisory services and a forum for the exchange of views on migratory matters.

Professional Staff: As of 1990, the IOM had a staff of 815, of whom 140 worked at its Geneva headquarters. The remainder of the staff were stationed in 50 offices throughout the world.

Qualifications: Persons seeking employment at the IOM should have a graduate degree, preferably in political science, international relations or business administration. The IOM generally requires that staff members have previous experience assisting refugees and migrants or have acted as a liaison with national and international authorities. Applicants must have knowledge of Spanish or French.

Internships: A limited number of internships for graduate students are available at the Geneva headquarters. Interns usually work in the field or do research.

Application Procedure: Persons seeking either professional employment or an internship should write to:

Chief, Division of Personnel
International Organization for Migration
17, route des Morillons
CH-1211 Geneva 19
Switzerland

INTERNATIONAL PEACE ACADEMY
New York, NY

The International Peace Academy is an independent, nonpartisan, international institution affiliated with the UN. Started in 1970, primarily as an organization to help train UN peacekeeping forces, the academy has shifted its emphasis more toward promoting the peaceful management and resolution of international and internal conflicts. The IPA functions as a facilitator: it provides the middle ground where opposing parties can meet in order to explore options for settling particular conflicts. In addition to the UN, the IPA works closely with regional and other international organizations, and draws on a worldwide network of statesman, business leaders, diplomats, military officers and academics.

Professional Staff: The IPA has a professional staff of 11 in the U.S. In the last year five persons were hired for the international department, which is reported to be growing.

Qualifications: Persons applying to the IPA should have a JD, MA, MIA, MPA, MS or PhD. The preferred field of study depends on the program in progress. Previous work experience in an international environment is required, and persons with a strong background in international affairs stand the best chance of being hired. Although proficiency in a foreign language is not required, knowledge of French, Arabic or German is preferred. Willingness to travel or live abroad is not a requirement for employment.

Internships: Internships are available to college students and graduate students enrolled in international studies or related areas of study. Interns are assigned work on ongoing projects and are given varied responsibilities, depending on their past experience and the nature of the project.

Application Procedure: Persons interested in applying for internships should write to the Development Director. Employment applicants should write to:

> Administrative Assistant
> International Peace Academy
> 777 UN Plaza
> New York, NY 10017
> (212) 949-8480

UNITED NATIONS CHILDREN'S FUND (UNICEF)
New York, NY

Unicef is a semiautonomous UN organization with a mandate to address the problems of children in both industrialized and developing countries. With emphasis on child survival and development in the less-developed nations, Unicef cooperates with governments in planning and designing low-cost healthcare services for the benefit of children and their mothers. It finances training programs for professional groups and others involved with children's needs, provides supplies and equipment and, in emergency situations, provides disaster relief. Unicef receives all of its income from voluntary contributions, with about 80% coming from governments and intergovernmental organizations.

Professional Staff: Unicef has a professional staff of 1,672, including 153 U.S. citizens, stationed in its main offices (New York, Geneva, Copenhagen and Tokyo) and in 100 field offices in the Third World. There are 298 people at the New York headquarters. In the past year, 88 professionals were hired from the outside.

Qualifications: Unicef usually requires a graduate degree—an MA, MBA, MD, MIA, MPA, MS, MPH, RN or PhD—and experience in fields such as health, nutrition, water, sanitation, education, administration, finance and personnel. Knowledge of French, Arabic, Spanish or Portuguese is required. Preference is given to those who have had experience administering assistance programs in developing countries. Willingness to live and work abroad is essential.

Application Procedure: The UN circulates vacancy announcements internally and occasionally in professional journals. It requires the standard UN application, the Personal History Form, which is available from:

> Chief, Recruitment and Staff Development Section
> UNICEF
> Room: H-5F
> 3 United Nations Plaza
> New York, NY 10017
> (212) 326-7000

UNITED NATIONS DEVELOPMENT FUND FOR WOMEN (UNIFEM)
New York, NY

Unifem, founded by the UN General Assembly in 1976 as the Voluntary Fund for the UN Decade for Women, changed its title in 1985. Working in partnership with UNDP, Unifem assists women in developing countries who are trying to raise their standard of living. It provides women involved in cooperative activities, food production, fuel and water supply, health services, small business, and management and planning, with access to credit, training and technologies. The fund encourages grass-roots participation in the political process and aims to ensure that women are involved in both national policy planning and the decision-making process of mainstream development programs.

Professional Staff: Unifem has a professional staff of 16 in New York and 10 stationed overseas in Thailand, India, Pakistan, Senegal, Zimbabwe, Brazil, Ecuador and Barbados. In the last year, one person was hired for the international department.

Qualifications: Unifem generally hires people with an MS or PhD. Gender and development, social studies and economics are the preferred fields of study. Depending on the demands of the specific job, management and technical expertise or experience in program and project development is most useful. A minimum of four to five years of previous work experience is essential and, depending on the assignment, applicants should have worked in Asia, Africa or Latin America/Caribbean. Unifem also prefers applicants who have had experience managing women's programs for developing countries. Foreign languages, while not required, are preferred, especially French, Spanish and Arabic.

Training Program: While Unifem does not have its own formal training program, it collaborates with UNDP in providing staff members with gender-training programs. In order to ensure that both genders receive consideration when large-scale assistance is given to developing countries, these programs examine the needs and responsibilities of women and men in their respective countries.

Internships: Unifem offers summer and year-long internships to graduate students who are interested and trained in gender studies. Interns are selected to assist program officers with research projects.

Applications: For an intern position, send a resume and cover letter to:

UN Development Program/Division of Personnel
DC-1-1864
New York, NY 10017

For a professional staff position, applications should be addressed to:

Director
United Nations Fund for Women
304 East 45th Street
New York, NY 10017
(212) 906-6400

UNITED NATIONS DEVELOPMENT PROGRAM (UNDP)
New York, NY

UNDP is the principal coordinator and central source of grants for UN development activities. It assists developing countries in raising productivity, improving living standards and using assets in a more effective way. With a network of 115 field offices, UNDP is the most broadly based UN organization, with a presence in virtually every developing country. Its projects include agricultural and rural development, educational systems and economic and community planning. UNDP funds and monitors the implementation of these projects, which are, for the most part, executed by the specialized UN agencies. The agencies are responsible for hiring their own technical personnel (usually referred to as experts) and purchasing equipment for the projects. At present, there are some 20,000 experts (international and national) working on more than 1,000 UNDP-financed projects.

There are three main opportunities for employment with UNDP: the Junior Professional Officer Program (JPO), the Management Training Program (MTP), and other regular staff appointments. Other short-term opportunities may exist for specialized consultants.

The JPO Program accepts about 75 people annually for two- or three-year assignments in the UNDP field offices. Only nationals of participating donor countries, or those selected from developing countries by the donors, may be considered for this program. Because the U.S. has declined to participate, there are no American JPOs. Qualified Americans, however, are eligible for other employment (see below).

Professional Staff: UNDP has a professional staff of approximately 960, of whom 700 are based overseas. Their primary responsibility is to manage the technical cooperation projects described above. About 95 have been hired in the past year; most openings occur on the entry-level or junior levels. UNDP recruits worldwide from graduate programs.

Qualifications: UNDP requires a graduate degree. Economics, development-related disciplines, public administration, anthropology and international business are the preferred fields of study. Knowledge of at least two official UNDP languages (English, Spanish, French) is required; Arabic, Chinese, Russian and Portuguese are also useful. Experience in a development-related field, especially in a Third World country, is strongly preferred. A willingness to live and work abroad is necessary, as well as an ability to work with people from different countries and cultural backgrounds.

Training Program: The Management Training Program has approximately 20 participants per year who attend an initial four-week training course at UNDP headquarters. They are then assigned to a UNDP field office as a Program Officer or Assistant Resident Representative—the first steps on the professional career ladder.

Internships: Unpaid summer internships are available to first-year graduate students pursuing a development-related degree. Interns carry out project and program evaluation and research and analysis and should speak two UNDP official languages.

Application Procedure: Applications for all positions should be sent to the address below. List specific positions or programs, if applicable.

> Chief, Recruitment Section
> Division of Personnel
> United Nations Development Program
> One UN Plaza
> New York, NY 10017
> (212) 906-5279

UNITED NATIONS ENVIRONMENT PROGRAM (UNEP)
Nairobi, Kenya

UNEP, which has been described as the "environmental conscience" of the UN, aims to initiate, stimulate, support, complement and accelerate action at all levels of human society on all issues of environmental concern. Whenever possible, UNEP acts as focal point for environmental action and coordination within the UN. It exists as a catalyst, working through and with other organizations, including UN agencies and governments, to seek a balance between national interests and the global good. UNEP aims to unite nations in confronting common environmental problems and to forge a global partnership in order to finance solutions. UNEP's main areas of study have included the ozone layer, climate, wastes, marine environment, water, land degradation, forests, energy, chemicals, education and environmental law. It also acts to ensure that programs are effectively implemented and managed.

Professional Staff: UNEP has a professional staff of 8 in the U.S. and 267 overseas, approximately 60 of whom were hired in the last year. Overseas staff are stationed in Kenya, Austria, Canada, France, Greece, Jamaica, Mexico, Saudi Arabia, Thailand, Egypt, Britain, Germany, Switzerland and Bahrain.

Qualifications: UNEP requires that applicants have a college degree and expertise in environmental protection, in the broadest sense. Applicants should have at least two years experience relevant to UNEP's activities. A willingness to travel and live abroad is essential. Knowledge of foreign languages is required; English, French and Spanish are preferred.

Internships: Unpaid internships, lasting from three to six months, are available to college and graduate students. Interns should be required by their university to undertake practical training in their field of study.

Application Procedure: Persons seeking internships or professional employment should write to:

> Chief, Recruitment Unit
> United Nations Environment Program
> PO Box 30552
> Nairobi, Kenya

UNITED NATIONS HIGH COMMISSIONER FOR REFUGEES (UNHCR)
Geneva, Switzerland

In 1949 the UN decided to assume more-direct responsibility for international action in favor of refugees. The UN established Unhcr as a subsidiary organ of the General Assembly. Unhcr's mandate is subject to periodic review.

Unhcr shelters, feeds and protects some 17 million refugees who have fled civil wars, political persecution and upheaval. It offers international protection to refugees while searching for permanent solutions to their problems. Unhcr, which has its headquarters in Geneva, Switzerland, has more than 100 offices worldwide staffed by professionals, including lawyers, program officers, administrators and public information specialists. Overseas staff administer refugee camps in Asia, the Middle East, Central America and Africa. They provide legal assistance, coordinate humanitarian aid and negotiate with governments on behalf of refugees.

Professional Staff: Unhcr has a professional staff of 2,500 stationed in 80 countries worldwide. The New York and Washington, DC, offices have a total professional staff of 10. In the last year one professional was hired in the U.S. Both foreign nationals and U.S. citizens are hired for overseas positions.

Qualifications: Successful applicants usually have graduate degrees in law and/or political science, with an emphasis on international affairs, administration or economics. At least five years previous work experience in law, administration or economics is preferred. Willingness to travel and live overseas is necessary as is foreign-language competency. French and Spanish are preferred.

Internships: Semester-long unpaid internships are available to college and graduate students. Interns work in public information and refugee resettlement programs. There are also internships for second- and third-year law students.

Application Procedure: To work in U.S. offices apply to:

> Washington Liaison Office
> UNHCR
> 1718 Connecticut Avenue, NW
> Suite 200
> Washington, DC 20009

For all other locations, write to:

> Office of Recruitment, Career Development and Placement
> UNHCR
> 154, rue de Lausanne
> CH-1202 Geneva
> Switzerland

UNITED NATIONS INDUSTRIAL DEVELOPMENT ORGANIZATION (UNIDO)
Vienna, Austria

Unido, which became the sixteenth specialized agency of the UN system in 1986, promotes industrialization in the developing world by providing technical assistance, training and expertise, and assisting with the exchange of industrial information, the purchase of equipment and investment promotion. Unido's worldwide contacts, in both the public and private sector, and experience in technical cooperation enhance its role as a neutral intermediary, which promotes cooperation among governments, intergovernmental and nongovernmental organizations, financial institutions and private enterprises. Unido maintains the Industrial and Technological Information Bank, which provides information on investment opportunities in developing countries.

Professional Staff: Unido has a staff of approximately 1,400, including those assigned to offices in New York and Washington, DC. Of the personnel at Unido's Vienna headquarters, 450 are professionals. In addition, Unido recruits about 2,000 experts and consultants for assignments in its technical cooperation program in developing countries.

Qualifications: Unido requires an advanced degree for employment and three to five years experience in a field such as economics; chemical, industrial or mechanical engineering; technical-assistance project formulation; management; industrial investment; biotechnology; metallurgy; environment and energy; or administration. Longer experience is required for many positions. Technical experience in the Third World is an asset but not a requirement. Knowledge of English or French is essential. Employees should be willing to work and travel abroad. Unido is interested in hiring more women and welcomes applications from qualified applicants.

Internships: See Chapter Ten.

Application Procedure: Internship applicants must be nominated by the U.S. Mission to the UN or by their college or university. Schools may initiate the application by contacting the Chief, Language Training, Personnel Services Division, at the address listed below. Persons interested in professional positions at the headquarters may request the appropriate application forms by writing to the Chief, Recruitment Section, at the same address. Applicants for expert posts in the field should write to Project Personnel, Recruitment Section, also at the address below. Applications do not need to be made for specific vacancies. Qualified candidates' names will be retained on a computerized roster, which is Unido's major source of recruitment when posts become vacant.

> Vienna International Centre
> PO Box 300
> A-1400 Vienna
> Austria
> (43-1) 21131
> Facsimile: (43-1) 232156

UNITED NATIONS INSTITUTE FOR TRAINING AND RESEARCH (UNITAR)
New York, NY

Unitar, an autonomous UN organization, sponsors training and research programs to improve the effectiveness of the UN in maintaining peace and security and promoting economic and social development. Unitar's programs, which currently focus on training, stress international cooperation, multilateral diplomacy and development. They also prepare participants for assignments within the UN or in other international organizations. A recent addition to the program relates to training in peacekeeping, peacemaking and overall conflict resolution. Training programs last from three days to one year. About 3,000 national and UN officials working in the areas of diplomacy, international law and development economics are accepted into the programs each year.

Unitar also sponsors research projects on issues related to the functions and objectives of the UN and does research for the Secretary-General and for organizations that request it. Since its founding in 1963, Unitar has published over 230 books. Topics have included the arms race, the environment, pollution, technology transfer and development aid, international law, human rights, management and public administration.

Professional Staff: Unitar currently has a professional staff of about 50. Staff are based overseas in Geneva, Switzerland; Rome, Italy; Nairobi, Kenya; and at New York headquarters. Those based in Geneva carry out training programs and perform liaison work. Those based in Rome and Nairobi carry out special projects.

Qualifications: A JD, MBA, MPA, MIA, MA or PhD in international relations, political science, economics or international administration is most useful. Knowledge of at least one UN working language is required, English being the most important. Previous work experience is required.

Internships: Unpaid internships are available to graduate students and junior officials on a summer and semester basis. Interns serve as training assistants and perform research in existing UNITAR projects.

Application Procedure: Applications should be addressed to:

Chief, Program Support Service
United Nations Institute for Training and Research
801 United Nations Plaza
New York, NY 10017
(212) 370-1122

UNITED NATIONS RELIEF AND WORKS AGENCY FOR PALESTINE REFUGEES IN THE NEAR EAST (UNRWA)
Vienna, Austria

Unrwa was created after the Arab-Israeli conflict of 1948 to assist homeless Palestinian refugees. Education, health and relief assistance are provided today to refugees in Jordan, the West Bank and Gaza Strip, Lebanon and Syria. Much of Unrwa's budget is spent on education, vocational and professional training and university scholarships. Its medical centers, which stress preventive medicine and community health, handle more than 4 million patients annually. Unrwa also provides food, small grants and some shelter repair for the most needy. The agency is financed by voluntary contributions, primarily from governments but also from international organizations, voluntary agencies, corporations and individuals.

Professional Staff: Unrwa has a professional staff of 153, all but one of whom are based overseas, either at Vienna headquarters or in Lebanon, Syria, Jordan or Israel. Twenty-four internationally recruited people have been hired in the past year. At present there are 17 U.S. citizens working for Unrwa.

Qualifications: In addition to its own staff, Unrwa has on loan medical staff recruited by WHO and educational specialists hired by Unesco. Unrwa desires a graduate degree in personnel administration, finance, engineering, or technical or relief-oriented disciplines. Knowledge of languages is preferred, with Arabic, French and German in greatest demand. Unrwa requires a minimum of five years experience, preferably with other international or governmental organizations and preferably in the Middle East. Experience can be in international relief work, finance, personnel and administration, law, supply and transport logistics or public information.

Application Procedure: In addition to distributing vacancy notices within the UN, Unrwa sometimes advertises openings in large city newspapers. The UN standard employment application, the Personal History Form, should be sent to:

Chief, Personnel Services Division
United Nations Relief and Works Agency
Vienna International Centre
PO Box 700
A-1400 Vienna
Austria

UNITED NATIONS VOLUNTEERS (UNV)
Geneva, Switzerland

The UN Volunteers (UNV) program is the international volunteer-sending arm for the UN and is dedicated providing technical assistance to developing nations. The U.S. Peace Corps assists UNV headquarters in Geneva with recruitment, processing, and cosponsorship of U.S. citizens applying to the UNV program. The majority of UN Volunteers, approximately 75%, serve in Africa. The remainder serve in Asia and the Pacific. Only about 6% of the program is located in Latin America.

The average tour of duty is two years. UNVs work in a variety of capacities and train local personnel to carry on when their assignment is completed. The Peace Corps provides U.S. volunteers with transportation to and from the country of assignment. UNV provides a monthly living stipend (equivalent to $600 to $800 a month), housing and health and life insurance. Upon completion of their service, UNVs receive a resettlement allowance equivalent to $200 for each month they have served.

Professional Staff, UNV Positions: UNV recruits mid- to upper-level professionals with specialized and technical skills. Approximately 2,000 UNVs, including 55 U.S. citizens, are currently serving in UNV positions in developing countries. (For information on Peace Corps staff openings, see discussion of Peace Corps in the U.S. Government chapter.)

Professional Staff, UNV Headquarters in Geneva and Support Staff Overseas: The UNV has a professional staff of 200 at UNV headquarters in Geneva. Seven Americans hold positions as support staffers, managers and directors. These positions are filled by UN headquarters. The UNV has an additional 200 to 500 professional staff members throughout the world serving as support staff to the volunteers. They also coordinate with national authorities to establish UNV programs and work with government ministries, NGOs, local and regional organizations and other UN agencies in managing, evaluating and revising UNV programs. These positions are generally filled by other UN organizations, such as the UNDP. For information on these positions, individuals should contact UNV/Geneva directly at:

> UN Volunteers
> Palais des Nations
> Ch-1211 Geneva 10
> Switzerland

Qualifications For UNVs: Volunteers must be 21 or older and fluent in at least one of the UNV working languages: English, French or Spanish.

Language training is not provided. Candidates will be considered for UNV projects only if they are fluent in the language of the post. (Post languages include English, French, Spanish, Arabic and Portuguese.) Volunteers must be in good health, have a minimum of two to five years of full-time experience in their field and a college degree or technical diploma. The following is a partial list of desired UNV fields: accounting, agronomy, architecture, business administration, computer programming/science, community development, economics, engineering, fishery, forestry, health education, irrigation, library science, mechanics, nursing and general practice, nutrition, university-level English teaching, urban and regional planning, veterinary science and technical and vocational training.

Application Procedure: U.S. citizens must apply for volunteer positions through the Peace Corps. (Non-U.S. citizens should contact UNV/Geneva directly for application procedures.) Applicants must meet all Peace Corps requirements for cosponsorship, complete a Peace Corps application through a Peace Corps Recruiting Office, and have an interview and reference checks. Candidates must also complete a UNV application, which should be channeled through the UNV office in Washington, DC. Once candidates receive Peace Corps cosponsorship, their applications are sent to the UNV headquarters in Geneva. If accepted by UNV/Geneva, the applicant's name is placed on a roster according to his or her field. UNVs are then selected from the roster based on the suitability and competitiveness of their skills and how their work experience matches the needs of a particular country. Applicants do not apply for specific vacancies. UN Volunteers must be cleared by appropriate UN agencies and host country authorities and must pass a medical examination. The entire application procedure takes a minimum of six months, and once on the roster, it is difficult to determine when or if the candidate will be selected for a post. For further information, please contact:

> Peace Corps
> United Nations Volunteers
> 1990 K Street, NW
> Washington, DC 20526
> (800) 424-8580, ext. 2243

THE WORLD BANK GROUP
Washington, DC

(See Chapter Three: International Finance and Banking)

WORLD HEALTH ORGANIZATION (WHO)
Geneva, Switzerland

PAN AMERICAN HEALTH ORGANIZATION (PAHO)
Washington, DC

WHO is the specialized UN agency that seeks to improve public health throughout the world. Since 1977 WHO's basic concern has been to ensure that individuals everywhere have access to affordable health services that will enable them to lead socially and economically productive lives. In support of this objective WHO collaborates with member countries in immunization programs, promotes and coordinates research on tropical diseases and sexually transmitted diseases, sets standards for the control of drugs and vaccines, and disseminates substantial data on health matters in the form of books, journals, technical publications and primary health care material, including training manuals. It also supports the development of, health services, fosters community involvement in health issues, and provides advice and technical assistance to governments.

WHO's activities and programs are financed by the annual contributions of its more than 166 member countries. A large part of its work is carried out through its six regional offices in Brazzaville, Congo; New Delhi, India; Copenhagen, Denmark; Alexandria, Egypt; Manila, The Philippines; and Washington, DC. The Washington office is known as the Pan American Health Organization and is an independent inter-American organization in its own right.

Professional Staff: WHO has a professional staff of about 1,550 of whom 614 are in Geneva and 936 in the regional and field offices. PAHO has about 296 professionals, many of whom are stationed in Latin America. During the past year, WHO hired 207 people (including Associate Professional Officers or APOs) and PAHO, 25. About 20% of WHO and PAHO staff are U.S. citizens.

Among the technical staff, many are medical and public health specialists, but nursing, pharmacy, dentistry, veterinary medicine, sanitary engineering, biology, chemistry, economics, statistics and library science are also represented. The supporting services include specialists in information, budgeting and accounting, management techniques, procurement of supplies and personnel. Because of the exceptional language requirements of an international organization, linguistic staff provide important supporting services, and at WHO headquarters there are many translators and editors.

Qualifications: Most positions in WHO are filled by persons highly specialized in health fields. General practitioners or surgeons will not be considered for employment. The desired specialties for physicians, public health officials, nurses, scientists and health-care technicians are extremely varied.

A graduate degree (MA, MBA, MD, PhD) is normally required for employment plus a minimum of five years of relevant work experience. Previous overseas experience is particularly helpful. Knowledge of languages, Spanish for PAHO and French for certain areas, is required. Applications from women are particularly welcome.

Associate Professional Officers (APOs): WHO has signed an agreement with 11 donor countries for the employment of APOs. APOs are qualified young professionals with limited experience, especially in developing countries. Their assignment (for one to three years) is financed by donor countries. Most of them are medical officers assigned to field projects where they get significant on-the-job training before returning to their country of origin.

Application Procedure: Persons interested in employment as an APO should contact Head, ASC, Personnel Division, at the address below. Those interested in other professional positions should write to:

> Head, Manpower Resources
> Personnel Division
> World Health Organization
> 20 Avenue Appia
> CH-1211 Geneva 27
> Switzerland

Applications to PAHO may be sent to:

> Chief, Manpower Planning and Staffing Unit
> Department of Personnel
> Pan American Health Organization
> 525 23rd Street, NW
> Washington, DC 20037
> (202) 861-3200

WORLD INTELLECTUAL PROPERTY ORGANIZATION
Geneva, Switzerland

The World Intellectual Property Organization became a UN specialized agency in 1974. Dedicated to the promotion and protection of intellectual property, WIPO maintains services for obtaining protection of inventions, trademarks and industrial designs. It also encourages the conclusion of new international treaties and the modernization of national legislation. The international bureau in Geneva, the secretariat of WIPO, administers the various "unions," or multinational treaties, and works to promote increased international cooperation among its 125 member states.

In addition, WIPO assembles and disseminates information and provides technical assistance to developing countries. WIPO is responsible for helping to ensure that developing countries will benefit economically, socially and culturally from new technology.

Professional Staff: WIPO has one person stationed in the U.S. and 125 in Geneva, Switzerland, and Vienna, Austria. In the last year 18 professionals were hired for the international department, which reportedly is growing.

Qualifications: Persons with a graduate degree in law who have specialized in intellectual property, or with a graduate degree in international relations stand the best chance of being hired. Most professional positions at WIPO require that staff have a legal background and a minimum of three, but often more, years of experience in the industrial property or copyright fields. Staff members must be willing to travel and to live abroad. Foreign languages are required. French and Spanish are preferred.

Application Procedure: Vacancies for professional posts at WIPO are generally advertised through the appropriate offices of member states and in WIPO periodicals, which are available at the Geneva headquarters. Those seeking employment should contact:

Personnel Recruitment Section
World Intellectual Property Organization
34, chemin des Colombettes
1211-Geneva 20
Switzerland

Chapter Ten

INTERNSHIPS

INTRODUCTION

Finding a job is often frustrating: You are told you need work experience to land the position, but you cannot gain experience without getting work. Even though entry-level jobs can be filled by people without experience, employers are hesitant to hire someone with no employment credentials, particularly when others who have worked are available.

So how does one get work experience? The answer is through an internship. An internship provides you with the opportunity to learn firsthand about a company or organization by working for it on a short-term basis. The exposure helps you decide if the field is right for you. An internship also provides you with professional work experience, which will help you pursue a permanent position. Finally, an internship helps you make contacts. If you got along well with your supervisor, he or she might be willing to help you find a permanent job, write you a recommendation or even hire you permanently.

Internships vary a great deal. Some are paid; others provide a small stipend or commuting expenses; some pay nothing. They are available for periods a short as a four-week winter break from college or for up to a year or two. Internships are filled by high-school, college and graduate students and by older people reentering the work force or changing careers.

Some organizations sponsor formal internship programs and take a set number of interns each term, train them and give them specific tasks. Other firms may take interns for a specific project. A few companies hire interns and let them provide help where they see a need. In general, a more structured internship provides more responsibility and a better learning experience than one in which duties or supervisors are unspecified.

Some companies take interns as part of their recruiting process and may hire former interns as permanent employees. Other companies are only interested in getting some temporary help. An internship should be a mutually beneficial relationship. The company should benefit from the work of the intern, and the intern should gain experience and exposure to the firm's work.

INTERNSHIP ETIQUETTE

In an internship you must display initiative. Ask for projects that you can work on, volunteer your services to staff members, and be helpful around the office. Each internship situation varies, however, and in some your supervisor may not appreciate your doing someone else's work. Like a guest in someone else's house, be courteous and get to know your surroundings before volunteering for additional chores. Be careful to listen to and follow your supervisor's instructions. One reason some organizations are wary of taking interns is that they can cause more harm than good if they fail to follow instructions.

Interns' jobs run the gamut from clerical work to aiding staff on a variety of stimulating projects. Before accepting an internship, it is wise to find out what work is available and what is expected of you. With the help of your supervisor, you should write down your learning goals. This would identify your interests for your supervisor and help him or her assign work for you. Make clear that you welcome criticism. This is the only way you will learn to do a better job.

Many colleges and graduate schools offer credit for one- or two-day-a-week internships during the fall or spring semester, and some programs require part- or full-time internships in order to receive a degree. Other schools give credit for summer internships, which are usually full-time positions. Before you decide on an internship, find out what your school expects of you and make sure your employer understands this. A student receiving credit should write learning goals with the help of his or her school's intern coordinator and supervisor.

Finally, many internships are unsalaried, but this does not mean they "don't pay." The experience, the opportunity to test a field, the contacts and supervisors' references are all valuable. You need not fear that taking an unpaid internship carries less prestige than a paid one—it doesn't. If you must earn money, look for a paid internship but understand that these are harder to find, or get a second, paying job. Think about living at home or with a relative in order to save money. And ask if the company will pay for your transportation or lunches.

INTERNING IN INTERNATIONAL FIELDS

In some fields an internship is a virtual prerequisite for employment. In journalism, for example, summer jobs and even work during the term are very important for getting a permanent position. Most students in law, business and public-policy graduate programs hold paid summer internships, and companies often use the intern pool to recruit permanent staff. In some nonprofit work, so many applicants have internships that those without them are not considered serious candidates.

Internships in banking, finance and some business fields are less important because many companies offer training programs. But because internships show you have initiative and drive, they are useful in getting into a training program, which can otherwise be difficult. Businesses are most interested in hiring staff who are competent and will work hard. Any work experience you have will help convince employers of your potential.

It is often difficult to find internships in the international departments of businesses. You are encouraged to try, but do not be disappointed if you have to settle for an internship in the home office. Later on you can get into international work.

For positions in the United Nations and related organizations, previous professional experience is essential. Few internships are offered by these organizations, and they are usually for highly qualified people. For a job in the U.S. government, an internship can help establish your credentials, but it is generally not considered on a par with professional experience, which is useful for entry-level and required for mid- and upper-level positions. The same holds true for the field of development assistance. Nevertheless, internships are a good way to get experience in these difficult-to-enter fields.

INTERNSHIPS ABROAD

Internships are an excellent way to gain critical overseas work experience, develop contacts and language proficiency, demonstrate your resolve and cultural adaptability, and experience firsthand living and working overseas. Internships overseas, however, differ from U.S. internships in several ways:

Arranging an internship overseas can be considerably more difficult than arranging an internship in the U.S. Give yourself plenty of lead time, and research the field thoroughly. Internships abroad are the employment equivalent of a blind date since most people do not visit the organization or meet with the people with whom they will be working. In most cases internships must be applied for at least three to six months before the start of the internship, and travel and living arrangements must also be taken care of.

Other aspects such as language proficiency, work schedule and time commitment must be considered. In most cases fluency in the native language is essential, as is a willingness to work full time. Persons looking for the opportunity to travel while interning might be disappointed by the five-to-six-day work week required by many internship programs, and they should reexamine their goals. In most cases it is best to travel before and/or after the internship. Allow time for adjustment. In a three-month internship abroad, you may spend a good part of the time familiarizing yourself with your surroundings and duties. A six-month or one-year commitment may be more beneficial for both you and the sponsoring organization.

Finally, many overseas internships are unpaid. This usually means that travel and living expenses come out of the intern's pocket. Some internship programs listed below ask for a flat fee, paid in advance, which can be costly. But many organizations provide information about how to apply for financial aid, and some make all living and travel arrangements as well as provide a stipend. Some colleges and universities offer financial aid for overseas internships.

If you have considered all of the above and you still think an internship overseas is right for you, there are several ways to proceed. If you are an undergraduate or graduate student, check with your college or university to see if they have any overseas internship programs. Advantages of university-sponsored programs are that even if they are unpaid, academic credit is almost always assured, and because the programs are well-established, they may be more substantive. If you are not currently enrolled in college, or your institution does not have an internship program, you can turn to the listings found in this chapter and those in the sources listed in the bibliography.

If all these sources do not produce your ideal internship, you may want to try to forge your own path. Jeffrey B. Wood, director of the career development and alumni office at the Monterey Institute of International Studies in Monterey, CA, suggests several methods of arranging or creating your own internship overseas in his article, "Going

International: An Overseas Business Internship May Be Within your Reach." Although aimed at business internships, the information can apply to almost any field.

- Approach U.S. companies with overseas offices. First use your career counselor or alumni office for contacts at overseas offices of U.S. companies, or contact the international division head-quarters for an introduction.

- Offer your services as a research or teaching assistant to faculty members engaged in international research projects.

- Start your own international business club, or organize an international business seminar on campus and invite members of the faculty and the business world to participate. It is an excellent way to develop contacts.

- Join a professional association for information, training and contacts.

INTERNATIONAL BUSINESS

AIESEC UNITED STATES, INC.
New York, NY

Founded in 1948, Aiesec is an international, nonpolitical, nonprofit, student-run independent educational association comprised of students interested in economics and management. Aiesec seeks to develop people's understanding of foreign economies, business environments and cultures through exchange programs, conferences and other initiatives and programs.

The International Trainee Exchange Program is Aiesec's largest program. Working through local representatives at 750 universities and colleges in 74 countries, companies worldwide hire more than 6,000 master's students, recent graduates and upperclassman for two- to eighteen-month internships. U.S. students must attend and be active with the chapter at one of the more than 70 affiliate colleges and universities to qualify for an overseas internship. Established companies like Unisys, Xerox, AT&T, IBM, Arthur Andersen, as well as emerging international businesses, employ interns in accounting, finance, management, economics, marketing and related fields. Before students enter the exchange program they must demonstrate managerial competence and pass a screening by executive advisers and Aiesec officials. Aiesec helps the intern arrange housing, transportation and insurance and organizes social and cultural assimilation events.

For more information and a list of participating schools contact:

> AIESEC United States, Inc.
> 135 West 50th Street
> New York, NY 10020-1202
> (212) 757-3774

THE AMERICAN-SCANDINAVIAN FOUNDATION (ASF)
New York, NY

ASF is a nonprofit organization that promotes international understanding through educational and cultural exchanges between the U.S. and Denmark, Iceland, Norway and Sweden. ASF's programs include fellowships and grants for American and Scandinavian students, trainee placement, publishing of a journal and cultural activities.

ASF arranges short-term training opportunities in some Scandinavian countries. The programs are designed to provide American students with cross-cultural contacts and practical work experience. Opportunities exist primarily in the fields of engineering, computer science, agriculture and horticulture. Short-term positions are available during the summer for two- to three-month periods. Between 50 and 100 positions are available each summer.

Interns receive a stipend to cover living expenses during the period of training but are expected to cover air fare costs. ASF cooperates with the host organization to provide housing, for which interns pay $120 to $385 per month. Once an assignment is confirmed, ASF also arranges for a work permit to be issued to the intern.

Applicants must have at least three years of undergraduate studies with a major in the field in which training is sought. Knowledge of English is sufficient, but interns are encouraged to gain a basic proficiency in the language of their chosen country by the time the internship begins.

To apply, send a resume to ASF along with a cover letter specifying the field and country in which you wish to train. List appropriate skills and dates of availability. A nonrefundable application fee of $50 is required at the time an application is submitted. The deadline for applying for the short-term program is December 15.

For more information, contact:

Training Program Coordinator
The American-Scandinavian Foundation
725 Park Avenue
New York, NY 10021
(212) 879-9779

CDS INTERNATIONAL
New York, NY

CDS International is a private, nonprofit organization whose goal is to promote the interests of international business through international professional training. It serves companies with global interests by organizing and administering a variety of work-training and educational exchange programs. Most of the programs are between the U.S. and Germany, although one—the UNIDO (United National Industrial Development Organization) program—involves people from developing nations. Three noteworthy CDS programs are:

Internship Program: American college seniors or recent graduates with some practical work experience and majors in business or technical fields are eligible to participate. Knowledge of German is required.

Interns spend one month in an intensive German language course while staying with German families. Thereafter, interns work with a German company for five months. Interns are generally paid by the company; if not, limited stipends are available. Programs start in January, March, April, September and October. Applications must be submitted four months in advance of the program commencement date.

Career Training Program: This program offers young professionals intensive language training plus paid work experience in Germany. The program begins with one to three months of intensive language training. During this time participants board with a German family, gaining extensive language and cross-cultural experience. Language training is followed by on-the-job training in a German company for 12 to 18 months. Applicants should possess U.S. citizenship, an undergraduate degree in a business, engineering or technical field or training in the hotel business or as a bilingual secretary, one to two years of full-time work experience and a good working knowledge of German.

Congress-Bundestag Youth Exchange Program: Sponsored by the U.S. federal government, this competitive exchange program provides for two months of intensive language training, four months of study at a German technical or trade school or university, and a five-month internship in Germany. Participants also have the opportunity to reside with a host family. Placement is arranged throughout Germany. Program duration is late July through mid-July of the following year. Interested applicants must be U.S. citizens between the ages of 18 and 24 at the start of the program and have clear career goals and practical work experience. German language ability is not required but is recommended. In addition to the above-mentioned, the program also provides air fare, health insurance and stipends toward local transportation and host family compensation.

For more detailed information about these and other CDS programs, contact:

> Program Officer
> CDS International, Inc.
> 330 Seventh Avenue
> 19th Floor
> New York, NY 10001
> (212) 760-1400
> Washington, DC 20062
> (202) 463-5731

DEPARTMENT OF STATE
Washington, DC

The State Department Internship Program reports a growing demand for candidates with economics, business administration and finance backgrounds to do research and to work as administrative, economic and commercial officers. They encourage BS and MBA candidates interested in international economics, finance and business to apply for internships. (For more information, see U.S. Department of State entry in U.S. government section below.)

EDUCATIONAL PROGRAMS ABROAD (EPA)
Yorktown Heights, NY

EPA is a nonprofit organization that promotes and organizes internships in Europe. Most positions are in advertising, business, law, education, health care, politics, social sciences, theater and urban planning.

EPA offers internships throughout the year in Bonn, Cologne, London, Madrid, Paris and at the European Parliament in Strasbourg, France.

Interns work three or four days a week during the fall and spring and take two classes related to their field of interest, for which they may receive academic credit. Internships are usually for one semester. Full-time internships are also available for 10 weeks during the summer. EPA places 80–100 interns annually.

There is a fee for each program, ranging from $1,780 to $6,300, depending on how long the stay, where the internship is and what U.S. university is awarding credit. These fees include room and board. Students are not paid for the internship work, although some receive financial aid from their undergraduate school.

Prospective interns should be juniors, seniors or graduate students with a GPA of 3.0 or above. Fluency in German, French or Spanish is required for internships in, respectively, Bonn, Paris or Madrid. Applications are accepted throughout the year and should include a transcript, two letters of reference and an essay outlining career goals. There is a nonrefundable application fee of $25. For more information contact:

> Educational Programs Abroad
> 540 Giordano Drive
> Yorktown Heights, NY 10598
> (914) 245-6882

FMC CORPORATION
Chicago, IL

FMC produces machinery and chemicals for industry, agriculture and government, with 107 manufacturing facilities and mines in 26 states and 14 countries. FMC is involved in five broad markets: industrial chemicals, petroleum equipment and services, defense systems, performance chemicals and specialized machinery.

FMC offers a summer internship program for students who have completed their first year toward an MBA. Interns are placed in departments according to the company's current needs. Some interns work on international marketing projects and international competitor analyses. The corporation looks for strong analytic skills and some experience in a manufacturing environment. Research skills are also important, and a foreign language may be helpful. Interns, who are sometimes hired as full-time staff after graduation, are paid a competitive salary, and are usually employed in the main office in Chicago. About 20–25 interns are employed annually.

FMC contacts local graduate schools when positions are available. However, resumes with cover letters are also accepted and should be mailed in January or February to:

MBA Recruiting
FMC Corporation
200 East Randolph Drive
Chicago, IL 60601
(312) 861-6000

GENERAL ELECTRIC COMPANY (GE)
Fairfield, CT

GE is a diversified technology, manufacturing and services corporation with 13 major businesses: aerospace, aircraft engines, National Broadcasting Company (NBC), electrical distribution and control, communications and services, motors, financial services, industrial and power systems, lighting, transportation systems, appliances, medical systems, and plastics.

Recruiting for permanent employment as well as internships in GE is decentralized. Many of the GE divisions hire graduate and undergraduate students as interns at various offices around the world. Basic qualifications are high academic standing and demonstrated leadership ability. GE offers interns competitive monthly salaries.

Resumes and cover letters are accepted at GE offices around the country. It is recommended that the cover letter include the type of position or work desired. Resumes for intern positions should be sent to:

General Electric Company
Recruiting and University Development
1285 Boston Avenue, Building 23CE
Bridgeport, CT 06601
(203) 382-2000

INTERNATIONAL BUSINESS MACHINES
CORPORATION (IBM)
Armonk, NY

IBM is one of the leading corporations in the field of information-handling systems. It produces information-processing products and computer systems and software, telecommunications systems, and educational and testing materials. Its products are widely used in business, government, science, space exploration, defense, education and medicine.

Through IBM's CO-OP and summer preprofessional programs, college students are hired to work at IBM locations around the country on engineering, programming and marketing projects. Because the program is large and decentralized, the number of students participating varies with location.

Undergraduate and graduate students with backgrounds in engineering, mathematics, science or computer science who are interested in IBM's field of operation and who have a good GPA and oral and written skills are preferred candidates. Former interns are often hired after graduation.

Interested students may submit a resume and cover letter to either an IBM central employment office (located in major cities) or a local IBM office. A cover letter should indicate the position in which you are interested and the location where you would like to work. IBM responds to every employment inquiry. To locate the address of the nearest IBM office look in your local directory. Address all inquiries to the Manager of Personnel.

MONSANTO COMPANY
St. Louis, MO

Monsanto Company produces a diversified line of chemical and agricultural products, pharmaceuticals, low-calorie sweeteners, industrial process controls, man-made fibers and plastics. Its five operating units are Monsanto Chemical Company, Monsanto Agricultural Company, Fisher Controls International, G.D. Searle and NutraSweet, doing business in over 100 countries.

Monsanto sponsors a summer corporate internship program for undergraduate students between their junior and senior years and for graduate students. It places emphasis on employment of minority and female students, to whom it offers approximately 30 out of a potential 35 internships. Interns are integrated into a variety of ongoing projects in various departments including manufacturing, engineering, management information systems, and finance and accounting. Interns are offered travel expenses and a competitive salary and are often hired back for permanent employment.

To qualify, a student must have a high GPA and a relevant major, such as engineering, computer science, a life science or accounting. Resumes with cover letters should be sent by February to:

Monsanto Company
Professional Recruiting
G4EE
800 North Lindbergh Boulevard
St. Louis, MO 63167
(314) 694-2702

THE U.S. CHAMBER OF COMMERCE
Washington, DC

The U.S. Chamber of Commerce is the world's largest national organization of business, trade and professional associations. It represents the interests of the American business community through lobbying, media campaigns and public-policy research. It makes recommendations to Congress based on the views of its membership. The chamber's international division publicizes the organization's views on international issues to Congress, the executive branch, foreign governments and the media.

The chamber offers unpaid semester-long internships to undergraduate juniors and seniors. Approximately 85 interns are hired each year, most of whom work in the international division, the chamber's largest division. The international division is broken down into regional departments. Language ability is helpful and will allow the student to gain more from the internship, but is not required.

Interns work on research projects, monitor bilateral economic issues, prepare directories of organizations, write articles for a monthly newsletter, attend congressional hearings and follow legislation. To be considered for the internship program, the applicant must have good writing and research skills and be studying international relations, economics or a geographic specialization. Internships can result in full-time employment if an opening occurs. If interested, contact:

> Personnel Department, Internship Coordinator
> The U.S. Chamber of Commerce
> 1615 H Street, NW
> Washington, DC 20062
> (202) 659-6000

U.S. AND FOREIGN COMMERCIAL SERVICE (U.S.&FCS)
Washington, DC

The Department of Commerce's U.S.&FCS was established in 1982, the product of the merger of the U.S. Commercial Service and the Foreign Commercial Service. Headquartered in Washington, DC, the 48 domestic offices of U.S.&FCS are linked to 124 overseas posts in 68 countries. It represents an integrated organization serving as the department's delivery arm to encourage, service, and support U.S. exports and to assist directly American businesses in their international trade activities.

U.S.&FCS sponsors a work-study intern program, which provides a limited number of summer internships abroad for 10 to 12 weeks to highly qualified university or college junior, senior and graduate students.

The objective of the program is to encourage students to consider careers in international trade and to assist the department in its mission of creating a career professional international trade specialist corps that recognizes the needs and meets the demands of the U.S. business community. The work-study program is a volunteer service program and is subject to the regulations and restrictions of the Office of Personnel Management. Internships in this program are considered to be adjunct to an applicant's education, therefore internships are open only to currently enrolled students who are taking at least one-half of a full-time academic workload, and who will be returning to complete their education immediately upon termination of their internships. Internships are nonpaid and all living, travel and other expenses are absorbed by the intern.

All internships under U.S.&FCS work-study program are at Foreign Service posts abroad.

Interns will be assigned to junior-level professional duties such as conducting market research, preparing reports, drafting replies to correspondence and promoting and recruiting exhibitors for trade events.

Applicants should submit a completed SF-171; a certified copy of college transcripts and two letters of reference from professors; and a 500- to 700-word autobiography indicating the applicant's objective in seeking an internship, a description of relevant study and involvement in area issues and indication of no more than three (in order of preference) U.S.&FCS posts desired. The autobiography must also indicate that the applicant will be continuing studies in the fall semester immediately after the internship. If this is not indicated, the application will not be considered. Interns must also be of 21 years of age before the date of assignment overseas; have completed some course work relevant to international trade; be a continuing junior, senior or graduate student; and be able to pass a thorough security background investigation.

Recruitment for the program takes place September 1 through November 1 of the previous year. Applications postmarked after November 1 cannot be accepted.

Send applications to:

> Work-Study Internship Program
> Office of Foreign Service Personnel
> U.S. and Foreign Commercial Service
> PO Box 688
> Ben Franklin Station
> Washington, DC 20044-0688
> (202) 482-2000

INTERNATIONAL CONSULTING

BEIJING-WASHINGTON, INC.
Bethesda, MD

Beijing-Washington is an export consulting firm that represents about 40 American, Canadian and European firms in the People's Republic of China (PRC). Beijing-Washington specializes in marketing and selling electronic and electrical production equipment to the PRC. In addition, it supplies installation and service for the production and assembly-line equipment sold to China.

The firm uses an average of two interns every year for a period of four to six weeks in the fall, spring or summer. The internships are not paid but can often lead to employment with the company. Interns start with clerical duties such as typing, word processing, filing and mailing. Later they may assist project managers by researching and responding to requests from customers in China.

Interns should have an active interest in China and speak and write Mandarin Chinese. The internship is open to college juniors or seniors. No previous work experience is required, but interns should have good typing and writing skills and be familiar with word processing. There is no formal deadline to submit applications, which should include a cover letter and resume and be sent to:

> Assistant to the President
> Beijing-Washington, Inc.
> 4340 East-West Highway
> Suite 200
> Bethesda, MD 20814
> (301) 656-4801

INTERNATIONAL BUSINESS-GOVERNMENT COUNSELLORS, INC.
Washington, DC

IBC is an international consulting firm that provides assistance in intelligence, research, counseling and problem solving to corporations, foreign institutions and governments. IBC analyzes government trade and investment policies and international political and economic developments affecting business operations. It provides strategic counseling, early alert, forecasting of future international developments and information on government activities.

IBC takes 9 to 10 interns annually, during the fall, spring and summer. There is no stipend, but college credit may be arranged. Interns assist IBC staff with research projects, monitor government activity in countries of interest and provide background information on certain countries for clients.

Applicants must be college juniors or seniors. Cumulative GPA should be 3.5 or above. Previous experience is helpful, although not required. Applications must include a college transcript, writing sample, a cover letter and resume. There is no formal deadline, but early applications are encouraged. For more information, contact:

> Intern Coordinator
> International Business-Government Counsellors, Inc.
> 12th Floor
> 818 Connecticut Avenue, NW
> Washington, DC 20006
> (202) 872-8181

RUDER FINN, INC.
New York, NY

Ruder Finn is a large independent public relations agency with offices in New York City, Chicago, Washington, DC, Los Angeles and Raleigh, NC, and international partners worldwide. The firm serves corporations, foreign institutions and governments and nonprofit organizations.

Ruder Finn takes 27 interns a year, 9 each fall, spring and summer. Interns work full-time at the New York office and receive a salary of $300 a week. Interns may have an opportunity to write press releases and "pitch" letters, develop media lists and contacts, conduct research, participate in planning and coordinate special events and press conferences. Interns attend training sessions on different aspects of public relations such as international business, product promotion, tourism promotion, government relations, sports marketing, broadcast communications and design. Although interns are not sent abroad, they might work with overseas clients. Ruder Finn views internships as a training ground for entry-level public relations professionals and has hired 50% of its former interns.

The internship is very competitive: about 200 applications are received for each session. Applicants must be graduates of four-year colleges who majored in the liberal arts disciplines, such as English, political science or languages, or law, advertising or business management, or professionals interested in changing careers. Knowledge of a foreign language can be useful, as can previous experience in public relations and a demonstrated interest and ability in communications. At least a "B" (3.0 GPA) average is preferred. Applicants should send a resume and request an application at least two months prior to the application deadline. In addition to taking a writing test, which is included with the application, applicants must arrange for an interview during which they will be asked to analyze a public relations case study. The deadlines are April 1 for the summer program, June 15 for the fall program and November 15 for the spring. For more information, contact:

> Intern Coordinator
> Executive Training Program
> Ruder Finn, Inc.
> 110 East 59th Street
> New York, NY 10022
> (212) 715-1584

INTERNATIONAL FINANCE/BANKING

CHASE MANHATTAN BANK
New York, NY

Chase is divided into three core businesses: global banking, national banking and consumer banking. With operations in over 100 countries, the corporation offers a comprehensive range of financial services to corporations, individuals, financial institutions and governments around the world.

Chase offers 20 summer internships to MBA candidates between their first and second years and 20 internships to undergraduate students between their junior and senior years. The 10-week program integrates interns into business teams or projects that involve analysis of financial data and writing reports. Weekly seminars are planned with the officers of the bank. All positions are salaried.

Occasionally there are internships in international departments of domestic branches. There are also a few positions available in offices abroad. Candidates for the latter positions should have at least two years experience working or living in the country for which they apply and have good command of the language of that country.

Graduate interns are recruited on business-school campuses around the country. Interested students should send a resume and cover letter to:

Director of Summer Internship Programs
Professional Recruitment
Chase Manhattan Bank
One Chase Manhattan Plaza
New York, NY 10081
(212) 552-3262

THE FIRST BOSTON CORPORATION
New York, NY

The First Boston Corporation, headquartered in New York City, is a leading international investment banking organization which provides a broad array of financial services to corporate clients; city, state and foreign governments; and institutional and substantial individual investors.

The summer associate program hires 40 to 50 MBA candidates between their first and second years to serve as interns each summer. Interns learn about sales and trading through projects, informal sessions and rotational assignments on the trading floor. Interns support the professional staff in projects requiring quantitative analysis skills and are paid a competitive salary. The program lasts approximately 10 weeks.

First Boston seeks students with a well-rounded background and some financial experience. Preference is given to interns with two to five years experience in investment banking. Interns are recruited from business schools throughout the country, and resumes with cover letters are accepted from October through February. They should be sent to:

Manager of MBA Recruiting
The First Boston Corporation
Park Avenue Plaza
55 East 52nd Street
41st Floor
New York, NY 10055
(212) 909-2482

EXPORT-IMPORT BANK OF THE UNITED STATES (Eximbank)
Washington, DC

Eximbank is an independent U.S. government agency that facilitates the export financing of U.S. goods and services. It supplements and encourages, and does not compete with, commercial financing. By neutralizing the effect of export credit subsidies from other governments and by absorbing risks that the private sector will not accept, Eximbank enables U.S. exporters to compete effectively in overseas markets on the basis of price, performance, delivery and service. To achieve its export finance mission, Eximbank has authority to provide loans, guarantees and insurance.

Eximbank takes approximately 15–20 summer and semester interns each year. Interns assist bank staff in the areas of accounting, economics, financial analysis and computer work. Seminars, field trips and on-the-job experience in special projects connected with each intern's major field of study are arranged.

Applicants should be undergraduate or graduate students. Interns are placed in different departments so relevant fields of study vary although finance, economics, marketing, computers and business administration are most common.

Applicants should send the personnel form SF-171 (available from the Office of Human Resources Management and Development) together with a copy of college transcripts no later than March 31 to:

> Export-Import Bank of the United States
> Office of Human Resources, Room 1005
> 811 Vermont Avenue, NW
> Washington, DC 20571
> (202) 566-8834

INTERNATIONAL JOURNALISM

AFRICA NEWS SERVICE
Durham, NC

Africa News Service offers up to 10 internships of varying duration every year to those interested in journalism and African issues. The organization supplies news and analysis about Africa to the public through a radio broadcast service for public and commercial stations, by responding to requests for research and writing, and through *Africa News,* a biweekly digest of African affairs. The service gears its broadcasts, reports and publications to both the specialist and the novice in African affairs.

Although Africa News Service does not have a preference about the level of education completed, interns must be 18 years or older. Interns have a variety of duties including maintenance of the information base by monitoring or transcribing short-wave radio broadcasts, and reading, note-taking or filing incoming clippings, magazines and reports. Interns also assist in researching articles and help to answer outside research requests with resources from the organization's own files. Depending upon experience and interests, the intern may write articles, edit and copy tapes for the audio service, or participate in other relevant activities. If desired, interns may devote up to 20% of their time to a research project of their own choosing, making use of *Africa News* information resources. Academic credit may be arranged with the home institution. Internships often lead to permanent positions with the organization.

Africa News Service is unable to provide financial support for interns, but would assist in finding inexpensive living accommodations in Durham. Applicants should submit a personal letter describing background, interests and goals; one letter of recommendation; a transcript of courses and grades; and a writing sample. Knowledge of any African languages is preferred. For more information, contact:

Internship Program
Africa News Service
Box 3851
Durham, NC 27702
(919) 286-0747

AMERICAN SOCIETY OF MAGAZINE EDITORS (ASME)
New York, NY

ASME is a New York-based association of more than 650 senior magazine editors. It sponsors a well-known and competitive 10-week summer internship program in which about 50 college students work on magazine editorial staffs. Most interns are assigned to positions in New York; a few elsewhere. About 50 magazines are associated with ASME, including *Business Week, Glamour, Life, Newsweek, New York* and *U.S. News & World Report.*

Interns perform editorial tasks such as evaluating unsolicited manuscripts, researching articles, checking facts, writing leads and captions, proofreading, copy editing, interviewing and covering press conferences. Interns indicate the magazine to which they would like to be assigned, but editors' preferences prevail in the final choice. Each intern must submit a final report commenting on his or her experience. Interns receive a minimum $275 weekly stipend and are responsible for travel and living costs. ASME arranges housing in New York University dormitories for students who need it. The approximate cost for a room is $1,500 for the summer.

While the program does not necessarily lead to employment, it does provide the intern with excellent journalism experience, which can be used to secure future employment.

Announcements of the program are sent to deans and university internship offices around October 1 of each year or can be requested by a student. Any U.S. college or university may nominate one prospective intern each year and students must be so nominated to apply. Applicants should have a demonstrated interest in journalism—such as courses in journalism, participation on a campus publication and previous journalism internship experience. Applications must include an application form, one letter expanding on the application, a letter of reference (from the school and from a former intern if possible), writing samples, a photograph and a self-addressed stamped postcard for notification of application receipt. The deadline is December 15. For more information, contact:

> Executive Director
> American Society of Magazine Editors
> 575 Lexington Avenue
> Suite 540
> New York, NY 10022
> (212) 752-0055

THE INSTITUTE FOR CENTRAL AMERICAN STUDIES (ICAS)
San Jose, Costa Rica

ICAS is dedicated to peace, justice and the well-being of the people and land of Central America. ICAS seeks to disseminate accurate and reliable information about political and socio-economic development in Central America. ICAS has no partisan allegiances. It is supported by subscriptions to its publication *Mesoamerica*, a six-page newsletter containing information and analysis, by income from educational programs and by contributions.

ICAS offers approximately 12–18 internships each year that offer practical experience in journalism and Latin American studies by working on *Mesoamerica*. The work includes researching and writing articles as well as clipping and filing. Interns have the opportunity to participate in seminars, attend press conferences, lectures and workshops, and take university classes. The program requires a minimum commitment of six months, with a minimum work load of 20 hours per week. Internships can begin at any time. Because internships are nonremunerative, most interns find jobs teaching English 10–15 hours a week to help pay for room and board. However, it is necessary to have additional income or savings to meet expenses. Interns should expect to pay $200 monthly for room and board and $100 monthly for miscellaneous expenses. There is an additional administration fee of $200.

Most interns are recent college graduates, but some are undergraduates or graduate students. Interns must have working knowledge of Spanish and a good command of English and proficient writing skills.

For more information and application procedures, contact:

> The Institute for Central American Studies
> Apartado 300
> 1002 San Jose, Costa Rica

THE MACNEIL/LEHRER NEWSHOUR
New York, NY
Washington, DC

The MacNeil/Lehrer NewsHour is the only one-hour, nationwide evening news program on U.S. television. It is carried by 297 public television stations, which comprise 93% of all PBS stations nationwide and reach 97% of the nation's television households. Approximately 3 million viewers watch the *NewsHour* each weeknight. The *NewsHour* has two programs for aspiring journalists.

The desk assistant program is designed for recent college graduates looking for entry-level job experience in the newsroom. The program runs approximately five to six months and pays minimum wage. It is a full-time position requiring eight hours a day on the job. Four desk assistants are accepted twice a year.

The Washington, DC, and New York offices hire 24 research interns each year. The New York office annually hires 3 graphic arts interns as well as 12 research interns. The Washington office has 12. The following terms are available: fall (September through December); spring (January through May); and summer (June through August). Four interns are hired for each of these terms.

Interns assist at the news desk, help assemble background material and answer viewer mail. In New York, interns report to senior producers responsible for national affairs, the economy, science, medicine, environment and special features. Graphic arts interns help produce maps, charts, photos and slides by researching, ordering materials and assisting in graphic production. Washington interns perform similar tasks.

The program requires that interns receive college credit. They must be available 20 hours per week. There is no monetary compensation. Former interns are sometimes hired for permanent positions.

Undergraduate students with a strong interest and experience in news and excellent oral and written English skills are desired. To apply you most complete a questionnaire (available from *NewsHour* offices) and send it along with your resume, and a letter from your school stating that you will be able to receive college credit for the internship.

For summer internships the deadline is March 1. The deadline for fall is July 31 and for the spring, November 1.

For the graphic arts internships, contact the Art Director; for all others contact the Internship Coordinator:

> The MacNeil/Lehrer NewsHour
> 356 West 58th Street
> New York, NY 10019
> (212) 560-3113

For information on the Washington internship, contact:

> Intern Coordinator
> The MacNeil/Lehrer NewsHour
> 3620 27th Street South
> Arlington, VA 22206
> (202) 998-2837

THE NATIONAL COUNCIL ON U.S.-ARAB RELATIONS/THE JOE ALEX MORRIS JR. JOURNALISM INTERNSHIP PROGRAM
Washington, DC

Founded in 1983, the National Council on U.S.-Arab Relations is an American nonprofit organization dedicated to improving American knowledge and understanding of the Arab world. The council seeks to improve U.S.-Arab relations through people-to-people exchanges and through a wide variety of educational and informational programs in the U.S.

Through a rigorous competition process, U.S. journalism graduates (with bachelor's or master's degrees), and communications graduates are selected for semester and summer internships as reporters and photographers with English language newspapers and magazines in the Arab world.

Interns are offered both travel expenses and a stipend. Up to 10 interns are accepted a year. Foreign language ability is not necessary. Interns are sometimes hired for permanent positions abroad.

For the application procedure contact:

> Journalism Internship Coordinator
> National Council on U.S.-Arab Relations
> 1735 Eye Street, NW
> Suite 515
> Washington, DC 20006
> (202) 293-0801

THE NATION INSTITUTE
New York, NY

The Nation Institute, in conjunction with *The Nation* magazine, provides a practical and comprehensive internship program for college students and recent graduates interested in magazine journalism and publishing. *The Nation*, America's oldest weekly magazine, is a journal of politics and the arts that focuses primarily on foreign and domestic policy, civil liberties and literature.

To gain editorial experience interns read and evaluate manuscripts, check facts, do research and are encouraged to write editorials, articles or reviews for the magazine. On the publishing side interns assist the advertising, circulation and promotion staffs with day-to-day business, and in creating and carrying out developmental and research projects for the magazine and the institute. Interns' duties also include filing, photocopying, running errands and other routine office work. An additional position is available in *The Nation's* Washington office. This intern will work closely with the magazine's Washington editors, attending press conferences and Congressional hearings as well as doing some clerical work.

Weekly seminars are another important part of the program in New York. Among the authors and journalists, politicians and political delegations invited to discuss selected topics with the interns were New York Governor Mario Cuomo, Senator George McGovern, muckraking author Jessica Mitford, *60 Minutes* producer Mimi Edmunds, Jamaican Prime Minister Michael Manley, and I.F. Stone, former publisher and editor of *I.F. Stone's Weekly*. Nation staff members also hold seminars on editorial and publishing skills.

Internships are full-time, five days a week. The total number of internships each year is 24. There are three cycles each year: fall, winter/spring and summer. Each cycle has eight interns, seven in New York City at *The Nation* offices and one in the Washington, DC, office.

There are nonspecific requirements. Each applicant is evaluated on the basis of his or her resume, recommendations, writing samples and interview. Applicants of all ages are welcome, although most interns have completed their junior year of college.

Whenever possible, *The Nation* will assist interns in arranging for academic or work-study credit. The internship carries a small stipend.

In addition to a cover letter indicating your interest in *The Nation* and describing your prospective career goals, send a resume, two letters of recommendation (from professors or former employers) and two writing samples. Published clips are preferred, though academic papers and creative writing samples are acceptable. All application materials become the property of *The Nation*. Contact *The Nation* for application deadlines.

Send application materials to:

> The Nation Institute Intern Program
> 72 Fifth Avenue
> New York, NY 10011
> (212) 242-8400

TIME, INC. MAGAZINES
New York, NY

Time, Inc.'s summer editorial intern program is designed for undergraduate students interested in magazine journalism. The nine-week paid internship offers several students an opportunity to work as reporter-researchers, picture researchers, or as assistants in editorial support areas including the picture collection and photo lab. The majority of students are assigned internships in New York and are placed on one of the magazines or in a general service area. Students have also been assigned to Time-Life Books in Alexandria, VA.

Each year, Time Inc. Magazines invites several colleges and universities to participate in the program. The school publicizes the program on campus, accepts applications according to Time, Inc. Magazines' specifications, and prescreens the candidates. Each institution is allowed to nominate two individuals, students who will be between their junior and senior years. Candidates are asked to submit an academic transcript, a resume, and a 300-word essay describing their interest in the Time, Inc. Magazines internships. In addition, nominees may include up to three non-returnable "clips," i.e. published writing samples. Senior editorial staff members review the nominees' files and select the individuals who will be offered an internship. For further information contact:

Executive Assistant, Human Resources
Time, Inc. Magazines
1271 Avenue of the Americas
New York, NY 10020
(212) 522-2752

INTERNATIONAL LAW

There are virtually no internships in the field of law. There are some internships in law-related fields, such as human rights, or with the government. We have listed what little we found below.

Most law students work for a law firm at least one summer during law school. For a listing of law firms that accept summer associates, as summer law students are called, see the October supplement in *The American Lawyer* (600 Third Avenue, 2nd Floor, New York, NY 10016). Each year the supplement is dedicated to either first-year associate programs, third- and fourth-year associate programs, or "mid-level" associate programs. The 1992 supplement has information on mid-level associate programs. The supplement can be purchased separately for $20.00, but most law-school career offices receive it. The October supplement rates the firms on the basis of "how interesting work was," "importance of work," "client contact," "library research," and "accept or reject a full-time offer."

Nonlaw students who want to work in a law firm to decide if the field is right for them might want to consider working as a paralegal or legal assistant. Paralegal work varies greatly but is mostly clerical. It does, however, afford an inside look at the field. For more information contact:

American Bar Association
750 North Lake Shore Drive
Chicago, IL 60611
(312) 988-5000

or:

National Association of Legal Assistants, Inc.
1601 South Main Street, Suite 300
Tulsa, OK 74119-4464
(918) 587-6828

LAWYERS COMMITTEE FOR HUMAN RIGHTS
New York, NY

The international human rights program has four law school student interns each summer. The tasks of a summer intern vary and depend largely on the needs of staff. Summer interns will be assigned to work on a specific region, though they may receive assignments during the course of the summer from any of the five regions currently covered by committee staff: Soviet Union/Eastern Europe, Asia, Africa, Middle East and the Americas. They can expect to assist in research projects and drafting letters to government officials, appeals to aid foreign lawyers and judges who are threatened and harassed because of their legal work, and help in monitoring bodies like the United Nations Commission on Human Rights, the Inter-American Commission on Human Rights and the Africa Commission on Human and Peoples' Rights.

The committee frequently hosts meetings with foreign lawyers and human rights activists, and summer interns are encouraged to attend these meetings. Members of the international human rights program staff also give weekly talks to summer interns, describing their work and methodology.

The usual length of a summer internship ranges from eight to ten weeks. The committee cannot pay its summer interns but offers travel expenses. In the past interns have received funding from various sources including fellowships, law school summer public interest programs, foundation grants and work-study funds.

If you are interested in applying for a position as a summer intern, send a copy of your resume and a recent writing sample (4–10 typed pages) before March 1 to:

> Deputy Director
> Lawyers Committee for Human Rights
> 330 Seventh Avenue, 10th Floor
> New York, NY 10001
> (212) 629-6170

NATIONAL AUDUBON SOCIETY
Washington, DC

The National Audubon Society, an organization committed to the conservation of wildlife and its habitat, offers internships to law students and recent graduates. Legal interns in Audubon's Washington office are part of the professional staff, learning and assisting in the fields of water resources, pollution control and international affairs. Each intern works with a member of the legal staff who supervises his or her work. Legal interns do research, write legal memoranda, assist in the development of litigation strategy, attend meetings and hearings, draft pleadings, testimony, legislative language, legislative history and administrative rule-making comments. Legal interns can work with nonlegal program staff in issue areas of interest and assist in the other work of the office. Each intern is exposed to a variety of issue areas and undertakes different types of assignments, the goal being to show the intern the full range of work undertaken by the staff attorneys.

Legal interns are expected to work full-time, preferably for three to six months. Interns who are participating as part of their law school curriculum can work on a part-time basis, if necessary. Interns are reimbursed for any out-of-pocket expenses incurred in connection with work but are not offered a stipend.

Applicants must display a high degree of initiative, maturity, motivation and responsibility. Knowledge of the general environmental field and some exposure to administrative and/or legislative process is helpful. The ability to write, conduct legal research and analyze legal problems is essential.

Interested individuals should submit a resume, legal writing sample and a letter stating special interests and availability. References should be available on request. For those interested in summer legal internships, applications should be submitted by March 1. Send them to:

National Audubon Society
666 Pennsylvania Avenue, SE
Washington, DC 20003
(202) 547-9009

OFFICE OF THE GENERAL COUNSEL, OFFICE OF THE SECRETARY OF DEFENSE
Washington, DC

The Office of General Counsel is the chief legal organization in the Department of Defense. The office is responsible for advising high-level policymakers in the Office of the Secretary of Defense. In addition, the office works closely with senior attorneys and policymakers from the military departments, and with officials from the Departments of Justice, State, Treasury, and other government agencies. The issues considered by the office involve virtually all areas of law, with particular focus on international relations, the Uniform Code of Military Justice, the Department of Defense (DOD) counternarcotics program, the acquisition process, the appropriations process, constitutional issues, environmental law, property law, administrative procedure, dependents and military education, labor management relations, industrial security, counterintelligence policy and national intelligence. The office frequently works on special projects for the Secretary of Defense. Within the office, 36 full-time lawyers are distributed among six sub-offices; international and intelligence; logistics; legislative reference; fiscal and inspector general; legal counsel; and personnel and health policy.

The Office of General Counsel offers two types of internships: paid summer internships lasting at least 10 weeks, and semester and summer unpaid externships. Interns generally work full-time, while externs' schedules are more flexible. Most summer externs, however, work full-time. Approximately eight summer internships are available; the number of externships varies widely.

Interns and externs perform the same duties: assisting in drafting and commenting on legislation, regulations, congressional testimony, litigation materials and legal opinions. Interns also have the opportunity to assist in the process of formulating DOD legal policy on topics of current interest. Interns are given substantial opportunities to enhance research and drafting skills by working closely with members of the office.

Interns should have a bachelor's degree from an accredited college or university, Although some preference is given to students who will have completed two years of law school before the summer, consideration will be given to first-year law students who have particularly strong employment or academic experience. Persons who will be graduated from law school prior to the fall semester of 1992 are not eligible for the program. However, persons who will be graduated from law school in the spring and who will begin a judicial clerkship in a federal or state court by November may be considered.

Externs must have a bachelor's degree from an accredited college or university and have completed at least one year of law school. In addition, externs must be enrolled in a law school or graduate program in an accredited college or university, and have the permission of that institution.

Applicants for both internships and externships must submit a resume; a federal application, Standard Form 171 (SF-171); a law school transcript; and OPM Form 1170/17 (Supplemental Qualifications Statement); a statement of class rank; and a writing sample. If class rank is not maintained by the law school, a statement to that effect will suffice. An unofficial transcript may be submitted as part of the initial application, but an official transcript will be required before a final offer is made.

Applications should be addressed to:

Office of General Counsel (P&HP)
Department of Defense
The Pentagon
Room 3E999
Washington, DC 20301-1600
(703) 695-3657

U.S. ARMY JUDGE ADVOCATE GENERAL'S CORPS
Fort Belvoir, VA

The U.S. Army Judge Advocate General's Corps hires 25 first- and 75 second-year full-time law students each summer as temporary civil service employees to work as legal interns in Army legal offices in installations throughout Germany and possibly any area where the Army has a JAGC office, including Italy, Korea and Panama.

Under the supervision of an attorney, interns assist in preparing civil and criminal cases by performing legal research, writing briefs and opinions, conducting investigations, interviewing witnesses and other activities.

The Judge Advocate General's Corps summer intern program seeks law students with proven scholastic ability and demonstrated leadership potential. Because these are not military positions, interns must pay all costs of housing and travel to their job location. Interns are appointed sponsors from the office in which they will work who assist with locating housing and other arrangements.

Applicants should send the DAJA-PT Form 13 and Standard Form 171, resume and undergraduate and law school transcripts. An interview should be arranged with a JAGC Field Screening Officer prior to the application deadline (November 1 for second-year students and March 1 for first-year students).

For further information write or contact:

Army JAGC Professional Recruiting Office
(Summer Intern)
Building 1834
Franklin Road
Fort Belvoir, VA 22060-5818
(800) 336-3315

TRANSLATING AND INTERPRETING

There are few internships in translating and interpreting for students during the beginning of their training. Students are rarely proficient enough in languages to be of help to professional translators. The best way to break into the field is through language practice and advanced translator/interpreter training. (For more information on internships and a listing, see Chapter Six.)

NONPROFIT ORGANIZATIONS

Research and Education

AMERICAN INDONESIAN CHAMBER OF COMMERCE
New York, NY

The chamber is an independent organization that promotes trade, investment, financial and other business services between Indonesia and the U.S. Its activities include sponsoring luncheons with business experts, publishing analyses of U.S.-Indonesian business relations and organizing meetings and seminars between official and private representatives of Indonesia and the U.S. Its membership comprises over 100 corporations, including banks, petroleum companies, shipping lines, law firms and trading firms.

The chamber uses up to a total of six interns per year, two in the fall, two in the spring and two in the summer. Interns prepare periodical indexes for reference use, write synopses of articles and books dealing with U.S.-Indonesian business relations, respond to inquiries and do research. There is a stipend of $4 per hour when funds are available. The internship does not lead to future employment with the chamber.

Undergraduate or graduate students majoring in internationally related fields may apply. They should have a good knowledge of economic, business and cultural issues affecting U.S.-Asian relations. No foreign languages are required. Apply early in the semester for the following

semester's program by submitting a resume and setting up an interview.
Write to:

> Intern Coordinator
> American Indonesian Chamber of Commerce
> 711 Third Avenue
> 17th Floor
> New York, NY 10017
> (212) 687-4505

AMERICAN SECURITY COUNCIL (ASC)
Washington, DC

ASC is a prodefense citizen's lobby, and the ASC Foundation is a group
that works with other educational institutions to improve public understanding of national security issues. The foundation serves as the research
and educational staff of the National Security Caucus, a bipartisan
alliance of prodefense leaders who support the adoption of a national
strategy for peace-through-strength. The caucus includes over 200
members of Congress. In addition to defense and foreign policy issues,
ASC concentrates on programs related to economic growth, energy
security, the space program, human rights and world trade.

The ASC intern program involves research assignments, writing
reports, and assisting with ASC events. Projects center around the
production of national security reports and putting together the annual
ASC Voting Index. Interns also attend weekly briefings and open
discussions given by ASC staff members which address various defense
and foreign policy issues. ASC accepts four unpaid interns each fall,
spring and summer.

Undergraduates may apply for the internship program. Knowledge of
Spanish is preferred but not required. Applicants should submit writing
samples and a cover letter anytime during the year. To obtain an
application and further information, contact:

> Executive Director
> American Security Council
> 916 Pennsylvania Avenue, SE
> Washington, DC 20003
> (202) 484-1676

AMERICAS SOCIETY
New York, NY

A national nonprofit private organization, the Americas Society is dedicated to informing the people of the U.S. about the societies and cultures of their neighbors in the Western Hemisphere. The society does this through a variety of programs offered by its three major divisions: Latin American affairs, Canadian affairs and cultural affairs. Also, affiliated with the Americas Society is the Council of the Americas, which is a U.S. business organization made up of multinational corporations with interests in Latin America and the Caribbean.

Paid summer and semester internships are available in the society's Latin American affairs, Canadian affairs, literature, visual arts and programs departments. Interns handle public relations work, assist personnel with clerical tasks and in the organization of programs and study groups as well as conduct research. High school, college and graduate students may apply. Proficiency in Spanish or French is preferred. There is no formal deadline for applications. For further information, contact:

> Director of Personnel and Administration
> Americas Society
> 680 Park Avenue
> New York, NY 10021
> (212) 628-3200

THE ATLANTIC COUNCIL OF THE UNITED STATES
Washington, DC

Founded in 1961, the Atlantic Council of the United States is a nonprofit center that seeks to address "the advancement of U.S. interests engaged in the issues now before the Atlantic and Pacific communities." Its purpose is to identify challenges and opportunities, illuminate choices and foster informed public debate about U.S. foreign, security and international economic policies. It is also dedicated to the education of "the generations that will succeed to America's international leadership." The council is national in its membership, bipartisan in orientation and centrist and consensus-building in nature.

The council engages the American government, corporate, professional and educational communities in an integrated program of policy studies and roundtable discussions, briefings, dialogues, conferences and publications designed to support selected membership and other constituencies.

Internships are regularly available in the office of programs and projects, the office of education, the NATO information office, public affairs and policy education, East-West studies, the program on nuclear nonproliferation, development, and Atlantic-Pacific program. Interns are responsible for assisting program directors and staff in planning, organizing and running the council's programs and projects. Interns also conduct research, attend hearings and meetings, help prepare proposals and help conduct conferences of varying sizes.

Approximately 30–40 unpaid internships are offered each year. The council traditionally seeks junior and senior undergraduates with a demonstrated interest in the public and foreign affairs of the nations of the Atlantic alliance and the Pacific basin. Applicants should have excellent writing and communications skills, and must be familiar with WordPerfect 5.1 word processing.

For more information or to apply for an internship contact:

> Internship Coordinator
> The Atlantic Council of the United States
> 1616 H Street, NW
> Washington, DC 20006
> (202) 347-9353

CARNEGIE ENDOWMENT FOR INTERNATIONAL PEACE
Washington, DC

The Carnegie Endowment is an operating foundation that conducts its own programs of research, discussion, publication and education in international affairs and U.S. foreign policy. Focusing on contemporary policy issues, the endowment addresses topics such as arms control, economic development and regional issues. Projects are carried out by senior and resident associates and are directed to both general and professional audiences. The endowment publishes the quarterly journal *Foreign Policy.*

The endowment has a professional staff of approximately 30; there are no entry-level positions. Endowment scholars come from a wide variety of backgrounds, including government, journalism and public affairs. Most have worked overseas.

The student intern program is designed to provide a substantive work experience for students who have a serious career interest in international affairs. It is open only to college seniors or persons who have completed their undergraduate degree within the past academic year. Internships last six months and pay a stipend of $1,500 a month. They usually involve work with the journal *Foreign Policy,* or some ongoing project at the endowment. Each year, about 10 interns are selected in a highly competitive selection process. Applicants should have a substantial background in international politics or economics, must be nominated by their university and must complete a formal application procedure. The application deadline is January 15.

There are also limited opportunities throughout the year for volunteer interns.

For information on the programs, write to:

> Intern Coordinator
> Carnegie Endowment for International Peace
> 2400 N Street, NW
> Washington, DC 20037
> (202) 862-7900

CENTER FOR STRATEGIC & INTERNATIONAL STUDIES (CSIS)
Washington, DC

CSIS is a policy research institute whose activities include public seminars, roundtable meetings across the U.S. and publications and programs for scholars, the media and foreign leaders on a variety of international issues.

CSIS hosts 60 unpaid interns throughout each year. Interns do library research, help coordinate conferences and assist with administrative duties. Internships can be arranged on a part-time or full-time basis. The program occasionally leads to employment with CSIS.

Applicants must be undergraduate or graduate students with a background in international relations. No previous experience is required. There is no formal deadline for applications.

Applications must include a resume, writing samples and a cover letter, and should be sent to:

> CSIS Intern Coordinator
> 1800 K Street, NW
> Washington, DC 20006
> (202) 887-0200

COUNCIL ON ECONOMIC PRIORITIES (CEP)
New York, NY

CEP is a nonpartisan, nonprofit organization that makes impartial analyses of the vital issues facing the nation.

CEP provides policymakers and the media with information on energy issues, military spending, employment practices and the environment. Its employees publish studies, reports and newsletters; write op-ed articles for U.S. newspapers; testify before Congress; and participate in economic conferences. CEP has up to 10 interns at one time who work for a minimum of three months. Most interns receive a weekly stipend to cover expenses. Internships run during the summer and academic semester. Interns work on various projects in such areas as corporate accountability, environment and the economic commission.

Most interns work in the New York office. Undergraduates and graduate students may apply for the internship program throughout the year. Applicants should have good analytical, research and writing abilities and personal computer experience. Prospective interns may send a resume or call CEP to discuss their interests. Contact:

> Administrative Director
> Council on Economic Priorities
> 30 Irving Place
> New York, NY 10003
> (212) 420-1133

COUNCIL FOR INTER-AMERICAN SECURITY (CIS)
Washington, DC

CIS is an independent, nonpartisan, nonprofit foreign policy research and educational organization specializing in development and security issues that affect the Western Hemisphere. Organized in 1976, CIS now has over 250,000 members nationwide. CIS provides up-to-date information on political, economic and military affairs in Latin America. CIS publishes a newsletter, *West Watch,* with a monthly circulation of over 100,000.

CIS hosts both part-time and full-time interns year-round. The internships are suited to the interest, background and abilities of the applicant. Internships at CIS provide substantial opportunities to research, write and publish within the intern's field of interest. In addition to having good research and writing skills, applicants should be dependable and able to accept responsibility quickly. For more information contact:

Director of Research
Council for Inter-American Security
122 C Street NW
Suite 710
Washington, DC 20001
(202) 393-6622

FREEDOM HOUSE
New York, NY

Founded in 1941, Freedom House is a private, nonprofit, bipartisan organization that monitors human rights and political freedoms worldwide. Internationally, Freedom House focuses attention on human rights violations by oppressive regimes, both on the left and on the right. Domestically, it stresses the need to guarantee all citizens equal rights under law and equal opportunity for social and economic advancement.

Freedom House takes as many as 50 paid interns a year. Work-study arrangements are also acceptable. Interns do a number of tasks including research, writing, proofreading, copy editing, typing and filing. Most interns do research for the annual "Survey of Freedom in the World."

Applicants must be a junior, senior or graduate student and should be studying economics, history, journalism or law. Send a current resume stating areas of interest and expertise and references from recent employers and/or instructors. For more information contact:

Intern Coordinator
Freedom House, Inc.
120 Wall Street
26th Floor
New York, NY 10005
(212) 514-8040

HUMAN RIGHTS WATCH/
EVERETT PUBLIC SERVICE INTERNSHIPS
New York, NY

Human Rights Watch offers three internships during the summer in conjunction with the Everett Public Service Internship Program.

Interns are assigned to one of Human Rights Watch's divisions: Africa Watch, Americas Watch, Asia Watch, Helsinki Watch (covering Europe and North America), Middle East Watch, the Fund for Free Expression and the Women's Rights project. Interns may be asked to undertake a variety of tasks, including research on human rights conditions, assistance in drafting human rights reports and help in related advocacy efforts. Interns work closely with the research staff, under the direction of the regional director.

Weekly events will be held for interns both in the Human Rights Watch offices and outside by the Everett Program. In addition, interns will be encouraged to attend regularly held Human Rights Watch staff and board meetings at which current human rights developments and organization policy are discussed.

The internships last from eight to twelve weeks, at a minimum of 30 hours per week. A small stipend of $125 per week for undergraduates and $150 per week for graduate students will be provided to offset expenses.

Forward a resume, one writing sample, one letter of reference and a cover letter stating your geographic region of expertise, any specific skills and foreign language ability and your reasons for seeking an internship in the field of human rights to:

> Intern Coordinator
> Human Rights Watch
> 486 Fifth Avenue
> New York, NY 10017
> (212) 972-8400

JOINT BALTIC AMERICAN NATIONAL COMMITTEE (JBANC)
Rockville, MD

Jbanc coordinates and represents the interests, views and policies of three major Baltic organizations in the U.S.—the Estonian American National Council, the American Latvian Association and the Lithuanian American Council. Jbanc monitors developments in Estonia, Latvia and Lithuania and provides the government, press and interested persons with information, analysis and guidance on issues important to its members. Jbanc also operates a 24-hour hotline of political and economic events in the Baltics, information on legislation pending in the Baltic parliaments as well as in the U.S. Congress, and other information concerning developments in the area of Baltic and U.S. relations.

Jbanc offers a 10-week unpaid internship program for college students year-round. A limited number of stipends, awarded on a merit basis, are available from Jbanc's parent organizations. Usually not more than three stipends in the amount of $1,500-$2,000 are awarded each year.

Applicants must be undergraduate students and possess excellent writing skills. Preference is given to students with a working knowledge of at least one of the Baltic languages. If selected, applicants will be responsible for their own transportation and housing needs (access to the office is difficult without a car).

Interns are required to complete at least one major project or research an assigned subject during their employment. In some cases, this work may be used to complete a requirement for class. Interns will also take part in the day-to-day activities of Jbanc, including reporting on hearings in Congress, tracking legislation, preparing information for grass-roots activists, answering phone and written inquiries and maintaining databases of information. Interns should expect to be assigned clerical work and other office tasks as needed.

All applicants must submit a letter outlining their interest in Jbanc, a resume, writing sample and two references from professors. Applicants with proficiency in Estonian, Latvian or Lithuanian should submit an additional writing sample (no more than five pages in length) demonstrating the level of their ability in the given language. Students applying for a stipend should forward an additional copy of their application materials specifying the organization from which they wish to request a stipend.

Application materials should be sent to:

Director of Public Relations
Joint Baltic American National Committee
400 Hurley Avenue, PO Box 4578
Rockville, MD 20849
(301) 340-1954

MERIDIAN INTERNATIONAL CENTER
Washington, DC

Meridian International Center is a nonprofit educational and cultural institution promoting international understanding through the exchange of people, ideas and the arts. It holds conferences and seminars and makes cultural presentations for international visitors, diplomats and newcomers to the U.S. Meridian International Center sponsors programs for the Washington community and the international business and academic world. In addition to the diplomatic corps, foreign dignitaries and visitors, participants in Meridian International Center activities include students and the business community.

Meridian International Center is interested in undergraduate and graduate students with an international background, writing abilities and computer skills. Knowledge of a foreign language is desirable. Former interns are occasionally hired to join the organization's 100-member staff. There is no formal deadline to apply. Applicants should submit a resume and a cover letter with their application and send it to:

Director of Personnel
Meridian International Center
1630 Crescent Place, NW
Washington, DC 20009
(202) 667-6800

THE MIDDLE EAST INSTITUTE
Washington, DC

The Middle East Institute is a nonprofit organization founded in 1946 with the purpose of improving public knowledge and understanding of the area. It strives to do this through lectures, conferences, language courses, publications, the Islamic Affairs Program, the Sultan Qaboos Research Center and the George Camp Keiser Library.

MEI is looking for interns interested in the Middle East and Islam. Internships are available in a wide range of areas including working on the *Middle East Journal*, in the Middle Eastern languages and cultural programs department and in the Middle East political programs department. *MEJ* interns cite information from hundreds of worldwide Middle East publications in the "Bibliography of Periodical Literature" section of the journal, proofread articles and book reviews, and learn first-hand how a scholarly journal is published. Programs department interns help research, plan and administer lectures, conferences, language courses, publications and outreach materials. They are responsible for planning either a luncheon lecture or a research paper, keeping a journal of their activities, and writing articles for the MEI newsletter.

Internships are available to college and graduate students throughout the year and last from three to four months. Fifteen to twenty interns are taken per term. While some interns work full-time, others find an internship at MEI a valuable complement to their studies or other employment. The institute is unable to offer monetary compensation to interns beyond a small stipend to cover local commuting. Interns are, however, eligible to take courses tuition-free in Arabic, Persian, Hebrew and Turkish; are given full MEI membership privileges for one full year; and often receive university credit for the internship.

Applicants are requested to submit a cover letter with a resume, a college transcript and a letter of recommendation. Interns with strong writing, organizing and word processing (WordPerfect) skills are preferred. Journalism and/or course work in Middle Eastern Languages, history or politics is helpful. For more information on the Middle East Institute and the internship program, contact:

Internship Coordinator
Middle East Institute
1761 N Street, NW
Washington, DC 20036
(202) 785-1141

RADIO FREE EUROPE/RADIO LIBERTY (RFE/RL)
Washington, DC

RFE/RL is a nonprofit radio station funded by grants from Congress through the U.S. Board for International Broadcasting. It disseminates national news and other developments in the world at large in order to encourage a constructive dialogue with the peoples of Eastern Europe and the former Soviet Union. RFE/RL has offices in Washington, DC, and in Munich, Germany, from where it broadcasts in 21 languages to the former Soviet Union, Bulgaria, Czechoslovakia, Hungary, Poland and Romania. The RFE/RL Research Institute and its publications are fundamental resources for anyone with a serious interest in Eastern Europe and the former Soviet Union.

RFE/RL offers 10 summer internships abroad. Research internships are located in Munich, and engineering internships, depending on the needs at the time, in Germany, Portugal or Spain, usually at transmitting stations. Internships last between 8 and 12 weeks. Interns are provided with round-trip air transportation, a daily stipend and living quarters.

Graduate students or highly qualified undergraduates in East European or Soviet studies or international communications with appropriate foreign language competence (East European and former Soviet area languages for research and German, Portuguese or Spanish for engineering) are sought.

Application deadlines are usually in mid-February. Resumes should only be sent after consulting the current program announcement available from:

Summer Internship Program
RFE/RL, Inc.
1201 Connecticut Avenue, NW
Washington, DC 20036
(202) 457-6936

or

Intern Program
RFE/RL, Inc.
Personnel Division, Box 86
Oettingenstrasse 67
D-8000 Munich 22
Germany
49-89-21020

WOMEN'S INTERNATIONAL LEAGUE FOR PEACE AND FREEDOM (WILPF)
Philadelphia, PA

Since its founding is 1915, Wilpf has worked toward a world free of violence, poverty, pollution and domination. Wilpf works toward these goals through its publications, forums, study groups, workshops and lobbying.

Several internships are offered in its Philadelphia headquarters: assistant to the executive director, helping the executive director with the national coalition's liaison work, researching and writing federal budget issues and how they effect women, and corresponding with other peace and women's organizations and Wilpf branches; program assistant, working with the program director in the development and implementation of national priorities; the peace and freedom editorial assistant, who helps the editor of Wilpf's publication to locate and solicit copy, edits and rewrites news items, researches and writes occasional stories, checks facts, etc.; membership assistant, who is involved in every phase of membership development; and development assistant, who works with the development director and other staff on aspects of articulating the needs for Wilpf's national political campaigns. Each internship requires different qualifications, so contact Wilpf for further details before applying.

The legislative office located in Washington, DC, offers a legislative internship covering the following categories: disarmament, civil rights, the Middle East, and Latin America, with emphasis on undoing racism and sexism and on women's perspectives. Interns typically focus on one bill or legislative issue. The internships range from 12 weeks to a year, and interns are asked to work a minimum of 15 daytime hours per week. Contact Wilpf for further information about qualifications.

For internships in the Philadelphia headquarters send a resume, writing sample, internship goals and date available to:

Women's International League for Peace and Freedom
1213 Race Street
Philadelphia, PA 19107-1691
(215) 563-7110

For legislative internships in Washington send a resume, writing sample, internship goals and date available to:

Legislative Director
WILPF
710 G Street, SE
Washington, DC 20003

WASHINGTON OFFICE ON AFRICA (WOA)
Washington, DC

WOA is a church- and trade-union-sponsored antiapartheid lobbying and research organization. Founded in 1972, WOA has lobbied on a number of issues including: sanctions, developmental aid and stability in the region.

An undetermined number of summer, semester and year-long internships are offered to college and graduate students. A stipend is available. Due to staffing constraints, WOA currently focuses on two legislative issues: maintaining sanctions against South Africa, and normalizing relations with the government of Angola. Thus, interns are primarily responsible for tracking legislation related to those issues; working with congressional staff on strategy development; carrying out work related to such strategy; working with WOA's coalition partners in the Southern African Working Group to further the work goals; and maintaining the Africa Hotline that provides weekly updates about relevant legislation and events in southern Africa. Interns are also responsible for administrative assignments in addition to their specific legislation work.

WOA looks for interns who are self-starters, motivated and well-organized. Interns are sometimes hired for permanent employment.

Contact WOA for an application:

Executive Assistant
Washington Office on Africa
110 Washington Avenue, NE
Suite 112
Washington, DC 20002
(202) 546-1545

WASHINGTON OFFICE ON LATIN AMERICA (WOLA)
Washington, DC

WOLA was founded in 1974 to monitor "human rights practices and political developments in Central and South America and the formulation and implementation of the United States' Latin America policies." It provides information and analysis to policymakers, the media, academics and others in an effort to promote informed debate on U.S. policy in Latin America, and it sponsors seminars and conferences in which prominent Latin Americans and area experts are invited to address issues such as human rights and social justice. WOLA also publishes pamphlets and newsletters, including *Enlace*, a Spanish-language newsletter.

WOLA accepts four interns per semester to work with its program and administrative staffs. WOLA prefers interns who can work 30–40 hours per week but can occasionally arrange more-flexible hours. Interns work with staff members who monitor events in the region; assist administrative staff in providing clerical support, perform other duties necessary to the day-to-day operation of a small nonprofit human rights organization.

Interns should have a demonstrated interest in and knowledge of human rights issues and Latin America; flexibility; the ability to work in a fast-paced, crowded environment with a changing agenda, a heavy influx of international visitors and busy telephones; good organizational skills; excellent oral and written communication ability; and some office skills. Command of Spanish is helpful, but not required.

Applicants should send a cover letter, resume, three references and a short writing sample. The letter should specify preference for work on Central or South America and should include a statement that the applicant understands the internship is unpaid. College transcripts are useful but not required.

Send materials to:

Intern Coordinator
Washington Office on Latin America
110 Maryland Office, NE
Washington, DC 20002-5695
(202) 544-8045

Development Assistance, Environment and Relief

AMIGOS DE LAS AMERICAS
Houston, TX

Amigos de las Americas is a private, nonprofit organization that places young people in summer health projects in Latin America. A nationwide network of more than 18 Amigos chapters trains and raises funds for the volunteers. Projects in Latin America are decided on by the Amigos field staff and the host countries.

More than 550 volunteers participate in the program each summer. Volunteers start by taking a course, which can be done through a chapter or through the mail, prepared by Amigos. The course includes conversational Spanish, Latin American culture and history and human relations training. Volunteers are sent to countries such as the Dominican Republic, Costa Rica, Mexico, Ecuador, Paraguay and Brazil. They participate in projects involving dental hygiene, community sanitation, immunization, vision screening, animal health services, environmental education and other projects as requested by the host countries. Each volunteer is supervised by "a route leader", who visits the community each week and monitors the health and safety of the participants.

Volunteers pay a substantial fee to participate in the program. Prices for 1991 were: Central America and the Caribbean $2,385, Ecuador and Paraguay $2,535 and Brazil $2,965. The fee covers round-trip air fare, accommodations and transportation in the host country, training and fund-raising materials and orientation. Programs start in mid-June and end in August.

Volunteers must be at least 16 years old, but there is no upper age limit. One year of high school Spanish or the equivalent is also required. Potential volunteers should contact their local Amigos chapter or the international office in Houston for information.

Recruiting
Amigos de las Americas
5618 Star Lane
Houston, TX 77057
(800) 231-7796
or (713) 782-5290

MINNESOTA STUDIES IN INTERNATIONAL DEVELOPMENT (MSID)
Minneapolis, MN

MSID sponsors internship programs in Kenya, Senegal, Morocco, Ecuador, India and Jamaica. To participate, interns must be University of Minnesota students, students of other schools or those with a special interest or experience in international development. MSID's primary goal is to contribute to the training of potential development workers through practical experience and cultural exchange. Interns work on local development projects, participate in village-level planning, study communications patterns, promote housing projects and conduct lectures, demonstrations and literacy programs for primary and secondary schools.

The MSID program includes two predeparture courses, which must be taken through the University of Minnesota. The internship abroad runs for a period of five to six months beginning in January, followed by outreach activities on return to Minnesota. Thirty interns participate each year. Interns work full-time and pay University of Minnesota tuition and program fees. Students may apply for financial aid through the University of Minnesota and receive college credit.

Interns may choose the country in which they want to work. Interns interested in Ecuador, India, Kenya, Morocco and Senegal will receive additional instruction in the language of their country.

To participate, students must have completed a minimum of 90 quarter credits (junior standing) and have a cumulative GPA of at least 2.5. Other criteria include specialized skills, background knowledge of the country, recommendations, ability to work well with others, maturity and cultural adaptability. The application deadline is May 15. To apply, or for more information, contact:

> Program Associate
> Minnesota Studies in International Development
> Global Campus
> 106 Nicholson Hall
> University of Minnesota
> Minneapolis, MN 55455
> (612) 625-3379 or (612) 625-9383

NATIONAL AUDUBON SOCIETY
New York, NY

The National Audubon Society is a private nonprofit conservation organization dedicated to the preservation of wildlife and its habitat in the

U.S. and abroad; educating the public on a broad range of environmental issues; and working legislatively toward more ecologically sensitive laws and regulations. Audubon's Science and Sanctuaries Division maintains over 100 wildlife sanctuaries, totaling more than 150,000 acres of protected land. Sanctuaries in Maine, Connecticut, Kentucky, South Carolina, Florida, Arizona, New York and California offer internships

The internship program was created to help individual sanctuaries meet their need for additional personnel—to do everything from leading walks to running visitor centers; from data collection to original research; and from manual labor to building displays. Internships are usually arranged for semester or summer periods. Interns are paid and provided with furnished housing, utilities and uniforms. At any one time, the society may have up to 100 interns.

Applicants must contact the individual sanctuaries to apply. For more information about the sanctuaries and the internships they offer, contact the National Audubon Society for their intern program pamphlet at:

National Audubon Society
950 Third Avenue
New York, NY 10022
(212) 832-3200

NATURAL RESOURCES DEFENSE COUNCIL (NRDC)
Washington, DC

NRDC, an organization with over 130,000 members, is dedicated to the wise management of natural resources through research, public education and the development of public policies. The council typically offers unpaid internships to college students and recent graduates during the fall, spring or summer semesters, although longer internships can be arranged. Interns work with attorneys, scientists and policy specialists on activities in several departments, including agriculture, air quality, endangered species, global warming, international environment, nuclear weapons, public health and toxins and water quality.

Experience in environmental work, science, policy issues, languages (especially Russian or Spanish) computers, grass-roots organizing or communications is helpful. Assignments usually require solid writing, research and communications skills. Part-time positions may be available, although some NRDC departments prefer a minimal commitment of 30 hours per week.

To apply, send a cover letter indicating two or three of the aforementioned departments in which you are interested in working, a starting date, hours per week you are available to work and summarize relevant experiences and background. Also include a resume, writing sample and transcript (if available). Students are urged to apply at least three months before their preferred starting date to increase chances of being selected. Summer positions are more competitive. Send application materials to:

Intern Coordinator
Natural Resources Defense Council
1350 New York Avenue, NW
Suite 300
Washington, DC 20005
(202) 783-7800

NRDC also offers internships at its other offices, in San Francisco, Los Angeles and New York City. Contact these offices for more information.

SOCIETY FOR INTERNATIONAL DEVELOPMENT (SID)
Washington, DC

The Society for International Development is a professional association for people with an interest in international economic, political and social development. SID was founded in 1957 and now has members in 120 countries and territories, forming a network of over 95 national and local chapters. The Washington chapter of SID is the largest with over 1,400 individual and 49 institutional members. SID is a multidisciplinary, nonprofit, nonpolitical organization.

The Washington chapter operates a small office with one full-time staff member and one part-time assistant to handle the maintenance of membership records and the coordination of programs and publications. From September to June, SID offers 15–20 programs per month. The monthly calendar of events and the monthly newsletter, *Development Connections,* are edited and prepared by the staff and volunteers. Other major events include the SID annual conference, in the spring, and the SID annual dinner in June.

Two to four nonpaid internships are available per semester. Some interns do receive academic credit. Each internship is tailored to the needs of the individual intern and the needs of the chapter office. The staff will try to structure interns' tasks according to personal interests. All interns are expected to help with general office duties as well as other assigned special projects.

An intern needs to have a strong interest in the field of international development, good writing skills, flexibility and a willingness to help out with a wide variety of tasks. SID also looks for persons who are self-starters and who are dependable. A basic familiarity with office procedures is a plus.

Send a resume, a writing sample and a short cover letter explaining your interest in international development issues and SID to:

> Executive Director
> The Society for International Development
> 1401 New York Avenue, NW
> Suite 1100
> Washington, DC 20005
> (202) 347-1800

VISIONS IN ACTION
Washington, DC 20007

Visions in Action is an international nonprofit organization that coordinates year-long volunteer internships in urban areas of developing countries. Visions is a nonsectarian, nonpolitical organization operating programs in Kenya, Uganda and Zimbabwe and introducing programs in India and South Africa in the 1992–93 program year.

Visions matches interns according to their skills, interests and experience to one of any number of overseas nonprofit organizations. Interns work in such diverse fields as housing, development, journalism, project management, youth group coordination, community development, women's concerns and environmental and health issues.

Applicants must have completed their second year of college or have the equivalent experience—most interns are graduates or graduate students. No experience or special skills are required. Approximately 15–30 interns are accepted into each country program.

Costs including living expenses for the internships are borne by the intern. Housing costs and air fare can total up to $5,000, so fund raising is encouraged. Interns receive nominal stipends for their work.

For more information and application deadlines contact:

> Visions in Action
> 3637 Fulton Street, NW
> Washington, DC 20007
> (202) 625-7402

Health and Population

Because many health organizations only employ medical professionals, medical students and public health experts, they normally do not offer internships. There are a few research-oriented internships for graduate students studying public health or in marketing, fund-raising or education/outreach departments. There are some internship opportunities for medical, nursing or other health-provider students. (See Chapter Seven for more information.)

THE POPULATION INSTITUTE
Washington, DC

The Population Institute is a nonprofit organization that assists institutions, the media, policymakers and the public in their understanding of global population issues. The institute is developing an extensive communications network with the ultimate goal of recruiting 1 million Americans to speak out on population issues. To this end, the institute sponsors the Future Leaders Program with 32,000 volunteers, who support U.S. assistance for international family-planning programs. Institute staff also write articles and editorials, organize world population days on campuses across the U.S. and distribute media awards.

Up to eight interns serve for each six-month session of the Future Leaders Program. Internships run during the fall and spring and offer a stipend of $800 per month plus medical and dental insurance. Interns build and activate national networks of community leaders to promote institute programs, serve as liaison with congressional staff and research possible projects. The majority of interns work on the Future Leaders Program, but a few are assigned to the public information and education division or to the public policy division. Interns stand a good chance of being hired by the institute.

Applicants for the positions must be at least 21 years of age to be eligible. Participants are selected on the basis of their leadership skills, written and oral communication skills, and their ability to set goals and aggressively pursue them. Applications should include a cover letter and a resume. For more information, contact:

> Director of Future Leaders Program
> Population Institute
> 107 2nd Street, NE
> Washington, DC 20002
> (202) 544-3300

ZERO POPULATION GROWTH (ZPG)
Washington, DC

ZPG is a national nonprofit membership organization that works to mobilize broad public support for sustainable balance among the earth's population, its environment and its resources. ZPG focuses on the role Americans can play in achieving this goal both in the United States and abroad.

Internships can cover a wide range of activities including research, writing policy analysis, organizing, teacher training, and monitoring specific legislation. Interns may choose one of ZPG's four program areas: population education, which provides training and classroom materials for teachers; media and public relations, which increases public awareness of population issues through publications and print and broadcast ventures; government relations, which works with Congress to foster policy initiatives on population and domestic and international family planning; and field and activist services, which coordinates chapter activities, volunteer efforts and public outreach events.

Full-time internships are preferred, but part-time internships can be arranged. Interns may work for a semester or a summer. Stipends are offered. ZPG accepts undergraduate and graduate students throughout the year. Students should have a strong interest in population and environmental issues, and should send a resume and three references along with a statement describing their interest in the internship to:

> Internship Program
> Zero Population Growth
> 1400 16th Street, NW
> Suite 320
> Washington, DC 20036
> (202) 332-2200

Youth Programs

AFS INTERCULTURAL PROGRAMS
New York, NY

AFS is a nonprofit, nongovernmental organization that provides cultural exchange programs for high school students and teachers in more than 60 countries. Many AFS positions are hired internally, therefore an internship provides an entrance into the AFS world with the possibility for future employment.

College and high school student internships are available in area studies, international program administration, research in intercultural learning, finance, marketing, public relations, publications, fund raising, personnel, program support, etc.

Interns must be college sophomores, juniors, seniors or graduate students with a minimum GPA of 2.5 and must have good academic standing with their college. Internships will be two or three days per week. Generally, internships will be unpaid, unless AFS has signed a contract with the college for work-study students. Students are paid a stipend for lunch ($5.00 per work day of 5 hours or more) plus transportation to and from AFS.

Internships are also offered to college graduates who seek an internship for work experience. The number of internship positions varies with demand from semester to semester. In any one period as many as 20 interns are hired.

While students are invited to submit general applications for positions, from time to time AFS will publicize specific internship assignments. You can call for current assignments. The internships are offered in the spring, summer and fall.

Send applications to:

Internship Program Coordinator
AFS Intercultural Programs
Personnel Department
313 East 43rd Street
New York, NY 10017
(212) 949-4242

U.S. GOVERNMENT

COMMISSION ON SECURITY AND COOPERATION IN EUROPE (CSCE)
Washington, DC

Created in 1976 as an independent advisory agency based in the U.S. Congress, CSCE, commonly known as the Helsinki Commission, is charged with monitoring and encouraging compliance with the provisions of the Final Act of the CSCE, signed in 1975 in Helsinki by the heads of state of the U.S., Canada, the Soviet Union and 32 European countries.

(The CSCE now includes 48 countries, including the now-independent states of the former Soviet Union.)

The commission plays a significant role in formulating and implementing U.S. policy in the CSCE process, holding extensive meetings with the officials of the executive branch, and participating in bilateral consultations with other signatories and in international diplomatic forums. The commission conducts hearings and meetings and provides a regular flow of reports and information to the Congress, the press and public on issues involving Helsinki Final Act implementation (recent reports, for example, include those on elections or political developments in the republics of the U.S.S.R. and Eastern Europe, or on the situation of minorities in CSCE states).

Part-time undergraduate internships are available during the fall and spring semesters. A limited number of paid summer internships for undergraduates are available. While there are no specific requirements, a background in international relations (particularly the former Soviet Union and Central/Eastern Europe) are strongly recommended.

Interns' duties include research on issues related to the Helsinki Final Act (including daily compilation of newspaper articles), assisting in preparation of reports, hearings and meetings, and general office work. Those interested in fall or spring internships should contact the Commission one month before the beginning of the semester. Prospective summer interns should submit resumes and academic transcripts before April 1 to:

Commission on Security and Cooperation in Europe
237 Ford House Office Building
Washington, DC 20515
(202) 225-1901

EXPORT-IMPORT BANK OF THE UNITED STATES
Washington, DC
(See Chapter Three, International Finance and Banking.)

COOPERATIVE EDUCATION PROGRAM (CO-OP)

CO-OP programs, which combine periods of study with periods of study-related employment in federal agencies, expose students to career opportunities and acquaint them with various work environments. Available to students working toward any degree—from a high school diploma to a PhD—CO-OP offers an opportunity for employment with the federal government in one's field of study.

Schools must have a continuing CO-OP, and candidates must meet the academic requirements for that school's program. The school recommends its candidates for positions, providing transcripts, descriptions of majors and programs, and other relevant academic information. Each agency has its own criteria for choosing among these candidates.

CO-OP jobs are paid according to the GS schedule, and salary is dependent upon the education and work experience possessed by the student. High school CO-OP students must work during school terms and may not work more than 20 hours per week. They are hired at grade GS-1.

Associate-degree students must be enrolled full-time at their schools to participate in CO-OP. They are hired at GS-2 and GS-3 and may be promoted if their work is satisfactory. Some associate-degree students are employed for specified occupations, and may be given a career-conditional appointment on a noncompetitive basis at GS-4 level after completing their studies.

Bachelor-degree CO-OP students are hired at grades GS-2 through GS-5. Graduates may be appointed to professional, technical or administrative positions noncompetitively at grades GS-5 or GS-7.

The CO-OP program for graduate students is used by agencies as a recruiting ground to meet long-range staffing needs. The employing agency may convert graduate interns to career service positions after interns successfully complete the program. To be eligible, graduate students must be enrolled in a field of study related to the position to which they would be appointed, and they must meet all other qualification requirements, which vary from agency to agency. Appointments are made at GS-5 or GS-7, the entry-level for professional positions.

Students who are interested in CO-OP should consult the CO-OP office at their school, where they may receive lists of available CO-OPs and other relevant information.

Private firms also participate in CO-OP programs similar to those offered by the government. Programs are normally established between firms and individual colleges and universities. Interested students should contact their college or university career office. CO-OPs in the private sector normally last several terms, with the students alternating between the CO-OP and the classroom on a semester-by-semester basis.

THE LIBRARY OF CONGRESS, THE HISPANIC DIVISION
Washington, DC

The Hispanic Division of the Library of Congress has available throughout the year a limited number of internships through which students may be trained in working in the field of Luso-Hispanic studies. Internships carry no stipend, but most interns receive academic credit.

Interns are trained in the day-to-day activities of the Hispanic Division, including bibliographic and reference work, reader service, working with *The Handbook of Latin American Studies*, classifying pamphlets and assisting foreign scholars. Time may also be spent on a specific bibliographic project or working with the Archive of Hispanic Literature on Tape.

Send a resume and two letters of recommendation to:

Hispanic Division
Library of Congress
Washington, DC 20540
(202) 707-5400

THE PRESIDENTIAL MANAGEMENT INTERN PROGRAM (PMI)
Washington, DC

PMI provides highly qualified recipients of graduate degrees with a means of entry into the federal service. Interns should be committed to management and analysis of public policies and programs. The program emphasizes the career development of the interns through a variety of work assignments, seminars, discussion groups and other activities designed to expose them to a wide range of federal management issues. Interns receive on-the-job training, which may include training courses; rotational assignments within the agency as well as between headquarters, regional offices, and field sites; and short-term assignments to other federal agencies. PMI also offers the intern a career-development program including three conferences which focus on developing the managerial competencies needed for working in a federal agency; one Congressional briefing seminar; one foreign affairs briefing seminar; two international policy institute embassy seminars; and participation in a career development group facilitated by a high-level federal manager.

In addition to these programs, the intern designs an individual learning agreement to identify his or her career objectives, training needs and the opportunities available within the internship.

PMIs are employed in all cabinet departments and with more than 60 federal agencies. The majority of available positions are in domestic policy agencies, but there are some available in the Departments of State and Defense and the International Trade Administration. There are also increasing numbers of positions becoming available within the international affairs offices of domestic agencies. Positions are available in both functional areas and general management. Although the majority of internships are in the Washington, DC, area some positions are available in regional offices and in scientific and military installments around the country.

PMIs receive two-year appointments. In some cases a one-year extension may be granted. Regardless of prior federal service or work experience, all PMIs start at GS-9 (approximately $25,717 in 1991). After the first year, they may advance to GS-11; after completing the two year program, PMIs are eligible for noncompetitive conversion to a GS-12 permanent federal position.

To be eligible for the program, an applicant must be a U.S. citizen and must have received or expect to receive a graduate degree during the current academic year. The course work of the degree should emphasize analysis and management of public policies and programs. Agencies are interested in employing interns from a wide range of academic disciplines (economics, business, law, public administration, etc.), as long as they have demonstrated a commitment to public service.

To apply, applicants must be nominated for the program by the dean or chairperson of their graduate degree program. Any graduate degree program may nominate up to 25 percent of its proposed graduating class if the degree or courses are related to public management, or the applicant has completed a public service internship as part of the graduate degree requirements. After being nominated, candidates undergo a preliminary review: they are evaluated by a committee of government officials and academicians on their potential for a career in public policy and program management and on their academic performance. Semifinalists are then invited to a regional screening, which includes completion of a writing sample and individual and group problem-solving exercises to test skills in oral communication, leadership, planning, organization and decision making. After this screening process, the PMI finalists are selected from the pool of candidates.

All finalists must pass a basic background investigation. They then receive a handbook of positions, which lists the positions available in the given year at over 60 participating agencies. The book includes contact names and addresses. Finalists may set up interviews at the agencies for the positions of their choice. At the same time, PMI coordinators distribute profiles of the finalists to the agencies, who contact finalists in whom they have a particular interest. Although PMIs are not guaranteed a position, it is rare that a selected intern who actively seeks a position does not get placed with an agency.

More information on PMI and application materials may be obtained by calling the Career America college hotline on (900) 990-9200 or by contacting:

Presidential Management Intern Program
U.S. Office of Personnel Management
PO Box 164
Room 315
Washington, DC 20044
(202) 504-2622

U.S. DEPARTMENT OF STATE
Washington, DC

The Department of State and its constituent bureaus and offices in the Washington, DC, area annually sponsor various internships (both domestic and overseas), in which a limited number of highly qualified college or university junior, senior and graduate students can gain firsthand knowledge of the Department of State's work and foreign affairs. Internships are considered an adjunct to the applicant's education and are therefore only offered to currently enrolled students planning to return to their studies upon completion of the internship.

Interns are assigned junior-foreign service officer type duties, e.g., attending meetings, answering cable traffic from embassies, filling in for absent desk officers, researching special projects, responding to inquiries from the public, participating in policy discussions and assisting in preparation of briefing materials and may be involved in areas such as financial management, intelligence, computer sciences, security and assistance and domestic and international law.

All prospective interns must be a continuing college or university junior, senior or graduate student; be a U.S. citizen; have completed some academic studies relevant to the type of work desired in the department; and be able to pass a background investigation. In addition, many bureaus have their own eligibility requirements, usually some special interest, experience or academic course work in a relevant field.

The department hires both paid and unpaid interns who serve for one semester or quarter during the academic year, or 10 weeks during the summer. Paid interns will be appointed to positions at the GS-4 through GS-7 grade levels, based on their individual qualifications and availability of funds.

All applicants must submit: a completed Standard Form SF-171 (Personal Qualification Statement), indicating the bureau or office in which you are interested in working in item 1 of the form (a separate application package must be submitted for each bureau of interest up to the maximum of two. Indicate the type of internship—paid or unpaid— after each bureau or office listed); a copy of college or university transcripts; a 500–750 word autobiography, which includes a statement of objective and a discussion of relevant studies and involvement in area issues; a Standard Form 1386 (Background Survey Questionnaire 79-2) and Standard Form 256 (Self Identification of Handicap). If you are applying after receiving an undergraduate or graduate degree, be sure to indicate that you will be continuing your studies following your internship or your application will not be considered.

To receive all the necessary forms and an informative pamphlet that provides additional details about the individual internship programs and the bureaus/offices that offer them write to:

> Intern Coordinator
> U.S. Department of State
> PO Box 9317
> Arlington, VA 22219

(Completed application forms may also be sent to this address).

Deadlines for receipt of internship applications are as follows:

> Summer Internship—November 1
> Fall Internship—March 1
> Spring Internship—July 1

After confirming that the applications are complete, the State Department sends them on the bureaus/offices in which the applicants are interested. The bureaus/offices all have their own internship coordinators who screen the applicants according to the needs of their office, and contact those who are accepted into their program. The following bureaus/offices offer internships:

- Bureau of Administration
- Bureau of African Affairs
- Art Bank Program
- Art in Embassies Program
- Bureau of Consular Affairs
- Bureau of Diplomatic Security
- Bureau of East Asian and Pacific Affairs
- Bureau of Economic and Business Affairs
- Bureau of European and Canadian Affairs
- Family Liaison Office
- Bureau of Finance and Management Policy
- Office of Foreign Mission
- Foreign Service Institute
- Bureau of Human Rights and Humanitarian Affairs
- Office of Information Management

- Office of Inspector General
- Bureau of Intelligence and Research
- Bureau of Inter-American Affairs
- Bureau of International Communications and Information Policy
- Bureau of International Narcotics Matters
- Bureau of International Organization Affairs
- Office of the Legal Adviser
- Bureau of Legislative Affairs
- Bureau of Near Eastern and South Asian Affairs
- Bureau of Oceans and International Environmental and Scientific Affairs
- Bureau of Personnel
- Policy Planning Staff
- Bureau of Politico-Military Affairs
- Office of the Chief of Protocol
- Bureau of Public Affairs
- Bureau of Refugee Programs

Applicants should also contact the bureaus/offices in which they are interested in working individually. Most offer additional information about their own internship program.

OTHER GOVERNMENT

DELEGATION OF THE COMMISSION OF THE EUROPEAN COMMUNITIES
Washington, DC

Internships with the delegation are intended to provide students with the opportunity to acquire considerable knowledge of the European Community, its institutions, activities, laws and statistics.

Interns are asked to perform the functions of information officers, under the supervision of the permanent staff. Examples of topics researched by interns include: political, economic, monetary and trade relations with the U.S.; relations with other industrialized countries, developing countries and Eastern Europe; and policies in the fields of agriculture, social and regional development, energy, transport, high-technology, education and culture.

Occasionally, interns are asked to assist with specific research projects, e.g., collection of speeches by relevant political figures; analysis of the responses received for specific information campaigns, etc.

Internships are offered three times a year: from the beginning of September until the third week of December (fall semester); from the beginning of January until the end of May (spring semester); and from the beginning of June until the end of August (summer session).

Interns are not paid, and preference is given to students available on a full-time basis. Part-time internships are, however, available.

Applications should contain a curriculum vitae, a copy of a recent transcript and a cover letter indicating the reasons for pursuing an internship with the European Community. A daytime number should also be included. Submit applications at least two months prior to the beginning of the internship. Applications should be addressed to the attention of "Academic Affairs" (Students in the fields of journalism and communications should contact *Europe Magazine* or the "Speakers' Bureau" directly for information about internships with these departments at the same address.)

Delegation of the Commission of the European Communities
2100 M Street, NW, 7th Floor
Washington, DC 20037
(202) 862-9500

THE HANSARD SOCIETY FOR PARLIAMENTARY GOVERNMENT
London

The Hansard Society promotes knowledge of parliamentary democracy. The society's internship program is open to college students interested in enlarging their knowledge of the British political system. A maximum of 17 unpaid summer and semester internships are available. Travel expenses are offered to interns.

For more information, contact:

General Secretary
The Hansard Society for Parliamentary Government
16 Gower Street
London WC1E 6DP
UK
01-323-1131

UNITED NATIONS/
INTERNATIONAL ORGANIZATIONS

Opportunities for internships at the United Nations are limited and require superior qualifications. The work is often interesting and substantive, but internships are almost always unpaid. Agencies require that interns work full-time and pay their travel expenses to and from the site of work, whether in the U.S. or abroad.

Most UN agencies require highly qualified interns, often with work experience in technical fields, developmental economics, agricultural economics, public or health administration, engineering or finance. For the most part, interns are expected to have graduate degrees or be currently enrolled in graduate school.

With the exception of the UN Headquarters Internship Program described below, the Secretariat makes no formal provision for internships. Internship programs do exist through the specialized programs and agencies on an ad hoc basis. Below are listed the major United Nations internship programs:

THE UNITED NATIONS HEADQUARTERS
INTERNSHIP PROGRAM

The purpose of the program is to promote among the participants a better understanding of major problems confronting the world and to give them an insight into how the United Nations attempts to find solutions to these problems. The program also provides departments at headquarters with the assistance of outstanding young students specializing in a relevant field, such as economics, international law, international relations, journalism, political science, population studies, public administration, social affairs and translation and terminology.

The program consists of three two-month periods throughout the year: mid-January to mid-March, mid-May to mid-July, and mid-September to mid-November. In exceptional cases, individual internships may be extended for up to one month upon written request from the department concerned

Interns are fully involved in the work program of the department or office of the Secretariat that has selected them for an internship, carrying out their assignments under the supervision of a professional staff member. A number of informational briefings on the role and objectives of the organization is included in the program.

Applicants should be currently enrolled in a graduate school, or if pursuing studies in countries where higher education is not divided into undergraduate and graduate studies, should have completed at least three years of university studies. Those with a second-level university degree will not be considered, and applicants should not be more than 30 years of age. Internships are not paid. Costs of travel and accommodation, as well a living expenses, are the responsibility of interns or their sponsoring institutions.

Graduate students who are interested in an internship at UN headquarters in New York should submit a completed application form with Part II filled out by the office of the dean of the graduate school or by the Permanent Mission to the United Nations. Grade transcripts or lists of courses taken and, if available, a sample of research work in English or French should accompany the application. Applicants should also submit an essay, written in English or French, stating the purpose of the internship. The deadline for receipt of applications is six months prior to the starting date. Late or incomplete applications will not be considered.

Application forms can be obtained by contacting:

> Coordinator, Internship Program
> Room S-2500E, United Nations
> New York, NY 10017
> (212) 963-1223

AD HOC INTERNSHIP PROGRAM

The purpose of the Ad Hoc Internship Program is to promote among the participants a better understanding of international problems and an insight into the workings of the United Nations; and to provide departments with the able assistance of young students specializing in a field related to their work.

The program is open to graduate (and, in special cases, to exceptional undergraduate) students. Interns are expected to work a minimum of two months.

For more information write:

> Internship Coordinator
> Recruitment Programs Section
> Room 2475
> Office of Personnel Services
> United Nations
> New York, NY 10017

UNITED NATIONS INSTITUTE FOR TRAINING AND RESEARCH (UNITAR) INTERNSHIP PROGRAM

UNITAR accepts a small number of interns for work in research, training or administration for periods varying between two months and one year.

Application forms are available at the office of the dean of the relevant graduate schools or at permanent missions to the UN. Applications should be sent to:

> Executive Director of UNITAR
> 801 United Nations Plaza
> New York, NY 10017

UNITED NATIONS DEVELOPMENT PROGRAM (UNDP) SUMMER INTERNSHIP PROGRAM

UNDP summer internships last from eight to ten weeks and are aimed at on-the-job training for a limited number of qualified young students undertaking development-oriented graduate studies. Participants will obtain firsthand practical experience in the operations of the largest program of technical assistance in developing countries. At the beginning of the program, interns receive three days of formal training.

To qualify for an internship with UNDP, applicants should be studying at the post-graduate level in development-related studies and be proficient in two of UNDP's main working languages (English, French and Spanish) and have a keen interest in the field of development.

Applications should be sent to:

> Chief of Recruitment Section
> Summer Internship Program
> Division of Personnel
> UNDP, One United Nations Plaza
> New York, NY 10017

UNITED NATIONS INDUSTRIAL DEVELOPMENT ORGANIZATION (UNIDO)
Vienna, Austria

UNIDO, the 16th specialized agency to the United Nations, promotes industrial development in developing countries. It provides a forum for developing and industrialized countries to meet and discuss industrialization and assists these countries in obtaining external financing for industrial projects. UNIDO provides technical assistance, training and expertise, and assists with the exchange of industrial information, the purchase of equipment and investment promotion.

About 50 unpaid internships are available per year on an ad hoc basis. Applicants are normally expected to have a graduate degree or to be enrolled in an advanced-degree program. Departments in which interns work include: external relations, public information, language and documentation service, industrial operations, program and project development, industrial promotion consultations and technology and occasionally in the director general's office or administration. Interns work under the guidance of the professionals in the respective departments and either assist them in their day-to-day work or are given specific research assignments.

Internship applicants must be nominated by the U.S. Mission to the UN or by their college or university. Schools should initiate the application at least three months in advance by contacting:

> Personnel Services Division
> UNIDO, Room E0554
> Vienna International Centre
> PO Box 300
> A-1400 Vienna, Austria
> (43-1) 211 31

Chapter Eleven

GRADUATE PROGRAMS

INTRODUCTION

On December 6, 1991, President Bush signed the National Security Education Act of 1991, the largest new higher-education initiative of its kind since 1958. The act provides funds for undergraduate study abroad, curriculum grants to colleges and universities for programs in international and area studies and foreign languages, and fellowships for graduate students in those fields. Government is recognizing, with some prompting from academia and business, the urgent need in every economic sector for people with international training. Careers in world affairs require skills in language, politics and economics, and call for cultural understanding and sensitivity. Education—together with study or work abroad and internships in organizations that do international work—is the best way to establish your credentials and open the door to an international career.

In recent years undergraduate majors in international affairs have proliferated. These majors, which include interdisciplinary programs combining history, political science, languages and other fields, are a good start for someone already committed to international work: they provide a general background in international studies and are helpful in finding internships. However, for most fields a graduate degree is essential. Most international firms and organizations require or a least encourage applicants to obtain graduate degrees. Some will not hire without one.

DOCTORATES VS. MASTERS AND "ACADEMIC" VS. "PROFESSIONAL" DEGREES

When considering a graduate program, students are faced with a choice between a "professional" and an "academic" degree. It is important to know what type of work you are most interested in pursuing. Knowing what your priorities are and what you want from a graduate degree will make it easier to sort through the many options available today.

In general, the student of international relations follows one of two paths. An "academic" course prepares the student to continue on to a PhD* degree and will usually lead to a career in university-level teaching or research. Some PhD recipients go on to work for international organizations and international financial institutions, both governmental and private, as well as think tanks and consulting firms or enter policy-oriented careers where a PhD may be useful or required. For most internationally oriented jobs, however, a PhD is not necessary.

PhD programs in international studies are based on two traditional academic disciplines—politics and economics—and may also include psychology, sociology, history and regional studies. If you have decided to follow the PhD path, it is important to be aware of the difference between single-discipline-based doctorates, which better equip a student for a traditional academic career, and interdisciplinary doctorates, which generally equip students for a more policy-oriented career.

The employment outlook for PhD recipients in teaching and research appears quite promising. According to Gerard F. Sheehan, Associate Dean at Tufts University, "...data regarding the availability of college/university-level teaching jobs is much more positive than it was in 1986/87." A report published in 1989, "Prospects for Faculty in the Arts and Sciences" by William G. Bowen and Julie Ann Sosa, predicted an increased demand for qualified professors by 1992, and projected that by 1997 there would be only seven eligible candidates for every ten available positions in the social sciences and humanities.

The second or "professional" path usually terminates with a master's degree, although some students continue on to doctorates. Masters pro-

---

* See glossary of degrees at the end of the chapter.

grams generally run one to two years, with a bachelor degree as a prerequisite. Some universities offer more-specialized graduate degrees in such fields as international development, area studies and economics. The most prominent masters programs, however, are the MPA and the MAIR/MIA.

The MAIR and MIA programs usually draw on five academic disciplines: politics, economics, history, law and business. They also include many interdisciplinary courses, e.g., "law and policy in international business." These programs are often combined with regional or functional concentrations, sometimes both. The MIA and MAIR tend to take a social science approach to international relations and to pay close attention to area studies.

Graduate schools that offer public policy programs tend to consider themselves professional schools, the trainers of tomorrow's decision makers. The degree was originally created to offer students interested in government service professional training similar to that available to business, law and medical students. The courses concentrate less on history and theory than on teaching students to create and analyze public programs and policies and bring economic, statistical, organizational and political analyses to bear on current issues. The MPA/MPP programs attempt to blend the academic rigor of an MIA/MAIR program with the practical disciplines of an MBA.

The difference between MIA/MAIR and MPA/MPP programs begins to blur once one examines the requirements and course offerings of many of the schools. Many MIA/MAIR programs are considered *professional*, because they emphasize the practical application of theory in their curriculum, and a number of international relations courses offered by the MPA/MPP programs could just as easily fit into the curricula of their more academic counterparts.

Two questions that can help you determine if a school or program is appropriate for you are: First, what careers have alumni of the program chosen? If you are interested in an academic path and most of the alumni are in business, it may not be the best program for you. Second, does the school belong to any organization or consortium, such as the Association of Professional Schools of International Affairs (ASPIA) or the National Association of Schools of Public Affairs and Administration (NASPA)? These organizations usually have guidelines or common policies concerning educational goals, curriculum and admissions.

MBAs AND JDs

Many banks, financial institutions, consulting organizations and businesses require or prefer a Master of Business Administration (MBA)

The number of recipients of MA/PhDs in International Relations and MA/PhDs in Public Policy

	International Relations		Public Policy	
	MA	PhD	MA	PhD
86-'87	1415	61	4967	91
87-'88	1213	63	5188	106
88-'89	1516	50	5150	130
89-'90	1535	87	5123	117

Source: Department of Education, National Center of Educational Statistics

for employment. The MBA is a two-year graduate-degree program that covers accounting, finance, microeconomics, macroeconomics, statistics, computers, marketing, administration and management. In response to an increasingly global business environment, more MBA programs are emphasizing international courses.

Besides being useful for entry into business, an MBA can also lead to work in the public sector, nonprofit organizations and other nongovernmental organizations. Top-notch management and problem-solving skills are also sought by public-sector organizations like the World Bank, the United Nations Development Program and the Congressional Budget Office and nonprofits like the Ford Foundation and others. Work experience in the public sector does not hinder movement into the private sector. "Many forecasters who attempt to predict the business environment in the next century believe that the top business leaders will have worked in the public arena at least once and some will flow back and forth several times," according to Peter Veruki and Candy Mirrer in their article, "An Alternative Career for MBAs—The Public Sector."

The JD, or law degree, is a three-year program in which graduate students are trained in the fundamentals of the U.S. legal system. The law degree has traditionally been a passport to politics, government and business. While it is still useful in these fields, some people consider other degrees more relevant—such as the MBA for business and the MPA for government.

JOINT DEGREES AND STUDY ABROAD

Joint-degree programs call for simultaneous studies in two fields leading to two separate degrees. The benefit of pursuing two degrees concurrently is that, at most schools, some courses will be credited to both degrees. Consequently, the program can be completed in a shorter time. A joint law and international relations program, for example, takes four years. If pursued consecutively, the degrees would require five years. Joint degrees are popular because they allow a student to combine two interests and gain greater depth in both fields. If you are unable to find a joint degree program in the fields of your choice, some schools offer ad hoc joint degree programs or allow you, under direction, to create your own.

Studying abroad not only increases language skills but also provides an understanding of foreign cultures that is not attainable from simply reading and studying about them. Undergraduates interested in international affairs might consider spending a semester or year abroad. Many undergraduate institutions allow students to count credits earned abroad toward their BA degree. Some also provide financial aid for foreign study. Programs for graduate students are less common but do exist. Some schools sponsor foreign programs; others may allow their students to participate in outside programs, with arrangements made on an ad hoc basis.

Most colleges and graduate schools have information about study-abroad programs and can advise students in planning their travel. The Information Center at the Institute of International Education (IIE) can also assist students, scholars and teachers in finding opportunities to study or teach abroad. Information is not given out over the phone. The Information Center is located at 809 UN Plaza, New York, NY 10017, (212) 883-8200. The center is open Monday through Friday from 10 AM to 3:45 PM.

STANDARDIZED TESTS, APPLICATION PROCEDURES

For business and law, there are separate standardized tests. Most business schools require the GMATs, and law schools insist on the LSATs. Other graduate schools require the GREs for admission to doctoral and master's programs. Joint degree programs may require a combination of two tests. Because they are part of your application package, doing well on these tests is important.

Use of the GRE test scores varies considerably from institution to institution. Some admissions departments give test scores equal weight with other parts of the student's application, including personal essay, letters of recommendation, relevant work experience, etc. Others weight scores heavily, while others do not require the tests at all.

The general GRE now has three sections, analytical, quantitative and verbal. The highest possible score in each section is 800. Some universities are only interested in scores for one or two of the sections. Find out from the university what scores they are most interested in and what they consider an acceptable score.

Information about these tests can be obtained from your undergraduate school career office, from the graduate school to which you are applying or from Educational Testing Services (ETS), Princeton, NJ, (609) 771-7670. Look into the tests early because they are only offered a few times a year. They can be difficult and you will want time to study. You might consider preparing for the tests by taking a practice course. If you find the course fees prohibitive, GRE study aids are available in most book stores or directly from ETS.

LANGUAGE TRAINING

As private and public enterprises become more and more global, the need for individuals with language skills increases. In recognition of this, many graduate programs require foreign language proficiency at the time of graduation. Some schools even require prospective students to prove a certain degree of language skill before admission.

Intensive training, preferably abroad, is still the best way to learn a language. There are too many university-sponsored and private study programs in the U.S. and abroad to list here, but two summer programs in the U.S. deserve special mention.

Middlebury College offers an MA in French, German, Italian, Russian or Spanish, which can be earned through a series of 12 courses taken over several summers. A Master of Modern Languages degree (MML) may be earned by taking an additional 12 courses beyond the MA degree and passing comprehensive written and oral examinations. A DML degree (Doctor of Modern Languages) is available. It requires proficiency in two languages and a thesis. Middlebury also offers nondegree language programs in Arabic, French, Chinese, German, Italian, Japanese, Russian and Spanish. These summer programs are roughly the equivalent of one year of undergraduate study in the language. The address is: Middlebury College, Middlebury, VT 05753, (802) 388-3711.

The **Monterey Institute of International Studies** offers an MA in Teaching Foreign Language or in Teaching English to Speakers of Other Languages in an intensive program over three summers. It also offers intensive eight- and nine-week summer programs at the first- and second-year college level in Arabic, Chinese, English, French, German, Italian, Japanese, Korean, Portuguese, Russian and Spanish. The institute's Training for Service Abroad program enables executives and representatives of American and foreign firms, journalists and students to acquire language proficiency and cross-cultural business skills. The institute's Center for Language Services offers court-interpreter training. The address is: Monterey Institute of International Studies, Admissions Office, 425 Van Buren Street, Monterey, CA 93940, (408) 647-4123.

HOW TO USE THIS CHAPTER (Read carefully!)

Following are brief explanations of the contents of each graduate program/school entry. It is important to contact admissions departments for updates on admission requirements, deadlines for application, program changes and other critical information. Please note that the lists do not include political science degrees, doctoral programs, international education programs or programs at universities abroad. These are simply too numerous to include. We have tried to make the lists complete, but as of this writing there are well over 200 programs in international and public policy studies. We apologize in advance for any inadvertent omissions, and encourage students to explore programs not mentioned here.

Degrees: The entry lists established international and related fields of study that result in a master's degree.

Joint Degrees: The entry indicates what joint degrees are offered in international and related fields. Be sure to contact the school for information concerning special application and admission requirements for joint programs. Degree acronyms are spelled out at the end of the chapter.

Areas of Specialization: The entry lists available fields of concentration, major and minor. The areas are usually subdivided into regional and topical issues. Most masters programs encourage or require students to concentrate on one area. We have not indicated whether such specialization is required or optional.

Number of Applicants and Entering Class: Unless otherwise indicated, applicant and enrollment numbers are representative of two-year masters programs only. The entering class figures do not include the total number of students enrolled in the program or school, **nor do they reflect the total number of students admitted into the school/program**. Entering class figures are anywhere from 50%-75% of the number of students accepted.

Entrance Requirements: The entry indicates test requirements and desirable applicant qualities as described by the university. It is very important to check with the university before applying to make certain that there have been no recent changes in entrance requirements. When GRE is listed as a requirement, this refers to the general test. Requirements for subject tests must be obtained from the college or university.

Financial Aid and Internships: The entry indicates what special financial aid may be offered by the university, school or program. University financial aid on the graduate level usually comes in the form of teaching assistantships, research assistantships, work-study, grants, fellowships and scholarships. In some cases, universities make the distinction between need-based and merit-based financial aid. Individual fellowships and scholarships are not listed. Specific information about these must be obtained from the university. Be aware that some schools are more likely to fund a student after he or she has successfully completed a semester and demonstrated his or her academic ability.

This section does not include information about the availability of federal and state funds, such as guaranteed student loans. Some work-study programs are also federally funded, and some schools offer combination packages comprised of both government and private money. Most universities have facilities to help students apply for federal and state financial aid in the event they do not qualify for, or there is a lack of, university-sponsored financial assistance.

Career Development: The entry indicates any special career development resources the school or university may offer, including career centers, career fairs and on-campus recruiting.

Study Abroad: The entry lists special programs that are available to enrolled students to spend a semester, summer or entire year abroad while earning credits toward a master's degree. Many graduate programs allow students to devise their own study-abroad program for academic credit. Applicants should consult the graduate school for this information; only formal programs have been listed here.

THE AMERICAN UNIVERSITY
School of International Service
4400 Massachusetts Avenue, NW
Washington, DC 20016
(202) 885-1600

Degrees: Master of Arts in International Affairs, Master of Arts in International Communication, Master of Arts in International Development; Master of Science in Development Management
Joint Degrees: JD/MAIA
Areas of Specialization: International politics, international law and organization, international political economy, peace and conflict resolution, U.S. foreign policy, international economic policy, comparative and regional studies, international communication, international development, development management.
Number of Applicants Fall 1992: 999
Entering Class Fall 1992: 320
Entrance Requirements: GRE. Students applying for the JD/MA program may submit LSAT scores in lieu of the GRE. Applicants must have a cumulative average of at least 3.3 on a 4.0 scale; should have completed at least 24 credit hours of social science work relevant to international relations.
Financial Aid and Internships: Students may apply for financial aid on the basis of merit. Due to the school's location, internships are plentiful. The school also offers international internships.
Career Development: The American University's Career Center offers career education, resources and preparation, cooperative education and placement programs. A team of placement and cooperative education coordinators serve SIS students exclusively. Throughout the school year, special programs are tailored to specific majors and professional fields.

THE AMERICAN UNIVERSITY
School of Public Affairs
4400 Massachusetts Avenue, NW
Washington, DC 20016
(202) 885-2940

Degrees: Master of Public Administration, Master of Science in Human Resources, Master of Science in Public Financial Management, Master of Science in Justice (A Master of Arts in Political Science is also available.)
Joint Degrees: JD/MS in Justice

Areas of Specialization: (Note: Not all specializations are offered for every program.) American politics; comparative politics; law and society; court management; corrections; law enforcement; drugs, justice and public policy; procurement management; management-information systems; international development; policy analysis; human resources development; public financial management; and urban affairs.

Number of Applicants Fall 1991: 419

Entering Class Fall 1991: 165

Entrance Requirements: The school is divided into three departments: Government, Public Administration and Justice, Law and Society. Applicants must apply directly to appropriate departments, which have different entrance requirements. Generally a 3.0 average in the last 60 semester hours is required. The LSAT and GRE are required for the JD/MS in Justice.

Financial Aid and Internships: Merit-based and minority fellowships and assistantships are available. Paid internships are available for graduate students.

Study Abroad: International Co-op (work-study) opportunities are available in Britain, France, Belgium, Spain, Germany, Costa Rica, Barbados, Jamaica, the Dominican Republic and Japan.

BAYLOR UNIVERSITY
PO Box 97276
Waco, TX 76798-7276
(817) 755-3588

Degrees: Master of Arts in International Relations, Master of International Management, Master of International Journalism, Master of Business Administration in International Management

Areas of Specialization: International business, international relations

Number of Applicants Fall 1992: NA

Entering Class Fall 1992: 84

Entrance Requirements: Applicants should have an undergraduate GPA of at least 2.7. The GRE is required for the MAIR programs; the GMAT for the MBA-IM and either the GRE or GMAT is acceptable for the MIM.

Financial Aid and Internships: There are about ten research assistantships. Work-study is also available.

Career Development: On-campus recruiting by the U.S. government, Texas state government and major corporations.

BOSTON UNIVERSITY
Graduate School Center for International Relations
152 Bay State Road
Boston, MA 02215
(617) 353-9278

Degree: Master of Arts in International Relations
Joint Degrees: MAIR/JD, MAIR/MBA, MAIR/ICOM, MAIR/REM
Areas of Specialization: East Asia, Latin and Central America, Middle East, Europe, security studies
Number of Applicants Fall 1992: 445
Entering Class Fall 1992: 89
Entrance Requirements: GRE. The LSAT for the MAIR/JD, and the GMAT for the MAIR/MBA programs.
Financial Aid and Internships: Three fellowships and 14 graduate assistantships are available. No work-study is available.
Career Development: There is a career development center at Boston University that runs on-campus recruiting programs and advises students.

BRIGHAM YOUNG UNIVERSITY
David M. Kennedy Center for International Studies
237 Herald R. Clark Building
Provo, UT 84602
(801) 378-3377

Degrees: Master of Arts in International and Area Studies
Joint Degrees: MA/MBA and MA/JD
Areas of Specialization: American studies, Asian studies, international development, international relations, Near Eastern studies
Number of Applicants Fall 1992: 72
Entering Class Fall 1992: 20
Entrance Requirements: GRE scores required, as is a minimum undergraduate GPA of 3.2, some undergraduate background in an international field, completion of 16 undergraduate hours in a foreign language or other evidence of conversational fluency. Pre-law students may submit LSAT scores and joint MBA students may submit GMAT scores.
Financial Aid and Internships: Most students have research or teaching assistantships. The David M. Kennedy Graduate Fellow Award goes to two outstanding first-year students. The center also provides first-year full-time financial assistance in the form of tuition scholarships to as many students as possible. International Studies Association, publications and the study abroad program hire graduate students for work-study and internships.

Career Development: A placement program helps students seeking employment.
Study Abroad: London, Austria, Israel, Russia and elsewhere.

UNIVERSITY OF CALIFORNIA, BERKELEY
Graduate School of Public Policy
2607 Hearst Avenue
Berkeley, CA 94720
(510) 642-4670

Degree: Master of Public Policy
Joint Degrees: MPP/JD, MPP/MPH
Areas of Specialization: The program emphasizes domestic policy. Students with international goals may take electives from other departments on campus.
Number of Applicants Fall 1992: 389
Entering Class Fall 1992: 32
Entrance Requirements: none
Financial Aid and Internships: Teaching assistantships are available to second-year students. The graduate division and the Public Policy department also provide funds.
Career Development: Regular on-campus recruiting.

CALIFORNIA STATE UNIVERSITY, SACRAMENTO
International Affairs Graduate Program
6000 J Street
Sacramento, CA 95819-6072
(916) 278-7254

Degree: Master of Arts in International Affairs
Number of Applicants Fall 1992: 36
Entering Class Fall 1992: 18
Entrance Requirements: GRE. There are also language, economics and statistics requirements which may be fulfilled while enrolled; credits do not count toward the degree.
Financial Aid and Internships: There are no research assistantships, teaching assistantships or work-study. Internships have been arranged with state and local government, the Port of Sacramento and the private sector.
Career Development: Individual faculty consultations with on-campus recruiting facilities.

Study Abroad: The International Program Center works with students to coordinate one-year programs, mainly in Europe.

UNIVERSITY OF CALIFORNIA, SAN DIEGO
**Graduate School of International Relations
and Pacific Studies (IR/PS)**
9500 Gillman Drive
La Jolla, CA 92093-0520
(619) 534-5914

Degree: Master of Pacific International Affairs
Areas of Specialization: Concentrations in international management, international relations and comparative public policy; regional concentrations in China, Japan, Korea and Latin America.
Number of Applications 1992: 400
Entering Class Fall 1992: 89
Entrance Requirements: Strong academic record, previous professional employment, a history of meaningful international experience and demonstrated leadership ability are a plus. The GRE is required, but scores from the GMAT may be substituted.
Financial Aid and Internships: Financial aid is available in the form of merit-based awards, research and teaching assistantships and need-based financial aid.
Career Development: IR/PS offers career-support programs, including Career Services Strategic Planning Committee, the IR/PS Resume Book, Professional Development Workshop Series, Career Advising Panels, Career Forums, Career Services Library Resources, and others.

THE CLAREMONT GRADUATE SCHOOL
Center for Politics and Policy
170 East 10th Street
McManus Hall 225
Claremont, CA 91711-6163
(714) 621-8171

Degrees: Master of Arts in International Studies, Master of Arts in Politics, Master of Arts in Public Policy
Joint Degrees: All three masters programs can be combined with masters programs in psychology, economics, history, management, information science, mathematics, education, philosophy and religion.
Areas of Specialization: International studies (international political economy, foreign policy, defense policy), comparative politics, public

policy, political philosophy, American politics, criminology, criminal justice system, public law and judicial process. Other concentrations can be developed individually in consultation with faculty.

Number of Applicants Fall 1992: 221

Entering Class Fall 1992: 48

Entrance Requirements: GRE

Financial Aid and Internships: There are approximately 20 research assistantships and teaching assistantships available each semester. The center also offers a number of partial and full fellowship awards and work-study. Internships are required of policy students.

Career Development: The Office of Career Services provides career-development services particularly for non-academic jobs.

CLARK UNIVERSITY
International Development Program
950 Main Street
Worcester, MA 01610
(508) 793-7201

Degree: Master of Arts in International Development

Joint Degrees: MAID/MARP (with Rehovot Development Center in Israel)

Areas of Specialization: Natural resources management, rural development, women and development, development theory, international political economy, household economic behavior, local organization and participation, comparative economic relations, anthropology, and development management. A student may also design a course sequence that results in a new focus. Originally oriented primarily toward Africa, the program also offers courses, field work and internship opportunities for Latin America, the Caribbean and South Asia.

Number of Applicants Fall 1992: 140

Entering Class 1992: 12

Entrance Requirements: GRE not required. International work experience, especially abroad, is preferred.

Financial Aid and Internships: Every year research assistantships and teaching assistantships are available to graduate students. A special scholarship is offered to a returning Peace Corps volunteer. No work-study is available. Internships, especially overseas, are encouraged and earn credit toward the degree. Assistance in procuring them is provided.

COLUMBIA UNIVERSITY
School of International and Public Affairs (SIPA)
420 West 118th Street
New York, NY 10027
(212) 854-4737

Degrees: Master of International Affairs, Master of Public Administration
Joint Degrees: MBA/MIA, MS in Journalism/MIA, JD/MIA, MPA/MIA, MIA/MPH, MIA/MSW, and MA in Teaching/MIA, MPA/JD, MPA/MSW, MPA/MPH
Areas of Specialization: (MIA program) Regional—Africa, East Asia, East Central Europe, former Soviet Union, Latin America and Iberia, Middle East, Southern Asia, Western Europe. Functional—environmental policy studies, international economic policy, economic and political development, human rights and international law, international business, international economics, international finance and banking, international media and communications, international political economy, international security policy, international policy analysis and public management. **(MPA program)** Advanced management techniques, advanced policy-analysis techniques, urban planning policy, health policy, environmental science and technology policy, social services and welfare policy, international affairs policy, education policy, legal and public policy, and self-designed policy concentration.
Number of Applicants Fall 1992: MIA-1400, MPA-350
Entering Class Fall 1992: MIA-291, MPA-84
Entrance Requirements: The GRE is highly recommended but not obligatory. All joint programs have separate application procedures. Applicants for the MIA must have some language proficiency. Some requirements can be fulfilled while enrolled.
Financial Aid and Internships: The school has a merit/need system of financial aid. Fellowship competition is open to all students. Work-study and internships are available to all students who qualify.
Career Development: On-campus and off-campus recruiting. Separate career offices for SIPA.

CREIGHTON UNIVERSITY
Graduate School
24th and California
Administration Building, Room 235
Omaha, Nebraska 68178
(402) 280-2870

Graduate Degree: Master of Arts in International Relations
Areas of Specialization: International politics and economics, Europe in world affairs, the U.S. in world affairs, the less-industrialized world
Number of Applicants Fall 1992: 21
Entering Class Fall 1992: 8
Entrance Requirements: Students must have taken the GRE, 24 semester hours of upper-division social science and have had the following courses: survey history, introductory political science, and fundamentals of economics. A modern foreign language is recommended but not required for admission. However, language competency is required to graduate. Language credits do not count toward the degree.
Financial Aid and Internships: Program has no special fellowships or teaching assistantships. Some internships have been arranged.
Career Development: Most students at Creighton Graduate School are employed full-time, a majority by the U.S. military.

UNIVERSITY OF CONNECTICUT
Division of International Affairs
843 Bolton Road
Storrs, CT 06269
(203) 486-3152

Degrees: Master of Arts in International Studies
Joint Degrees: MAIS/MBA
Areas of Specialization: Latin American and Caribbean studies, Slavic and East European studies, Western European studies, African studies
Number of Applicants Fall 1991: NA
Entering Class Fall 1991: NA
Entrance Requirements: The GRE is required for all graduate programs and the joint MAIS/MBA program also requires the GMAT. A "B" average in undergraduate studies is also essential.
Financial Aid and Internships: Teaching assistantships and research assistantships are available and awarded on the basis of merit. There are limited funds for work-study, which is reserved for U.S. citizens and permanent residents of the U.S.
Career Development: On-campus career development facility.

CORNELL UNIVERSITY
Mario Einaudi Center for International Studies
170 Uris Hall
Ithaca, NY 14853-7601
(607) 255-6370

The Center: The Mario Einaudi Center for International Studies facilitates cooperation in international work among the independent academic units at Cornell. It is basically an administrative entity, not a separate school.

Degrees: There are over 25 international masters degree programs, including a Master of Professional Studies in International Development, Master of Public Administration with area concentration, and concentration in international relations.

Areas of Specialization: At present there are over 20 international programs, including 5 national resource centers: African, Latin American, South Asia, Southeast Asia, and Western studies, as well as 13 development and topical studies programs. There are also several MPS and MPA programs available for the mid-career professional.

Number of applicants 1991: NA

Entering Class Fall 1991: NA

Entrance Requirements: The GRE is required by most fields. Many fields also require a score from an appropriate subject test. Exam requirements differ according to the graduate field.

Financial Aid and Internships: There are numerous teaching and research assistantships, work-study positions and fellowships available to graduate students. Travel grants are also offered.

Career Development: The graduate school has a career center.

UNIVERSITY OF DENVER
Graduate School of International Studies (GSIS)
2201 S. Gaylord Street
Denver, CO 80208
(303) 871-2324

Degree: Master of Arts in International Affairs

Joint Degrees: MA/JD, MIM, MA/MSW, MA/MA in Mass Communications

Areas of Specialization: Global conflict, development, human rights, technology, policy analysis, international political economy. Regional concentrations: Africa, Latin America, former Soviet Union/Eastern Europe, Middle East and East Asia, Western Europe. Fields: international economics, international politics, comparative politics.

Number of Applicants Fall 1992: 450

Entering Class Fall 1992: 90

Entrance Requirements: GRE required for all general and joint masters programs with the exception of the MIM and MA/JD programs, which require the GMAT and the LSAT respectively. A minimum undergraduate GPA of 3.0 is necessary. There is a foreign-language requirement for the

program but not for admission. Language credits count toward the degree. **Financial Aid and Internships:** GSIS offers 35–40 academic scholarships each year to U.S. and international students based on merit and need. For second-year students, teaching and research assistantships are available. Internships with Denver-area businesses, government agencies and nonprofits are plentiful and earn credits toward the degree. Workstudy is extremely limited, and based on need for U.S. citizens.
Career Development: There is a Central Career Services Office and a yearly recruiting fair. GSIS also has its own small career services office. Study Abroad: Germany, France, Chile and Costa Rica.

DUKE UNIVERSITY
Sanford Institute of Public Policy
4875 Duke Station
Durham, NC 27706
(919) 684-6612

Degree: Master of Arts in Public Policy Studies
Joint Degrees: MA/JD, MA/MBA, MA/MEM, MA/MD and others available.
Areas of Specialization: International policy, health policy, environmental policy, education policy, communications, tax policy, management.
Number of Applicants Fall 1992: 250
Entering Class Fall 1992: 27
Entrance Requirements: GRE. For the joint JD/MA and MA/MBA the LSAT and GMAT, respectively, are necessary.
Financial Aid and Internships: The department administers merit-based fellowship support; need-based loans are available from the graduate school. Teaching and research assistantships are based on work-study eligibility. Internships are required during the summer after the first year.
Career Development: Full-time internship and placement director and staff. There is regular on-campus recruiting and a reading and resource room.

FLORIDA INTERNATIONAL UNIVERSITY
Graduate Program in International Studies (GPIS)
DM-497A
University Park
Miami, FL 33199
(305) 348-2455

Degree: Master of Arts in International Studies
Areas of Specialization: Development (four functional fields): international relations and development, sociopolitical change and development, economic development, Latin America/Caribbean.
Number of Applicants Fall 1992: 105
Entering Class Fall 1992: 27
Entrance Requirements: The general GRE and a 3.0 undergraduate GPA are required.
Financial Aid and Internships: There are a number of teaching and research assistantships available in participating departments and merit-based scholarship funds.
Career Development: There is a career office on-campus.
Study Abroad: Caribbean

GEORGETOWN UNIVERSITY
The Edmund A. Walsh School of Foreign Service
The Graduate Division
7th Floor, Intercultural Center
Washington, DC 20057-0999
(202) 687-5763

Degree: Master of Science in Foreign Service
Joint Degrees: MSFS/MA in History, MSFS/MA in Economics, MSFS/JD, MSFS/BS in Foreign Service
Areas of Specialization: U.S. foreign policy and diplomacy (including security studies), international trade, finance, development, and business diplomacy; regional: Africa, Asia, Europe, Latin America, Middle East and Russia.
Number of Applicants Fall 1992: 1,000
Entering Class Fall 1992: 65
Entrance Requirements: GRE. Applicants for the MSFS/MA in Economics must take the economics subject test. The LSAT is required for those interested in the MSFS/JD degree. Microeconomics and macroeconomics, four semesters of a romance language or six to seven semesters of a non-romance language. These requirements cannot be fulfilled while enrolled.
Financial Aid and Internships: Tuition scholarships are awarded based on academic merit and financial need. All applicants for scholarship assistance must submit the FAF or the GAPSFAS (federal financial aid forms) in addition to the Georgetown financial aid form. Students can apply for teaching or research assistantships once they have matriculated in the MSFS Program. There are many on- and off-campus work-study

positions. An MSFS internship coordinator is available to provide information about public- and private-sector firms and organizations.

Career Development: The MSFS Program has a Career Resource Center. The center provides career reference material and information and other resources. The career officer and intern coordinator identify career opportunities in the public, private and nonprofit sectors and assist students in developing career plans and timetables for implementing them. Students' professional-contact skills are defined through workshops, mock interviews and videotaping, as well as informational interviews. Students are introduced to a network of alumni, faculty and the MSFS Advisory Panel who provide insights and advice in either one-on-one sessions or by participating in discussions on-campus. A weekly newsletter, *Briefing,* provides announcements about programs, internship positions and jobs, and advertises regular events such as employer presentations and receptions, speakers, seminars and alumni panels. Public, private and nonprofit organizations recruit from the MSFS Program.

Study Abroad: All over the world including: Austria, France, Germany, Republic of China, Netherlands and Canada.

THE GEORGE WASHINGTON UNIVERSITY
Elliott School of International Affairs
Stuart Hall Room 107
2013 G Street, NW
Washington, DC 20005
(202) 994-7050

Degrees: Master of Arts in International Affairs, Master of Arts in East Asian Studies, Master of Arts in European Studies, Master of Arts in International Development, Master of Arts in Security Policy Studies, Master of Arts in Latin American Studies, Master of Arts in Russian and East European Studies, Master of Arts in Science, Technology and Public Policy.

Joint Degree: JD/MA with the National Law Center

Areas of Specialization: International politics, international economics, comparative politics, modern political theory, U.S. foreign policy, history of strategy and policy, international economic development, international business, international health and development, international law, political psychology, science, technology and public policy. Students may specialize in a disciplinary area—history, economics or politics—of the following regions: Western Europe, Eastern Europe, Middle East, Africa, former Soviet Union/Russia, South and Southeast Asia, China, Japan, Latin America.

Number of Applicants Fall 1992: 1300
Entering Class Fall 1992: 230
Entrance Requirements: GRE. The LSAT and GRE are both required for the JD/MA program. The school emphasizes a strong background in the social sciences and at least one foreign language for applicants, although languages are not required for admission. Economics requirements can be fulfilled while enrolled and credits count toward the degree.
Financial Aid and Internships: Resources include fellowships and assistantships, loans and work-study. A wide variety of internships are available in the Washington, DC, area.
Career Development: The Career and Cooperative Education Center maintains up-to-date listings of full-time, part-time and summer positions. Career consultants are available to discuss career issues and concerns and to critique resumes and cover letters. More than 200 companies visit the center each year, and an alumni network of contacts is maintained on a computerized data base in the center.

HARVARD UNIVERSITY
John F. Kennedy School of Government
79 John F. Kennedy Street
Cambridge, MA 02138
(617) 495-1122

Degrees: Master in Public Policy, Master in Public Administration (one-year), Master in City and Regional Planning.
Areas of Specialization: Business and government policy; human resources; labor and education; health care policy; housing, urban development and transportation; crime and criminal justice; international affairs and security; international trade and finance; political and economic development; environment and natural resources; science, technology and public policy; press and public policy.
Number of applicants 1992: 1015 (excluding one-year MPA)
Entering Class Fall 1992: 263 (excluding one-year MPA)
Entrance Requirements: GRE or GMAT is accepted. Applicants to the one-year MPA program must have a minimum of seven years experience in the public sector.
Financial Aid and Internships: Need-based grants and fellowships are available. Work-study positions are available to second-year students. External summer internships are offered between the first and second year.
Career Development: Professional career development staff offers a range of resources, including career development workshops, an

on-campus recruiting program, lists of current job openings and the Career Resource Room.

THE JOHNS HOPKINS UNIVERSITY
The Paul H. Nitze School of Advanced International Studies (SAIS)
1740 Massachusetts Avenue NW
Washington, DC 20036
(202) 663-5600

Degrees: Master of Arts in International Relations, Master of International Public Policy
Joint Degrees: BA/MA, MA/MBA (Wharton), MA/JD (Stanford), MA/MHS
Areas of Specialization: International relations, American foreign policy, international economics, social change and development. Area studies: Africa, Asia, Canada, Europe, Latin America, Middle East, Russia and Eastern Europe.
Number of Applicants Fall 1992: 1400
Entering Class Fall 1992: 269
Entrance Requirements: GRE. Joint degree applicants must meet the exam requirements of the second institution: Wharton—GMAT, Stanford—LSAT. Two years of college-level preparation in a foreign language or the equivalent and microeconomics and macroeconomics are required for entry.
Financial Aid and Internships: SAIS provides a combination of merit- and need-based scholarships, guaranteed student loans and college work-study to meet demonstrated needs. College work-study jobs include research assistants, administrative aides and general clerical support on- and off-campus. Students are encouraged to pursue internships, although they do not receive academic credit. The school has extensive information about internships available in Washington, DC, and elsewhere.
Career Development: The SAIS Career Office is a resource center, which provides information on employment opportunities, counseling and job hunting skills, and training for masters degree candidates and alumni. Staff assists in evaluation of potential career paths and provides programs featuring SAIS alumni and other professionals who help students explore different careers. A limited number of private-sector, government and nonprofit institutions recruit on campus.
Study Abroad: Italy, the People's Republic of China; academic arrangements available with universities in Latin America, Europe and Asia.

UNIVERSITY OF KENTUCKY
The Patterson School of Diplomacy and International Commerce
Patterson Office Tower, Room 455
Lexington, KY 40506-0027
(606) 257-4668

Degree: Master of Arts in International Affairs, Master of Arts in International Business
Areas of Specialization: Diplomacy, international development, international economics, international commerce, foreign and security policy, international affairs.
Number of Applicants Fall 1992: 175
Entering Class Fall 1992: 20
Entrance Requirements: GRE foreign language proficiency. Experience abroad is preferred.
Financial Aid and Internships: Fellowships, which pay for tuition and provide a small stipend, are available for two thirds of each entering class. Work-study employment is available. The school encourages and assists students to find appropriate summer internships.
Career Development: On-campus recruiting is carried out by all agencies of the U.S. government and businesses.

UNIVERSITY OF MARYLAND
Department of Government and Politics
College Park, MD 20742
(301) 405-4156

Degree: Master of Arts in Government and Politics
Areas of Specialization: International relations, American government, comparative politics, political theory and political economy. Subsidiary fields—national security, international political economy, ex-Soviet/Eastern European studies, and conflict resolution.
Number of Applicants Fall 1992: 300
Entering Class Fall 1992: 35
Entrance Requirements: The GRE is required, with aggregate scores for three parts in the 1800 to 1900 range. Undergraduate GPA should be at least 3.4.
Financial Aid and Internships: Graduate school fellowships and departmental assistantships provide a stipend and tuition. An internship with the state of Maryland is available with a stipend plus tuition. Work-study is also available.
Career Development: The department has a faculty member who assists students in securing academic placement.

UNIVERSITY OF MIAMI
Graduate School of International Studies
Coral Gables, FL 33124-3010
(305) 284-4173

Degrees: Master of Arts in International Studies, Master of Arts in Inter-American Studies
Joint Degrees: By individual agreement with other schools, including School of Business and the School of Communication.
Areas of Specialization: Area fields—Inter-American studies, Middle East studies, European studies (includes Eastern Europe, former Soviet Union, European Community, and Iberia). Functional fields—international relations, international business, international security and conflict, international economics, comparative development.
Number of Applicants Fall 1992: 170
Entering Class Fall 1991: 46
Entrance Requirements: GRE. Joint program with MBA requires GMAT. Minimum undergraduate GPA of 3.0.
Financial Aid and Internships: Graduate assistantships (research assistantships) are available. There are also work-study and project-related positions, depending on student skills and project funding.
Career Development: On-campus recruiting, workshops and individual counseling.
Study Abroad: Colombia

UNIVERSITY OF MICHIGAN
Institute of Public Policy Studies
440 Lorch Hall
Ann Arbor, MI 48109
(313) 764-3490

Degree: Master of Public Policy
Joint Degrees: MBA/MPP, JD/MPP and MPA/Masters from the School of Public Health
Areas of Specialization: International studies and other policy specializations.
Number of Applicants Fall 1992: 475
Entering Class Fall 1992: 67
Entrance Requirements: GRE. Applicants to the MPP program must have a minimum of three years of full-time professional work experience in the public sector. Students interested in joint degree programs must be admitted to both programs separately.

Financial Aid and Internships: IPPS offers financial aid to some students in the form of tuition grants, stipends for living expenses and assistantships (teaching, research and staff).

Career Development: Some on-campus recruiting and a resume book.

UNIVERSITY OF MINNESOTA
Hubert H. Humphrey Institute of Public Affairs
Humphrey Center
301 19th Avenue South
Minneapolis, MN 55455
(612) 625-9505

Degrees: Master of Arts in Public Affairs, Master of Planning in Public Affairs

Joint Degrees: MP/JD, MA/JD, MP/MSW, MA/MSW

Areas of Specialization: management of public and nonprofit organizations, planning, policy analysis, social policy, economic and community development, land use and human settlements, technology, energy and environmental policy, foreign policy and international affairs.

Number of Applicants Fall 1992: NA

Entering Class Fall 1992: NA

Entrance Requirements: GRE. Students must have taken a course in intermediate microeconomic theory and are encouraged to be familiar with college-level algebra, basic quantitative methods and the characteristics of the American political system. Some of these requirements can be fulfilled while enrolled without credit. Applicants for joint degree programs must be accepted to each program separately and take the required tests, i.e. the LSAT for the MP/JD. The MSW program requires one year work experience, either voluntary or paid, a 3.0 minimum GPA and biology and statistics courses.

Financial Aid and Internships: The institute offers both need-based and merit-based funding. Teaching, research and administrative assistantships are available. Several fellowships are also available. A three-month full-time internship is a required component of the degree plan.

Career Development: Placement services include job posting, workshops, resume and networking counseling and some on-campus interviews.

MONTEREY INSTITUTE OF INTERNATIONAL STUDIES
425 Van Buren Street
Monterey, CA 93940
(408) 647-4123

Divisions: The institute has four divisions: International Management, International Policy Studies, Language Studies, and Translation and Interpretation.

Degrees: Master of Business Administration in International Management, Master of Arts in International Policy Studies, Master of Public Administration in Development Management, Master of Arts in Teaching Foreign Language, Master of Arts in Teaching English to Speakers of Other Languages, Master of Arts in Teaching Foreign Language, Master of Arts in Translation, Master of Arts in Translation and Interpretation, Master of Arts in Conference Interpretation.

Areas of Specialization: Area studies associated with the languages of Asia, Latin America, Near East, Russia and Western Europe.

Number of Applicants Fall 1992: 906

Entering Class Fall 1992: 594

Entrance Requirements: GRE. The GMAT is required for the MBA program. A minimum undergraduate GPA of 3.0 and two years of college-level second-language study is required. Some requirements may be fulfilled while enrolled but credits do not count toward the degree.

Financial Aid and Internships: Work-study and merit-based scholarships are available. Internships are encouraged. The International Management Division has exchange programs with four European business schools. The programs are offered to a limited number of students, and internships are usually arranged by the European school.

Career Development: The Career Development and Alumni Office presents workshops and provides assistance on job search strategies, internships, resumes and cover letters, interviewing and self-assessment. It lists worldwide internships and full-time and part-time positions and maintains a career research library. It also publishes *Career Connections* and an alumni directory as well as coordinating on-campus employer interviews.

STATE UNIVERSITY OF NEW YORK AT BINGHAMTON
Department of Political Science
Director of Graduate Studies
PO Box 6000
Binghamton, NY 13902-6000
(607) 777-2167

Degrees: Master of Arts in Public Policy Analysis and Administration
Areas of Specialization: Public policy analysis
Number of Applicants Fall 1992: 84
Entering Class Fall 1992: 32

Entrance Requirements: GRE. Candidates for the Masters programs should have an undergraduate GPA of 3.0 and an average of 3.2 for the last two years.

Financial Aid and Internships: There are 18–20 research/teaching assistantships available, and 7 underrepresented-minority fellowships based on a university-wide competition.

NEW YORK UNIVERSITY
Robert F. Wagner Graduate School of Public Service
4 Washington Square North
New York, NY 10003
(212) 998-7414

Degrees: Master of Public Administration, Master of Urban Planning, Master of Science Management

Joint Degrees: BA/MPA, JD/MUP, JD/MPA, MS (in Engineering)/MPA

Areas of Specialization: Management for public and nonprofit organizations, financial management and public finance, public policy analysis. The MPA degree offers concentrations in public administration and health policy. Within these two concentrations there are specialty course offerings or "specialty clusters." Following are the specialty clusters for the public administration concentration: comparative and development administration, international administration, nonprofits and arts management, performance and information systems auditing, information resource management, environmental policy and management, urban development, housing policy, transportation policy and poverty, race and class. The health policy clusters are: health services management, health policy analysis and financial management.

Number of Applicants Fall 1992: 684

Entering Class Fall 1992: 266

Entrance Requirements: GRE or GMAT scores are optional for masters programs. Applicants should have an undergraduate GPA of 3.0 or better. Students wishing to enter joint degree programs must meet the entrance requirements of the other school.

Financial Aid and Internships: The school offers merit-based scholarships and need-based financial assistance in the forms of fellowships, graduate assistantships, Dean's scholarships and other program-related scholarships. Appropriate work-study is limited. Although there are no formal internships, the school encourages and gives credit for on-the-job experience.

Career Development: The Office of Career Development has a program consisting of workshops, seminars, special events, off- and on-campus recruiting and other resources. While the focus is on permanent placement for graduating students, the office also assists students who seek internships and part-time employment to help finance their education. There is an on-campus recruitment program for internships and full- and part-time employment.

UNIVERSITY OF NORTH CAROLINA AT CHAPEL HILL
Master of Public Administration Program
CB #3265, 318 Hamilton Hall
Chapel Hill, NC 27599-3265
(919) 962-0425

Degree: Master of Public Administration
Joint Degrees: JD/MPA, MPA/MRP
Areas of Specialization: Concentrations include public management and public-policy analysis. Students in both concentrations may select specializations in international affairs, international development or others.
Number of Applicants Fall 1992: 160
Entering Class Fall 1992: 27
Entrance Requirements: GRE. The public management concentration requires three credits in American government and three hours of economics. Public-policy analysis requires three credit hours in probability and statistics and three in intermediate microeconomics. Admission to the joint JD/MPA and MRP/MPA programs must be gained independently of admission to the MPA program.
Financial Aid and Internships: The program offers research assistantships (out-of-state students may qualify for in-state tuition rates), Graduate School Merit Awards, the Woodrow Wilson Program in International and Public Policy, several scholarships and one substantial fellowship. The MPA program requires all students to have had a full-time professional field experience in a public service agency.
Career Development: There is some on-campus recruiting.

OHIO UNIVERSITY
Center for International Studies
56 East Union Street
Athens, OH 45701-2987
(614) 593-1840

Degree: Master of Arts in International Affairs

Areas of Specialization: International administrative studies, African studies, Latin American studies, international development studies, Southeast Asian studies, communication and development studies.
Number of Applicants Fall 1992: 250
Entering Class Fall 1992: 199
Entrance Requirements: There is no exam required for entrance. Applicants must have at least a 3.0 undergraduate GPA. Language requirement may be filled while enrolled and credits count toward the degree.
Financial Aid and Internships: Each program has a limited number of scholarships, which pay for tuition only. Graduate assistantships and work-study are also available.
Career Development: Career Planning and Placement Office. Internships are facilitated through the Center for International Studies.
Study Abroad: Ohio University works with the International Students' Exchange Program (ISEP) to place students in 100 universities worldwide.

UNIVERSITY OF OREGON
International Studies Program
Eugene, OR 97403-5206
(503) 346-5051

Degree: Master in International Studies
Joint Degrees: MBA/MAIS, MAIS/MAPA, MAIS/MSPA, MAIS/JD, MAIS/MAAS
Areas of Specialization: International development, development and environment, international education, cross-cultural communication, international business, Asian and Pacific studies, Southeast Asian studies.
Number of Applicants Fall 1992: 85
Entering Class Fall 1992: 17
Entrance Requirements: The GRE is highly recommended but not required. Students must take the LSAT or GMAT as appropriate for joint programs. International experience and language background are important. Study of less-common advanced languages such as Japanese, Chinese, Indonesian and Thai is credited toward the degree.
Financial Aid and Internships: There are several assistantships including: competitive university-wide assistantships for minorities, second-year graduate assistantships, assistantships for teaching languages such as Japanese, Spanish, etc. Students with an interest in Southeast Asia are eligible for several fellowships and assistantships. There is also a modest fellowship for a first-year student. All students without extensive

international work experience are required to have an internationally oriented internship. Internships abroad are available.

Career Development: All new graduate students must complete a three-course sequence related to professional development. Occasional on-campus recruiting exists.

Study Abroad: Europe, Pacific Basin, Latin America, Africa and elsewhere.

UNIVERSITY OF PENNSYLVANIA
The Joseph H. Lauder Institute
Lauder Fisher Hall
256 South 37th Street, 2nd Floor
Philadelphia, PA 19104-6330
(215) 898-1215

Joint Degree (only): MAIS/MBA
Areas of Specialization: East Asia, Latin America, Western Europe, U.S. and the former Soviet Union. (All regional specializations include a language component.)
Number of Applicants Fall 1992: 325
Entering Class Fall 1992: 52
Entrance Requirements: GMAT. An oral proficiency interview is not needed to apply but is required prior to admission.
Financial Aid and Internships: Merit-based awards are available from the institute; need-based packages are available from Wharton. Corporate internships are built into the program. Internships should be taken in the country/area of specialization.
Career Development: Career Development and Placement Office at Wharton.
Study Abroad: Russia, France, Germany, China, Japan, Brazil or Mexico.

UNIVERSITY OF PITTSBURGH
Graduate School of Public and International Affairs
GSPIA-3L03 Forbes Quad
Pittsburgh, PA 15260
(412) 648-7640

Degrees: Master of Public Administration, Master of Public and International Affairs, Master of Urban and Regional Planning
Joint Degrees: Law/MPA, Law/MPIA, Law/MURP; School of Social Work: MSW/MPA, MSW/MPIA, MSW/MURP

Areas of Specialization: Environmental management and policy, management of nonprofit organizations, personnel and labor relations, international security studies, international political economy, area studies in conjunction with the University Center for International Studies.

Number of Applicants Fall 1992: 707

Entering Class Fall 1992: 182

Entrance Requirements: The GRE exam is not necessary, but the LSAT is required for joint law degrees.

Financial Aid and Internships: Graduate student assistantships available, as well as specialized fellowships. Opportunities for student employment and loans are available. Internships are required and are coordinated through the Office of Career Services.

Career Development: The Office of Career Services offers career counseling, resume review, on-campus recruiting and internship assistance; compiles a resume book; publishes a student guide to career services, a biweekly newsletter *Career Notes*, and in cooperation with local alumni, a "Career Series" of presentations. Also, the university's Central Placement Office offers resume review and mock interviews.

Study Abroad: The university has exchange arrangements with the Institute of Social Studies at The Hague, The Institute of Public Administration in Rio de Janeiro, the University of Wales and the University of Lancaster.

PRINCETON UNIVERSITY
Woodrow Wilson School of Public and International Affairs
Princeton, NJ 08544
(609) 258-4836

Degree: Master in Public Affairs, Master in Public Affairs and Urban and Regional Planning

Joint Degrees: MPA/JD (with Columbia and New York University law schools), MPA/MBA (with select business schools), MPA/URP

Areas of Specialization: International relations, development studies, domestic policy, economics and public policy

Number of applicants 1992: 620

Entering Class Fall 1992: 63

Entrance Requirements: GRE. For the joint degrees in law and business, the LSAT and GMAT are required, respectively. Princeton emphasizes strong academics, motivation and focus. A core curriculum consisting of microeconomics, macroeconomics, statistics and political and organizational analysis must be fulfilled during the first year. Credits count toward the degree.

Financial Aid and Internships: Students are funded to meet their individual need. Students are required to take an internship for the summer between their first and second years.
Career Development: On-campus recruiting is available. Other resources include alumni panels, trips to Washington, DC, and New York, and individual career counseling by a professional staff.

SAN FRANCISCO STATE UNIVERSITY
International Relations Program
1600 Holloway Avenue
San Francisco, CA 94132
(415) 338-2055

Degree: Master of Arts in International Relations
Areas of Specialization: Regional, economic development, political economy, and intelligence and covert activity.
Number of Applicants Fall 1992: 100
Entering Class Fall 1992: 35
Entrance Requirements: The GRE and an undergraduate GPA of at least 3.25. Some language requirements can be fulfilled while enrolled. Credits do not count toward the degree
Financial Aid and Internships: The university does not offer any special financial aid. There are a limited number of teaching internships and internships within the community.
Career Development: Career center and course in international careers.
Study Abroad: Europe, Asia and Africa

SCHOOL FOR INTERNATIONAL TRAINING
Kipling Road
PO Box 676
Brattleboro, VT 05302
(802) 257-7751

Degrees: Master in International Administration, Master of Arts in Teaching
Areas of Specialization: Development management, international education, intercultural training, teaching English to speakers of other languages, French and Spanish.
Number of Applicants Fall 1992: 250
Entering Class Fall 1992: 130

Entrance Requirements: GMAT and GRE are not required. A bachelor's degree or equivalent, intercultural experience or professional experience are helpful.

Financial Aid and Internships: There are grants and work-study available based on need. Merit scholarships are awarded competitively. Internships are required and are identified and negotiated by the student, but assistance is available.

Career Development: The Professional Development and Resource Center contains resources and provides services, including career counseling and an alumni information network. There is little on-campus recruiting.

UNIVERSITY OF SOUTHERN CALIFORNIA
School of International Relations
Von Klein Smid Center 330
Los Angeles, CA 90089-0043
(213) 740-6278

Degree: Master of Arts in International Relations
Joint Degrees: MA/JD, MSIPA/MAIC
Areas of Specialization: International political economy, international security studies, foreign policy analysis, international politics and diplomacy, regional studies
Number of Applicants Fall 1992: 320 (includes PhD)
Entering Class Fall 1992: 25 (includes PhD)
Entrance Requirements: GRE. The MA/JD also requires the LSAT.
Financial Aid and Internships: The school offers financial aid in the form of merit-based fellowships, teaching and research assistantships. All admitted students are automatically considered for the school's merit-based financial awards. First year graduate students do not normally receive teaching and research assistantships. Scholarships, grants and part-time work-study employment is also available through the USC graduate school. Students are encouraged to seek outside funding for graduate studies.
Career Development: The school has its own career services office that provides internship notices; resume, cover letter and interview assistance; and access to the school's alumni network. It also hosts a career event in cooperation with the Political Science Department and the School of Public Administration.

UNIVERSITY OF SOUTH CAROLINA
Department of Government and International Studies
Columbia, SC 29208
(803) 777-3109

Degrees: Master of Public Administration, Master of International Studies
Areas of Specialization: International relations theory and practice, foreign policy analysis, comparative politics and area studies.
Number of Applicants Fall 1992: MIS-200, MPA-77
Entering Class Fall 1992: MIS-18, MPA-28
Entrance Requirements: A course in elementary statistics is a prerequisite but this requirement can be filled while enrolled in the program. Credits do not count toward the degree.
Financial Aid and Internships: Teaching assistantships are available from the department. Research assistantships are available from the Institute of International Studies. Fellowships are available from the university. Internships are available on a case-by-case basis. UN, USIA, State Department and international business are the major sources.
Career Development: The university maintains a career development and placement center and internship office. The department has a placement officer, mainly to serve PhD students. The university also provides an on-campus recruiting schedule.
Study Abroad: Germany, France, Britain

SYRACUSE UNIVERSITY
Maxwell School of Citizenship and Public Affairs
Syracuse University
Syracuse, NY 13244-127
(315) 443-2252

Degree: Master of Arts in International Relations, Master of Public Administration
Joint Degrees: MA/JD, MA/MPA, MA/MBA
Areas of Specialization: **(MAIR program)** Foreign policy, war and conflict resolution, international law and organizations, international political economy, intercultural communications, international development; area concentrations—Africa, Asia, Europe, former Soviet Union, Latin America. **(MPA program)** State and local government financial analysis and management, health policy and administration, public management, technology and information management, development administration.
Number of Applicants Fall 1992: MAIR-223, MPA-NA
Entering Class Fall 1992: MAIR-35, MPA-70

Entrance Requirements: GRE. For the joint MA/JD and the joint MA/MBA programs, the LSAT and the GMAT respectively will be accepted in lieu of the GRE. Applicants should have two years of undergraduate language training. English is acceptable for non-native speakers.

Financial Aid and Internships: There are a limited number of research assistantships. Non-college work-study is available as well. Internships are widely available and encouraged.

Career Development: The Maxwell School has a full-time placement director and on-campus recruiting.

THE UNIVERSITY OF TEXAS AT AUSTIN
Lyndon B. Johnson School of Public Affairs
Drawer Y, University Station
Austin, TX 78713
(512) 471-4962

Degree: Master of Public Affairs
Joint Degrees: MPA/JD, MPA/MBA, MPA/MS in Engineering, MPA/MA in Asian Studies, MPA/MA in Middle Eastern Studies, MPA/MA in Latin American Studies
Areas of Specialization: Students may develop their own areas of specialization such as environmental and regulatory policy, international or foreign affairs, human resources and social policy, urban and metropolitan policy, strategic management, governance and fiscal policy, health policy.
Number of Applicants Fall 1992: 600
Entering Class Fall 1992: 108
Entrance Requirements: Applicants must have a combined score of at least 1000 on the GRE and have an undergraduate GPA of at least 3.0. The LSAT and GMAT are required for joint MPA/JD and MPA/MBA programs, respectively. Courses in economics (two semesters), government (two semesters), math and statistics are suggested but not required.
Financial Aid and Internships: All applicants are considered for merit fellowships. Need-based grants are given to those who are eligible. There are a few assistantships for second-year students. Work-study is available. Paid internships are arranged for every student. Some internships are overseas.
Career Development: The school sponsors brown-bag lunches, where speakers, recruiters and alumni present job information. A resume book is sent to potential employers by the career development coordinator annually. The development coordinator also provides information on job opportunities.

THUNDERBIRD: THE AMERICAN GRADUATE SCHOOL OF INTERNATIONAL MANAGEMENT
15249 North 59th Avenue
Glendale, AZ 85306-6003
(602) 978-7210

Degrees: Master of International Management, Executive Master of International Management, Master of International Health Management (with University of Arizona), Master of International Management of Technology (with Arizona State University).
Joint Degrees: MBA/MIM (with Arizona State University or University of Arizona), MIM/MPA, MIM/Master of Accountancy, MIM/Master of Economics, MIM/Master of Science in Information Systems (with the University of Arizona).
Areas of Specialization: For the MIM: International marketing, international finance and banking, international management, international executive management. Other degrees and joint degrees: International marketing, international finance, international management, international health management, international executive management.
Number of Applicants Fall 1992: 2,000+
Entering Class Fall 1992: 450
Entrance Requirements: GMAT. Arizona State University Department of Industrial Engineering requires the GRE. Foreign Language proficiency not required for admission but is for graduation. Basic business courses may be completed before admission but are also offered at Thunderbird; however, a limited number is counted toward graduation requirements. Undergraduate degree, showing acceptable performance in previous formal education, work experience and international exposure.
Financial Aid and Internships: Teaching and research assistantships are offered as well as work-study appointments. Scholarship awards based on merit available to all students. Internships, both in the U.S. and abroad, are available through the career center.
Career Development: Career Services Center assists in career management skills and provides the following programs: graduate associate, open employer forums, on-campus recruiting, career assessment and management workshops and off-campus recruiting forums.
Study Abroad: Japan, Germany, Finland, Spain, Mexico, China, Thunderbird European campus in France.

TUFTS UNIVERSITY
The Fletcher School of Law and Diplomacy
Medford, MA 02155
(617) 628-7010

Degrees: Master of Arts in Law and Diplomacy, one-year MA (for midcareer professionals)
Joint Degrees: MA/MALD, DVM/MALD, JD/MALD with Harvard and UC Berkeley law schools (other ad hoc programs possible by petition with about ten other U.S. law schools), MBA/MALD (with the Amos Tuck School at Dartmouth)
Areas of Specialization: The Fletcher School has 21 fields of specialization, with regional and functional concentrations.
Number of Applicants Fall 1992: 1542
Entering Class Fall 1992: 140
Entrance Requirements: The GRE for MA and MALD programs. For joint JD or MBA programs, applicants must also take the LSAT or GMAT, respectively. Students should also have a strong background in a foreign language. If career interest is in the business/economics fields, students should have a solid basis in economics and demonstrated quantitative aptitude.
Financial Aid and Internships: Substantial scholarship funds, university loans and work-study are available to students based on merit and financial need. There are approximately 30 research assistant positions at Fletcher and 25 teaching assistantships at Tufts. The school annually provides 40 or more travel grants to students who have obtained unpaid internships overseas in the public or nonprofit sectors.
Career Development: The Office of Career and Student Services offers a range of services, including on-campus recruiting, career trips to New York City and Washington, DC, weekly career speakers and an on-line career data base.
Study Abroad: Exchange program with the Graduate Institute of International Studies in Geneva, Switzerland.

TULANE UNIVERSITY
Department of Political Science
New Orleans, LA 70118
(504) 865-5166

Degrees: Master of Arts in International Relations
Joint Degrees: MA in Political Science/MA in Latin American Studies, MA in Political Science/JD
Areas of Specialization: Comparative politics with emphasis on Latin American politics, public policy, international relations, political philosophy.
Number of Applicants Fall 1992: 67 (includes PhD)
Entering Class Fall 1992: 22 (includes PhD)

Entrance Requirements: GRE. The LSAT for the MA/JD. A minimum of 3.2 undergraduate GPA is required.
Financial Aid and Internships: Graduate fellowships and assistantships carry a stipend and a tuition waiver. Some students only receive tuition waiver. There is no work-study or internship program offered by the university.
Career Development: Tulane has a Career Placement Center that coordinates credentials. There is some on-campus recruiting, but not a great deal.
Study Abroad: Germany and France

UNIVERSITY OF VIRGINIA
Woodrow Wilson Department of Government and Foreign Affairs
232 Cabell Hall
Charlottesville, VA 22901
(804) 924-3358

Degrees: Master of Arts in Government, Master of Arts in Public Administration, Master of Arts in Foreign Affairs
Joint Degrees: MA/JD and MA/MBA
Areas of Specialization: American government, comparative government, international relations, political theory.
Number of Applicants Fall 1992: 533 (includes PhD)
Entering Class Fall 1992: 77 (includes PhD)
Entrance Requirements: GRE with a combined score of 1200. Subject GREs in economics, political science and history are preferred. For the MA/JD, the LSAT is accepted in lieu of GREs, and GMAT is also accepted for MA/MBA candidates. A minimum undergraduate GPA of 3.2 is required.
Financial Aid and Internships: A handful of the most qualified candidates receives offers of substantial aid (i.e. tuition plus stipend). However, most university aid goes to returning students in the form of teaching assistantship or research assistantship positions or fellowships. Work-study is available, but limited.
Career Development: The university's Office of Career Planning and Placement offers interviews and other assistance.

UNIVERSITY OF WASHINGTON
Henry M. Jackson School of International Studies
Thomson Hall, DR-05
Seattle, WA 98195
(206) 543-4370

Degrees: Master of Arts in International Studies
Joint Degrees: MAIS/MBA, MAIS/JD, MAIS/MFR, MAIS/MPA, MAIS/MPH, MAIS/MMA
Areas of Specialization: China, Eastern Europe, International Studies, Japan, Korea, the Middle East, Russia, South Asia and comparative religion.
Number of Applicants Fall 1992: 450
Entering Class Fall 1992: 92
Entrance Requirements: GRE. For the joint MAIS/MBA, the GMAT is required and can be substituted for the GRE. Joint MAIS/JD applicants must take both the GRE and LSAT. The university also requires an undergraduate GPA of at least 3.0 in the last 90 quarter- or 60 semester-credit hours. Regional programs require at least one year of study of a relevant language (e.g., one year of Chinese for China studies); the Russia and Eastern Europe programs require two years. For the general International Studies program, intermediate economics and language knowledge are preferred. Professional schools have additional requirements.
Financial Aid and Internships: A number of fellowships are available that pay stipend and tuition. Teaching and research assistantships and work-study are also available. The Jackson School administers an Asia internship program offering paid assignments with businesses in East Asia for six months. Foreign language proficiency equivalent to two years of college-level study is required.
Career Development: The school has a career/internship adviser and offers on-campus recruiting.

UNIVERSITY OF WYOMING
International Studies Program
Box 3197, University Station
Laramie, WY 82071
(307) 766-6484

Degree: Master of Arts in International Studies
Number of Applicants Fall 1992: 44
Entering Class Fall 1992: 11
Entrance Requirements: Applicants should have a combined minimum of 900 on the GRE, and have a background in social sciences or humanities. A language requirement equivalent to 12 undergraduate hours must be completed before graduation, but is not required for admission. Credits do not count toward the degree.

Financial Aid and Internships: Several assistantships which pay full tuition and a stipend are usually available. Work-study opportunities may also be available.

Career Development: The university has a placement center which sponsors some recruiting on-campus. The International Studies Program only provides access to materials on careers.

YALE UNIVERSITY
Yale Center for International and Area Studies
85 Trumbull Street
13A Yale Station
New Haven, CT 06520
(203) 432-3410

Degrees: Master of Arts in International Relations
Joint Degrees: MAIR/MPPM, MAIR/FES, MA/JD, MAIR/OM. There is also a three-year informal joint degree program with the Divinity School.
Areas of Specialization: Law, epidemiology, public health, forestry and environmental studies, and religion.
Number of Applicants Fall 1992: 269
Entering Class Fall 1992: 27
Entrance Requirements: GRE. Entering students must have had introductory courses in microeconomics and macroeconomics. Both the GRE and LSAT must be taken for the joint MAIR/JD program, and the GRE and GMAT are needed for the joint MAIR/MPPM program.
Financial Aid and Internships: Fellowships, summer fellowships, teaching assistantships and research assistantships are available.
Career Development: A resource room and adviser are available to students. There is some on-campus recruiting.

GLOSSARY OF ABBREVIATIONS

BA: Bachelor of Arts
BS: Bachelor of Science
DVM: Doctor of Veterinary Medicine
GMAT: Graduate Management Admissions Test
GRE: Graduate Record Examination
JD: Juris Doctor
LSAT: Law School Admissions Test
MA: Master of Arts

MAIA: Master of Arts in International Affairs
MAIC: Master of Arts in International Communications
MAID/MARP: Master of Arts in International Development and Master
    of Arts in Rural Planning
MAIPS: Master of Arts in International Policy Studies
MAIR: Master of Arts in International Relations
MAIR/FES: Master of Arts in International Relations and Forestry
    and Environmental Studies
MAIR/ICOM: Master of Arts in International Relations and International
    Communication
MAIR/OM: Master of Arts in International Relations and Organization
    and Management
MAIR/REM: Master of Arts in International Relations and Resources
    and Environmental Management
MAIS: Master of Arts in International Studies
MALD: Master of Arts in Law and Diplomacy
MARP: Master of Arts in Regional Planning
MAT: Master of Arts in Teaching
MBA: Master of Business Administration
MBA/IM: Master of Business Administration and International
    Management
MEM: Master of Environmental Management
MFR: Master of Forest Resources
MGA: Master of Government Administration
MHS: Master of Health Science
MIA: Master of International Affairs
MIM: Master of International Management
MIMOT: Master of International Management of Technology
MMA: Master of Marine Affairs
MPA: Master of Public Administration
MPH: Master of Public Health
MPIA: Master of Public and International Affairs
MPP: Master of Public Policy
MPPM: Master of Public and Private Management
MPS: Master in Professional Studies
MPS/ID: Master of Professional Studies in International Development
MS: Master of Science
MSFS: Master of Science in Foreign Service
MSIE: Master of Science in Industrial Engineering
MSW: Master of Social Work
MSSW: Master of Science in Social Work
MURP: Master of Urban Regional Planning
TESOL: Teaching English to Speakers of Other Languages

Chapter Twelve

JOB-HUNTING STRATEGIES

Self-assessment, the difficult process of examining your strengths and weaknesses, your interests and objectives, is the first step in job-hunting. For those considering an international career it is especially important because of the special demands an international job may make. The most innovative career books on the market are not career books in the traditional sense of explaining a field, how to get into it and what to expect. Instead, they concentrate on helping you to make decisions about yourself and your values and goals. The assumption is that once you do, you will be able to pursue a job that suits and satisfies you. Factors to think about include:

- which skills you are best at and most enjoy using,
- your values and to what extent your work must reflect them,
- what kind of atmosphere you want,
- how important is the size of the salary,
- how important are possibilities of advancement,
- how much free time you like to have and what hours you like to work,
- where you want to live,

- how successful you want to be,
- how much supervision you like.

Sometimes these interests clash, so you must determine your priorities.

You should have a good idea of what kind of a job you want before beginning your search. A potential employer is unlikely to hire someone who only "thinks, sort of, that the job would be interesting." Employers look for enthusiasm and direction and need to be convinced that you want the job. Furthermore, unless you know what job you want, you run the risk—in a fit of job-hunter's frustration—of settling for *any* job and regretting your decision later. Some introspection and truthfulness with yourself now can go a long way.

INFORMATIONAL INTERVIEWING

To help decide whether a field is right for you, it is a good idea to set up informational interviews. The purpose of an informational interview is to meet people working in the field and to question them about it. The cardinal rule is not to ask the people you meet for a job. Remember that you have asked them to tell you about their field, not to find you a job, and you must keep your word. If you make a good impression, they might tell you about openings when they hear of them.

A good way to find people to interview is to go through your college or graduate-school alumni or career office. Many colleges compile work histories and addresses of alumni and make them available to other alumni. Many alumni are delighted to help "one of the fold" or to meet the younger generation. Talk with people in a variety of jobs and at different levels, if possible. It may be difficult to find senior-level people to talk to you, but junior personnel may be just as helpful because they know the current job market.

Informational interviews are important in developing a network of people in your field. In the 1980s networking was a hot topic; in the 1990s it is a survival skill. Look to everyone you know—friends, former colleagues, relatives, friends' relatives—as a potential contact or source of contacts. Use the network to help keep yourself informed of job openings and to keep abreast of developments in the field.

You don't have to have contacts to call up an organization. Explain your interest in its work and ask to come meet the people who are doing the jobs which are meaningful to you. Be prepared to tell them why it is in their interest to meet you—for example, what you can bring to the organization—but stress that you are most interested in learning about the field and not necessarily applying for a job.

If you call a company where you have no contacts, try to avoid ending up in the personnel department. You need to speak directly to the people who have jobs comparable to those in which you are interested. This is particularly important in larger organizations, where personnel or recruiting departments may be out of touch with the other offices. Be sure to do your homework about the organization before you go for an interview.

A key question to ask in any informational interview, after you have thoroughly exhausted your inquiries about the field, is, "Do you know anyone else to whom I should talk?" Often people eager to help will give you names of colleagues or other alumni and organizations. By following these referrals, you could eventually run into someone who has a job to offer or who knows of one.

WRITING AND WIELDING A RESUME

Once the informational interviews have helped you decide on your field and you have established a few contacts, you are ready to apply for a job. Your first step is to write a resume (or curriculum vitae, which is generally longer, more detailed and for people with more experience). Resumes are a necessary evil: employers use them to narrow the field of candidates for a job. The main purpose of the resume is to obtain an interview; it is pure advertisement. Your resume should make the reader want to meet you and ask about your experience, your qualifications and, importantly, what you can do for the company.

There are many different resume styles and numerous books offering advice on how to write them. The chronological resume—also referred to as the "obituary," "traditional" or "business" resume—is the most common. It lists your work experience, starting with your present job, and specifies your duties. As can be observed from the different nicknames, experts have varying opinions on the effectiveness of the chronological format. Some experts feel this kind of resume is not effective for those entering or changing careers, or those with employment gaps, because the reader can only see what you have done, not your qualities or strengths. Employers, however, are most familiar with this type, and for the most part expect chronological resumes.

Functional resumes concentrate on qualifications, skills and accomplishments, and de-emphasize dates, positions and specific responsibilities. They are harder to write—and read—because there is less to latch onto. ("Effective organizer who grasps a concept well" is much less concrete than "copyreader" or "associate editor.") The combination resume joins the two styles, stressing skills and competencies as well as providing names and dates. People tend to write functional resumes to mask their work inexperience; people tend to write chronological resumes when they have a lot to communicate. Functional and combination resumes take longer to read but may be perused more carefully and communicate more. In general, you must play up your strengths and minimize your weaknesses.

Whatever format you choose, there are a few basic rules to follow. Make your resume neat, accurate (word processing and laser printing are now the standard presentation), and no longer than a page unless you have significant experience or publications to list. Make sure the layout can be readily scanned. Leave out personal data, names and addresses of references and lengthy paragraphs. Make your accomplishments obvious and your career objective or profile clear: tailor your resume to the job for which you are applying. (You may want to prepare more than one resume.) Above all, make your resume distinctive without resorting to gimmicks. For additional tips and examples of resumes, you might want to refer to one of the many publications on the subject. For a list, see the bibliography (Chapter Thirteen).

Getting your resume read is your next objective. Ways to search for a job include asking friends, relatives and teachers to help you; answering newspaper or journal ads; and using a state or private employment agency, a professional association or a union. The traditional job-hunting approach is to mail hundreds of resumes and hope for responses. Richard Bolles, author of *What Color Is Your Parachute?* and a critic of this method, claims that it does not work: "...in this country, only one job offer is tendered for every 1,470 resumes that the average company receives." By sending your resume cold, you are inviting rejection. The specialists agree that your strongest selling point is yourself—your intelligence, personality and enthusiasm—not your resume.

Statistics indicate that 85% of all jobs are never formally advertised. They are publicized instead to a few people by word of mouth. If you are not in touch with the people who have heard of an opening, you are out of luck. According to Richard Lathrop, author of *Who's Hiring Who: How to Find that Job Fast!* you have a 50–50 chance that your job will be landed through personal contacts; 1 chance in 4 that the job will come from "cold" contacts; 1 in 20 using help-wanted ads and 1 in 25 through an employment agency—all reasons why conducting informational interviews and networking are so important.

Just as the "don'ts" of job hunting are fairly consistent among the experts, so are the "dos." Both Bolles and Lathrop suggest that using your personal contacts is probably the most effective way to land a job. Second best is meeting face-to-face with those people who most likely will be able to hire you and not relying entirely on mail or telephones to get a job. Lathrop suggests "direct personal contact with people who supervise personnel with qualifications similar to yours," especially if they were recommended by a friend, relative or acquaintance. And lastly, perseverance. Job hunting is a full-time job and should be treated as such.

COVER LETTERS

If you have to send your resume, send a cover letter with it. Most specialists agree that the cover letter is at least as important as the resume. Cover letters should be straightforward, interesting without being gimmicky, typed neatly, personally addressed and should say something that will make the reader want to meet you. They should also be brief. A mistake often made is writing cover letters that only discuss the applicant's wants and desires. Explain why you will be useful to the firm and what experience you will bring to it. Avoid duplicating wording from your resume. In closing, suggest an interview and inform the reader that you will be calling him or her on a particular date. Then, don't forget to call.

INTERVIEW

Once you get an interview, your objective is to demonstrate your knowledge of the organization, your understanding of where you fit in and how you can help. Never go into an interview unprepared. To research a company, read current business magazines, visit your library and use the research directories listed in the bibliography in Chapter Thirteen.

It is also a good idea to practice answers to some commonly asked questions. For example, if you have quit a job, be prepared to explain why without sounding negative.

H. Anthony Medley, in his excellent book on interviewing, *Sweaty Palms Revised,* suggests some interview rules:

- dress neatly and appropriately,
- arrive early,
- be certain of the time and place of the interview and the name of the interviewer,
- bring a pen and notebook,
- remember the interviewer's name,
- be enthusiastic, sincere, tactful and courteous,
- remember you're selling yourself and your goal is to strike a good feeling in him/her about you,
- get the interviewer to talk about himself/herself early,
- talk intelligently about something in which the interviewer is concerned,

- learn as much as you can about the company,
- be positive.

In general, keep the interview amicable, even if the interviewer tries to create a stressful atmosphere, and make your answers short if the interviewer's attention begins to wander.

FOLLOW-UP LETTERS

After your interview, write a thank-you letter immediately. If you have made some contacts in the field, you might want to keep them posted on how your job hunt is going. When you do find a job, let these same people know. These letters need not be long or detailed. Their purpose is to say thanks and to keep you in the interviewer's or the contact's mind.

Chapter Thirteen

ANNOTATED BIBLIOGRAPHY

GENERAL CAREER BOOKS

The Almanac of International Jobs and Careers, by Ronald L. Krannich and Caryl Rae Krannich. Manassas Park, VA, Impact Publications, 1991. 330 pp. $14.95 (paper).
Gives the names, addresses and telephone numbers of over 1,000 key employers in the international arena. Briefly describes the functions of firms in a number of fields: federal government, international organizations, research institutes, business, consulting, non-profit, embassies and consulates and more. Each chapter provides strategies for job-hunting in the specific field.

The American Almanac of Jobs and Salaries, by John W. Wright and Edward J. Dwyer. New York, Avon Books, 1990. 664 pp. $15.95 (paper).
This book discusses pay scales for a wide variety of professions, including business, government, health, banking, consulting, science and technology. For each of the hundreds of jobs listed, additional data is given on qualifications, salary range and history, advancement chances, number of people employed, etc. Also includes information on employment trends.

The Berkeley Guide to Employment for New College Graduates, by James I. Briggs. Berkeley, CA, Ten Speed Press, 1984. 188 pp. $7.95 (paper).

This book does not discuss specific fields, but offers good advice on job-hunting techniques, such as self-assessment, goal-setting, "finding out about the world of work" and evaluating a job offer.

Careers in International Affairs, Maria Pinto Carland and Daniel H. Spatz, Jr., eds. Washington, DC, School of Foreign Service, Georgetown University, 1991. 308 pp. $15.00 (paper).

One of the most knowledgeable sources of information on internationally related careers, this book covers the usual topics with unusual savvy. There are chapters on careers in U.S. government, commercial banking, consulting, trade and professional associations, research organizations, nonprofit organizations and other fields.

Careers and the Study of Political Science: A Guide for Undergraduates, 5th ed., Mary H. Curzan, ed. Washington, DC, American Political Science Association, 1992. 51 pp. $3.50 (pamphlet).

Easy reading for the undergraduate who is thinking about or is already majoring in political science, the pamphlet discusses different fields for which "poli-sci" is useful and gives a brief idea of the sort of competition and application processes that can be expected.

The Complete Guide to International Jobs and Careers, by Ronald L. Krannich and Caryl Rae Krannich. Manassas Park, VA, Impact Publications, 1990. 320 pp. $13.95 (paper).

The guide (the companion book to **The Almanac of International Jobs and Careers**) focuses on identifying and assessing the international job arena, and includes chapters on jobs in the fields of government, international business, nonprofits, international organizations and more. The book provides a general explanation of the field and a list of firms and addresses, and is useful in organizing a job search and in understanding the evolving international job market.

The Damn Good Resume Guide, by Yana Parker. Berkeley, CA, Ten Speed Press, 1989. 46 pp. $6.95 (paper).

Outlines the author's personal resume style, which is different from (and, the author argues, more effective than) the "traditional" resume.

Directories in Print, 9th ed. Detroit, MI, Gale Research Co., 1991.
Helpful industry book, published every year, gives pertinent
information on about 14,000 other research directories.

Encyclopedia of Associations 1993, 27th ed., Deborah Burek, ed.
Detroit, MI, Gale Research Co., 1993.
Published annually, the encyclopedia lists about 23,000 associations. Chapters are arranged by topic and a master index includes
references by topic, keyword or organization name. Each entry
includes contact information, description of publications and
function, key officers and budget.

The Foundation Directory, 15th ed. New York, The Foundation Center,
1992.
The definitive book on private, nonprofit, grant-making foundations
in the U.S. is published every year. It lists foundations by state,
subject and types of support. Good for researching possible
employers.

From College to Career, by Donald Asher. Berkeley, CA, Ten Speed
Press, 1992. 183 pp. $7.95 (paper).
One of the best resume books we came across. Asher gives
step-by-step instructions for resumes, curricula vitae and technical
resumes and provides many good examples. There are also chapters
on cover letters, interviews, job-search techniques and other
job-hunting topics.

**Guide to Careers, Internships & Graduate Education In Peace
Studies.** Amherst, MA, Hampshire College, Five College Program in
Peace and World Security Studies, 1990. 71 pp. $4.50 (paper).
A short but informative guide that introduces the reader to the field
of peace studies. The guide provides useful information on various
options available, from traditional and nontraditional careers to
internships. The guide also lists graduate programs, organizations
and reference publications.

The Harvard Guide to Careers, by Martha P. Leape and Susan M.
Vacca. Cambridge, MA, Harvard University Press, 1991. 222 pp. $12.95
(paper).
This book has sections on the fundamentals of choosing a career,
job-hunting, resumes and interviewing, plus indexes listing
bibliographical references, general employment directories and
specific career fields.

High Impact Resumes & Letters, 5th ed., by Ronald L. Krannich and William J. Banis. Manassas Park, VA, Impact Publications, 1992. 249 pp. $12.95 (paper).
Advocates a resume that combines the chronological and functional styles. Shows not only how to write resumes and letters, but also how to distribute them for maximum impact. Written for those who want to spend a few days assessing their skills and goals before writing a resume.

How To Get The Job You Want Overseas, by Arthur Liebers. Babylon, NY, Pilot Industries, Inc., 1990. 39 pp. $4.95 (paper).
A brief but informative book for individuals considering working overseas. While the book is not as detailed as others, it does offer refreshing and straightforward advice that should help the overseas job-hunter.

International Affairs Directory of Organizations: The ACCESS Resource Guide, Bruce Seymore II, ed. Santa Barbara, CA, ABC-CLIO, Inc., 1992. 326 pp. $75.00 (paper).
Easy to use and providing excellent information on overseas organizations, the guide contains information on 865 organizations, specialists and resources in 81 countries. Each entry includes: organization's purpose statement, information strengths, resources produced, in-house specialists etc. Includes a section listing about 250 relevant directories, dictionaries, research guides and periodicals. Six indices help the user locate organizations by topic, product or service.

International Jobs: Where They Are, How to Get Them, by Eric Kocher. Reading, MA, Addison-Wesley Publishing Co., 1989. 384 pp. $12.95 (paper).
A general book that looks at numerous fields: government, nonprofit organizations, business, banking, communications, the United Nations, teaching and law. Kocher is an informed writer whose advice is useful.

Jobs in Washington, DC, by Greg Diefenbach and Philip Giordano. Manassas Park, VA, Impact Publications, 1992. 256 pp. $11.95 (paper).
A good book for recent graduates, it features first-hand descriptions of job-hunting and what to expect in a first job by people currently holding entry-level positions. The authors also include descriptions of DC nightlife, nearby recreation and prospects for living arrangements. Chapters cover a broad range of fields—the arts, business and finance, law, media, etc.—and list organizations, addresses and

telephone numbers. For some organizations, the authors include salaries, contact names, positions and testimonials from employees.

Occupational Outlook Handbook, 1992–93 ed. Washington, DC, U.S. Department of Labor, Bureau of Labor Statistics, 1992. 473 pp. $23.00 (paper).

While this standard book does not specifically discuss international jobs, it identifies and describes about 250 occupations that reportedly account for seven out of eight of the current jobs in the U.S. Its introductory essays provide data on job availability, outlook and growth, salaries and industries.

Professional's Job Finder, by Daniel Lauber. River Forest, IL, Planning Communications, 1992. 506 pp. $14.95.

Written to help readers find the jobs that are rarely found in the classifieds. Leads readers to periodicals, job banks and job hotlines that announce professional jobs in over 50 specialties. It provides sources for professional jobs listed state by state. Also includes chapters on developing effective resumes, cover letters and performing well in interviews.

The Resume Catalog: 200 Damn Good Examples, by Yana Parker. 1988. Berkeley, CA, Ten Speed Press, 1988. 314 pp. $15.95 (paper).

A companion book to Parker's seminal **Damn Good Resume Guide.** Provides examples of resumes written by real people for jobs in fields from accountant to writer. Should satisfy anyone's need to see more examples of Parker's resume style.

Standard Periodical Directory, 15th ed. New York, Oxbridge Communications, Inc., 1992.

For those who do not know where to begin, this reference lists the basic periodicals in a number of fields, including international affairs, banking and finance, journalism and international trade.

Sure-Hire Resumes, by Robbie Miller Kaplan. New York, AMACOM, 1987. 177 pp. $14.95 (paper).

This resume guide differs from others in that it includes 25 sample resumes, along with the author's suggestions and comments in the margins, as well as the improved finished version. Also has a chapter on cover letters.

Sweaty Palms Revised, by H. Anthony Medley. Berkeley, CA, Ten Speed Press, 1992. 254 pp. $9.95 (paper).

For those truly panicked at the prospect of an interview, the myriad interviewing strategies in this book are quite soothing.

The Three Boxes of Life And How to Get Out of Them, by Richard N. Bolles. Berkeley, CA, Ten Speed Press, 1981. 466 pp. $14.95 (paper).
This book discusses "life/work planning," a method of achieving a life-style balanced between work, play and learning. Written by one of the recognized experts in career and life planning, it is not meant to be skimmed. Reading it, the author admits, takes effort and reflection.

Washington '93, 10th ed., John J. Russell, ed. Washington, DC, Columbia Books, 1993. 1,119 pp. $75.00 (paper).
A "guide to the power structure of [that] vibrant American city." Lists approximately 4,000 important institutions, firms, companies, governmental offices and other organizations. Each entry includes a brief description of the organization's purpose, address and telephone number, as well as the names and titles of the ranking officers.

What Color is Your Parachute? A Practical Manual for Job-Hunters and Career-Changers, by Richard N. Bolles. Berkeley, CA, Ten Speed Press, 1993. 421 pp. $14.95 (paper).
One of the first to propose "alternative" job-hunting ideas (e.g. not sending out 200 resumes or consulting the want ads as your first and only job-hunting strategy), Bolles' book, now in its 20th edition, is a classic. With its annual edition, it also remains an innovator in the career-guidance field. It is a must for every job-hunter to read at the beginning of the job search.

Where to Start: Career Planning, 1991, 8th ed., Carolyn Lloyd Lindquist and Diane June Miller, ed. Princeton, NJ, Peterson's Guides, Inc., 1991.
Provides complete bibliographical information for a variety of fields, including business, communications, international affairs, health and medicine, journalism and overseas employment.

Who's Hiring Who? 12th ed., by Richard Lathrop. Berkeley, CA, Ten Speed Press, 1989. 266 pp. $9.95 (paper).
This book has a misleading title: instead of focusing on which jobs are more available than others (some information on the subject is given toward the end of the book), it discusses "alternative" job-hunting methods and processes. Its sections have something to say to everyone, including former military personnel, people

reentering the job market and older job-seekers, but it is especially worth reading for those just beginning to look for a job.

Work, Study, Travel Abroad: The Whole World Handbook, 1992–93, edited by Del Franz and Lézaro Hernéndez for the Council on International Educational Exchange. New York, St. Martin's Press, 1992. 502 pp. $12.95 (paper).
Recommended for those thinking about going abroad and trying to decide whether to travel, study or find work. Once you have made a decision, there are other books with more information, but this is a good start. For each country or area of the world it offers information on academic programs, travel books, visas, currency, hotels and other accommodations, plus a host of worthwhile facts to ease travel. There are useful comments in the introduction about long-term employment possibilities.

Work Your Way Around the World, 6th ed., by Susan Griffith. Princeton, NJ, Peterson's Guides, 1993. 432 pp. $17.95 (paper).
This book describes ways in which the enterprising traveler can earn money, such as driving a truck, working on a ship or as an air courier or teaching English. The book, which is appropriate for the noncareer-minded, lists jobs by countries.

NEWSLETTERS AND PERIODICALS

Career Opportunities News, Garrett Park Press, PO Box 190M, Garrett Park, MD 20896. $30.00/year prepaid (six issues).
Contains interesting articles on opportunities in a variety of fields, plus book reviews, job tips and information aimed at women and minorities. While we cannot guarantee that every issue will have something for the internationally oriented job-seeker, the issues we received included many relevant tips. Especially useful for career counselors.

International Employment Hotline, PO Box 3030, Oakton, VA 22124-9030. $25.00 for a six-month subscription, $36.00 for one year.
An eight-page monthly newsletter with current international job openings with nonprofit, governmental and other international agencies and informative articles about various international employment topics.

International Employment Gazette, Global Resources Org., Ltd., 1525 Wade Hampton Boulevard, Greenville, SC 29609. $95/year (26 issues).

Each 64-page issue, published biweekly, lists over 400 current international job openings by geographical area and occupational field. Every entry includes a description of the job and where to apply. Since it was first published four years ago, the **International Employment Gazette** has listed jobs with over 15,000 employers.

International Employment Opportunities, The Brubach Corporation, 1100 Connecticut Avenue, NW, Suite 700, Washington, DC 20036. $29 for minimum 2-month subscription (4 issues).
A 34-page newsletter, published biweekly, with lots of international opportunities in all fields of endeavor, including internships. An excellent resource for finding international jobs that is also useful for monitoring the job market and learning what qualifications are most sought after. Also publishes **Opportunities in Public Affairs**.

Overseas Employment Opportunities, PO Box 460, Town of Mount Royal, Quebec, Canada H3P 3C7. $105.00/year (24 issues). Shorter subscriptions are available.
This newsletter lists business-related positions abroad. Most positions listed are for people with considerable experience.

INTERNATIONAL BUSINESS

Careers in Business, by Lila B. Stair and Dorothy Domkowski. Chicago, IL, National Textbook Company, 1992. 208 pp. $12.95 (paper).
A general discussion of the fields of finance, marketing, insurance, real estate, consulting, management, accounting and data processing. Good for those who have yet to decide in what business career they are interested, those who want an overview of the field or those who are interested in starting a small business.

Craighead's International Business Travel and Relocation Directory to 71 Countries, 6th ed. Detroit, MI, Gale Research Co, 1992, $425.
Up-to-date information on organizations doing business abroad. The directory is divided into two parts. The first provides background information for personnel officers and employees, for example, guidelines for choosing employees for overseas assignment, tips on moving and legal information. The second gives detailed information on 71 major countries including customs regulations, currency restrictions, leisure activities, background information and health and medical tips. A section on travel safety explains how to travel in politically unstable countries.

Directory of United States Importers, 1992–93 ed. Phillipsburgh, NJ, The Journal of Commerce, 1992. $400/set.

The export/import business is perfect for those who like to deal with foreign cultures. The directory, although oriented toward professionals and not job-seekers, gives a reader an idea of the field, including over 35,000 entries and 120,000 names. It lists companies engaged in importing products to the U.S., commodities handled, customs and import regulations, world ports and other relevant information.

Directory of American Firms Operating in Foreign Countries, 12th ed., 3 vols. New York, World Academy Press, 1991. $195.00.

Lists more than 2,600 U.S. corporations, along with their 19,000 subsidiaries and affiliates operating in 127 countries. The first volume lists the firms alphabetically and includes relevant management names, addresses and telephone/facsimile numbers, principal products and services, and the countries in which foreign operations are located. The second and third volumes list firms by country. Each country list contains, alphabetically, the name, address and phone number of the U.S. parent firm, its principal product or service, and the name and address of its subsidiaries or affiliates in that country.

Major Companies of Europe, R.M. Whiteside, ed. London, Graham and Trotman Ltd., 1992.

Volume I of this annual publication lists 5,000 companies in the European Community (EC), with basic information on management, finances, subsidiaries, and activities. Volume II lists 1,500 companies outside the EC. Other volumes by this press cover companies in Africa, the Far East, the Middle East and Latin America.

Moody's International Manual, New York, Moody's Investors Service, Inc., 1992.

This annual directory gives pertinent fiscal and geographical data on foreign countries and profiles of major companies.

Principal International Businesses 1992: The World Marketing Directory. New York, Dun and Bradstreet International, Ltd., 1991.

This is a selective annual directory of firms chosen on the basis of size, national prominence and international business. Information listed includes sales volume, number of employees, management, import/export ratios and business activities. Firms (50,000 in 143 countries) are listed alphabetically, geographically and by product classification.

Standard & Poor's Register of Corporations, Directors and Executives, 3 vols. New York, Standard & Poor's, 1992. Published annually.
This annual directory gives basic information on 55,000 U.S. corporations. Volume I is an alphabetical listing, which includes company name, address and telephone number; a products and business description; lists of the top officers and outside directors; annual sales; number of employees; and the subsidiary companies it owns. Volume II contains biographies of 70,000 businesspeople. Volume III consists of a cross-listing of Standard Industrial Classification Codes, a geographical index and a series of corporate "family trees" showing subsidiary relationships.

INTERNATIONAL CONSULTING

Consultants and Consulting Organizations Directory, 12th ed. Janice McLean, ed. Detroit, MI, Gale Research Co., 1992.
This directory lists 17,000 firms, people and organizations involved in 400 consulting specialties. Cross-listings are by location, company name, officers and function. Published annually in May, the directory has a supplement which comes out in November entitled "New Consultants and Consulting Organizations."

How to Make it Big as a Consultant, 2nd ed., by William A. Cohen. New York, AMACOM, 1990. 336 pp. $26.95 (hardcover).
Discusses the field of consulting, how to get clients, negotiate, propose, make presentations, price services, write contracts, plan the project, run the consulting business and provide the services for which you were hired. The book is well-written and easy to read.

The International Consultant, rev. ed., by H. Peter Guttman. Washington, New York, Wiley & Sons, 1987, 184 pp. $22.95 (hardcover).
A practical, how-to guide on international consulting in all fields. The advice runs the gamut from how to identify prospects to negotiating a contract. Special chapters for managers discuss staffing, financing, incorporating and administering multinational operations. The final sections contain listings of prospective employers.

INTERNATIONAL FINANCE AND BANKING

Moody's Bank and Finance Manual, New York, NY. Moody's Investors Service, Inc., 1992.

Lists thousands of U.S. banks, savings and loans, insurance companies and international banks and profiles 100 of the largest banks in the "free world." For each bank, the directory provides a history, principal business activity, names of management, stock, income, balance sheets, foreign business and subsidiaries.

The Thomson Bank Directory, 3 vols. 1992. Skokie IL, Thomson Financial Publishing, 1992.
A broad listing of banks in the U.S. and abroad, this directory contains information on directors, officers, subsidiaries and financial conditions. Volumes I and II list U.S. banks by state and city; volume III lists international banks by country and city.

INTERNATIONAL JOURNALISM

Career Opportunities for Writers, by Rosemary Guiley. New York, Facts on File Publications, 1992. 232 pp. $14.95 (paper).
Writing jobs surveyed include newspaper and news services, magazines, television and federal government positions. Salary ranges, employment and advancement prospects, education and experience needed and opportunities for women and minorities are discussed for each position.

Editor & Publisher International Yearbook. New York, The Editor & Publisher Co., 1992.
This directory publishes the circulation, advertising rates, price and names of corporate and editorial management for a large number of U.S. and foreign newspapers. It also includes information on news and syndicate services, mechanical equipment suppliers and services and other news-related organizations, including journalism schools and professional societies.

Gale Directory of Publications and Broadcast Media. Detroit, MI, Gale Research Company, 1992.
This annual sourcebook lists U.S. publications that appear four or more times a year. It provides information such as editor and publisher, circulation and advertising rates and cross-lists by subject matter and by city and state of publication.

The International Directory of Little Magazines and Small Presses, 28th ed., Len Fulton and Ellen Ferber, eds. Paradise, CA, Dustbooks, 1992. 900 pp. $42.95. (hardcover), $26.95 (paperback).

Lists small presses and magazines alphabetically, by subject and by state. Useful for someone trying to cover all the local employment possibilities in publishing.

Journalism Career and Scholarship Guide, 32nd ed. 1992. Available from the Dow Jones Newspaper Fund, PO Box 300, Princeton, NJ 08543-0300 or by calling 1-800 Dow Fund. 183 pp. $3.00.
Aimed at encouraging young people to consider careers in journalism, this annual book offers general information on journalism careers and the qualifications necessary to succeed. Most of the book is devoted to listing and describing undergraduate programs in journalism. A final section discusses scholarships, internships and many grant programs, and lists scholarship programs for minorities. This is a very good book for the beginner.

Literary Market Place 1992. New York, The Directory of American Book Publishing, R.R. Bowker, Co, 1991.
Directory lists book publishers, clubs, associations, awards, grants, services, suppliers, events, conferences and courses. Also lists direct-mail promotion companies, book manufacturers and includes information on magazine and newspaper publishing. Bowker also publishes **Publishers International Directory-International Literary Market Place,** which also lists publishers abroad.

INTERNATIONAL LAW

Directory of Opportunities in International Law, 9th ed. Charlottesville, VA, The John Basset Moore Society of International Law, University of Virginia School of Law, 1991. 75 pp. $20.00 (paper).
This directory is useful mainly for its list of law firms with international practices. It also has a partial listing of U.S. law schools that provide some international training.

Guide to Education and Career Development in International Law, Jonathan Clark Green, Denise M. Hodge and Robert F. Kemp, eds. Washington, DC, International Law Students Association, 1991. 246 pp. $39.95 (paper). $29.95 (students).
An informative and easy-to-read guide for both lawyers and students. Through essays and surveys the guide provides insight into international law and its job opportunities. Also includes two lists on the varied educational options for those interested in international law.

TRANSLATING/INTERPRETING

Opportunities in Foreign Language Careers, by Theodore Heubener. Lincolnwood, IL, VGM Career Horizons, 1992. 160 pp. $10.95 (paper).
A useful guide for those seriously interested in translating, interpreting or otherwise using their language skills. Areas covered include world trade, government, tourism and several other international careers.

NONPROFIT ORGANIZATIONS

Community Jobs: The Employment Newspaper for the Nonprofit Sector. ACCESS: Networking in the Public Interest, 50 Beacon Street, Boston, MA 02108. $39.00/6 months (individual rate).
This monthly newspaper lists jobs in the nonprofit sector by region, including "foreign" meaning overseas, and internships. Most job listings include organization and job descriptions, qualifications, size of staff, budget and contact. Also includes articles on employment trends in the nonprofit sector, book reviews and profiles of nonprofit organizations

Doing Well by Doing Good: The Complete Guide To Careers In the Nonprofit Sector, by Terry W. McAdam. Rockville, MD, Fund Raising Institute, 1986. 199 pp. $24.95 (hardcover).
A straightforward book that gives background on the nonprofit sector, examining both the positive and negative aspects of employment in this field. The author defines the values by which nonprofit organizations operate, and what this means for society. Examines many effective job-search strategies, including 42 action steps that are meant to motivate. Includes a sample list of nonprofit organizations, job-search checklists, evaluation forms and many other additional information resources.

The Environmental Career Guide: Job Opportunities with the Earth in Mind, by Nicholas Basta. New York, John Wiley & Sons, Inc., 1991. 195 pp. $14.95 (paper).
An excellent book for people considering entering the "green-collar" workforce. With a chapter on the recent history of environmentalism, the author provides a good background for people who are new to environmental issues. Explains the structure of environmental businesses, while detailing and describing different professions, from biologist to lobbyist. The author provides job strategies for entering the different sections of the environmental market. An

appendix lists many federal, state, nonprofit and educational organizations.

Great Careers: The Fourth of July Guide to Career, Internships and Volunteer Opportunities in the Nonprofit Sector, Devon Smith, ed. Garrett Park Press, PO Box 190M, Garrett Park, MD, 20896. 1990. 600 pp. $35.00 (paper).

Developed by a team of over 40 college career planning directors, the book lists hundreds of organizations, resource publications and suggestions for career planning in public, community and international service. Includes sections on animal rights, environmental and renewable energy fields, government, research centers, peace/disarmament and others.

Nonprofits' Job Finder by Daniel Lauber. River Forest, IL, Planning Communications, 1992. 320 pp. $14.95.

The third in a series of job-hunting books (the first two cover government and general positions). It gives complete information on how to use over 1,000 sources to obtain nonprofit sector jobs, internships and grants in dozens of specialties. State-by-state listings of job-matching services, job hotlines, specialty periodicals with job ads, salary surveys and directories. Covers many subjects including agriculture, environment, education, media and social services. Includes chapters on sample resume and cover-letter preparation and interviewing.

OPTIONS. Project Concern International, 3550 Afton Road, San Diego, CA 92123. $25.00/year (six issues). Cost includes membership fee plus the referral services.

This newsletter is the international health-professional recruitment and referral service of Project Health International. OPTIONS provides volunteer opportunities linking health and development specialists with programs, hospitals and clinics worldwide.

Research Centers Directory, 17th ed., Karen Hill, ed. Detroit, MI, Gale Research Co., 1992.

A comprehensive listing of nonprofit and university-related organizations. Includes 12,800 foundations, institutes and centers that provide contact information, function and purpose, officers' names, budget and a description of publications. Organizations are cross-referenced by subject, geographic area or keyword.

Volunteer! The Comprehensive Guide to Voluntary Service in the U.S. and Abroad, by Majorie Adoff Cohen, with the Council on

International Educational Exchange and the Commission on Voluntary Service and Action. New York, Council on International Educational Exchange, 1991. 142 pp. $6.95 (paper).

Describes work programs abroad and in the U.S. for people interested in voluntary services. Discusses a wide variety of possibilities, ranging from work camps that require few qualifications to programs for which applicants need advanced degrees. Most programs listed are aimed at young people, ages 16–30. The only qualification is a willingness to work.

Voluntary Foreign Aid Programs: Report of American Voluntary Agencies Engaged in Overseas Relief and Development Registered with the Agency for International Development, by the Bureau for Food and Humanitarian Assistance. 1992. Available free from the Public Inquiries Division, U.S. Agency for International Development, 320 21st Street, NW, Room 2884, Washington, DC, 20523-0062.

An invaluable resource for researching possible employers in international development. The registry provides short descriptions of the organizations including what they do and where they currently have projects overseas. Also provides a summary of the agencies' budgets and the percentage of funds received from non-U.S. government sources.

U.S. GOVERNMENT

The Almanac of American Government Jobs and Careers, by Ronald L. Krannich and Caryl Rae Krannich. Manassas Park, VA, Impact Publications, 1991. 392 pp. $14.95 (paper).

Primarily a directory to federal, executive and legislative agencies and to Congress. It describes the work of each agency, including examples of positions, and provides contact information on specific agencies and employers. It also includes information on all members and committees of Congress. While the focus of the book is clearly on federal employment, it also includes information on state and local job opportunities.

Capitol Jobs: An Insider's Guide to Finding a Job in Congress, by Terry Dumbaugh and Gary Serota. Washington, DC, Tilden Press, 1986. 123 pp. $6.95 (paper).

An informative study, the book describes what kinds of jobs are available; the work entailed; salary levels; the ins and outs of finding jobs—including some excellent thoughts on networking, Capitol Hill-style; the resume, application and interview process;

and other topics vital to a savvy Hill job-hunter. Although last published in 1986 and now out of print, this book remains valid and useful.

Congressional Staff Directory 1992, Ann L. Brownson, ed. Mount Vernon, VA, Staff Directories, Ltd., 1992. 1,152 pp. $59.00 (hardcover). Published annually and updated later in each year, this indispensable guide to Congress includes the staff and committee assignments as well as 3,200 biographies. It also lists 9,000 U.S. cities by district and representative, including a listing of all governors and the mayors of the 65 largest cities in the U.S. Finally, a 125-page index section has separate indexes for staffers and for subject keywords.

Federal Career Directory 1992. Order from the Superintendent of Documents, U.S. Government Printing Office, Washington, DC 20402. (202) 783-3238. Stock # 006-000-01339-2. $31.00. 265 pp. looseleaf. Published to help prospective applicants learn about federal job opportunities in general and answer the most commonly asked questions. It profiles every federal agency and department, and lists the college majors most desired by that department. Also included in each profile are occupational titles and GS levels There is also a very helpful index of college majors and fields of study, and what offices hire from those fields. It discusses pay systems, internship opportunities and methods of application, but does not list current openings.

Federal Career Opportunities, Federal Research Service, Inc. PO Box 1059, Vienna, VA 22183-1059. (703) 281-0200. 64 pp. $38.00 for 6 biweekly issues, $75.00 for 12, $160.00 for 26. The Federal Research Service is a private organization not affiliated with the U.S. government. It publishes a biweekly listing of over 4,000 federal job openings, listed by government agency. Each includes a very brief description, wage scale and address contact. Most jobs are at GS-9 through 13, most are in the U.S., and nearly a third are with the Department of Defense. While this is a useful publication, it should be noted that all of this information can be obtained free of charge from the individual government agencies, although it may be difficult to track down.

Federal Job Opportunities List. Available from any Office of Personnel Management or Federal Job Information Center. In New York area, at the Jacob K. Javits Federal Building, 26 Federal Plaza, Room 2-100, New York, NY 10278, (212) 264-0422. Mail in request for a free copy.

A short, computerized list of federal jobs available in New York state and northern New Jersey. Other OPM offices around the country offer a similar service; federal job seekers are encouraged to call or write. Positions are listed by job title with a very brief description. Contact information is also provided. Addresses of other FJICs are listed in the federal government section of the blue pages in the telephone book.

Federal Personnel Guide, 1992. Washington, DC, Key Communications Group, Inc., 1992. 154 pp. $8.00 (paper).
This book is filled with hard-to-find information on government regulations concerning salaries, training, insurance benefits, leave, retirement, incentive awards, Social Security, etc. Published annually.

Federal Staff Directory, 1992, Ann L. Brownson, ed. Mount Vernon, VA, Staff Directories, Ltd., 1992. 1,540 pp. $59.00 (hardcover).
Lists over 32,000 staffers, with biographies for 2,600 of them. Every federal office is included, with an explanation of its responsibilities and a listing of its personnel and titles. Indexes by person and by keyword.

Find a Federal Job Fast, 2nd ed., by Ronald L. Krannich and Caryl Rae Krannich. Manassas Park, VA, Impact Publications, 1992. 196 pp. $9.95 (paper).
Helps readers navigate the new, decentralized federal employment procedures. Provides strategies for getting a federal job at all of the stages, including an entire chapter on writing an effective SF-171 form. An appendix provides job hotline and personnel office telephone numbers for federal agencies.

Government Job Finder, by Daniel Lauber. River Forest, IL, Planning Communications, 1992. 322 pp. $14.95 (paper).
An extensive listing of periodicals, job banks and job hotlines that announce government jobs in over 50 specialties. Also provides sources for local and state government jobs by state, as well as separate sources for overseas jobs. In addition to resource listings, it includes chapters on developing effective resumes and cover letters, and on performing well in interviews.

How to Find an Overseas Job with the U.S. Government, by Will Cantrell and Francine Modderno. Oakton, VA, Worldwise Books, 1992. 421 pp. $28.95 (paper)

An extensive look at the key employers overseas: the Departments of State, Commerce and Defense, USIA, AID and the Peace Corps. Also contains information on employment with many other agencies. Entire sections devoted to the Foreign Service exam and filling out the SF-171 form are helpful, but most useful is the occupational index, listing agencies that employ individuals in the various professions and specialties. Each of the major agencies receives its own chapter, complete with a look at how the agency functions, for what overseas positions it hires, how to qualify and where to apply.

How to Get a Federal Job, 7th ed., by David E. Waelde. Vienna, VA, Federal Research Service, 1990. 186 pp. $15.00 (paper).
If you are confused about or discouraged by the maze of federal employment-application procedures, this book can help. It includes detailed job information about OPM requirements, how to locate job openings and how to fill out the forms. A special section discusses options for government employees facing a "reduction-in-force," or RIF, in a period of budget cuts. A good resource for guidance through the OPM process.

The United States Government Manual, 1991/1992. Available from the U.S. Government Printing Office, Washington, DC 20402, (202) 783-3238. 926 pp. $23.00 (paper).
Billed as the "official handbook of the federal government," this useful source lists all U.S. federal agencies, independent establishments, government corporations, quasi-official agencies and selected multilateral and bilateral organizations. For each, it typically gives a principal personnel list (which is unavoidably out of date in some cases), a summary of the organization's purpose, a brief history and a description of its programs and activities.

Washington Information Directory, 1991/1992. Washington, DC, Congressional Quarterly Inc., 1991. 1,100 pp. $89.95 (hardcover).
This useful directory lists thousands of Washington-based U.S. government agencies, congressional committees, private associations and more by subject, so that someone interested in a particular topic can easily find organizations similarly inclined. Also cross-indexes alphabetically. Phone numbers, addresses and contact names are provided for all organizations.

UNITED NATIONS

Basic Facts of the United Nations, New York, Department of Public
Information, United Nations, 1991. 237 pp. $5.00 (paper).
This book provides lots of facts and information on the UN, its
activities, resolutions, members and structure.

INTERNSHIPS

Directory of International Internships: A World of Opportunities,
Charles A. Gliozzo, Thomas D. Luten, Timothy J. Aldinger, eds. East
Lansing, MI, Career Development and Placement Services, Michigan
State University, 1990. 131 pp. $20.00 (paper).
Explains the international internship process, including questions a
person should ask in the attempt to find a "quality" internship. Lists
the many educational, government and private institutions that offer
internships, providing descriptions, objectives, location, duration
and eligibility.

**International Internships and Volunteer Programs: International
Options for Students and Professionals,** Will Cantrell and Francine
Modderno. Oakton, VA, Worldwise Books, 1992. 223 pp. $18.95 (paper).
A good listing of internships with government and international
organizations, college and university sponsored internships

Internships 1993. Princeton, NJ, Peterson's Guides, Inc., 1993. 416 pp.
$28.95 (paper).
A comprehensive guide to nearly 15,000 organizations that offer
short-term opportunities in more than 25 career fields. Includes
articles with tips on resume writing and interview preparation.

Internships and Careers in International Affairs, James P. Muldoon,
Jr., ed. New York, United Nations Association of the U.S.A., 1989. 68
pp. $7.50 (paper).
This short booklet lists internship possibilities with the U.S.
government, nonprofit and voluntary organizations and the UN.
Some of the entries are out-of-date, but the introductory advice is
helpful.

National Directory of Internships, Barbara E. Baker and Bridget B.
Millsaps, eds. Raleigh, NC, National Society for Experiential Education
(NSEE), 1991. 440 pp. $24.50 (paper).

Published by the NSEE, an organization devoted to promoting experiential education, this directory lists internships for people with a wide range of experience, from high-school graduate to established professional. For each organization the number of positions, applicant qualifications, duration of position, application procedure, deadlines and a description of the internship are provided. There is also a section listing resources for international internships. This book is noteworthy for the geographical diversity of its entries and for its listing of little-known (and thus not so competitive) programs.

GRADUATE PROGRAMS

Barron's Guide to Graduate Business Schools, 8th ed., Eugene Miller. Woodbury, NY, Barron's Educational Series, Inc., 1992. 786 pp. $14.95 (paper).
Informative and useful for those interested in learning more about the application procedure and the market for the degree they are about to pursue.

Barron's Guide to Law Schools, 10th ed. Woodbury, NY, Barron's Educational Series, Inc., 1990. 362 pp. $14.95 (paper).
Includes information about applying to, choosing between and getting into law schools and finding a job after law school in the U.S. It offers rankings and descriptions of over 175 ABA and non-ABA law schools and profiles of lawyers' starting salaries.

Graduate Admissions Essays—What Works, What Doesn't and Why, by Donald Asher. Berkeley, CA, Ten Speed Press, 1991. 131 pp. $9.95 (paper).
Provides excellent advice on choosing a school or program, planning and managing your application process, letters of recommendation and, of course, how to write a smashing essay. Includes sample essays for several different graduate programs and scholarships, residency and fellowship applications. Highly recommended.

Guide to American Graduate Schools, 6th ed., by Harold R. Doughty and Herbert B. Livesey. New York, Penguin, 1992. 485 pp. $20 (paper).
An overview of all graduate programs offered at U.S universities. A subject index facilitates finding schools that offer programs in particular fields.

Guide to Graduate Study in Political Science. Washington, DC, American Political Science Association, 1992. 286 pp. $45.00.

Lists MA and PhD political science programs, including international relations, law and public policy, world politics and international organization, in over 300 U.S. and Canadian schools. Information provided includes degrees conferred, faculty and their specializations, program description and requirements for admission and degrees.

The Insider's Guide to the Top Ten Business Schools, 4th ed., Tom Fischgrund, ed. Boston, MA, Little, Brown and Co., 1990. 332 pp. $10.45 (paper).

Using quotes from former business-school students, this book tries to convey what it is like to attend one of the most prestigious business schools in the U.S. The book explains the methods of teaching, the academics, the social life, the work load, the grading system and the general life-style of each school. Each chapter is written by a graduate of the school and is thus subjective.

Journalism Directory, 1992–93. Columbia, SC, Association for Education in Journalism and Mass Communication (AEJMC), University of South Carolina, College of Journalism, 1992. 280 pp. $20 (paper).

Published annually in February, this directory lists American journalism and mass communications programs at all levels of education. It also lists journalism educational organizations; national funds, fellowships and foundations for journalists; and professional and student organizations.

Peterson's Graduate Guides to Graduate Study, 6 vols.

Often thought of as the definitive guide to higher education in the U.S., this series provides a reasonably comprehensive listing of graduate programs. The first volume is an overview; the other five list humanities and social sciences; biology, agricultural and health sciences; physical sciences and mathematics; and engineering and applied sciences. Published annually.

Top Business Schools: The Ultimate Guide, 1st ed., by Bruce S. Stuart and Kim D. Stuart. New York, Arco Press, 1990. 302 pp. $17.00 (paper).

Gives information on MBA programs, especially the admissions process and the GMATs.

SOME PRESSES THAT PUBLISH
USEFUL CAREER-ORIENTED BOOKS

AMACOM Books: 135 West 50th Street, New York, NY 10020. Business, management and other career books.

Council on International Educational Exchange: 205 East 42nd Street, New York, NY 10017. Books about study, travel and volunteer opportunities abroad.

Impact Publications: Careers Department, 9104-N Manassas Drive, Manassas Park, VA 22111. In addition to publishing its own career-related books, Impact publishes a briefly annotated 48-page catalogue of career-related publications, training programs, videos, audiocassettes and computer software.

Institute of International Education (IIE): Books, 809 United Nations Plaza, New York, NY 10017-3580. Books on international exchange and study abroad and reference books on grants, scholarships, fellowships and paid internships.

Peterson's Guides: PO Box 2123, Princeton, NJ 08540. Guides to educational institutions and career and job publications.

Ten Speed Press: PO Box 7123, Berkeley, CA 94707. General career and "career/life" planning publications.

INDEX

CAREER RESOURCES

Contact Impact Publications to receive a free copy of their annotated catalog of over 1,400 career resources (books, subscriptions, training programs, videos, audiocassettes, computer software).

The following career resources are available directly from Impact Publications. Complete the following form or list the titles and include your name and address. Include postage (see formula at the end), enclose payment, and send your order to:

IMPACT PUBLICATIONS
9104-N Manassas Drive
Manassas Park, VA 22111
Tel. 703/361-7300 or Fax 703/335-9486

Orders from individuals must be prepaid by check, moneyorder, Visa or MasterCard number. We accept telephone and fax orders with a Visa or MasterCard number. Most items ship within 24 hours.

Qty.	TITLES	Price	TOTAL

INTERNATIONAL AND TRAVEL JOBS

Qty.	TITLES	Price	TOTAL
___	Almanac of International Jobs and Careers	$19.95	___
___	Complete Guide to International Jobs & Careers	$13.95	___
___	Craighead's International Business, Travel and Relocation Guide to 71 Countries	$425.00	___
___	Directory of Overseas Summer Jobs	$14.95	___
___	Flying High in Travel	$16.95	___
___	Getting Your Job in the Middle East	$19.95	___
___	Guide to Careers in World Affairs	$14.95	___
___	Hoover's Handbook of World Business (annual)	$21.95	___
___	How to Get a Job in Europe	$17.95	___
___	How to Get a Job in the Pacific Rim	$17.95	___
___	How to Get a Job Overseas (audiocassette program)	$79.95	___
___	How to Get a Job With a Cruise Line	$12.95	___
___	International Consultant	$22.95	___
___	International Jobs	$12.95	___
___	Job Hunter's Guide to Japan	$12.95	___
___	Jobs For People Who Love Travel	$11.95	___
___	Jobs in Paradise	$13.00	___
___	Teaching English Abroad	$13.95	___
___	Travel and Hospitality Career Directory	$17.95	___
___	Work, Study, Travel Abroad	$16.95	___

JOB LISTINGS AND VACANCY ANNOUNCEMENTS

___ Federal Career Opportunities (6 biweekly issues) $38.00 ___
___ International Educator (4 quarterly issues) $28.00 ___
___ International Employment Gazette (6 biweekly issues) $35.00 ___
___ International Employment Hotline (12 monthly issues) $39.00 ___

KEY DIRECTORIES

___ Directory of Executive Recruiters (annual) $39.95 ___
___ Internships (annual) $28.95 ___
___ Moving and Relocation Directory $149.95 ___
___ National Directory of Addresses & Telephone Numbers $99.95 ___
___ National Trade and Professional Associations $69.95 ___
___ Occupational Outlook Handbook $22.95 ___

JOB SEARCH STRATEGIES, TACTICS AND SKILLS

___ Careering and Re-Careering For the 1990s $13.95 ___
___ Dynamite Answers to Interview Questions $9.95 ___
___ Dynamite Cover Letters $9.95 ___
___ Dynamite Resumes $9.95 ___
___ Dynamite Salary Negotiations $12.95 ___
___ Dynamite Tele-Search $10.95 ___
___ High Impact Resumes and Letters $12.95 ___
___ How to Get Interviews From Classified Job Ads $14.95 ___
___ Interview for Success $11.95 ___
___ Job Search Letters That Get Results $12.95 ___
___ *New* Network Your Way to Job & Career Success $12.95 ___
___ *New* Relocating Spouse's Guide to Employment $14.95 ___
___ Professional's Job Finder $15.95 ___

GOVERNMENT AND NONPROFIT CAREERS

___ Almanac of American Government Jobs and Careers $14.95 ___
___ Complete Guide to Public Employment $19.95 ___
___ Find a Federal Job Fast! $9.95 ___
___ Government Job Finder $14.95 ___
___ Great Careers $36.00 ___
___ Jobs & Careers With Nonprofit Organizations $14.95 ___
___ Jobs in Washington, DC $11.95 ___
___ Non-Profits' Job Finder $14.95 ___
___ Right SF-171 Writer $19.95 ___

SUBTOTAL ___

Virginia residents add 4½% sales tax ___

POSTAGE/HANDLING ($3.00 for first title and 75¢ for each additional book) $3.00

Number of additional titles x 75¢ ------------ ___

TOTAL ENCLOSED ---------------- ___

NAME _____

ADDRESS _____

FOREIGN POLICY ASSOCIATION PUBLICATIONS

FPA publications are an integral part of the Foreign Policy Association's commitment to educating the public on current international issues. Prepared by FPA's editors and foreign policy experts, they are informative, provocative, balanced and well-written. They excel at making complex world issues understandable to students and the general reader and are used in schools, colleges and universities, and by the public-at-large.

Headline Series

A valuable resource for teachers and students and a way to keep up-to-date on key foreign policy topics in the news…. Subscribe to the *Headline Series,* published four times a year.

Each issue
- is about a major world area or topic
- is written by an expert
- is brief (usually 64 pages)
- is highly readable
- includes basic background, illustrations, discussion questions and an annotated reading list

Great Decisions

Get the background you need to know more and do more about the events that shape our world. *Great Decisions,* a 96-page book prepared annually by FPA editors, increases your understanding of eight of the most important issues confronting this nation and gives you a way to make your opinions known to policymakers.

A Cartoon History of United States Foreign Policy: From 1945 to the Present

This book features more than 200 cartoons by America's leading cartoonists, past and present, accompanied by a text that sets the scene and offers a vivid portrait of U.S. politics at home and abroad.

Write or call for a **free** catalog.

Foreign Policy Association, c/o CUP Services
P.O. Box 6525, Ithaca, NY 14851
(800) 477-5836; Fax (607) 277-6292

0011